W9-BZA-412

The Structure of American Industry

TENTH EDITION

The Structure of American Industry

Walter Adams

Late Professor of Economics
Trinity University (Texas) and Michigan State University

James W. Brock

Moeckel Professor of Economics
Miami University (Ohio)

Prentice Hall

Upper Saddle River, New Jersey 07458

Library of Congress Cataloging-in-Publication Data

The structure of American industry / Walter Adams, James W. Brock, editors.—10th ed.

p. cm.

Includes index.

ISBN 0-13-017916-7

1. Industries—United States. I. Adams, Walter. II. Brock, James W.

HC106.S85 2001

338.0973—dc21

00-035958

Senior Editor: Rod Banister
Managing Editor (Editorial): Gladys Soto
Editor-in-Chief: P. J. Boardman
Editorial Assistant: Marie McHale
Assistant Editor: Holly Brown
Media Project Manager: Bill Minick
Senior Marketing Manager: Lori Braumberger
Production/Manufacturing Manager: Gail Steier de Acevedo
Production Coordinator: Maureen Wilson
Manufacturing Buyer: Natacha St. Hill Moore
Senior Prepress/Manufacturing Manager: Vincent Scelta
Cover Design: Bruce Kenselaar
Composition: BookMasters, Inc.

Copyright ©2001 by Prentice-Hall, Inc., Upper Saddle River, New Jersey 07458. All rights reserved. Printed in the United States of America. This publication is protected by Copyright and permission should be obtained from the publisher prior to any prohibited reproduction, storage in a retrieval system, or transmission in any form or by any means, electronic, mechanical, photocopying, recording, or likewise. For information regarding permission(s), write to: Rights and Permissions Department.

Prentice Hall

10 9 8 7 6 5 4 3
ISBN 0-13-017916-7

for Pedernales

Contents

Preface

A half-century ago, Walter Adams published the inaugural edition of this book. The collection's purpose, he wrote, was to provide "a laboratory for the analysis of industries illustrating various degrees of competition and monopoly." A kaleidoscopic survey of American business enterprise, the objective was to present a comprehensive, up-to-date view of American industry in its myriad forms of market structure and economic conduct. The means for achieving this would be the case study and individual industry approach: A selection of industries would be examined in depth in order to convey the distinctiveness of each while, at the same time, framing all of them within the paradigm of the structure-conduct-performance approach to industrial organization.

The book was intended not only for students in economics, business, law, and political science, but also for laypeople interested in learning more about the composition and functioning of American industry. To this end, Professor Adams urged the contributors to forsake the abstruse and abstract, the esoteric and scholastic, in order to render the book palatable to the broad audience at which it was aimed. The collection was directed, not at the professional grandstand but, instead, to the body of people—students and laypeople alike—interested in the key controversial issues of industrial organization and price policy. Methodologically, the chapters, individually and in combination, would constitute an exercise in induction—reasoning from the particular to the general—rather than a deductive process of interpreting facts and meanings, *a priori,* from abstract theoretical postulates and assumptions.

That initial edition featured a variety of industries, from cotton and bituminous coal to residential construction, chemicals, cigarettes, and ocean shipping. Through the ensuing nine editions, the mix of industries was adjusted in line with current issues and major antitrust actions: Newspapers, chemicals, aluminum, aerospace, food distribution, pharmaceuticals, physicians' services, major league sports, conglomerates (a "nonindustry"), casino gaming, and breakfast cereals variously debuted. Some industries included in earlier editions were subsequently replaced by other industries of greater contemporary interest; yet some of those industries were later re-added when they once again became contentious topics of national attention and public policy debate (including airlines, cigarettes, pharmaceuticals, and physicians' services).

Times and circumstances change. The array of specific industries has varied. But the book's transcending objectives, methods, and target audience remained constant throughout the succeeding nine editions which Professor Adams produced. In particular, generations of students (including most of the current contributors) cut their industrial organization "teeth" on various editions of this book.

Although Professor Adams passed away in 1998, this latest edition adheres to original intent: It offers, once more, a completely revised set of individual industry studies which, it is hoped, students and interested citizens alike will find useful for enhancing their understanding of important industries in the American economy. Each chapter, written by an expert in the field, continues to offer a "live" laboratory for clinical examination, comparative analysis, and assessment of major global forces and developments, as well as for evaluating domestic public policies and options. As such, the collection remains a useful supplement, if not a necessary antidote, to the economist's penchant for the abstractions of theoretical model building.

Finally, in producing this latest edition the editor has striven to achieve yet another goal confided long ago by Professor Adams—to produce the book without resort to dictatorial methods. For the contributors' generous and expeditious cooperation in this endeavor, the editor is most appreciative.

James W. Brock
Oxford, Ohio

About the Authors

Randall W. Bennett is Professor of Economics at Gonzaga University, Spokane, Washington. He has published numerous articles on the economics of sports, and has served as a consultant on antitrust issues.

James W. Brock is Moeckel Professor of Economics at Miami University (Ohio). He is the author of a number of books and articles on industrial organization and public policy, and has testified before various congressional committees on antitrust issues.

Kenneth G. Elzinga is Professor of Economics at the University of Virginia. He has served as Special Economic Advisor to the Justice Department's Antitrust Division, has published extensively on economic issues of antitrust policy, and has been an expert witness in numerous antitrust cases.

John L. Fizel is Professor of Economics in the Pennsylvania State University system. He has published articles and books on the economics of professional and collegiate sports, and has served as a consultant on antitrust and sports-related issues.

John Goddeeris is Professor and Chair of Economics at Michigan State University. He has published widely on the economics of health care, has served as an expert consultant for the State of Michigan on issues of public finance and access to health care, and has been a visiting scholar at the Congressional Budget Office.

Manley R. Irwin is Professor Emeritus of Economics at the University of New Hampshire. He has served as a consultant to presidential task forces on communications, as well as advising the governments of Canada and Taiwan, and has published extensively on the economics of telecommunications policy.

Adam B. Jaffe is Professor of Economics at Brandeis University, and member of the Board of Editors of the American Economic Review. He has served as Senior Staff Economist at the President's Council of Economic Advisors, as well as expert witness in the Minnesota tobacco litigation.

Barry R. Litman is Professor and Former Chair of Telecommunications at Michigan State University. He has published widely on economic and public policy issues concerning the video industry and electronic media.

Stephen Martin is Professor of Economics at the University of Amsterdam. He has served as Director of the Centre for Industrial Economics at the University of Copenhagen, and as Co-Managing Editor of the International Journal of Industrial Organization, while publishing numerous articles and textbooks in the field of industrial economics.

James McConnaughey is Senior Economist at the National Telecommunications and Information Administration, in the Office of Policy Analysis and Development, where he analyzes issues in telecommunications competition, regulatory reform, and universal service and Internet access.

Steven J. Pilloff is Economist in the Division of Research and Statistics of the Board of Governors of the Federal Reserve System, where he is involved in analyzing the competitive effects of bank mergers. He has published numerous articles on the economics of various aspects of commercial banking.

William G. Shepherd is Professor of Economics at the University of Massachusetts. He was Special Economic Assistant to the chief of the Antitrust Division at the Justice Department, is General Editor of the Review of Industrial Organization, has served as an economic expert in numerous antitrust and regulatory cases, and has published widely in the industrial organization field.

Daniel B. Suits is Professor Emeritus of Economics at Michigan State University. A Fellow of the Econometric Society and the American Statistical Association, he has published extensively in the areas of quantitative economic analysis and forecasting.

Don E. Waldman is Richard M. Kessler Professor of Economic Studies at Colgate University. He is the author of numerous books and articles on industrial organization and antitrust policy, and has been an economic consultant in antitrust cases involving price fixing, group boycotts and resale price maintenance issues.

CHAPTER 1

Agriculture

—DANIEL B. SUITS

As the supplier of most of the food we eat and the raw materials needed for industry, agriculture is clearly an important sector of the economy, but its importance extends even beyond this. In nations where farmers are unproductive, most workers are needed to grow food, and few can be spared for education, production of investment goods, or other activities required for economic growth. Indeed, one of the factors that correlates most closely with rising per capita income is the declining fraction of the labor force engaged in agriculture. In the poorest nations of the world, 50 to 80 percent of the population lives on farms, compared with less than 10 percent in western Europe, and barely more than 1 percent in the United States.

In short, economic development in general depends on the performance of farmers, and this performance, in turn, depends on how agriculture is organized and on the economic context, or market structure within which agriculture functions.

I. MARKET STRUCTURE AND COMPETITION

Number and Size of Farms

There are about 2 million farms in the United States today. This is roughly a third of the peak number reached 70 years ago, and as the number of farms has declined, the average size has increased. U.S. farms now average less than 440 acres, but this average can be misleading, for modern American agriculture is a large-scale business. Although only 5 percent of all farms contain 1,000 acres or more, these include more than 40 percent of total farm acreage. Nearly a quarter of all wheat, for example, is raised on farms of 2,000 acres or more, and 2.6 percent of the largest wheat growers raise half of all our wheat.

The size of the farm varies widely by product, but even where the typical acreage is small, production is concentrated. Nearly 65 percent of the tomato crop is grown on small farms, but the remaining 35 percent is marketed by 9 percent of the largest growers. Broiler chickens can be raised on small farms, but 2 percent of the largest growers produce 70 percent of all broilers.

In this age of large-scale commercial agriculture, the family farm, once the American ideal, is no longer common. Today, only about half of all farmers earn their livelihood entirely from operation of their farms; the others must supplement their farming with other jobs. Moreover, large-scale agriculture is increasingly carried out by large corporations. Although only 2 percent of farms are incorporated, these corporate farms operate 12 percent of all land in U.S. farms and market 22 percent of the total value of farm crops. In states like California, corporate farms manage a quarter of all farm acreage and market 40 percent of the value of all field crops (including 60 percent of all California sweet corn, vegetables, and melons). Even in a state like Kansas, over a third of all farm products are grown by corporations.

Competition in Agriculture

Despite the scale and concentration of production, modern agriculture remains an industry whose behavior is best understood in terms of the theory of pure competition. Although production is concentrated in the hands of a small percentage of growers, total numbers are so large that the largest 2 or 3 percent of the growers of any particular product still constitutes a substantial number of independent farms. For example, although 2 percent of the largest producers grow half of all U.S. grain, this 2 percent consists of some 27,000 farms. Numbers like this are a far cry from those for manufacturing. There are fewer than 300 firms producing men's work clothing, and only 200 cotton-weaving mills, but both these industries are recognized as highly competitive. Even if we ignore the competitive influence of the thousands of smaller farms growing each crop, we are still talking about nearly one hundred times as many independent producers as can be found in the most competitive manufacturing industries.

In addition, the number and size of existing farms are only partial indicators of competitiveness, for there are no special barriers to setting up and operating a new farm. In addition, most farms are adapted to a variety of crops and can easily shift production from one to another when the outlook for prices and costs is favorable.

Because of this competitive structure, even a huge modern farm is too small a part of the total to influence price or total output by its individual action. Each can only decide how much of which crops to grow and by what methods. The combined result of these thousands of individual decisions determines the total supply that reaches the market; that supply, in conjunction with demand, sets the market price.

Demand for Farm Products

Demand is an important element in the structure of agricultural markets. Potatoes are fairly typical and can be used as a convenient illustration.

Demand for Potatoes In Figure 1-1, the average farm prices of potatoes in the United States for the years 1989 to 1998 are plotted vertically against annual per capita consumption, measured horizontally. Each point represents the data for a recent year. The downward drift of points from upper left to lower right confirms the everyday observation that people tend to buy more at low than at high prices. During 1989, for example, when 100 pounds of potatoes sold at a price of $5.93, Americans, on the average, ate only 151 pounds of potatoes, whereas when the price fell to $3.13, average consumption rose to 190 pounds. Of course, a glance at the figure is enough to show that price is not the only influence on buying habits. In 1992, for example, Americans bought an average of 161 pounds of potatoes at a price of $3.93 per hundred pounds, but bought slightly more the next year, although the price rose to $4.27. Part of this variation can be traced to changes in buyers' incomes and in the prices of other vegetables that can be substituted for potatoes in the diet. Some of it arises from the appearance of packaged dried potatoes in the stores, and in the shifting popularity of such things as fries at fast-food outlets. Statistical procedures make it possible to abstract from the influence of these other things and to estimate the effect of price alone. The result is shown by the line drawn through the midst of the observations. Such a curve, called a *demand curve,* represents the quantities that buyers would be expected to purchase at each price, all other influences held constant.

Demand Elasticity The response of buyers to changes in price is measured by the *elasticity of demand,* which expresses the percentage change in amount purchased that would be expected from a 1 percent rise in price. Elasticity of demand can be estimated from demand curves by selecting two prices close together and reading the corresponding quantities from

FIGURE 1-1 Demand for Potatoes

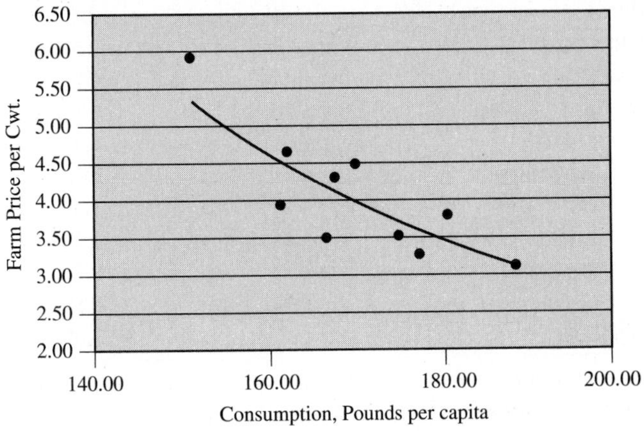

the curve. Elasticity is then the ratio of the percentage difference in quantity to the percentage difference in price. Applying this procedure to the demand curve of Figure 1-1, yields an estimated elasticity of −0.38.(Price elasticities are negative numbers because consumption tends to decline as price rises.)

Such exact measurement of elasticity is rarely needed, but we often need a general idea of how responsive buyers are to price. For this purpose, it is convenient to put elasticities into broad categories, using elasticity of −1, called *unit elasticity* as the dividing point. Demand with elasticity smaller than 1 (in absolute value) is termed *relatively inelastic* demand. If elasticity exceeds 1 in absolute value, it is referred to as *relatively elastic.* Accordingly, the demand for potatoes, with elasticity −0.38 is *relatively inelastic.* In contrast, the elasticity of demand for lettuce (see Table 1-1) has been estimated at about −2.58, so the demand for lettuce is *relatively elastic.*

Differences in Elasticity The way buyers respond to changes in price depends on the characteristics of products and on the buyers' attitudes toward them. Things like potatoes, that most people view as food staples, have relatively inelastic demands. People feel they need a certain amount

TABLE 1-1 Elasticity of Demand for Selected Farm Products

	Elasticity of Demand	
Product	***Price***	***Income***
Cabbage	−0.25	n.a.
Potatoes	−0.27	0.15
Wool	−0.33	0.27
Peanuts	−0.38	0.44
Eggs	−0.43	0.57
Onions	−0.44	0.58
Milk	−0.49	0.50
Butter	−0.62	0.37
Oranges	−0.62	0.83
Corn	−0.63	n.a.
Cream	−0.69	1.72
Fresh cucumbers	−0.70	0.70
Apples	−1.27	1.32
Peaches	−1.49	1.43
Fresh tomatoes	−2.22	0.24
Lettuce	−2.58	0.88
Fresh peas	−2.83	1.05

n.a. = not available.

Source: Estimated by the U.S. Department of Agriculture.

in their diet, so they are reluctant to cut back when price rises. By the same token, because they are already consuming about as much as they want, they find little use for more when price falls.

In contrast, things viewed as luxuries have relatively elastic demands, for people easily cut back when price rises, and are delighted at the chance to enjoy more when lower prices permit. Among farm products, the demand for fruits and fresh vegetables tends to be relatively elastic. The demand for fresh peaches, for example, is estimated to be −1.49, nearly five times that of potatoes.

Demand elasticity also depends on how products are related to each other. Products that have good substitutes tend to have relatively elastic demands, for even small increases in price lead large numbers of consumers to desert the product in favor of the now cheaper substitute. A vegetable like fresh peas has a relatively elastic demand because there are many other fresh vegetables that the family can eat when peas are expensive. These factors are reflected in the demand elasticities recorded in Table 1-l. We see that staple products like potatoes and corn have relatively inelastic demands, while the individual fruits and vegetables that are deemed less essential or that have many close substitutes have relatively elastic demands.

Elasticity of Derived Demand So far, we have been discussing the elasticity of demand for farm products purchased directly from the farm, most of which are bought by canneries, flour mills, cotton mills, and other processors. Even unprocessed fruit and vegetables require transportation, packaging, and retailing costs before they reach the table.

As Table 1-2 shows, on average, the original farm value is only about 20 percent of the retail price of food items. This small proportion further reduces the elasticity of demand for farm products. To see why this is so, consider frozen peas, a processed product with demand elasticity at retail of about −2.0. This means that a 5 percent reduction in the price of frozen peas at the supermarket will tend to induce buyers to increase their consumption of frozen peas by about 10 percent. If frozen peas are typical, however, the value of the raw peas is only about 20 percent of the retail price, and a reduction of 5 percent in the *farm* price of peas will produce only about a 1 percent reduction in the retail price of frozen peas. Given the retail elasticity of −2, consumers will buy only 2 percent more frozen peas, and pea growers will sell only 2 percent more raw peas to frozen food processors. At the farm level, then, elasticity of demand for raw peas is only −0.4, despite the highly elastic retail demand for frozen peas.

This relationship holds for all derived demands. In general, the smaller the farm share in retail price, the lower the elasticity of demand for the farm product, and demand for raw farm products tends to be inelastic even when retail demand for the final product is highly elastic.

TABLE 1-2 Shares in Final Retail Value of Food Products

	Billions of Dollars	*Percent*
Final retail value	$561.1	100.0
Processing and marketing		
Labor	216.2	38.5
Other costs	239.8	42.7
Raw farm products	105.1	18.8

Source: U.S. Department of Agriculture, *Agricultural Statistics, 1999* (Washington D.C.: U.S. Government Printing Office, 1999).

Commodities with Several Uses When products are used for more than one purpose, demand elasticity varies among uses, depending on whether buyers consider the particular use a "necessity" or a "luxury" and on whether the product has good substitutes for that particular use.

For example, wheat is used both for bread flour and for poultry feed. In its use for flour, wheat is a "necessity," and because of its gluten content, it has no good substitute. In fact, recipes for "rye," "corn," and other "nonwheat" bread calls for the addition of wheat flour to make the dough cohesive. As a result, demand for wheat at flour mills is relatively inelastic. As poultry feed, however, wheat is readily replaced by corn, oats, sorghum grains, and other substitutes, so the demand for wheat as feed grain is relatively elastic.

The overall elasticity of demand for the product is the average of elasticities in the several uses, weighted by the quantity purchased for each use. Because most wheat is used for flour, its overall demand is relatively inelastic, despite the relatively high elasticity of its demand for poultry feed.

Elasticity and the Allocation of Available Crops When the output of any crop declines, price rises and buyers purchase less, but not all uses are cut back equally. Consumption is reduced the most in uses with the highest elasticity: in the less essential uses, or where the product can be readily replaced by close substitutes. Conversely, when output expands, price falls and consumption increases, but the increase is relatively smaller where demand is inelastic and relatively larger for lower priority uses and for uses where the now cheaper product can replace expensive substitutes.

This principle can be seen in Table 1-3. When the wheat crop rose 15.6 percent in 1996, wheat for human food rose less than 1 percent. In contrast, the use of wheat for animal feed doubled.

TABLE 1-3 Allocation of Wheat in 1995 and 1996

	Total Food and Feed		*Human Food*		*Animal Feed*	
Year	*Million Bushels*	*Percent Increase*	*Million Bushels*	*Percent Increase*	*Million Bushels*	*Percent Increase*
1995	1037		883		154	
1996	1199	15.6	891	0.9	308	100.0

Source: U.S. Department of Agriculture, *Agricultural Statistics, 1999* (Washington D.C.: U.S. Government Printing Office, 1999).

Other Factors Affecting Demand

In addition to price, purchases are affected by the total number of consumers; by the incomes they have to spend; by the prices of substitutes; by fads, fashions, and consumer tastes; and—for things like soybeans that have important industrial uses—by the state of industrial technology.

Income Elasticity As with prices, the effect of changes in income on buying is expressed in terms of income elasticity of demand: the percentage change in quantity purchased in response to a 1 percent rise in real income. An income elasticity of 1 is characteristic of a commodity whose purchase expands in proportion to rising income. Income elasticity less than 1 is characteristic of staples that even low income families consume in quantity. Income elasticity is greater than 1 for fancy and luxury goods; lobster, for example, whose consumption expands greatly with rising income. (Unlike price elasticity, most income elasticities are positive numbers because consumption of most commodities rises with income.)

Income elasticities for a number of farm products are given in Table 1-1. It is clear that demand for basic staples like potatoes and onions has low income elasticity, whereas demand for cream, fruit, and fresh vegetables is characterized by high income elasticity.

We should note, however, that rising income affects the composition of demand more than it does the total amount of food consumed. Among families so poor that they have difficulty getting enough to eat, food consumption grows rapidly when their earnings increase, but once earnings exceed the poverty level, families tend to shift to more expensive food. For example, although high income families eat, on average, very little more food than do poor families, they eat nearly three times as much sirloin steak.

Demand Elasticity and Farm Incomes

Low elasticity of demand has important consequences for the behavior of farm incomes. Unlike most manufactured goods, which are priced first with production adjusted to whatever sales materialize, farm crops are grown first and then thrown on the market for whatever prices they bring. As production varies from year to year, low demand elasticity causes the prices of farm products to rise and fall more than in proportion to production, so the total dollar value of a smaller crop is greater than that of a larger crop.

This can be tested in Figure 1-1: According to the demand curve, the production of 170 pounds of potatoes per capita would bring a price of about $4 per hundredweight which would make the value of the crop about $7.16 per consumer, whereas a crop of 180 pounds per consumer would bring the price down to about $3.50, and the crop would be worth only $6.30 per consumer. In short, an increase of slightly less than 6 percent would reduce the total value of the crop to farmers by more than 12 percent.

For this reason, natural year-to-year fluctuations in growing conditions make farming very much a "boom-or-bust" proposition.

II. SUPPLY

Just as demand represents the reactions of buyers to prices, incomes, and other factors, *supply* represents the reactions of producers to prices and costs. There is, however, an important difference in the speed at which these reactions occur. Buyers tend to adapt quickly to new conditions, but producers often need time to revise plans and production schedules or to acquire new facilities and equipment. For this reason, it is useful to distinguish three different supply situations facing farmers.

Harvest Supply—The Very Short Run

Once crops are mature and ready for market, the maximum quantity available is fixed, and no action by farmers can yield output beyond that quantity. This sets an upper limit to what can be sold, but the maximum available is rarely harvested. It seldom pays farmers to strip fields so thoroughly that every last particle is collected. Some crops mature over a period of several weeks, and growers must decide when the time is best for harvest and whether it is worthwhile to return to the fields for a second harvest a week or so later. Clearly, high prices at harvest time make it profitable to harvest a greater proportion of the potential crop, whereas low prices make careful harvest unprofitable and often lead to outright abandonment of low-yield acreage where it would cost more to harvest than the crop would be worth.

Although there is some flexibility in the quantity of a given crop that is marketed, the relatively low cost of harvesting—roughly 20 percent of variable cost—severely limits variation in marketing. Once a crop is grown and ready for market, the harvested supply is extremely inelastic.

Short-run Supply and Production Costs

Cost Structure Like those of any business, the costs of farming are of two general types. Some costs, once incurred, are fixed regardless of output. Such *fixed costs* include taxes, interest on the farm mortgage, depreciation of equipment, and similar expenses that are not affected by the number of acres planted. Indeed, fixed costs would remain as charges against the farm even if production were abandoned entirely.

Variable costs, on the other hand, are zero as long as nothing is produced, but rise sharply when production is undertaken. This sharp initial increase includes the costs of planning, acquiring materials, and other costs that would not be incurred if the farm remained idle. An important component of this initial variable cost consists of the labor of the farm owner and family members, or the salaries of hired managers of corporate farms.

Once these start-up costs have been incurred, output can be expanded by relatively small increases in outlay for seed, fertilizer, herbicides, labor, fuel, and similar costs. These costs rise slowly as more output is produced, but there is a limit to what can be grown from given facilities. As this limit is approached, additional output can be obtained only by more intensive labor to provide greater care of the crop, the application of extra fertilizer, or by increases in the application of other inputs. All this means sharp increases in variable costs.

Costs of a Corn Grower Typical costs of growing corn on U.S. farms are given in Table 1-4. Clearly the more acreage planted, the more seed, fertilizer, and similar inputs are required, so these are variable costs. Altogether, variable costs amounted to $163.77 per acre planted.

Fixed costs are costs like interest on farm debt, depreciation of farm equipment and facilities, the rental value of land devoted to production, and other charges that once incurred do not vary with acreage planted. The fixed costs in the table are estimated for a typical farm of 500 acres.

Average and Marginal Costs Total cost is translated into average and marginal cost in Figure 1-2. *Marginal cost* (MC) is the rate at which total cost rises as production is increased. Once production is under way, additional corn can be raised for only the variable cost required to plant the additional acreage. This keeps marginal cost low until the whole acreage available to the farm has been planted. In the illustration, this yields about 65,000 bushels. To raise still more corn, greater and greater outlays are needed to extract additional output from existing land and facilities, and marginal cost rises more and more sharply.

TABLE 1-4 Costs of Growing Corn, Average of U.S. Farms

Item	***Cost (1996 $)***
Variable Costs per Acre Planted	
Seed	24.06
Fertilizer, lime, gypsum	53.13
Chemicals	26.82
Fuel, lube, electricity	21.14
Repairs	17.00
Hired labor	8.37
Other variable costs	10.19
Variable Cost per Acre Planted	***163.77***
Fixed Costs	
General farm overhead	7,520.00
Taxes and insurance	11,350.00
Depreciation	17,475.00
Interest	8,760.00
Land	42,740.00
Operator's labor	13,390.00
Fixed Cost	***101,235.00***

Source: Adapted from Resource Economics Division, Economic Research Service, *Farm Business Economic Report, 1996* (Washington D.C.: U.S. Department of Agriculture, April 1999).

FIGURE 1-2 Costs of a Corn Grower

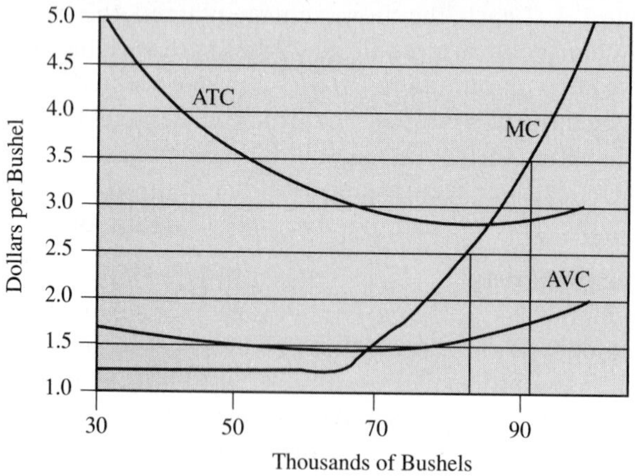

Average variable cost (AVC) is high at low levels of production because start-up costs are spread over limited output. As production expands, however, these start-up costs are spread over more and more bushels of corn, pulling down the average variable cost per bushel. As production enters the range where marginal cost rises steeply, however, average variable cost stops falling and begins to rise.

Because fixed costs do not change as output expands, *average fixed cost* is inversely proportional to output. *Average total cost* (ATC) is merely the sum of average variable and average fixed costs.

Profit Maximization and Supply Elasticity The most profitable production plan for the farm is to produce the output at which marginal cost is brought into equality with the price the farmer expects to get when the crop is finally harvested. When the farmer expects the price of corn to be $3.50 per bushel, a crop of about 92,000 bushels should be planned. If all goes according to plan, because this price is well above the average total cost, the farmer would reap a substantial profit. On the other hand, if the farmer expects a price of $2.50, the most profitable plan is about 85,000 bushels. Because resulting average total cost is about $3.60 a bushel, if everything works according to plan, the farmer will lose money. Despite the expected loss, the farmer continues in operation because fixed costs continue regardless of how much is planted. Because the expected price more than covers the variable cost of planting 85,000 bushels, the farmer will lose less by growing the crop than by abandoning production entirely. If the price falls below about $1.50, however, the farmer would be unable to recover even the farm's variable costs, and the farmer would be better off producing nothing.

At the price of $2.99 that prevailed during 1996 when the data of Table 1-4 were gathered, the farm would produce about 87,000 bushels, and would reap a small profit.

The cost curves in Figure 1-2 are consistent with the data of Table 1-4 and are typical of agricultural production. Marginal cost rises so steeply after all land is engaged in production that even wide year-to-year swings in price exert little influence on the output of any individual grower, at least as long as the farmer continues in operation. In other words, if a farm operates at all, it produces very nearly the capacity output obtainable from land and facilities. The result is a very low elasticity of supply. According to the figure, a 40 percent price increase from $2.50 to $3.50 induces only an 8 percent expansion of output. This amounts to a supply elasticity of only 0.2.

In fact, however, supply is more elastic than the costs would suggest, for many farms produce more than one crop. For example, corn and soybeans grow on the same type of soil and many farms grow both. Hog growers also typically grow corn. Some farms diversify production to protect against the failure of any one crop, and some grow several crops that mature at different times so that more efficient use of harvesting equipment can be made.

In any case, the proportions in which the different crops are grown vary in response to expected prices. For instance, the expectation of higher prices for soybeans compared to corn leads farms that grow both to devote more land to soybeans and less to corn. The expectation of high prices for hogs relative to corn leads hog growers to increase the number of hogs and to buy, rather than grow, the extra corn.

Market Equilibrium The interaction of short-run supply with demand governs the year-to-year behavior of production and prices. Equilibrium price and output comprise a sort of "target" in the market, indicating values toward which actual price and output are continually pushed, but it should be understood that equilibrium prices and outputs are rarely observed in practice. For one thing, supply deals with production *plans* rather than the eventual outcome of the plans. The most farmers can do is plant and cultivate crops in a manner calculated to earn the greatest return under normal conditions. How these plans turn out depends on weather, insect damage, disease, and other growing conditions. In addition, planting decisions are based on *expected* prices as they depend on expected demand, but consumers frequently do the unexpected. A shortage of substitutes, an unexpected rise in popularity, or the introduction of new ways to use the product—including new industrial uses—increases demand and raises prices above expectation. Likewise, declining demand leads to prices below expectation. An example of the resulting oscillation in price and output is shown in Figure 1-3.

Long Run Supply

The Role of Average Total Cost When low prices enable farms to recover more than their average variable costs but leave insufficient margin to recover total cost, farms will continue to operate at a loss. They can remain in business by letting buildings and equipment go without adequate repair and by digging into financial reserves to meet family-living expenses. Sooner or later, however, buildings become unusable and equipment wears out. At this point, farmers must decide whether to continue in operation. Unless the prospects are strong enough to promise recovery of the needed additional investment together with a satisfactory profit, it is clearly better to abandon the farm rather than to waste more money on a losing proposition.

This means that although the initial response to a fall in agricultural prices is small—we have estimated the elasticity of the short-run supply of corn at 0.2—if outlook for lower prices continues for several years, output will decline much more as farms abandon production. This makes long-run supply relatively elastic.

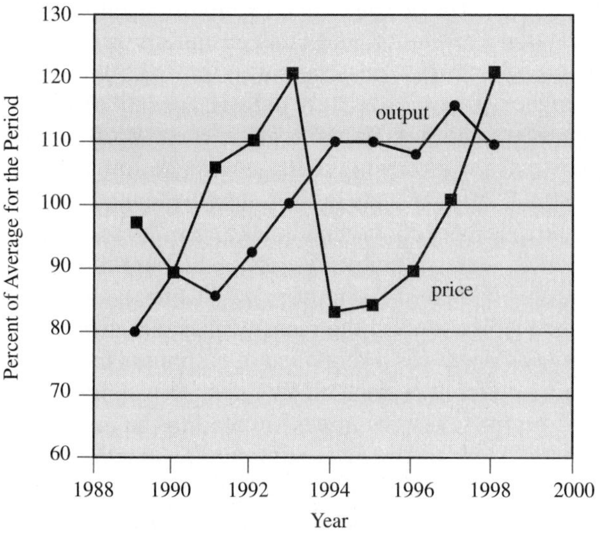

FIGURE 1-3 Price and Output of Onions

Response to Shifts in Demand Because of the three different supply situations that characterize agriculture, adjustments of prices and output to changes in consumer demand involve a sequence of events that takes several years to complete. Buyers whose demand has risen find themselves initially confronted by a very inelastic harvest supply. Although rising prices signal greater demand, growers can market only the result of production plans laid many months previously. The most they can do is to strip fields with greater care than would have been profitable at lower prices and to harvest low-yield acreage that otherwise would have been abandoned.

Despite their small immediate effect, the rising prices perform two important functions. First, rising prices reallocate available supplies among alternative demands. Buyers who can do so shift to (now) cheaper substitutes. The reduction of purchases by these buyers leaves more of the scarce crop for essential uses. Secondly, the higher prices encourage growers to plan for a larger crop next season by increasing the intensity of cultivation and by shifting some fields from other crops to the more valuable use. By the time of the next harvest, these plans will have materialized in greater output and prices will drop from the peak initially reached.

As the higher prices continue over several years, production is further expanded as farms invest in additional equipment, and new farms are attracted to the profitable crop. This expansion is accompanied by gradually declining prices, but continues as long as prices remain above average total cost.

This adjustment process has profound economic significance. Growing crops requires that land, labor, and other resources be diverted from manufacturing and other uses. Consumers who want the commodity signify by paying higher prices. However, time is needed to transfer resources from one use to another. The most growers can do at harvest time is to employ a few extra workers and a little extra gasoline to squeeze as much as possible from crops already in the field. By the next season, however, growers can expand production and make considerably more available. Over a period of years, still more resources can be transferred to the crop, and the transfer will continue until price falls to the level that just covers the average total cost of all the resources used in production.

Reduced demand produces a sequence of responses in the opposite direction. Declining demand is signaled by falling prices, indicating that consumers would prefer fewer resources devoted to the crop. However, most resources have been irretrievably sunk into production of the current crop. The most growers can do at this point is to save some small amount of labor and gasoline by abandonment of low-yield acreage and by less intensive harvest of the remainder. This saves a few resources, but in planning for the next season, growers who find that they can no longer expect to recover their average variable costs shift labor, fuel, and materials to other crops, or release them for employment elsewhere. Nothing can be done at this point about resources already sunk into buildings and farm equipment. As time passes, however, these wear out and are not replaced. Labor and other resources that would otherwise be employed in fabricating buildings and farm equipment are freed for employment elsewhere in uses more valuable to consumers.

III. IMPROVEMENT IN TECHNOLOGY

It is not enough for an industry merely to move resources in response to changes in demand. It must also keep the productivity of those resources as high as possible. The most important source of increasing productivity is the introduction of new, more efficient methods.

The rate of technical improvement in any industry involves two distinct aspects: (1) how rapidly firms in the industry originate and develop new methods; and (2) how rapidly firms adopt and put to use new methods as they become available.

On the first count, agriculture has a poor record. The intensely competitive structure and the relatively small scale of operation characteristic of farming simply do not lend themselves to research and development (R&D). Expensive laboratories and large research budgets, commonplace in many large industrial firms, are beyond the means of even the largest grower. If improvements had to wait until they could be developed on farms, agricultural productivity today would not be much ahead of what it was a century ago.

Fortunately, however, it has not been necessary for farms to develop their own technical improvements. Part of the job has been undertaken by the laboratories of state universities and government agricultural research stations. To a far greater extent, however, improvements have arisen from the work of farm equipment firms, chemical manufacturers, and other suppliers to modern agriculture. Although farmers originate little R&D themselves, they do provide a ready market for improvements once they have been developed and demonstrated. The result has been a rate of growth in productivity that has outstripped the rest of industry.

The Profit Incentive

The strong incentive to adopt better methods is the profit available to the first growers who introduce them. Suppose a corn farmer finds that by the outlay of, say, $4,000 for a new fertilizer, he can grow 3,000 more bushels of corn on his acreage. At a price of $3 per bushel, this adds $9,000 to the value of his crop, and $5,000 to his annual net income. Because his individual contribution to the total supply of corn is negligible, his action will not affect the price of corn, and until others take up the new method, the entire $5,000 is pure profit.

Innovation and Prices

Unfortunately for the corn grower, however, the new profitable situation carries within it the seeds of its own destruction. When other growers see the advantages of the new method, their own eagerness for greater profit leads them to imitate it. As more and more farms adopt the new method, the increase in supply becomes substantial, and prices fall. The price decline continues until a new equilibrium is approached at the new lower cost of production.

The long-run decline in price following technical innovation has a number of important consequences. First, it means that growers must be quick to change, because exceptional profits are available only to the first growers to introduce the new method. As other farms follow suit, the rising supply lowers prices and wipes out the extra gains. Just to break even, all farmers must now adopt the cheaper new method.

Ultimately, growers have no real choice about whether or not to adopt the new method. As prices fall toward the new lower-cost level, farms still using the old higher-cost methods are no longer able to cover costs of production. They must adopt the new method merely to survive, and if they hold back too long, they are driven out of business by losses.

Above all, as prices fall to the new lower level, the entire gain from the new method is passed on to consumers. Growers who first adopted the new method for the sake of extra profits and those who followed along in self-defense have combined in an action that has not only increased the productivity of resources but, with production at the new lower average total cost, has also eliminated extra profit and has delivered the entire cost saving to society at large in the form of lower prices.

Broiler Chickens: An Example of Innovation

Continual improvement in production methods is one of the most striking features of American agriculture. A good example is the revolution in the production of broiler chickens shown in Table 1-5.

It is probably difficult for modern readers to realize that 50 or 60 years ago, chicken was too expensive for everyday use and was generally served only on holidays and special occasions. In fact, during one presidential campaign, one of the candidates expressed his devotion to the prosperity of the voters by the promise of "A Chicken in Every Pot."

In those days, broiler chickens were raised on farms where they ran freely in yards; competed with one another for food; incurred heavy losses from accidents, predators, and disease; and required high labor costs for care. It took 16 weeks and 12 pounds of feed to raise one 3.5-pound chicken, and it took as much as 8.5 worker-hours per 100 pounds of output.

About 1950, a revolution began in commercial broiler production. Chickens were raised indoors in individual cages. This eliminated wasteful competition for feed, reduced disease and depredation, permitted automated delivery of feed, and substantially reduced labor costs. By 1980,

TABLE 1-5 Production Costs, Output, and Price of U.S. Broiler Chickens, 1934–1990

	Required per 100 lb of Chicken			
Year	*Feed (lb)*	*Worker-hours*	*Production (lbs per capita)*	*Price[1] ($ per lb)*
1934	n.a.	n.a.	0.76	0.457
1940	420	8.5	3.13	0.394
1950	330	5.1	12.82	0.342
1960	250	1.3	32.76	0.164
1970	219	0.5	52.27	0.135
1980	192	0.1	68.48	0.109
1990	n.a.	n.a.	103.44	0.083

n.a. = not available.

[1]Price of chicken divided by the Consumer Price Index to adjust for inflation.

Source: U.S. Department of Agriculture, *Agricultural Statistics, 1992* (Washington D.C.: U.S. Government Printing Office, 1992).

the labor time required per 100 pounds of chicken was barely 1 percent of what it had been 40 years earlier, and it now took only 7 weeks to bring a bird to market weight. These lower costs expanded supply, with a resulting fall in the market price of chicken. Adjusted for inflation, the price of chicken fell from $0.46 per pound in 1934 to $0.08 by 1990.

With the decline in price, consumers ate 140 times as much chicken in 1990 as they had 60 years earlier. Chicken, no longer a holiday dish, is now the cheapest meat in the store, and chicken has become the rival of hamburger in fast-food outlets.

Table 1-6 emphasizes that the story of broiler chicken is typical of what has happened to agricultural productivity. The continual introduction of new methods has reduced the production cost of virtually every crop.

TABLE 1-6 Productivity of Labor and Land in U.S. Agriculture: Selected Crops and Livestock, 1910–1998

Crop	*1910–1914*	*1945–1949*	*1965–1969*	*1982–1986*	*1996–1998*
Corn					
labor-hr per acre	35.2	19.2	6.1	3.1	n.a.
bu per acre	26.0	36.1	48.7	109.3	126.7
Wheat					
labor-hr per acre	15.2	5.7	2.9	2.5	n.a.
bu per acre	14.4	16.9	25.9	37.1	39.5
Potatoes					
labor-hr per acre	76.0	68.5	45.9	32.6	n.a.
cwt per acre	59.8	117.8	205.2	283.9	345.0
Sugar beets					
labor-hr per acre	128.0	85.0	35.0	20.0	n.a.
tons per acre	10.6	13.6	17.4	20.4	20.9
Cotton					
labor-hr per acre	116.0	83.0	35.0	5.0	n.a.
lb per acre	201.0	273.0	505.0	581.0	673.0
Soybeans					
labor-hr per acre	n.a.	8.0	4.8	3.2	n.a.
bu per acre	n.a.	19.6	24.2	30.7	38.9
Milk					
labor-hr per cow	146.0	129.0	84.0	24.0	n.a.
cwt per cow	38.4	49.9	82.6	127.3	164.8
Hogs					
labor-hr per cwt	3.6	3.0	1.6	0.3	n.a.
Turkeys					
labor-hr per cwt	31.4	13.1	1.6	0.2	n.a.

n.a. = not available

Source: U.S. Department of Agriculture, *Agricultural Statistics* (Washington D.C.: U.S. Government Printing Office, appropriate issues).

Today, it takes only a tenth as much labor to grow an acre of corn as it did 80 years ago, and that acre yields 4 times as much corn. Three times as much wheat can be raised with one-sixth the labor, and a worker-hour of effort yields 13 times as much milk and 100 times as much turkey as it did 80 years ago.

Scale of Operation

When technical innovation reduces farming cost by replacing labor with machinery, the result is lower variable costs, but higher charges for interest, depreciation, taxes, and other fixed costs. If lower average total cost is to result, these higher fixed costs must be spread over a larger output.

When farms grow larger, what happens to the total number in operation depends on demand for the product. As prices fall, total consumption increases in keeping with demand elasticity. Consumption also rises with growing population and increasing incomes. If demand is sufficiently elastic, and if income and population grow fast enough, the market for farm products can expand enough to maintain, or even to increase the number of farms in operation, despite the larger scale of operations.

The influence of technical development on the scale and number of U.S. farms is shown in Table 1-7.

Displacement of Farm Labor

Until about 1920, population and income grew faster than farm productivity, and the number of farms increased despite the growth in average size. After 1920 as technical improvement accelerated and population grew more slowly, the number of farms shrank as the average size in-

TABLE 1-7 Number and Size of Farms and U.S. Farm Employment, 1880–1990

Year	*Number of Farms*	*Average Acreage per Farm*	*Farm Employment (thousands)*
1880	4,008,000	133.7	10,100
1900	5,740,000	146.6	12,800
1920	6,453,000	148.5	13,400
1940	6,104,000	174.5	11,000
1960	5,388,000	215.5	7,100
1970	2,730,000	389.5	4,200
1990	2,140,000	461.0	2,891
1998	2,191,000	435.0	2,827

Sources: U.S. Department of Commerce, *Census of Agriculture* (Washington, D.C.: U.S. Government Printing Office, appropriate years). 1998 data from U.S. Department of Agriculture, *Agricultural Statistics, 1999* (Washington D.C.: U.S. Government Printing Office, 1999).

creased. In the last 30 years, the average size of U.S. farms has doubled, but the total number has been cut in half.

As the productivity of farm labor rises, any given amount of crop can be grown with the help of fewer people. Unless consumption expands proportionately, rising productivity means fewer people needed on farms. The history of declining farm labor is shown in the last column of Table 1-7.

It is the market that keeps the number of people engaged in agriculture in balance with productivity and demand. Increasing supply reduces farm prices and the earnings of farm workers. Farm people with marketable skills, especially young people, leave the farm for more profitable opportunities elsewhere. Those without other skills find themselves trapped in low-income farming or are forced off the farm into the city where, without marketable skills, many are added to the welfare rolls.

The fate of farmers is an excellent illustration of two important aspects of competitive markets. Competition generates inexorable pressure to extract greater output from available resources and passes these productivity gains on to consumers in the form of lower prices and higher standards of living. In doing so, however, the market operates without regard for the fate or the feelings of the people involved. The supply and demand for farm labor are rigorously balanced by the competitive market, regardless of what happens to families caught in the adjustment. Nowhere does the market, left to itself, take into account the human cost of this process.

Other Social Costs of Modern Agriculture

The increasing size of modern farms has brought profound changes to agriculture. Increasingly, farming is undertaken by large corporations, and the commercial farming of specialized crops is replacing the more diversified agriculture of the family farm.

Intense specialized farming, in turn, creates problems. It increases the danger of soil exhaustion as intensive use of fertilizer and single-crop operations replace crop rotation. In addition, contamination of streams and groundwater by runoff from chemical fertilizers and insecticides puts water supplies at risk and jeopardizes wildlife habitat.

The lower cost of mechanical harvest has led to the adaptation of many varieties of food to the requirements of machines, often at the expense of nutritional value and flavor.

Some of these problems reflect more on the tastes and preferences of consumers than they do on farm technology. If people are willing to buy cheap tomatoes with the flavor and consistency of red baseballs rather than pay a little more for flavorful tomatoes that are too delicate for anything more than hand harvesting, competitive agriculture will provide for their preferences. By the same token, more and more modern consumers are willing to pay for food raised organically without the use of artificial fertilizers, or chemical herbicides and pesticides—and the supply of such products is steadily increasing as farmers see the profit in the new opportunity.

Other problems, however, are fundamental to the nature of competitive agriculture, and consumers are powerless to change farming practice. These social costs arise because competitive producers pay attention only to costs that they themselves must pay. Any costs imposed on others count for nothing in the farm's calculations. If farmers can improve their own position by shifting costs from themselves onto society at large, competition will force them to do so if they want to stay in business. The competitive market provides no mechanism to balance gains in output and lower prices against higher social costs.

Sprinkler irrigation systems, in some areas at least, offer an example of the problem. The sprinkler provides a stable and ample water supply and does for crops what a lawn sprinkler does for a home garden. The adoption of the system increases the yield of the individual farm, yet widespread adoption of the technique creates problems for the rest of society. It depletes the water table, lowers the level of lakes and ponds, and increases the problems of municipal water supply, but no bill is presented to farmers for the wider consequences of their action. Individually, farmers take into account only the private profit potential of the method, and find themselves required by competition to adopt it, yet the collective result is higher cost to the rest of society.

There is increasing concern that extensive use of agricultural chemicals are dangerously polluting water and wildlife habitat and that consumer health is affected by growth hormones injected in cattle, by antibiotics used in animal feed, and by genetically modified crops. The market cannot prevent individual farmers from such practices. Indeed, the very forces of competition compel individual farmers to employ them. Any limitation or control must be imposed on all farmers from outside the market.

In 1999, methyl parathion and azinphon methyl, two pesticides that had long been used under heavy regulation, were banned outright for use on food crops ranging from apples to turnips. It would have been impossible for farmers themselves to abolish the use of these chemicals. As long as they are available, individual growers had to use them to stay competitive, despite the obvious damage inflicted. It took action by the government to outlaw their use.

Indeed, the alacrity with which competitive farmers utilize new technology poses serious problems. Genetically engineered crops, first introduced in 1992, have been welcomed enthusiastically, yet the long-run consequences of such crops are uncertain. Crops genetically altered to produce their own insecticide may destroy not only their own predators, but useful insects as well and poison birds and other animals that feed on them. Some scientists suspect that crops altered to be immune to viral diseases may interbreed with wild relatives and overwhelm the countryside with "super weeds" difficult to eradicate and expensive to control. In most cases, the long-run reaction of human health to the consumption of genetically engineered crops is unknown.

Although thorough discussion of issues of food safety and environmental pollution far exceeds the scope of this chapter, it is necessary to recognize that product safety and pollution are important aspects of the behavior of any industry. In this respect, untrammeled competition as exemplified by agriculture has a poor record.

IV. GOVERNMENT POLICY TOWARD AGRICULTURE

Price Supports

The problems wrought by untrammeled technical innovation has generated political pressure for governments all over the world to intervene in agriculture. Since it was first instituted in the 1930s as part of the New Deal, U.S. agricultural policy has largely focused on supporting prices at some target level above what would be determined on a competitive market. This was accomplished by a mixture of techniques. The government reduced supply by paying farmers to plant fewer acres than they otherwise would, or bought up enough crop to raise the price to the desired level. Under other laws, the government allowed farmers to produce and market their crops freely and then paid each grower a subsidy to make up the difference between the resulting market price and the target level. Finally, the government encouraged producers of certain products to join together in monopoly marketing organizations and agree among themselves about how much to produce and bring to market. At its peak, the support of agricultural prices directly cost taxpayers $18 billion per year. In addition, of course, consumers have had to pay more for the food on their tables.

But how much do farmers benefit from all this? The rationale for farm policy was to relieve the suffering caused by rapidly increasing agricultural productivity, yet the history of agriculture has been a continuous story of small farmers being driven out, and clearly those no longer on farms can hardly benefit from higher farm prices. Even most of those who remain on farms received few benefits from the program. The nature of price supports directs the benefits of the program toward the largest, most successful growers rather than toward the poor and weak who really need help.

A study made at the height of the program indicated that 50 percent of the smallest of all farms received less that 8 percent of total agricultural payments. This amounted to an average of only $250 per farm. In contrast, the largest 5 percent of farms received 25 percent of payments, which amounted to an average of almost $7,000 per farm. The three or four very largest farms received payments that ran to millions of dollars each!

This highly unequal distribution of benefits is a direct consequence of programs that pay for reduced acreage, that buy up excess production, and that directly subsidize prices. When the government pays to reduce acreage, the largest payments naturally go to the farms with the most acreage. When the government buys surpluses, or subsidizes prices, greatest payments go to farms with the largest production. Moreover, this is only part of the picture, for consumers must pay higher prices for food. Nobody knows how much this amounts to—it has been estimated at many times the value of the direct payments—but, whatever it is, it is distributed among farmers in proportion to the size of their operations, and so is concentrated in the hands of the largest producers.

Recent Governmental Policy: Partial Abandonment of Price Supports

The cost of price supports, the distortion of agricultural supply that they engender, and the obvious unfairness of the distribution of benefits has resulted in a new policy. The Agricultural Market Transition Act of 1996 was designed to wean the American farmer from price supports, and to stimulate a return to agriculture governed by market forces. The act does not suddenly remove all support from farmers, but rather reduces support and provides it in a way that leaves planting decisions unaffected. Farmers who contract to use their land exclusively for agricultural purposes, and who also agree to certain measures of conservation and wetland protection, are eligible for direct cash "transition" payments with no further strings attached. In other words, the new policy provides direct support to farmers, but in a way that will not affect agricultural supply or farm prices.

The total of annual payments to be made is reduced to a maximum that declines from $5.6 billion in 1996 to $4.0 billion in 2002. This total is allocated among growers of seven crops: about 26.3 percent is devoted to wheat, 46.2 percent to corn, 5.0 percent to grain sorghum, 2.2 percent to barley, 11.6 percent to upland cotton, 8.5 percent to rice, and 0.2 percent to oats.

The annual amount that each participating farm receives is based on a figure calculated by multiplying 85 percent of the acreage on the farm by a standard yield per acre of the commodity. The total number of dollars available for the crop is then prorated among participating farms on the basis of this calculation. Payments distributed this way are still in proportion to size of farm, but the act provides that no single farm can receive payments of more than $75,000 in any year.

How well the new farm policy will work in practice remains to be seen. During the first 2 years of the policy, commodity prices were high, and farmers were delighted to receive the transition payments in addition to their income from the sale of crops. When prices dropped in 1998 and 1999, however, farmers turned to the government for extra help. The prompt bi-partisan Congressional response was to grant billions of dollars in emergency aid to farmers. In 1999, this aid amounted to $8.7 billion, an additional expenditure roughly double the total prescribed for transitional payments. Without regard to long-run economic benefits, the question remains whether restoration of truly competitive agricultural markets is politically feasible.

Other Price-Support Measures

Although the government has abandoned price support for the seven commodities previously listed, other programs remain in place. Prices of peanuts and tobacco are supported by laws that restrict the acreage that can be devoted to these crops.

The prices of a broad array of commodities, ranging from citrus fruit to nuts, are set by marketing orders issued by the secretary of agriculture. These orders enable producers to organize *marketing boards,* which are given wide powers to control the production and marketing of designated commodities. Aside from certain professional sports, marketing boards are the only unregulated legal monopolies permitted in the United States. The boards limit production, sometimes by restricting the quality or sizes of product that can be shipped. Some boards prop up prices by assigning quotas to individual producers and requiring that any additional output be placed "in reserve," usually to be exported at low prices. The political advantage of marketing boards is that they impose the entire cost of the program directly on consumers, and avoid charges to the government budget.

The price of milk is supported by a combination of marketing order and government intervention. A marketing order by the secretary of agriculture sets the prices that dairies must pay dairy farmers for fluid milk destined for human consumption. The higher this price is set, the less milk dairies will buy, but the marketing order does little to control production. To deal with the result, all milk that farmers cannot sell at the fixed price is sold at whatever price it will bring as "industrial-grade" milk to be manufactured into butter, cheese, and dried milk. The demand for industrial-grade milk is, in turn, supported by loans extended to dairies by a government agency, the Commodity Credit Corporation (CCC). The CCC receives the manufactured dairy products in pledge for the loans.

When marketing conditions are poor, producers leave the products with the CCC rather than repay the loans, and the CCC accumulates a stock of the commodities. From time to time, the government passes on accumulated stocks of butter, cheese, and powdered milk to poor families.

Agricultural Policy and International Trade: The WTO

Intervention into agriculture is part of the policy of nearly every country in the world. The result, however, distorts production and prices away from what would result on truly competitive global markets. For example, under its former policy, the United States supported sugar prices by assigning import quotas among 41 sugar-producing countries. The effect was to impose the entire cost, estimated to be about $2.3 billion annually, on consumers, but the consequences of artificially high sugar prices extended well beyond the direct cost to consumers. In the world market, it meant that sugar came into the United States not from the most efficient producers, but from those lucky enough to come under an assigned quota. The import quotas also distorted our domestic markets. High prices induced many wheat growers to switch their operations to sugar beets. Perhaps the largest domestic impact was the extensive switch of consumers—particularly beverage manufacturers—away from sugar to substitutes, especially to high-fructose corn syrup (HFCS) and to low-calorie sweeteners. Sugar's share of the U.S. sweetener market fell from nearly 80 percent to barely more than 40 percent.

To make agriculture conform more closely to the free market ideal, the nations of the world in 1994 established the World Trade Organization (WTO), an international organization to deal with the rules of trade among nations. The main function of the WTO is to ensure that trade flows as smoothly and freely as possible.

To bring agriculture more into line with competitive global markets, the WTO agreement requires governments to abandon policies that encourage excess production, and to eliminate export subsidies that permit farmers to sell surplus production abroad at prices below the domestic market. Domestic policies that have a direct effect on production must be cut back by 20 percent by the year 2002.

Governments may continue direct payments to farmers as long as this is done in a way that does not stimulate production. (The shift in U.S. agricultural policy explained in the preceding section is in keeping with this provision.) In addition, governments can make certain direct payments that are accompanied by the requirement that farmers limit production. Governments may also continue to provide such services as advice to farmers, research, disease control, road construction, and the like, but subsidies that permit farmers to sell abroad at prices below the domestic level must be phased out.

Restriction of agricultural imports by quotas and other nontariff measures must be replaced by tariffs, which can be set to provide an equivalent level of protection. To this end, quantities that each nation imported under its old quota system are used to set "tariff quotas." Up to the amount of the tariff quota, imports are subject to greatly reduced tariffs, but imports in excess of the quota can be subject to higher (in some cases much higher) tariffs at the discretion of the importing country.

Friction and disagreements among nations about trade policies are channeled into an agreed dispute-settlement process where trade practices are examined for conformity to WTO agreements.

Consumer Safety and the WTO

One important aspect of the WTO agreement relates to the ability of governments to control the safety of imported food. Of course, all governments are obliged to protect their people from products that are harmful or unsafe. The difficulty is that some governments might allege problems of public safety as an excuse to shelter domestic growers from foreign competition, despite WTO provisions. The WTO agreement encourages member countries to use international food safety standards and guidelines where they exist, but countries are permitted to apply higher standards, the regulations say, *if there is scientific justification.* In other words, countries can set their own standards, but regulations cannot be arbitrary, and must be based on what somebody can point to as scientific evidence.

Unfortunately, this means not only that nations cannot use safety as a way around WTO regulations, but more important, it limits their ability to regulate imported food on the basis of a desire to err on the side of caution in untested areas. The question of what constitutes valid scientific evidence lies at the root of a recent controversy between the United States and the European Community. Several European nations, notably France, banned the importation of U.S. beef treated with growth hormones. The United States objected that there was no "scientific evidence" that growth hormones made beef unsafe for human consumption, and that the action was merely an attempt to protect European cattle raisers from imported United States beef. The United States appealed to the WTO, which concurred in the absence of "scientific evidence." Although the WTO cannot force the Europeans to buy hormone-treated beef, it ruled that the United States could, in retaliation, impose 100 percent tariffs on a list of luxury goods imported from Europe.

In an era of cloning, irradiation of food, genetic modification of food, and similar high tech innovations, many consumers are uncertain about food safety, and we can expect increasing controversy of this nature.

V. CONCLUSIONS

Left to itself, agriculture is a highly competitive industry, and its performance is, in many respects, almost ideal. Indeed, it is hard to imagine an industry better adapted to carry out the purely technical functions of producing products and allocating them among uses. Although harvest is subject to the vagaries of weather and random events, available supplies are rationed among users in accordance with consumer priorities as expressed by demand elasticities. At each stage of production, the greatest amount is extracted from available resources. In the very short run, when most costs have already been sunk into crops, relatively little can be done to adapt to consumer desires; however, given time, farmers shift output to match demand. Agriculture has a remarkable history of increasing the productivity of the resources it employs, and passing on the increases to consumers in the form of lower prices. At the same time, land, labor, and other resources have been released for the production of other products. All this has been accomplished with virtually no conscious collective planning, administrative direction, or political processes. Competitive pressure toward improvement is inexorable. New methods are not debated; rather, they simply impose themselves on the industry.

The same competitive process, however, sweeps along its own way, regardless of the fates of the people involved. The absence of social costs from the accounts of individual farms means that the search for cheaper methods can result in destroying the environment and imposing costs on society at large. Moreover, the same rise in productivity that has brought cheaper food and higher living standards to consumers has been accompanied by serious problems of human displacement. When productivity grows more rapidly than the demand for farm products, people who have devoted their lives to agriculture are driven off the farm to fend for themselves as best they can.

Governments the world over have adopted special programs to alleviate the plight of farmers, but these programs have done little for the people who most need help. Instead, the result was subsidy of the largest farms, inefficient use of land and labor, and economic chaos in the pattern of world trade in food and fiber. The World Trade Organization represents an attempt to bring world agricultural policy closer to conformity with the competitive ideal.

These are the economic forces working alongside the people, plows, and pickup trucks on the nation's fields and farms.

Suggested Readings

Adamantopolous, Constintinous. *An Anatomy of the World Trade Organization* (London: Kluwer Law International, 1997).

Bormann, F. Herbert, and Stephen R. Kellert. *Ecology, Economics, Ethics. The Broken Circle* (New Haven, CT: Yale University Press, 1991).

Burger, Anna. *The Agriculture of the World* (Brookfield, VT: Avebury, 1994).

Cameron, James, and Karen Campbell eds. *Dispute Resolution in the World Trade Organization* (London: Cameron, 1998).

Carlson, Gerald A., David Zilberman, and John A. Miranowski. *Agricultural and Environmental Resource Econom-*

ics (New York: Oxford University Press, 1993).

Cramer, Gail L., and Clarence W. Jensen. *Agricultural Economics and Agribusiness* (New York: Wiley, 1982).

Keesing, Donald. *Improving Trade Policy Reviews in the World Trade Organization* (Washington, D.C.: Institute for International Economics, 1998).

Marks, Stephen V., and Keith E. Maskus, eds. *The Economics and Politics of World Sugar Prices* (Ann Arbor: University of Michigan Press, 1993).

CHAPTER 2

Petroleum

—STEPHEN MARTIN

A company's most valuable asset is its customers.

—BUSINESS SCHOOL SAYING

Just as fossilized footprints mark the passage of a great dinosaur long after the dinosaur itself is gone, so the record of fluctuations in the price of crude oil marks passages in the world oil market. The tracks of major political events can be seen in Figure 2-1: the Arab-Israeli War of October 1973, the fall of the Shah of Iran in January 1979, and Iraq's August 1990 invasion of Kuwait. Economic changes, which for the most part occur less abruptly, also underlie the movements depicted in Figure 2-1. These are

- the shift in ownership and control over Mideast crude-oil reserves from vertically integrated, Western-based international oil companies ("the majors") to national oil companies;
- the development by the majors of new oil supplies outside OPEC control;
- the diffusion of energy-saving technologies on the demand side of the market and of high-technology production techniques on the supply side of the market;
- the vertical integration of national companies forward into refining and distribution;
- the return of international majors to nationalized oil provinces.

The market for oil is a world market, and one that is rich in lessons for students of industrial economics. It illustrates the ease with which firms may engage in limited collusion, and the difficulty with which they engage in complete collusion. It illustrates the endogeneity of market structure and the importance of vertical market structure for horizontal market performance. It illustrates governments' lack of understanding of and lack of faith in market processes.

We will examine the economic and political forces that have determined the performance of the world oil market and the U.S. submarket. Some of the questions we shall address are: What industry characteristics have allowed the exercise of market power, and by whom? What structural characteristics limit the exercise of market power? What has been

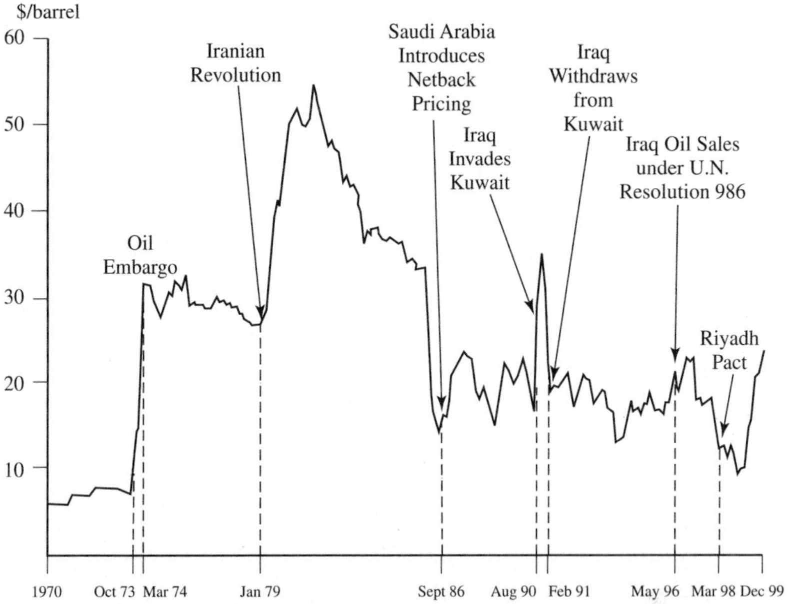

FIGURE 2-1 Real Price Per Barrel of Crude Oil (1999 Dollars)

the role of the major oil companies in the market, and that of smaller, independent companies? How have government policies affected the market? What does industrial economics suggest concerning likely future market performance?

I. STRUCTURE AND STRUCTURAL CHANGE

The petroleum industry is made up of four vertically related stages: production, refining, marketing, and transportation. Production involves the location and extraction of oil and natural gas from underground reservoirs; these may be so close to the surface that their oil seeps up through the ground, or they may require extensive drilling from platforms located miles offshore. The refinery segment manufactures finished products ranging from petroleum coke to motor gasoline and jet fuel. Wholesale and retail marketers distribute these products to consumers. Connecting these three vertical levels is a specialized transportation industry, including pipelines, tankers, barges, and trucks, which moves crude oil from fields to refineries and finished product from refineries to marketers.

In principle, these four vertically related segments might be supplied by independent firms, and at some times in some areas this has been the case, but throughout the history of the industry, the tendency has been for firms to integrate vertically and operate all along the line from production to distribution. These vertical links have been and continue to be critical in determining structure-performance relationships.

Domination by the International Majors

During the decade or so following World War II, the world oil market was dominated by the seven vertically integrated major oil companies. The Seven Sisters were actually eight, including the French firm Compagnie Française des Pétroles (CFP, later Total).[1] Five of these firms were based in the United States, and three of these five (Exxon, Mobil, and Chevron) were survivors of the landmark 1911 antitrust decision that dismantled the Standard Oil Trust.[2] The other two were British Petroleum (BP) and Royal Dutch/Shell. BP was half-owned by the British government. CFP was 25 percent owned by the French government, and effectively a public firm. Both are early examples of the persistent government belief that "oil [is] too important to be left to the oil companies."[3]

Together, these eight firms controlled 100 percent of 1950 world crude-oil production outside North America and the Communist bloc. Twenty years later, their combined share remained slightly above 80 percent.

The basis for this control was the system of joint ventures—partial horizontal integration—under which the vertically integrated majors divided ownership of the operating companies that exploited Middle East oilfields, the richest in the world (see Table 2-1).

This interconnecting network of joint ventures developed with the support of the home governments of the international majors, each concerned, for reasons of national security, to ensure the access of domestically based firms to crude petroleum reserves. Thus, the U.S. Department of State induced American firms to take part in the 1928 "Red Line Agreement" which formalized control of the Iraq Petroleum Company. The French government set up Compagnie Française des Pétroles to exploit its share of the Iraq concession.

The British government was similarly involved in the 1934 agreement that divided the Kuwait operating company between Gulf and BP. The U.S. government was instrumental in the 1948 reorganization of the Arabian-American Oil Company (Aramco) as a joint venture of Exxon,

---

[1]Such is the power of alliteration.

[2]In a certain sense, they were second-generation survivors, each being a combination of Standard Oil survivor firms. Exxon combined Standard Oil of New Jersey and the Anglo-American Oil Company; Mobil, for part of its life known as Socony-Vacuum, combined Standard Oil of New York and Vacuum Oil Company; and Chevron combined Standard Oil of California and Standard Oil of Kentucky.

[3]Anthony Sampson, *The Seven Sisters* (New York: Bantam Books, 1976), p. 68.

TABLE 2-1 Ownership shares in Middle East joint ventures, 1970

	Aramco	*Kuwait Oil Company*	*Iranian Consortium*	*Iraq Petroleum Company*
Exxon	30		7	11.875
Texaco	30		7	
Gulf		50	7	
Chevron	30		7	
Mobil	10		7	11.875
Royal Dutch/Shell			14	23.75
British Petroleum		50	40	23.75
CFP (Total)			6	23.75
Others			5	5

Source: S. A. Schneider, *The Oil Price Revolution* (Baltimore: Johns Hopkins University Press, 1983), p. 40.

Texaco, Chevron, and Mobil to produce Saudi Arabian crude. The Iranian consortium—which delivered Persian oilfields into the hands of the seven majors, CFP, and a handful of American independents—was established after a CIA-backed coup returned the Shah of Iran to power in August 1953 (reversing the nationalization of Iranian oil by the Mossadegh government). The fact that such a joint venture involving five American firms was contrary to U.S. antitrust law was set aside, at the urging of the department of state, for reasons of national security.

The continual contacts required for the management of these joint ventures resulted in a sharing of information and a communality of interest that is not characteristic of "arm's length" competition:

> [T]he international companies' vertical integration was complemented in practice by a degree of informal but effective horizontal integration. Their joint ownership of operating companies in the Middle East, and their voting rights under the complex operating agreements through which they controlled exploration, development, and offtake there, gave them a unique degree of knowledge of each others' opportunities to increase crude offtake, and some leverage to influence each others' opportunities.[4]

The Mideast joint ventures were operated under restrictions that had the effect of ensuring output limitations. For example, partners in the Iraq

[4]J. E. Hartshorn, *Oil Trade: Politics and Prospects,* (Cambridge: Cambridge University Press, 1993), p. 117. The economic and political tensions among the international cartel partners are described in Walter Adams and James W. Brock, "Retarding the development of Iraq's oil resources: an episode in oleaginous diplomacy, 1927–1939," *Journal of Economic Issues* (March 1993): 69–93.

Petroleum Company were obliged to file their requirements for crude oil 5 years in advance. Each partner thus gained definite information about the plans of every other partner. A firm that filed requirements for expanded output would telegraph its plans to rivals, exposing itself to immediate retaliation.[5]

With the international majors joined by an extensive network of horizontal and vertical linkages, the world oil market operated as a small-numbers oligopoly in which rivalry manifested itself in development of reserves, in marketing efforts, and in the development of brand names but not, in general, in price competition. The prosperity of the international majors depended on secure access to crude oil deposits. With concessions to produce from such deposits in many parts of the world, solid political support from their home country governments, and control over channels of distribution to final consumers, the majors were relatively immune to pressure by the governments of the less developed countries where the highest-quality deposits were located.

The same firms dominated supply on the world market and the U.S. submarket, but government regulations kept the two separate. From the 1930s until the 1950s, controls on oil production by state governments (importantly, the Texas Railroad Commission) held crude-oil prices in the United States at artificially high levels. These prices proved attractive to foreign suppliers, and by 1948 the United States became a net importer of refined oil products. Three congressional investigations of the matter in 1950 conveyed to the oil companies a congressional preference for low imports. When domestic oil producers raised the price of U.S. crude oil in June 1950, the U.S. coal industry, with the support of the petroleum industry, sponsored a bill to place import quotas on petroleum. The Eisenhower Administration set up "voluntary" import-restraint programs in 1954 and 1958, and when these proved ineffective, imposed mandatory quotas in 1959.

These formal and informal restrictions on the flow of oil into the United States meant higher prices for U.S. consumers, perhaps by as much as \$3 to \$4 billion a year.[6] At a time when the price of crude oil on the Eastern seaboard was about \$3.75 a barrel, a Cabinet task force estimated that the elimination of oil-import quotas would reduce the price of crude oil by \$1.30 a barrel.[7]

---

[5]M. A. Adelman, *The World Petroleum Market,* (Baltimore: Johns Hopkins, 1972), pp. 84–87. Stigler's theory of oligopoly explains why joint ventures affect market performance: the more rapidly cheating is likely to be detected, and therefore subject to retaliation, the less likely cheating is to occur. George J. Stigler "A Theory of Oligopoly," *Journal of Political Economy* Volume 72, Number 1, February 1964, pp. 44–61; reprinted in George J. Stigler *The Organization of Industry.* (Homewood, Illinois: Richard D. Irwin, Inc. 1968), pp. 39–63.

[6]S. A. Schneider, *The Oil Price Revolution,* (Baltimore: Johns Hopkins, 1983), p. 46.

[7]Subcommittee on Antitrust and Monopoly, Cabinet on the Judiciary, United States Senate, *The Petroleum Industry: Part 4, The Cabinet Task Force on Oil Import Control,* (Washington, D.C.: U.S. Government Printing Office, March 1970).

Although the quotas had been justified on national security grounds, the effect of high U.S. prices in a shielded market was to encourage the extraction of relatively high-cost U.S. crude oil, accelerating the depletion of U.S. reserves and conserving lower-cost reserves elsewhere in the world. It became clear, in 1973, that U.S. national security would have been better served if the pattern of extraction had been reversed.

Rise of Independent Oil Companies

One of the most important lessons of modern industrial economics is that market structure is endogenous, itself the product of economic forces. The world oil market provides more than one example. The domination of the world oil market by the international majors set in motion a process of entry by new firms in search of profit. This process occupied the period from the mid-1950s through 1973, and marked a transition from a market dominated by the international majors to a market dominated by the governments of producing countries.

The first step was the 1954 Iranian consortium, when the U.S. government insisted that the majors make room for nine independents. Having gained a toehold in the Middle East, the independents sought to expand their roles. Just as the majors had once been able to play host nation against host nation by shifting production from country to country to resist pressure to expand output, so host nations gradually gained the option of playing independent companies against major companies.

In 1956, Libya granted concessions to 17 firms. Independents subsequently accounted for half of Libyan output, and in due course products refined from this oil found their way to European markets.[8]

The activities of Enrico Mattei, head of the Italian national firm Ente Nazionale Idrocarburi (ENI), had far-reaching consequences. He sought access to oil supplies in Iran and elsewhere, and ultimately found it in the Soviet Union. After 1959, products refined from Russian oil joined the flow of independent oil onto world markets.

The increased flow of oil from these various independent sources created an excess supply at prevailing prices, despite rapidly expanding demand. The result was downward pressure on prices, which the international majors could not resist, but the governments of the oil producing nations collected taxes based on a "posted price" for oil, a price largely divorced from the reality of transactions in the marketplace. This posted-price system worked well as long as the market price of oil was level or rising. A falling market price combined with unchanging posted prices meant that an increasing share of profit went to host countries in the form of taxes that were levied based on the posted price.

---

[8]Anthony Sampson, *Seven Sisters* (New York: Bantam Books, 1976), pp. 174–175.

In August 1960, Exxon reduced its posted prices for oil. In due course, the remaining major firms followed suit. This reduction in the posted prices for oil was no more than a reflection of reductions in transaction prices. The reduction in transaction prices was the consequence of a more rapid expansion in supply than in demand. The more rapid expansion in supply than in demand was, in turn, a direct result of the actions of the host countries, which had granted independents access to crude supplies as a way of breaking the grip of the Seven Sisters on the world oil market.

The reduction in posted prices was, therefore, an inevitable consequence of the actions of host countries, but it appeared to them as a unilateral reduction in their own tax revenues, imposed by international corporations. The reaction came at a September 1960 meeting of Saudi Arabia, Iran, Iraq, Kuwait, and Venezuela, when it was agreed to establish the Organization of Petroleum Exporting Countries—OPEC.

The 13 years that followed the formation of OPEC saw a long dance between the two loosely coordinated oligopolies, one of the international majors and one of producing countries. At the start of this period, the balance of power lay with the companies; at the end, it lay with the countries.

Although OPEC member states were beneficiaries of this shift in power, they did not initiate it. The international companies had a long history of effective cooperation, and they were better at it than the producing countries. By negotiating on a country-by-country basis, the major companies were able to prevent the countries from combining their bargaining power. OPEC was able to prevent further declines in the posted price, but was not able to reverse the reductions that had induced OPEC's formation.

The catalyst for change was the interaction of independent companies and the revolutionary government of a relatively new oil province—Libya. Colonel Muamer Qadaffi's government took power in September 1969, and soon set about renegotiating the terms of Libyan oil concessions. As we have already remarked, independent oil firms had major roles in exploiting these concessions, and the independents were in a much weaker bargaining position, vis-à-vis the host countries, than the majors. Any one of the integrated majors, faced with an unattractive proposal from a producing country, could credibly threaten to reduce output in that country and turn to supplies elsewhere around the world. Independent companies had no such alternative.

In August 1970, Occidental Petroleum Company agreed to Libyan demands for higher prices and higher taxes. This example inspired other oil producing nations. In February 1971, oil companies agreed in Teheran to the higher price demanded by the Shah of Iran. The major oil companies revised the terms of their arrangement with Libya in April 1971.[9]

---

[9]*Ibid.*, pp. 253–272.

The oil producing countries had demonstrated their ability to control the terms upon which oil was lifted from their territories, but it was the major companies that, through their joint ventures, owned the operating companies (see Table 2-1). This too was to change.

Again it was the radical states, rather than OPEC, that led the way. Algeria nationalized 51 percent of French ownership in Algerian reserves in February 1971; Libya nationalized British Petroleum's interests in November 1971; and the Iraqi Petroleum Company was nationalized in June 1972. Long negotiations between Saudi Arabia, represented by Sheik Zaki Yamani, and Aramco followed. Aramco agreed to yield an initial 25 percent of its Saudi Arabian concession to Saudi Arabia.[10]

In the absence of intervening political developments, the transfer of world market control from the international majors to the producing countries would likely have continued at a gradual pace. The producing countries would have slowly replaced the international majors, with little change in market performance. In such a world, the Western "man in the street" would have remained blissfully unfamiliar with the nature of the world oil market. Events unfolded rather differently.

OPEC

The 1970s opened with the demand for oil increasing throughout the industrial world. Figure 2-2 shows the steady growth of the U.S. oil demand through the 1960s and early 1970s. Similar growth took place in Europe and Japan. In 1973, with simultaneous booms in North America, Europe, and Japan, world demand for energy—and oil—was at an all-time high.

At the same time, supply and the control of supply were increasingly concentrated in the low-cost Middle East. In 1970, proved reserves[11] of crude oil in the Middle East were 333,506 million barrels—versus 67,431 million barrels of proved reserves in the Western Hemisphere and 54,680 million barrels in Africa.

The location and development of crude oil reserves is a time-consuming process, particularly when oil fields are located offshore or in other hostile climates. Thus, the 1970s opened with a relatively small short-run supply of crude oil available from fringe, non-OPEC suppliers. These fringe suppliers faced substantially higher costs—development costs and operating costs—than Middle East producers (Table 2-2).

---

[10]*Ibid.,* pp. 278–282. On the eventual end of this process, see Youssef M. Ibrahim, "A U.S. era closes at Aramco," *International Herald Tribune,* April 6, 1989, p. 13.

[11]The American Petroleum Institute defines proved reserves as follows:

> Proved reserves of crude oil . . . are the estimated quantities of all liquids statistically defined as crude oil, which geological and engineering data demonstrate with reasonable certainty to be recoverable in future years from known reservoirs under existing economic and operating conditions.

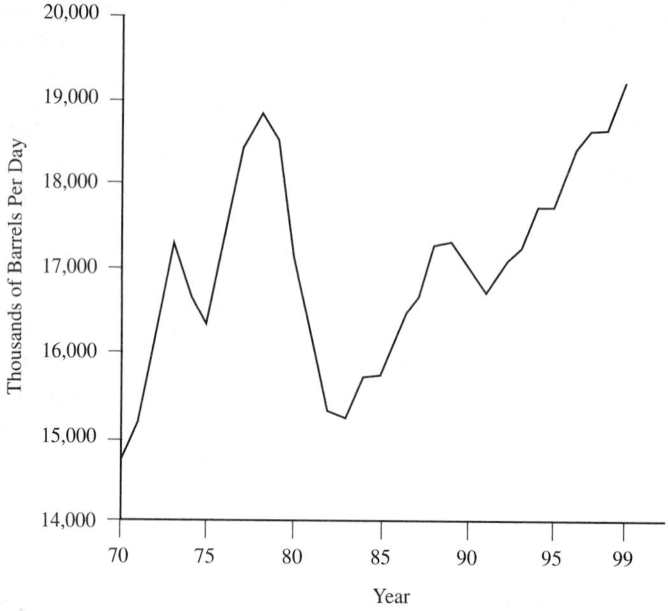

FIGURE 2-2 U.S. Demand for Refined Oil Products, (1999: first 3 months)

Source: Basic Petroleum Data Book, vol. 19, July 1999, Section 7, Table 2.

TABLE 2-2 Oil and Gas Production, Finding, and Development Costs, $ Per Barrel of Oil Equivalent

	$/Barrel
Saudi Arabia	≤2
Indonesia	6
Nigeria	7
Venezuela	7
Gulf of Mexico	10
North Sea	11
Russia	14

Source: The Economist 6 March 1999, p. 23.

This kind of market is illustrated in Figure 2-3(a). Fringe supply q_1^F is small relative to market size; the residual demand left for the cartel comprises the bulk of the market.[12] In such a market, a dominant firm or perfectly colluding cartel would maximize profit by selecting an output that equates marginal revenue along the residual demand curve—the market demand curve after subtracting fringe output—to marginal cost. In Figure 2-3(a), the corresponding cartel output is q_1^C, which would sell at price p_1. Because fringe supply is small, this is very nearly the monopoly position.

Because the economic interests of the OPEC member nations diverge in fundamental ways, OPEC was far from being able to act as a monopolist or a perfectly colluding cartel. It was a political rather than an economic event that triggered coordinated OPEC action and allowed it to take advantage of the demand-supply relationship depicted in Figure 2-3(a). In reaction to Western support for Israel during the

FIGURE 2-3 Fringe Supply and Cartel Output

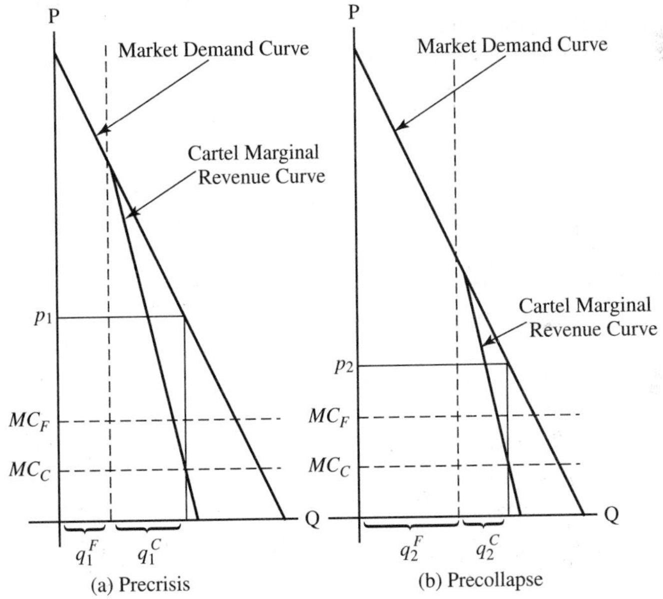

[12]It is an exaggeration to draw fringe supply as completely inelastic with respect to price—a vertical line—but only a modest one. Most of oilfield development cost is fixed and sunk, so that price would have to fall very low before fringe firms would reduce output. Given the constraints of location and development, even if price rises very high, it is not possible to expand output much in the short run. Thus the fringe supply curve will be nearly vertical.

Egypt-Israeli War of October 1973, Arab nations imposed production cutbacks and an embargo of crude oil supplies to the West.

The international oil companies were based in the West, and they had long benefited from the political support of their home governments, governments that sought to protect their perceived national security interest in a safe supply of oil. The international majors, however, administered the embargo of Western nations in accordance with OPEC directives, going so far as to provide Saudi Arabia with information on the shipment of refined oil products to U.S. military bases around the world.[13]

As the producing countries cut back the international majors' supplies of crude oil, the majors cut back supplies to independent companies. With their survival threatened, the independents turned to the market for oil not tied up by long-term contracts—the relatively narrow spot market. Independents bid up the spot-market price of oil, and official OPEC prices soon followed. The immediate result was the 1973 rise in official prices shown in Figure 2-1.

From this price increase flowed longer-run changes. OPEC revenue from the sale of oil rose from $13.7 billion in 1972 to $87.2 billion in 1974. Real U.S. gross national product, which grew 5.2 percent in 1973, fell 0.5 percent in 1973 and 1.3 percent in 1974.

Aside from the accelerated shift in control of production to the producing nations, there were remarkably few structural changes during the period following the first price increase. U.S. demand for oil fell slightly in 1974 and 1975, but then rose to new heights by 1978 (Figure 2-2). The share of imports in the U.S. market, and specifically imports from OPEC, peaked in 1977 but remained higher than in 1973 (Figure 2-4). The pattern of consumption and supply was much the same in other industrialized countries.

As shown in Figure 2-5, OPEC's share of world crude-oil production fell only about 5 percent over the period 1973 to 1979. World production of crude oil grew throughout this period, but OPEC's production was essentially level: 30,989,000 barrels per day in 1973, and 30,911,000 barrels per day in 1979.

Because of the length of time needed to develop new petroleum reserves and to install energy-saving residential and industrial equipment, the underlying market conditions that greeted the fall of the Shah of Iran in January 1979 were essentially the same as those that had greeted the Arab-Israeli War of 1973: peak demand, concentration of supply in the Middle East, and absence of spare capacity in the West.

The impact of the course of events on the market was also similar. Supply was disrupted. Independent refiners had their crude supplies cut

---

[13]Louis Turner, *Oil Companies in the International System* (London: Allen & Unwin, 1983), p. 136.

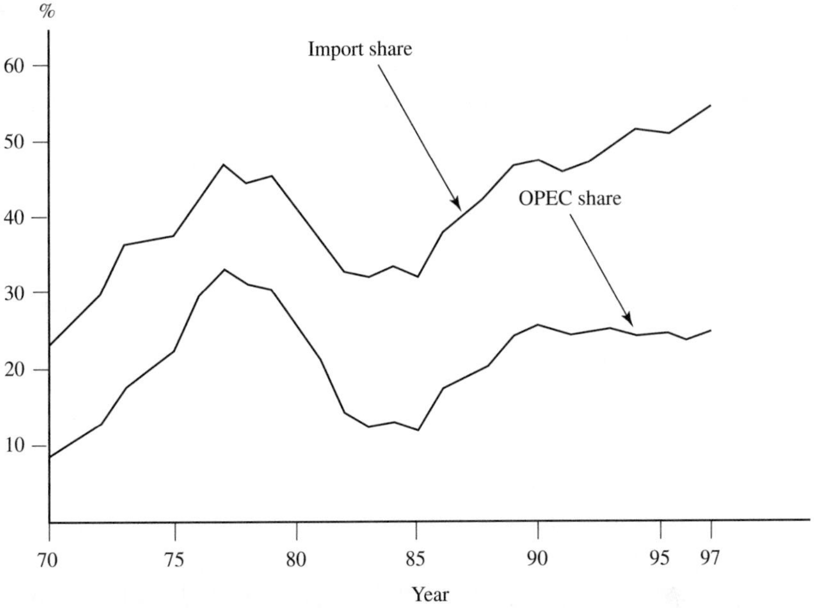

FIGURE 2-4 Import and OPEC Shares of the U.S. Petroleum Market, 1970–1997

Source: Basic Petroleum Data Book, vol. 19, July 1999, Section 7, Table 2; Section 14, Table 3.

FIGURE 2-5 Shares of World Crude Petroleum Production, 1970–1988

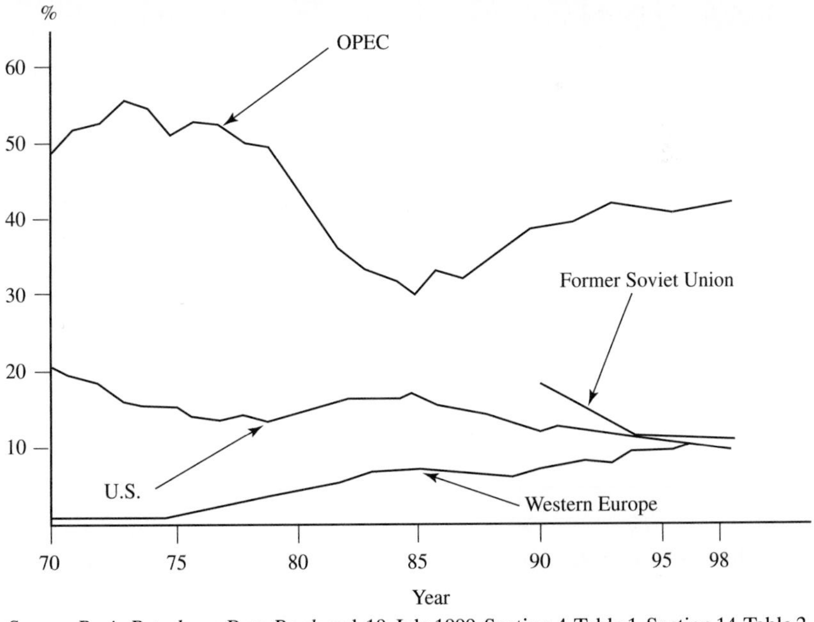

Source: Basic Petroleum Data Book, vol. 19, July 1999, Section 4, Table 1, Section 14, Table 2.

off. Desperate for crude oil, they turned to the spot market, and the price of oil, shown in Figure 2-1, shot up.

Cultivation of Crude Oil Supplies Outside OPEC

The response to the second oil-price shock, however, was substantially different from the response to the first oil-price shock. Differences occurred on both the demand side and the supply side of the market.

As shown in Figure 2-6, energy use in the United States declined slowly over the period from the first to the second oil price shock, but declined sharply thereafter. Energy use in the European Union and Japan was essentially unchanged over the period from the first to the second oil price shock, and has declined slowly since then.

These changes illustrate the long response time required to realize changes in the demand for energy resources. It indicates a long-term shift to greater efficiency in energy use, partly due to the greater real price of energy and partly due to increasing concern about the impact of energy consumption on the environment. This shift translates into slower growth in demand for energy from all sources, including petroleum.

A matching effect exists on the supply side of the market, described in Table 2-3. U.S. crude oil production peaked in 1970 and has followed a downward trend from that date. This trend will continue, mitigated by

FIGURE 2-6 Total Primary Energy Supply (in millions of tons of oil equivalent) Per Billion Dollars of Gross Domestic Product (measured in 1990 U.S. dollars)

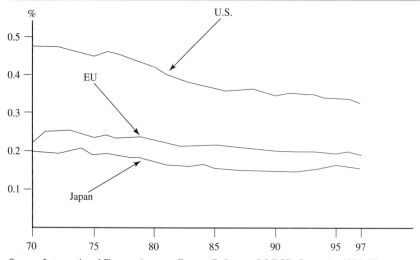

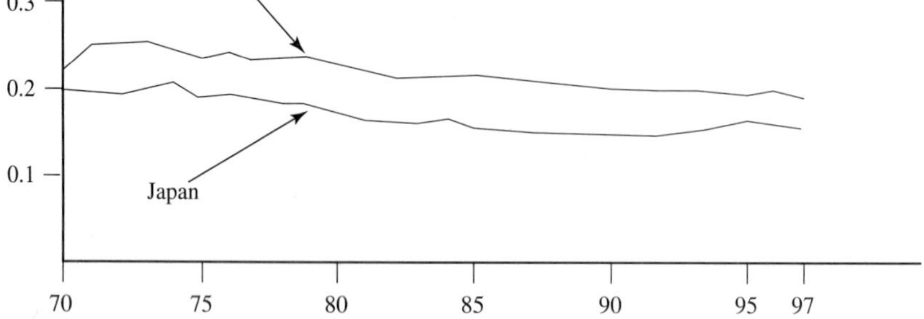

Source: International Energy Agency, *Energy Balance of OECD Countries 1996–97.*

TABLE 2-3 World Crude Production by Area, 1974 and 1998

	1974		*1998*	
	Million Barrels	***%***	***Million Barrels***	***%***
United States	3,203	15.6	2,326	10.6
Canada	617	3.0	737	3.4
Western Europe	142	0.7	2,301	10.5
Latin America	1,789	8.7	3,430	15.6
Asia	816	4.0	2,598	11.8
Eastern Europe	3,995	19.5		
Russia			2,564	11.7
Africa	1,990	9.7	2,497	11.4
Middle East	7,987	38.9	7,661	34.8
Total	20,538		21,983	

Source: American Petroleum Institute, *Basic Petroleum Data Book,* July 1999, Section 4, Table 1.

new technology but not by the discovery or exploitation of new reservoirs. Long isolated from the world market by protective quotas, the United States has been thoroughly explored. But output from Western Europe increased sharply over this period, as the North Sea oilfields of Britain and Norway came into production. North Sea oil output reached a plateau in the mid-1990s, and will decline (although technological progress continues to extend its potential beyond original expectations). The North Sea will remain an important source of natural gas.

Output in Latin America rose over this period, and this trend is likely to continue. Venezuela, a charter member of OPEC, continues to expand its oil reserves. It markets a coal-water mixture that is a good substitute for fuel oil, but that is exempt from OPEC output quotas. In addition, Venezuela has aggressively acquired networks of refineries and service stations, to ensure outlets for its oil. Other Latin American countries, including Peru and Columbia, continue to expand their oil industries; Mexico has increasingly cooperated with international oil companies to exploit its oil deposits.

Crude oil output from the rest of the world, including China and less developed countries (LDCs) in Africa, will increase. This reflects a convergence of interest between LDCs and the international majors. Nationalizations by OPEC member states cut the international majors off from the Mideast oilfields that were for generations the foundation of their dominant market positions. They will explore anywhere outside OPEC's sphere of influence for new reserves, which they can feed into their existing refining and marketing networks. They will do so as long as the new reserves can be developed at or below the spot market price for oil.

At the same time, LDCs know from bitter experience that it is their development efforts that are torpedoed by dependency on foreign sources of oil. For political reasons, LDCs will encourage the development of local oil supplies even if the cost seems likely to exceed the spot market price. Their national security, and often the lives of their leaders, depends on it.

The same applies to the world's newest group of less developed countries, the members of the Commonwealth of Independent States. Crude oil output from the former Soviet Union will decline during a transitory period, as the foundations of market economies are laid. Once that difficult transition is past, petroleum deposits will be viewed as much as a source of foreign exchange as a source of energy, and will be exploited accordingly. Independent oil companies are already establishing ties in this part of the world, despite the uncertain political and legal environments.

The international majors will, therefore, be welcome in the new oil provinces around the world. The supply of oil from less developed countries will increase, and to some extent this increase will result from political rather than economic considerations.

Along with the substantial increases in crude oil production outside OPEC has come the reduction in Middle Eastern output shown in Figure 2-5. By mid-1985, OPEC found itself in the kind of market illustrated in Figure 2-3(b). Fringe supply, after a decade of development efforts, was relatively large. Demand, after a decade of conservation efforts, had grown much less rapidly than expected. The residual part of the market left for OPEC was substantially reduced, compared with the situation of Figure 2-3(a). In such circumstances, the best OPEC could do would be to set a price p_2, much lower than p_1, and market a substantially smaller quantity q_2^C. Just as the international majors' long domination of the world oil market created an incentive for the entry and expansion of independent oil firms, so did OPEC's somewhat briefer period of control create an incentive for the development of new oil provinces.

The entry of independent firms undercut the resource base of the international majors, which reacted by seeking new supplies of oil. The entry of new oil-producing countries similarly undercut the power base of OPEC member states, forcing them to seek secure outlets for their oil. The result has been a renewed trend to vertical integration, by OPEC member states and by oil companies, with horizontal concentration reduced at all levels of industry.

The North Sea Markets

Perhaps the most ironic consequence of OPEC's assertion of control over the world crude market is the development of active spot and futures markets for Brent crude blend, which has made the price of North Sea crude a bellwether for the industry and ratified OPEC's inability to do more than slide down a contracting residual demand curve.

Sovereignty over North Sea oil deposits lies primarily with Britain and Norway. A large number of international oil companies exploit the North Sea oil fields through a complex web of joint ventures.[14] Concentration of production is high, although declining. Output is dominated by Exxon and Shell, whose combined market share was near 70 percent for much of the 1980s, and remained over 50 percent in 1993.[15]

North Sea oilfields benefit from a location near the major consuming centers of Europe and from a product with desirable physical properties from the refining point of view. North Sea oil is a good substitute for U.S. and OPEC products. For these reasons, and because the North Sea came "on line" at a time when international oil companies were scampering to acquire access to oil outside OPEC influence, the spot market for North Sea oil has assumed a central place in the interlocking world network of oil markets. The economic importance of the North Sea market is far greater than its share of world oil output (never more than 6 percent). The prices of many other transactions are tied to those on the North Sea market. In times of real or perceived shortage, surges of demand on the North Sea futures market (the market for oil to be delivered one, two, or more months in the future) can drive prices up rapidly, and often down again just as rapidly (examine Figure 2-1 for the time around the Iraqi invasion of Kuwait).[16] The role of the price of Brent blend as a marker price for the world petroleum industry confirms OPEC's long-run inability to control the world oil market. But the picture is not entirely rosy: the spot and futures markets for North Sea oil are subject to speculative binges, and price fluctuations on these markets often have little to do with the fundamentals of supply and demand.

Consolidation and Integration

The beginning of the twenty-first century sees three changes in market structure that, on balance, bode well for market performance on the crude oil market. Major oil companies are merging and restructuring their activities to reduce costs. State-owned oil firms—the product of the nationalizations of the 1970s—are integrating forward from production into refining and distribution, competing with the international majors at all vertical levels. And an increasing number of countries that nationalized their oil industries at the dawn of the OPEC era are allowing the international majors to return, on carefully controlled terms, to develop new

---

[14]Exxon and Shell, for example, are equal partners in all their North Sea assets.

[15]Paul Horsnell and Robert Mabro, *Oil Markets and Prices* (Oxford: Oxford University Press, 1993), pp. 25–28.

[16]See Steven Butler, "Oil traders devise strategies for the 21st century," *Financial Times* May 25, 1990, and Horsnell and Mabro, *Oil Markets and Prices.*

reserves. In a real sense, the structure of the world oil market is returning to what it was before the rise of OPEC, but with a larger number of players.

August 1998 saw the merger of British Petroleum (BP) and Amoco, a Standard Oil survivor company. Amoco was short of reserves of crude oil, and the merger would permit the combined firm to scrap outmoded refineries and reduce costs. Six months later, BP Amoco proposed to take over Arco, another Standard Oil survivor and a company pressed by low oil prices and the high cost of extracting oil from the North Slope of Alaska.

In December 1998, Exxon and Mobil, the two largest Standard Oil survivor companies, proposed to merge. Once again, low oil prices and the value of secure access to reserves lay behind the merger.

The Exxon-Mobil merger was approved by both Directorate General IV (DGIV) of the European Commission, the competition law enforcement arm of the European Union, and by the U.S. Federal Trade Commission (FTC). To obtain FTC approval, Exxon and Mobil agreed to sell off a refinery and nearly 5,000 retail gas stations, to avoid substantially increasing seller concentration in regional or local markets. The BP Amoco-Atlantic Richfield merger was approved by the European Union. In February 2000, the Federal Trade Commission announced its intention to block the merger, on the ground that the merger would create too great a concentration of sales of Alaskan crude oil and worsen performance in the West Coast market for supply of crude oil to refiners.[17] The companies made clear their intention to challenge the FTC action in court.

In December 1998, the French firm Total (formerly the eighth of the Seven Sisters, Compagnie Française des Pétroles) acquired the Belgian firm Petrofina. In October 1999, TotalFina proposed to take over the French firm Elf Aquitaine, a combination that would ensure European representation among the major private oil firms. DG IV approved the merger in February 2000, requiring the companies to sell off certain assets, including a number of retail outlets.

This wave of consolidation among private firms accompanies, and in a certain sense is a consequence of, the diversification of national oil companies out of production and into refining and distribution. These in-

[17]See U.S. Department of Energy, Energy Information Administration, "Price changes in the gasoline market: are Midwestern gasoline prices downward sticky?" for a review of the literature on the extent to which upward and downward fluctuations in the price of crude oil are passed on to the price of retail gasoline. The EIA finds that upward fluctuations in the price of crude oil are passed on to the retail price more rapidly than downward fluctuations, but that the full extent of crude oil price changes in both directions are ultimately passed through to the retail level.

clude Saudi Aramco, Venezuela's PDV, Brazil's Petrobas, and Norway's Statoil.[18]

Through a subsidiary of the Kuwait Petroleum Corporation, Kuwait owns two European refineries with a capacity of 135,000 barrels per day, together with 4,800 retail gasoline stations in seven different European countries. Kuwait has acquired a 22 percent ownership of British Petroleum, much to British government concern, and has sought refining assets in Japan.

Venezuela has employed joint ventures to acquire partial interests in refineries in West Germany, Sweden, Belgium, and acquired Citgo's refining and distribution operations in the United States.

Other OPEC members also integrated forward into the U.S. market. In November 1988, Saudi Arabia acquired half-ownership of Texaco, Inc.'s U.S. refining and distribution network. The three refineries involved had a capacity of 615,000 barrels per day; the distribution network included 11,450 retail gasoline stations. With this investment, the largest source of crude oil in the world moved to secure a market for its product. It also acquired an interest in maintaining profitability at the refining and distribution levels of the market, as well as at the crude level.

The motives for this forward integration are partly political and partly economic. A move forward into refining is a way of broadening the local industrial base while taking advantage of existing assets and skills. At the same time, a refinery associated with a national oil company of an oil-producing state has an almost insuperable advantage when compared with an independent refiner. The real cost of crude oil to the integrated refiner is the cost of crude production (regardless of the transfer price from the crude division to the refinery division). But the cost of crude oil to an independent, nonintegrated refiner is the much higher market price for crude oil. Refining and distribution networks associated with producing nations will always be able to undersell independents. When a surplus of crude oil exists, it will be tempting—and profitable—to do so.

The firms created by the merger wave of 1999 are large in an absolute sense, but small in proportion to the market. A combined Mobil and Exxon, the largest of the lot, accounts for only four percent of world crude production. Taking the rivalry of state-owned firms into account, the mergers among private firms seem unlikely to worsen performance on the world oil market.[19]

An encouraging structural change is the return of the international majors to oil provinces that were nationalized in the early 1970s. Several

---

[18]The merger of Statoil with the State's Direct Financial Interest (SDFI) was proposed by Statoil management to strengthen the company on the way to privatization.

[19]See U.S. Department of Energy, Energy Information Administration, "Price changes in the gasoline market: are Midwestern gasoline prices downward sticky?"

OPEC governments have confronted the harsh reality that the development of new reserves—their source of future oil revenues—is risky and expensive. For many such governments, the economic profits collected in the 1980s are gone, spent on wars, welfare, and development efforts; the option to work with the international majors has become more attractive than it once was. When the international majors are in place, the discretion of national governments to restrict output will be reduced.[20]

II. CONDUCT AND PERFORMANCE

The price increases of 1973 and 1979–82 are sometimes asserted to reflect no more than the working of competitive forces. In this view—favored in particular by oil producing nations—a price of oil at or near extraction cost fails to reflect the scarcity that current consumption imposes on future generations. A price substantially above marginal extraction cost, in this view, is to be desired, because it encourages conservation and spreads consumption of a finite resource over a long time period.

This argument might explain the price increases observed in 1973 and 1979–82. It cannot explain the price declines since then. Oil is, after all, as much a finite resource as it ever was, and if future scarcity produced a high price in 1982, it would, seemingly, produce a still higher price in the twenty-first century. Statistical tests do not support the argument that OPEC pricing is competitive.[21]

Some analysts suggest that the world oil industry is driven by a single dominant "firm"—Saudi Arabia. According to the figures in Table 2-4, Saudi Arabia holds 25 percent of the world's proven reserves. It is widely believed that Saudi Arabia substantially understates its reserve holdings. This quantitative description does not capture the fact that Saudi crude is by far the least expensive in the world, with an estimated cost of less than $1 a barrel.

These reserve holdings mean that Saudi Arabia will be a factor on the world oil market so long as there is a world market for oil. If Saudi Arabia were to act as a wealth-maximizing dominant firm, it would, in principle, restrict output and raise price above the cost of production. It would then gradually give up market share, as other producers expand

[20]The Iranian constitution prohibits granting concessions to foreign firms. Iran has therefore offered so-called "buyback agreements" to foreign firms. Under such an arrangement, foreign firms develop an oilfield for a fixed compensation, over a specified period, that is paid by Iranian receipts from the sale of oil. If the price of oil drops, Iran must sell more oil to pay the foreign developer.

[21]James M. Griffen "OPEC Behavior: A Test of Alternative Hypotheses," *American Economic Review* Volume 75, Number 5, December 1985, pp. 954–963.

TABLE 2-4 Estimated Proven Reserves of Crude Oil, 1999, (billion barrels)

Saudi Arabia	259.0
Iraq	112.5
United Arab Emirates	97.7
Kuwait	94.0
Iran	89.7
Venezuela	72.6
Russia	57.0
Mexico	47.8
Libya	29.5
China	24.0
United States	22.5
Nigeria	22.5
Norway	10.9
Algeria	9.2
Brazil	7.1
Angola	5.4
Oman	5.3
United Kingdom	5.2
Neutral Zone	5.0
Indonesia	5.0
Total World	1,034.7

Source: Basic Petroleum Data Book, vol. 19, July 1999, Section 2, Table 4.

output to take advantage of the opportunity for profit created by the price increase.[22]

A variation on this theme suggests that although no single OPEC member has sufficient control of reserves to exercise control over price, OPEC, as a group, is able to act as a collusive price leader. The predicted market performance is much the same as under the dominant-firm model. OPEC's share of the market should decline over time as independent producers respond to the incentive created by a price above the cost of production.

Figures 2-1 and 2-5 suggest that the dominant-firm and dominant-group models had a certain degree of explanatory power for perhaps 12 or 15 years after the 1973 oil shock. OPEC's share of world crude-oil

[22]Darius Gaskins "Dynamic Limit Pricing: Optimal Limit Pricing Under Threat of Entry," *Journal of Economic Theory* Volume 3, September 1971, pp. 306–322; Norman J. Ireland, "Concentration and the Growth of Market Demand," *Journal of Economic Theory* Volume 5, October 1972, pp. 303–305.

production fell very slowly from 1973 to 1979. As already noted, this is a reflection of the long lead times in discovery and development of oil reserves. OPEC's market share fell sharply in the 1980s, bottoming out at 30 percent of the world market in 1985 and rising to around 40 percent since then. OPEC has taken back some market share, at the expense of a lower price.

Cartel Dynamics

What the dominant-firm and dominant-group analyses fail to capture is the oligopolistic interactions that have flavored OPEC behavior. When price is raised above the cost of production, individual OPEC-member nations (not just independent producers) have an incentive to increase their own output.

The problem of OPEC, as with any cartel, is to achieve agreement on a course of action (raising price to some level) and then to secure adherence to the agreement. As is the case with any group, differences make for disagreements. OPEC has been plagued by differences in the urgency with which its members wish to turn their asset in the ground—crude oil reserves—into disposable income. Countries such as Saudi Arabia, Kuwait, and the United Arab Emirates have small populations, high GNPs per capita, and ruling elites that are well served by modernization at a slow pace. Their massive oil reserves ensure that they will earn oil revenue for the foreseeable future. Other OPEC members, such as Indonesia, Nigeria, and Algeria, have larger populations, smaller GNPs per capita, and substantially smaller oil reserves. Their best hope for economic development is through the maximization of short-run oil revenues. Political pressures reinforce this economic incentive. More than once, governments of OPEC nations have been overturned because of mismanagement of the oil sector, and the ousted leaders often do not survive to collect retirement benefits.

By 1985, OPEC's market share had fallen to 30 percent, mostly on the strength of output cutbacks by Saudi Arabia, which enjoyed an OPEC quota of 4.353 million barrels per day but was estimated to be producing only 2.5 million barrels a day in September 1985. OPEC's official price remained at $28 a barrel, but the spot market price for oil was no more than half that.

At this point, Saudi Arabia introduced a system of "netback pricing," under which the price paid for Saudi crude oil was determined by the market prices of the products refined from the crude. The immediate effect of the netback pricing system was to eliminate risk for the purchaser of Saudi crude: If the price of refined products should fall, the price of crude would fall proportionately. The consequence was a sharp increase in the demand for Saudi oil, output of which reached six million barrels a day by July 1986.

Other OPEC members soon adopted their own netback pricing schemes, and oil prices fell as low as $6 a barrel. By August 1986, OPEC members, with the exception of Iraq, which held out for a quota equal to that of Iran, reaffirmed their support for the quota schedule that they were all violating. A series of ineffective agreements followed, and crude prices stayed at levels which, while yielding OPEC members handsome profits, remained below the levels of the early 1980s.

Iraq's August 1990 occupation of Kuwait led to a brief spike in the price of oil (Figure 2-1), but otherwise caused hardly a ripple in the supply of oil to world markets. Supplies from Iraq and Kuwait were abruptly cut to zero, but Saudi Arabia increased output from 5.4 million barrels a day in August 1990 to 8.2 million barrels a day in November 1990, maintaining overall supply at a comfortable level. It was to insist on keeping output at this level for most of the rest of the 1990s.

Judging by its actions, Saudi Arabia perceives its own self-interest to be served by stable oil markets and prices that do not give too much encouragement to conservation efforts or the search for alternative fuels. At the time of the Iraqi invasion of Kuwait, Saudi Arabia was able to act in its own self-interest and expand output because it had excess capacity that allowed it to do so. Other OPEC members with significant petroleum reserves were not slow to draw the conclusion that bargaining power within OPEC is related to production capacity. In the immediate aftermath of the Gulf War, Kuwait (naturally enough), Abu Dhabi, and Iran all set in motion substantial investment programs aimed at increasing crude capacity. Not to be outdone, Saudi Arabia initiated an expansion of capacity to more than 10 million barrels a day.

OPEC's pattern of ineffective collusion continued after Iraq was driven from Kuwait in February 1991. Ecuador and Gabon (both small producers) withdrew as OPEC members. Amid bickering over how members would adjust (reduce) their own output as Kuwaiti oilfields returned to production and as Iraq began limited oil sales under U.N. supervision to raise funds for humanitarian needs, OPEC found its residual part of the market increasingly small.

In November 1997, OPEC oil ministers agreed to raise quota output by 1.5 million barrels a day (m b/d), to 27.5m b/d. A portion of this increase simply acknowledged reality—actual output was reported to be 27.0m b/d—but the decision was also based on a predicted increase in demand going into the Northern hemisphere winter. By expanding output, OPEC could supply the expected increase in demand rather than letting it go to suppliers outside the organization.

Alas, the Northern hemisphere winter of 1997–98 was mild, a severe economic slowdown in Asia reduced energy demand in that part of the world, and a large stock of crude oil was held in inventory. All three factors meant that crude oil prices fell sharply, and Saudi Arabia reached outside OPEC in pursuit of its long-term goals.

In March 1998, OPEC members Saudi Arabia and Venezuela agreed with nonmember Mexico to reduce output by 1.5m b/d, some 2 percent of world production. Additional output reductions were later pledged by other OPEC members and nonmembers (in particular, Norway), and producers came closer than in the past to meeting their commitments. The price of crude oil tripled in little more than a year (from about $9.40 a barrel in December 1998 to over $30 a barrel early in 2000). Jawboning by governments of consuming countries was initially ineffective in persuading OPEC member states to increase output, but in March 2000 the governments of moderate OPEC countries seemed ready to implement such increases in the interest of their own perceived self-interest in avoiding global economic disruptions.

III. PUBLIC POLICY

U.S. Antitrust Activity

Antitrust policy has been the traditional approach to the preservation of competition in the United States. As we have noted, in 1911 the Supreme Court upheld a finding that the Standard Oil Company had violated the Sherman Antitrust Act while acquiring a dominant position in the refining, marketing, and transportation of petroleum. The Court imposed a structural remedy, ordering the parent holding company to divest itself of controlling stock interests in 33 subsidiaries.[23] This first case was also the last successful major case involving the U.S. oil industry.

To be sure, the oil giants have from time to time attracted the attention of antitrust enforcers. In 1940, a case so broad that it became known as the "Mother Hubbard" case was filed.[24] Twenty-two major oil companies, 344 subsidiary and secondary companies, and the American Petroleum Institute were charged, in a Justice Department civil suit, with violating both the Sherman and Clayton Acts. The case was postponed because of World War II, and thereafter languished until it was dismissed in 1951 at the request of the Justice Department.

Throughout the postwar period, in fact, antitrust action against U.S. oil firms was suspended on grounds of national security. In the closing days of the Truman Administration, the government accused the five U.S.-based international majors (along with British Petroleum and Royal

[23]See Bruce Bringhurst, *Antitrust and the Oil Monopoly,* (Westport, Connecticut: Greenwood Press), 1979.

[24]*U.S.* v. *American Petroleum Institute et al.,* Civil No. 8524, (D.D.C., October 1940).

Dutch Shell, which were beyond the jurisdiction of U.S. authorities) of seeking to restrain and monopolize crude oil and refined petroleum products, in violation of the Sherman Antitrust Act. But the State Department urged that the oil companies receive antitrust immunity for their cooperation in setting up the 1954 Iranian consortium, and this immunity weakened the cartel case, which dragged on for years. Exxon, Texaco, and Gulf eventually settled for consent decrees, and charges against Mobil and Socal were dismissed. The last parts of the case were dropped by the Justice Department in 1968.[25]

Much of the vitality of American antitrust law derives from the possibility of private enforcement. A private antitrust suit filed in 1978 by the International Association of Machinists and Aerospace Workers (IAM) sought to apply U.S. antitrust law to OPEC. OPEC declined to appear when the case was heard, and the Department of Justice refused to submit the amicus curiae brief requested by the District Court. The District Court declined to hear the case on technical grounds, including that the IAM did not have "standing" to sue OPEC since IAM was not a direct purchaser from OPEC.

IAM appealed this dismissal to the Circuit Court of Appeals, which upheld the lower court refusal to hear the case on the grounds that the case would interfere with U.S. foreign relations. Once again, conditions of national security short-circuited the application of the antitrust laws.[26]

Government Policy Responses to OPEC

The fact that the oil crisis of 1973 was repeated just 6 years later is testimony that Western governments generally were unable to develop adequate energy policies the first time around. The founding of the International Energy Agency (IEA) in November 1974 suggests government recognition of the importance of cooperation among consuming countries. However, France refused to join the IEA, apparently preferring bilateral government-to-government negotiations with oil-producing nations. Such government-to-government negotiations became common during the tight crude markets of 1978–1980, when security of supply was a matter of concern. Since that time, as more and more oil became available on spot markets, sales with government involvement have declined.

Three interrelated aspects of the continuing debate over proper government policy toward the petroleum industry merit discussion. All reflect a failure to understand the way markets work.

---

[25]B. I. Kaufman, "Oil and Antitrust: The Oil Cartel Case and the Cold War," *Business History Review* Volume 51, Number 37, Spring 1977; Sampson, *Seven Sisters,* pp. 150–159.

[26]Irvin M. Grossack, "OPEC and the Antitrust Laws," *Journal of Economic Issues* Volume 20, Number 3, September 1986, pp. 725–741.

The International Energy Agency Twenty-one Western nations are members of the International Energy Agency.[27] They are pledged to share oil supplies if they determine that a shortage of oil has occurred or is likely to occur. "Shortage" is defined in terms of a physical interruption in supply, and it seems clear that the focus of the IEA is embargoes imposed for political reasons. Price increases, however, have been an important aspect of past oil shocks. It would be desirable to alter IEA procedures so as to facilitate a response to a sharp price increase as well as to a sharp supply decrease.

The Strategic Petroleum Reserves In 1975, Congress established a Strategic Petroleum Reserve (SPR) as insurance against future interruptions in foreign supplies. Targets, set in later detailed plans, were for 500 million barrels in storage by 1980 and a billion barrels by 1985. By March 1988, 545 million barrels were actually stored in salt caverns around the Gulf of Mexico. Modest sales from the SPR were made during the Gulf War. In view of the increases in supply from Saudi Arabia, such sales probably had little direct effect on oil markets. But it seems likely that the knowledge that the SPR existed had a calming effect on world oil markets. Adopting a policy of quietly building up the Strategic Petroleum Reserve during periods of low prices, as insurance against shortages and price spikes, would be desirable.

Low Price or Energy Independence? The debate on U.S. policy toward the petroleum industry has long been bedeviled by a failure to come to grips with the limitations imposed by the way markets work. Figure 2-7 shows a stylized demand curve for the world oil market. U.S. policymakers have long recognized the ills associated with a high oil price. Supply shocks mean short-run bursts of inflation, which eventually raise nominal interest rates. A high oil price raises the cost of all energy-intensive activity, by consumers and by industry. Economic growth is slowed, and the U.S. trade balance—because the high price applies to a good for which the U.S. is a net importer—is made worse. One might think, therefore, that low oil prices would be welcomed by U.S. policymakers. But solicitude for the domestic oil industry has led successive U.S. administra-

---

[27]See Douglas R. Bohi and Michael A. Toman, "Oil Supply Disruptions and the Role of the International Energy Agency," *The Energy Journal* Volume 7, Number 2, April 1986, pp. 37–50; David R. Henderson, "The IEA Oil-Sharing Plan: Who Shares With Whom?," *The Energy Journal* Volume 8, Number 4, October 1987, pp. 23–31; and George Horwich and David Leo Weimer, editors, *Responding to International Oil Crises,* (Washington, D.C.: American Enterprise Institute for Public Policy Research, 1988).

tions to defend a position that would have the U.S. at a point such as *Y* in Figure 2-7: a low price for oil, but we don't buy much of it, at least not from foreign suppliers.

What is striking is that OPEC member nations suffer from a symmetric failure to come to grips with the way markets work. In the long run, a monopolist or complete cartel can be anywhere on the demand curve. The constraint imposed by the market is that price and quantity are inversely related: A high price means a low quantity demanded, and a low price means a high quantity demanded. It is clear from endless public statements that OPEC oil ministers want very much to be at a point such as *X* in Figure 2-7. They want to charge a high price for oil and sell a great deal of oil, but over the long run, the market will not let them.

National Security: The Short Run

The current consumption of U.S. oil always increases future dependence on foreign oil, barrel for barrel. The only way to avoid this is permanent tariffs or quotas that artificially raise the price of oil in the United States and distort input/consumption choices in less efficient and productive ways. It is not in the national security interest of the United States to be protected from foreign oil that is cheaper than domestic oil.

FIGURE 2-7 Wishful Thinking at Home and Abroad

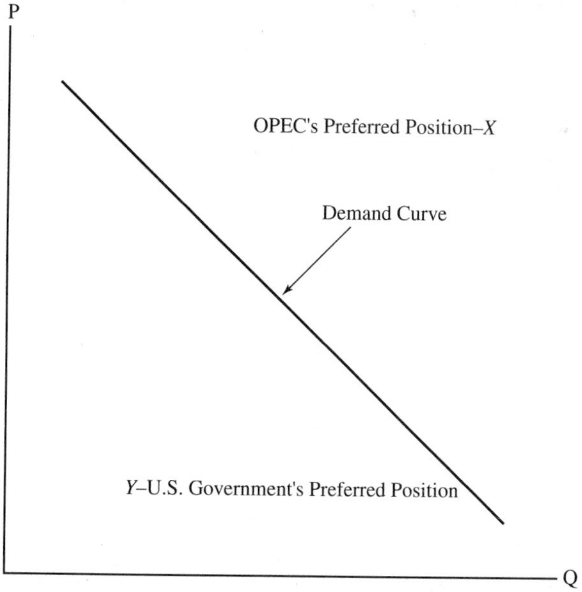

The specter is raised of unending Middle Eastern reserves and vulnerability to a cutoff of oil supplies from a politically unstable region of the world. The best response to this possibility is to diversify sources of supply away from politically unstable regions, and this diversification is increasingly feasible as new oil provinces open up around the world. The expansion of oil reserves outside OPEC implies that U.S. security interests lie in an open world market.

There is no *long-run* U.S. security interest in avoiding the current consumption of cheap foreign oil. There is a short-run U.S. security interest in neutralizing run-ups of oil price due to sporadic supply interruptions, and that is a problem that can be addressed, in the event, through proper use of the Strategic Petroleum Reserve.

National Security: The Long-Run

Secure energy supplies need not lie solely in oil reserves around the world. They may also lie in alternatives to conventional oil and natural gas-shale oil: coal gasification, solar power, nuclear fusion, and others. Experience shows that this sort of research cannot be left entirely to market forces. The costs of commercial-scale plants are far higher, and the development times far longer, than commercial enterprises can support. If government investment in a Strategic Petroleum Reserve to maintain short-run energy security is appropriate, then government support for the long-term research (20 to 50 years) needed to ensure long-run energy security is also appropriate.

IV. CONCLUSION

The oil price increases of 1973, 1979, and 1981 induced a permanent change in world demand for energy. The demand for energy will grow, as the world economy grows, but much less rapidly than would have been the case if the OPEC-administered price increases had never taken place. When the price of oil falls, the use of oil relative to other energy sources will increase, but industry will maintain the flexibility to reduce the use of oil in the event of oil price increases. The demand side of the world oil market, therefore, is permanently changed in a way unfavorable to any would-be cartel.

A critical change in structure is the expanded number of players. For generations, the world oil market was dominated by the Seven Sisters, the vertically integrated majors. For something more than a decade, the world oil market was dominated by OPEC member states. For the foreseeable future, events on the world oil market will reflect the actions of the OPEC member states (integrating forward toward the final consumer), the international majors (integrating backward through the development of OPEC and non-OPEC reserves), new supplying nations, and independent oil companies. These various firms and nation-firms will collude when they can and compete when they must. The increased number of suppliers reduces the likelihood of successful exercise of control of price.

Nonetheless, as events recently show, when the growth of demand and a reduction in independent supply presents the opportunity to extract monopoly profits, OPEC or (more likely) a group of high-reserve oil producers who are able perceive a common set of interests, OPEC members or not, the opportunity will be taken. Periodically, supply will be cut back and oil prices will rise. Future oil price shocks will occur.

Governments can—if they will—mitigate the effects of these shocks. The policy to do so will use the market as a trigger to release reserves over the short run, to share reserves among industrialized countries, and to supplement the market to develop long-run alternative sources of supply. Policies that fail to use the information provided by the market in the short run, and that rely on the market to develop new technology over the long run, will exacerbate future oil shocks.

Suggested Readings

Web sites

American Petroleum Institute—*http://www.api.org/*

International Energy Agency—*http://www.iea.org/homechoi.htm*

OPEC—*http://www.opec.org/*

Oxford Institute for Energy Studies—*http://associnst.ox.ac.uk/energy/*

Texas Railroad Commission—*http://www.rrc.state.tx.us/*

U.S. Department of Energy—*http://www.doe.gov/*

Publications

Adelman, M. A. *The Genie Out of the Bottle,* (Cambridge: MIT Press, 1995).

Blair, John M. *The Control of Oil,* (New York: Random House, 1976).

Boué, Juan Carlos. *Venezuela: The Political Economy of Oil,* (Oxford: Oxford University Press, 1993).

Chernow, Ron. *Titan: The Life of John D. Rockefeller, Sr.,* (New York: Random House, 1998).

Hartshorn, J. E. *Oil Trade: Politics and Prospects,* (Cambridge, England: Cambridge University Press, 1993).

Harvie, Christopher. *Fool's Gold: The Story of North Sea Oil,* (London: Penguin Books, 1995).

Heal, Geoffrey, and Graciela Chichilnisky. *Oil and the International Economy,* (Oxford: Claredon Press, 1991).

Horsnell, Paul, and Robert Mabro. *Oil Markets and Prices,* (Oxford: Oxford University Press, 1993).

Mabro, Robert, Robert Bacon, Margaret Chadwick, Mark Halliwell, and David Long. *The Market for North Sea Crude Oil,* (Oxford: Oxford University Press, 1986).

Sampson, Anthony. *The Seven Sisters,* (New York: Bantam Books, 1976).

Schneider, Steven A. *The Oil Price Revolution,* (Baltimore: The Johns Hopkins University Press, 1983).

Tarbell, Ida M. *The History of The Standard Oil Company* (Pittsburgh: McClure, Phillips and Co., 1904) *http://www.history.rochester.edu/fuels/tarbell/MAIN.HTM.*

Turner, Louis. *Oil Companies in the International System,* 3rd ed., (London: George Allen & Unwin, 1983).

U.S. Senate, Subcommittee on Monopoly. *The International Petroleum Cartel: Staff Report to the Federal Trade Commission,* (82d Cong., 2d sess., 1952).

Yergin, Daniel. *The Prize,* (New York: Simon & Schuster, 1991).

CHAPTER 3

Cigarettes

—ADAM B. JAFFE[1]

In 1997, Americans purchased 24 billion packs of cigarettes at a retail cost of $46 billion, almost 1 percent of household disposable income. Of this expenditure, about $6 billion went to the federal government, and about $8 billion went to state governments. In inflation-adjusted dollars, the 1997 expenditure represented an increase of about 14 percent over consumer expenditure 3 decades earlier in 1967. This increase is, however, due to increased real prices and increased taxes; aggregate domestic consumption of cigarettes has fallen by about 45 percent over this same period.

The domestic cigarette manufacturing industry had revenues of about $28 billion in 1997, or about .3 percent of gross domestic product (GDP). This represents a 27 percent decline, in real terms, from its 1967 revenues. Thus the economic significance of the cigarette industry has gradually declined, although its contribution to government revenues at both the state and federal level remains significant.

The cigarette industry is, however, a focus of public policy concern primarily because of the health impacts of smoking. It is estimated that more than 400,000 people die each year due to smoking-related illnesses, comprising almost 20 percent of all deaths in the United States. Smoking is the single largest preventable cause of death.

The health consequences of smoking make the analysis of the "performance" of the cigarette industry fundamentally different from that of other industries. Issues related to pricing, advertising, and product development in this industry all have complex public policy ramifications that go beyond the normal analysis of consumer benefit that would apply in other industries. In addition, the industry has been involved in litigation related to its health impacts that is unprecedented in scope and potential financial impact. In 1998, a group of state attorneys general settled a series of lawsuits seeking reimbursement for the costs of treating victims of smoking-related diseases. This settlement has large consequences for the conduct and performance of the cigarette industry in the coming decades.

---

[1]Jody Schmidt provided excellent research assistance for this chapter. The author served as an expert witness on behalf of a number of the states whose lawsuits against the cigarette companies were settled in 1998.

I. HISTORY

Mass Production and the Tobacco Trust

The economic significance of the cigarette industry and widespread prevalence of lung cancer in the population are both phenomena of the twentieth century. Prior to 1900, cigars, plug tobacco, and loose-smoking tobacco all had greater sales than cigarettes. It is unclear to what extent cigarettes are inherently more harmful than other forms of tobacco, and to what extent their low cost and high convenience facilitated the spread of the tobacco habit through the population, particularly among women who were not major users of other tobacco products.

The birth of the modern cigarette industry can be associated with the invention in the 1880s of a practical machine for mass production. Prior to this time, cigarettes were rolled by hand. Commercial cigarettes were produced by relatively small firms. It required skilled workmen to roll the cigarettes and significant supervision to oversee the quality of the product. In 1881 James Bonsack received a patent for a machine that could produce 12,000 cigarettes per hour, compared to the approximately 3,000 *per day* that could be rolled by a skilled workman. The patented Bonsack machine was leased to cigarette manufacturers at a price that reduced direct manufacturing cost by about half. Probably more important, the machine produced a standardized output so that large numbers of machines, together with relatively unskilled operators, could be combined on a large scale with relatively minimal supervision and quality-control efforts.

Mechanization of production thus removed the barrier to large-scale operation and laid the groundwork for both rapid industry growth and industry concentration. In particular, James B. Duke seized the opportunity created by the Bonsack machine, even though his W. Duke Sons & Co. had produced only loose-smoking tobacco prior to 1880. In return for large-scale commitment to the new technology, Duke was able to license the machine on favorable terms, giving him a cost advantage over his competitors. He then invested aggressively in manufacturing, and also in advertising and inducements to jobbers and retailers to promote his products. By 1889, Duke was the country's largest manufacturer of cigarettes.

The other makers of cigarettes found it difficult to compete with Duke's cost advantage and aggressive advertising. What ensued resembled the agglomeration that occurred in many manufacturing industries during the last 2 decades of the nineteenth century. Duke convinced all five major manufacturers of cigarettes to join him in the formation of the American Tobacco Company in 1890. At the outset, the "Tobacco Trust" controlled approximately 90 percent of U.S. cigarette production.

The trust acted aggressively to preserve this dominant market position over the next 2 decades. It purchased exclusive rights to the Bonsack machine and bought up patents on other machines. It was accused of using a variety of tactics to make life difficult for competitors, including trying to organize strikes among their workers, making exclusive deals with wholesalers and jobbers, and bidding up the prices for the tobacco leaf in those markets in which the independents were active. It also purchased a number of independents and added their brands to the trust. At the same time, in a pattern that has echoes in the modern market, the trust's heavy advertising and promotion succeeded in creating strong brand loyalty to its premier brands. The "Marlboro" of that era was called Sweet Caporal, which had a market share of approximately 50 percent at the turn of the century. Overall, the trust increased its market share to about 95 percent by 1899.

Antitrust Convictions

In its 2 decades of existence, the trust acquired approximately 250 previously independent companies. Some of these were shut down, but many continued to operate either as members of the trust or wholly owned subsidiaries of members. In 1911, the Tobacco Trust suffered the fate of its sisters in oil and other industries, and was found by the Supreme Court to have violated the Sherman Antitrust Act. As a result of this decision, the trust was broken up. The cigarette business and principal assets were put in the hands of four companies: the American Tobacco Company, RJ Reynolds Tobacco Company, Liggett & Myers Tobacco Company, and P. Lorillard Company.

The First World War seems to have facilitated the spread of cigarette smoking among men. During this period Reynolds introduced the Camel brand, which incorporated a new and supposedly premium blend of tobaccos. Reynolds abandoned the use of coupons that had previously been a major promotional tool, and explicitly advertised Camels as a more expensive smoke that was worth the price. This established the concept of premium brands at premium prices that continues to characterize the industry today. During the interwar period, the industry was dominated by Reynolds, American Tobacco, and Liggett & Myers, all of which had strong brands that were advertised heavily and priced at levels that yielded high margins. Cigarette smoking began to spread among women, who were explicitly wooed by advertising campaigns such as Lucky Strike's "Reach for a Lucky instead of a sweet."

The onset of the Great Depression set the stage for a series of events that eventually landed the descendants of the Tobacco Trust back at the Supreme Court. Despite falling tobacco-leaf prices and falling consumer incomes, the large tobacco companies raised cigarette prices in 1931, to a level that produced retail prices of approximately 14 or 15 cents per pack. Because of low-leaf prices, however, it was possible for small, new firms to produce a premium-quality cigarette that sold at retail for 10 cents. The size of the pricing gap and the pressure of bad economic times allowed these 10-cent brands to make significant inroads, capturing almost a quarter of the market by 1932. This pattern of high prices for premium brands creating an opportunity for what we would now call discount or generic varieties is one that we will see repeated in the 1980s and 1990s.

The major manufacturers then responded to the success of the 10-cent brands. In January 1933, American cut the price of Lucky Strikes by about 12 percent at wholesale, and this cut was followed by the other premium brands. In February, there was an additional 10 percent cut, which again was matched by the other majors. The large manufacturers also put pressure on distributors to reduce their margins so that the premium brands could sell at retail for 10 cents. The discount brands could not compete at pricing parity, and many of them disappeared. After a period of intense competition, Reynolds led a price increase in 1934 that brought the price of the premium brands partway back to where they were previously. It was later shown that during this "price war," Lucky Strike and Camel were being sold at a loss.

Despite the aggressive response of the Big Three to the incursion of the 10-cent brands, they were never able to restore the dominant market position that they enjoyed at the beginning of the 1930s. In addition to the 10-cent brands, incursions were made by Philip Morris & Co., an independent manufacturer that had never been part of the trust, and Brown and Williamson Tobacco Co., the U.S. subsidiary of the British American Tobacco Co. As a result, the combined share of Reynolds, American, and Liggett & Meyers, which had been 91 percent in 1930, fell to 69 percent by 1939. The emergence of Philip Morris and Brown and Williamson in the 1930s as significant national competitors represents the last time a new significant competitor would emerge in the U.S. cigarette industry. The "Big Six" of American, Reynolds, Liggett & Meyers, Lorillard, Philip Morris and Brown and Williamson would collectively dominate the industry through the modern era.

The apparently predatory pricing response to the growth of the 10-cent brands formed the core of new accusations that the top companies had engaged in monopolization and conspiracy in violation of the Sherman Act. The companies were convicted of these charges in 1941, and this conviction was eventually upheld by the Supreme Court. This time around, however, no structural remedies were imposed on the firms. They were required to pay fines and were subjected to restrictions on their abilities to communicate and coordinate their actions.

The Cancer Era

The competitive playing field was fundamentally transformed by the emergence in the early 1950s of significant concerns regarding cigarettes and cancer. Health concerns associated with tobacco and cigarettes were not entirely new; even back in colonial times there had been some who had criticized tobacco use as a filthy and dangerous habit, but these concerns had never been a significant aspect of the cigarette market. This situation changed dramatically in the decade following the end of World War II, as the emergence of cigarettes as a mass-produced product, the spread of the smoking habit through the population, and the development of new scientific research techniques led to scientific studies suggesting that cigarette smoking caused lung cancer. The evidence was of two types. Epidemiological studies, which use statistical techniques to analyze the connection or correlation in the population between various factors and the occurrence of disease, showed that smokers were much more likely to get lung cancer than nonsmokers. This statistical evidence was reinforced by experiments in which the constituents of cigarette smoke were condensed into a sludge that came to be known as cigarette "tar." This tar was then painted on the skin of laboratory mice and the mice developed tumors.

An article in *Reader's Digest* in 1953 summarized some of this research and led to widespread discussion and fear about the health consequences of smoking. For the first time, the major tobacco companies perceived these health concerns to be a major threat to their markets. The presidents of five of the Big Six companies met for 2 days at a hotel in New York to discuss the situation, the first time since the antitrust conviction of the 1940s that such a meeting had occurred. As is discussed later in detail, this meeting was the apparent genesis of an industry agreement on a collective response to the health "problem." With the exception of Liggett & Meyers, the companies joined together to create the Tobacco Industry Research Committee (TIRC), later renamed the Council for Tobacco Research. They published a statement, signed by the company presidents, in major newspapers throughout the United States, entitled "A Frank Statement to Cigarette Smokers."

In the Frank Statement, the industry disputed the evidence that cigarettes were harmful, but nonetheless accepted "an interest in people's health as a basic responsibility, paramount to every other consideration in our business," and promised to fund through the TIRC "research efforts into all phases of tobacco use and health."[2] The statement established a common public industry position on smoking and health that would stand for approximately 40 years. Although the precise expression of this position varied, it amounted to saying that the evidence that smoking was harmful was inconclusive, that more research was necessary, and that the industry was supporting such research in the hope of determining the truth.

---

[2] *State of Minnesota and Minnesota Blue Cross/Blue Shield* v. *Philip Morris, Inc.* et al., (1998), Trial Exhibit No. 14145.

Over the ensuing decade, the industry's position that the danger of smoking was unproven became increasingly untenable. In 1964, the U.S. surgeon general issued a report compiled by a special advisory committee that he had convened. After reviewing approximately 7,000 published studies, the report concluded that cigarette smoking was a cause of lung cancer and laryngeal cancer in men, a probable cause of cancer in women, and the most important cause of chronic bronchitis. Subsequent surgeon general's reports have confirmed these findings, and added other forms of cancer, heart disease, and emphysema to the list of diseases whose risk and mortality rates are significantly increased by smoking.

The 1964 Surgeon General report marked a watershed. From that time forward, reducing smoking has become a major public policy objective. No other legal product has ever been the target of such a large and sustained government effort to reduce its use. As shown in Figure 3-1, the incidence of smoking in the United States has declined significantly since the 1960s. Of all the people alive today who were ever regular smokers of cigarettes, approximately one-half have quit smoking. Looked at from the other side, however, 30 years after the government concluded that cigarettes kill people, approximately one-quarter of adult Americans still smoke cigarettes; many of those began smoking after the publication of the 1964 report. The story of how the industry has managed to mitigate the decline in smoking is the subject of the following sections.

FIGURE 3-1 Production and Consumption of Cigarettes

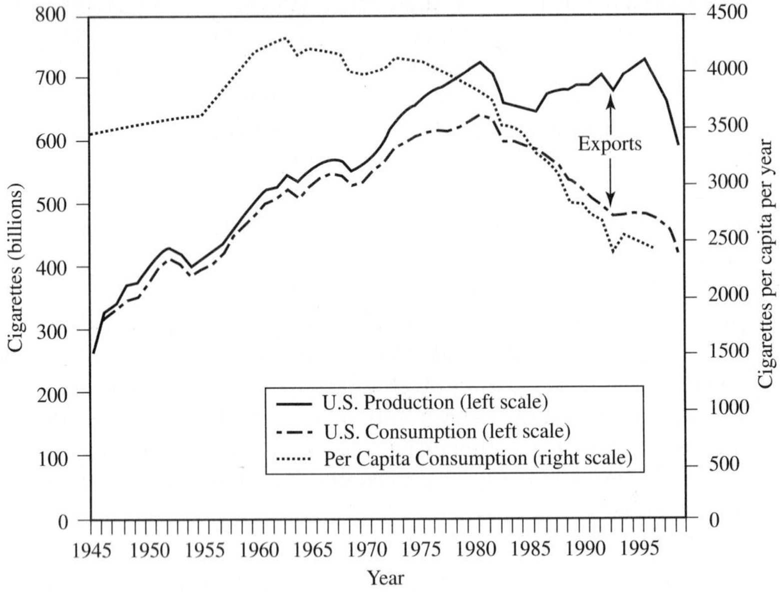

Source: Federal Trade Commission, 1997 and 1999.

II. MARKET STRUCTURE

As shown in Figure 3-2, the cigarette industry is one of the most concentrated industries in the United States, and has been so throughout the postwar period. In 1954, it was the ninth most concentrated manufacturing industry; in 1992, it was the fourth most concentrated, and it is the only industry that was among the ten most concentrated industries in both of these years. In 1996, following the acquisition of American Tobacco by Brown and Williamson, the remaining top 5 firms controlled 99.9 percent of the U.S. market, with the top 4 firms controlling 98 percent. In terms of manufacturing establishments, total U.S. cigarette production in 1997 came from only 13 manufacturing establishments, of which only 10 had 20 or more employees.[3] By any measure, the cigarette industry is structurally a tight oligopoly.

In addition to high concentration, the industry is characterized by significant barriers to entry. As noted previously, there has not been significant entry into the industry during the postwar period. There appear

FIGURE 3-2 Four Firm Concentration Ratio

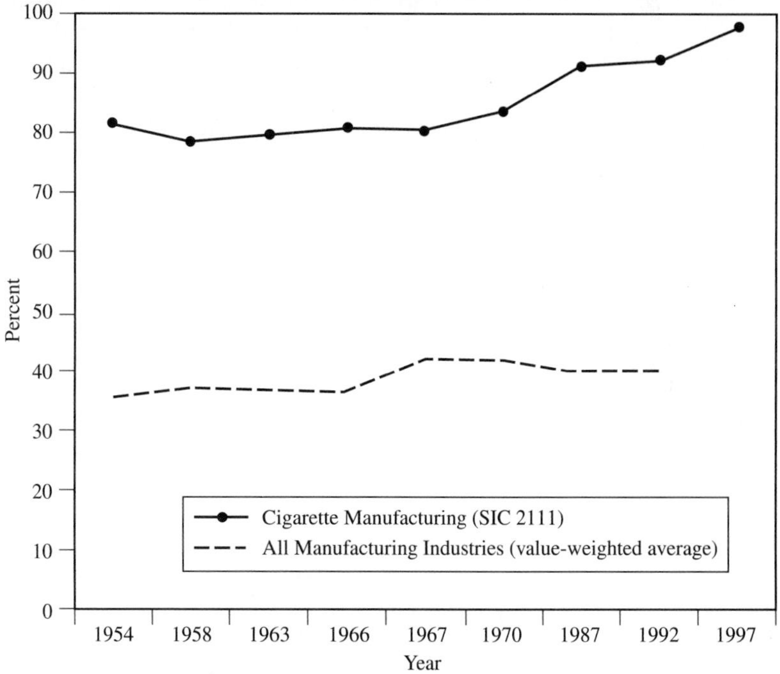

Source: U.S. Economic Census and Bulow and Klemperer, 1998.

[3]U.S. Census Bureau, *1997 Economic Census, Cigarette Manufacturing.*

to be several reasons for the lack of significant entry. First, smokers exhibit significant brand loyalty that would have to be overcome by a new entrant. It is estimated that less than 10 percent of smokers change brands in any given year.[4] This brand loyalty is sustained in part by massive advertising and promotion. Economies of scale in promotion make entry of a major new brand an expensive and risky proposition. In addition, one of the most cost-effective ways of launching a new national advertising campaign was taken away from the cigarette industry in 1970, when the Federal Trade Commission banned advertising of tobacco products on television and radio.

In addition to advertising and promotion, access to distribution would be a major hurdle for a new entrant. Cigarettes are distributed through thousands of wholesalers and over a million retail outlets. The major companies have large field-sales staffs that take orders, supervise stocking and point-of-sale displays, and provide a variety of incentives and promotions. A new entrant would have to choose between limited distribution, which would inherently limit brand growth, and a large investment in these distribution activities.

Finally, the fact that industry demand is in a long-run secular decline diminishes entry incentives, even in the face of high current industry profitability. This disincentive is exacerbated by the potential problems of legal liability for health impacts that would have to borne by any new entrant.

Another important aspect of market structure is the nature of demand. It is now well understood that the demand for cigarettes, at least on the part of regular smokers, is to a significant extent a demand for nicotine.[5] It is therefore not surprising that the elasticity of demand for cigarettes is low, estimated at approximately $-.4$ in the short run, possibly as large as $-.75$ in the long run if smokers take into account that smoking more today leads to addiction that will increase future cigarette purchases. On the other hand, despite relatively strong brand loyalty, episodes such as the 10-cent brands show that some smokers will switch brands in response to significant price differences, suggesting that the brand-level elasticity of demand is higher than the overall elasticity of demand for cigarettes.

---

[4]U.S. Surgeon General, *Reducing the Health Consequences of Smoking—25 Years of Progress: A report of the Surgeon General* (1989).

[5]In the inimitable words of William Dunn, a Philip Morris research psychologist who was known internally as the "nicotine kid," the cigarette should be thought of "not as a product but as a package. The product is nicotine. . . . Think of the cigarette pack as a storage container for a day's supply of nicotine." Minnesota Trial Exhibit No. 18089.

III. MARKET CONDUCT

Advertising and Promotion

Cigarettes are one of the most heavily advertised and promoted products in the United States. In 1997, the majors spent $5.7 billion on advertising and promotion, approximately 27 percent of wholesale revenues. This is an astounding expenditure for a product that does not have complicated performance characteristics or design changes that need to be communicated, and whose purchasers have, for the most part, been using the same brand of the product for years.

As shown in Figure 3-3, these expenditures have climbed significantly even as the number of smokers has declined. Advertising on television and radio was prohibited in 1970. This led to an initial decline in overall advertising and promotional expenditure, but beginning in the mid-1970s, promotional expenditures grew rapidly, quickly exceeding what had previously been spent on broadcast media. This category, which includes coupons and promotional payments to retailers, distribution of specialty gift items, and sponsoring of public entertainment, has been controversial because of its potential impact on children. As discussed in detail later, certain promotional activities have not been prohibited by the litigation settlement.

FIGURE 3-3 Cigarette Advertising and Promotional Expenditures (inflation adjusted)

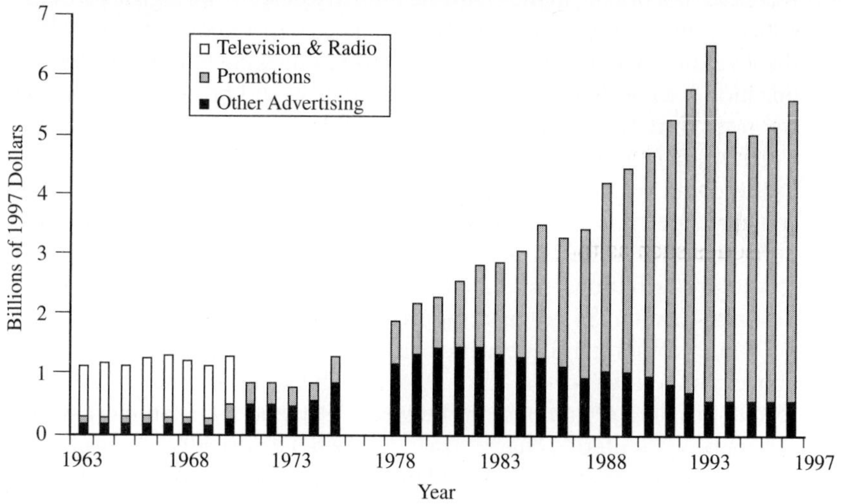

Source: Federal Trade Commission, 1999.

Note: Data for 1976 and 1977 are not available on a comparable basis.

An important aspect of the advertising history of the industry is the "Marlboro Man." Prior to 1954, Marlboro was an unimportant brand, and its owner, Philip Morris, was the fourth largest of the six major cigarette companies. In the mid-1950s, Philip Morris repositioned Marlboro as a man's cigarette, modifying its tobacco blend to produce a stronger flavor, and changing its packaging from white to the now-familiar red-and-white chevron design. At the same time, its advertising began to focus on men in supposedly tough and action-filled situations. Initially, the nature of these situations varied, but by the mid-1960s, the Marlboro Man was always a cowboy, photographed in the American West, identified as Marlboro Country. The Marlboro Man and Marlboro Country have now been used in ads and packaging in 150 countries; Marlboro has become by far the world's best-selling cigarette, and one of the best-known consumer brands of any product in the world.

A related dimension of industry conduct is the large and increasing number of varieties offered for sale. Over 1,200 varieties of cigarettes were offered for sale in 1997, up from under 600 in 1991.[6] This "brand proliferation" is due primarily to line extensions, as the sellers try to maximize the strength of popular brands by offering them in many different versions. The best-selling Marlboro brand, for example, was offered in 23 distinct varieties in 1997.

Pricing

It is clear that pricing in the cigarette industry, despite the high level of market concentration and significant barriers to entry, does not approximate the level that would occur if the firms were engaging in joint-profit maximization, i.e., setting prices at the level that would be chosen by a single cigarette firm. Indeed, a monopolist would never choose a price level at which the elasticity of demand is less than 1 (in absolute value); monopoly profits could always be increased by raising the price until the elasticity becomes greater. It is difficult to estimate what the monopoly price would be, because it requires extrapolation of demand outside of the range of observed prices, but one estimate is that a cigarette monopolist would raise the price to about $4 per pack, approximately twice the current level.[7]

On the other hand, there is certainly evidence that cigarette pricing is above competitive levels. The average real wholesale price of cigarettes rose approximately 40 percent between 1980 and 1997, an increase that cannot be attributed to changes in input costs. Historically, wholesale cigarette price changes have occurred infrequently, in no apparent relation to

---

[6]See annual reports by the Federal Trade Commission on the Tar, Nicotine, and Carbon Monoxide of the Smoke of Domestic Cigarette Varieties, various years.

[7]Jeffrey Harris, "American Cigarette Manufacturers' Ability to Pay Damages: Overview of a Rough Calculation," *Tobacco Control,* 5 (1996), pp. 292–294.

costs, and virtually simultaneously among the major manufacturers. As the Supreme Court noted as recently as 1993:

> The cigarette industry has long been one of America's most profitable, in part because for many years there was no significant price competition among the rivals. . . . List prices for cigarettes increased in lock-step twice a year, for a number of years, irrespective of the rate of inflation and changes in the cost of production, or shifts in consumer demand.[8]

An important aspect of pricing in the industry is the segmentation of the market into premium, discount, and deep-discount segments. The modern form of this segmentation was instigated by Liggett & Myers, who introduced low-price "generics" in the early 1980s. Somewhat reminiscent of the 10-cent brand episode of the 1930s, the other majors responded with the introduction of their own discount brands.[9] Today all of the majors sell discount brands, although they differ markedly in their dependence on discount sales. Although the discount brands account for only about one-quarter of industry sales, they do have an important impact on industry pricing.

Figure 3-4 shows the pattern of price changes, by segment, over the last decade. In the early 1990s, premium prices increased steadily, continuing the trend of the 1980s. Price cuts for deep discount and then discount brands therefore increased the price gap with the premium segment, so that by 1992, a price gap of approximately 40 cents had emerged between the premium and discount brands, compared to a manufacturing cost difference of only a few cents per pack. In addition to Liggett & Myers, discount brands were being heavily promoted by RJ Reynolds. As a result, the discount segment had grown to about 40 percent of the overall market, and the market share of Philip Morris's flagship Marlboro brand had slipped after climbing steadily for over 2 decades.

In 1993 Philip Morris responded by instigating a major realignment of prices on what has come to be called "Marlboro Friday." On that day, Philip Morris cut the price of its premium brands by 40 cents, eliminating the price differential between the premium and discount brands. As explained by Philip Morris in its 1993 annual report:

> We believe . . . that had we not responded promptly to this discount challenge mounted by our competition, our share losses in premium brands would have accelerated further, and damage to our premium brand franchises would have become irreversible.

---

[8]*Brooke Group, Ltd.* v. *Brown & Williamson Tobacco Corp.*, 509 U.S. 209 (1993), at 213.

[9]This resulted in the filing of an antitrust suit by Liggett & Myers alleging predatory pricing. The predatory pricing claim was eventually rejected by the Supreme Court (*Brooke Group* v. *Brown & Williamson, ibid.*).

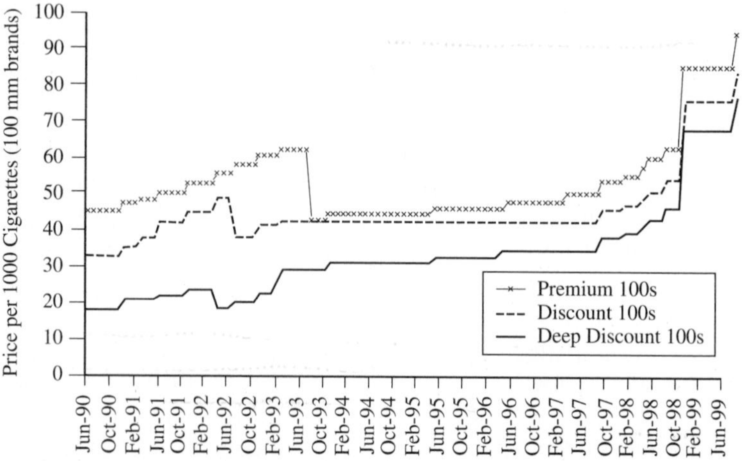

FIGURE 3-4 Wholesale Cigarette Price Revisions (not including taxes)

Source: U.S. Dept. of Agriculture, Economic Research Service, *www.econ.ag.gov/briefing/tobacco.*

The immediate financial consequences were enormous; Philip Morris stock declined 23 percent in one day, consuming $13 billion in shareholder equity. Philip Morris's decline in market share was reversed, however, and as can be seen in Figure 3-4, subsequent premium price increases have restored approximately half of the pre-1993 gap between the discount and premium brands. (The large price increases in 1998 are related to the litigation settlement and will be discussed later.) Further, the market share decline of the premium segment and Marlboro in particular have been reversed.

Product Development and the Health Issue

As discussed previously, the industry's public response to rising concern about cigarettes and health in the 1950s was to question the incriminating evidence and to call for more research. Privately, however, the companies understood the strength of the evidence against their product, and recognized that it had profound competitive implications. For example, a Philip Morris scientist wrote in 1958:

> Inasmuch as the evidence is building up that heavy cigarette smoking contributes to lung cancer . . .
>
> I'll bet that the first company to produce a cigarette claiming: a substantial reduction in tars and nicotine, or an ersatz cigarette whose smoke contains no tobacco tars, and with good smoking flavor, will take the market. Further, if he has the intestinal forti-

> tude to jump on the other side of the fence (provided he has some convincing experimental evidence to back him up) on the issue of tobacco smoking and health, just look what a wealth of ammunition would be at his disposal.[10]

In 1964, Helmut Wakeham, the research director of Philip Morris, authored a report for top company management on the "Significance of the Report of the Surgeon General's Committee." He stated that:

> [the challenge posed by the report] affords Philip Morris a splendid opportunity to gain a competitive edge through effective technical activity. Positive programs to cure ills cited in this report, whether real or alleged, are recommended, as little basis for disputing the findings at this time has appeared. . . .
>
> The hoped-for result of these efforts will be cigarettes with distinguishing new product properties which are biologically approved on all major health questions. Such products should be advertised vigorously on the basis of studies so conducted.[11]

Thus while the companies were publicly denying the significance of the health threat, internally they understood that consumers' desire for safer products created an opportunity to gain competitive advantage. Furthermore, they recognized that effective exploitation of that potential advantage required a "jump on the other side of the fence" on the health issue; that is, accepting the harmfulness of conventional cigarettes and arguing on that basis for the superiority of newly developed products.

This situation created a fundamental conflict between the *industry's* collective interest in minimizing the health threat, and *individual companies'* incentives to exploit consumers' demand for safer products. As a result of memoranda written at the time by employees of Hill and Knowlton, the public relations firm retained by the industry, we know that this conflict was discussed at the meeting of industry executives in New York in 1953. These Hill and Knowlton memoranda, combined with subsequent industry documents and behavior, demonstrate that the industry entered into a collusive agreement to suppress research that might have undermined their collective public position and led to the development of new competition that would exploit consumers' health concerns.[12]

This collusive agreement could not and did not shut down all efforts by the companies to compete in ways that exploited the health issue, but

---

[10]Minnesota Trial Exhibit No. 11662.

[11]Helmut Wakeham, "Smoking and Health: Significance of the Report of the Surgeon General's Committee to Philip Morris," Minnesota Trial Exhibit No. 10322. Similar expressions of market opportunity can be found in internal documents of other companies as well.

[12]Minnesota Trial Exhibit Nos. 18904 and 18905.

it did limit them in important ways. In particular, a number of documents originating in several different companies refer to the existence of a "gentlemen's agreement" to restrict certain kinds of research activities by the companies.[13] In the mid-1960s, a new research initiative at American Tobacco, which its scientists judged crucial to the technical progress and commercial success of the company, was terminated after intervention by company attorneys.[14] In the late 1960s, Reynolds undertook a series of experiments using animals to measure the effects of cigarette smoke. Philip Morris's Wakeham learned of these efforts, and brought them to the attention of top Philip Morris management, noting that they were inconsistent with the gentlemen's agreement, and arguing that Philip Morris should do the same. Instead, according to industry documents, the head of Philip Morris called the head of Reynolds and complained. The Reynolds animal research facility was shut down.[15]

In the late 1970s, Liggett & Myers had a prototype new-cigarette design that used a chemical catalyst to try to remove certain constituents of cigarette smoke that were suspected as carcinogens. Experiments showed that the "tar" from this cigarette caused dramatically fewer tumors when painted on the skin of mice. Contemporaneous Liggett & Myers documents indicate that the company perceived this new product to have huge market potential, but the project was abruptly terminated and the product never commercialized. An outside attorney who worked on the project for Liggett & Myers has testified that the Liggett general counsel was pressured by attorneys from the other firms not to introduce the product.[16]

The most important product development attempting to reduce the harmfulness of cigarettes was a product called Premier, test-marketed by Reynolds in 1988. Premier was a new concept in cigarette design; indeed one could question whether it was really a cigarette. Instead of burning tobacco, Premier burned a small core of graphite, which heated tobacco extract and a substrate containing nicotine in order to produce a smoke-like aerosol containing nicotine and tobacco aroma. Reynolds undertook a large research program that demonstrated that the "smoke" from Premier showed dramatically reduced biological activity, using essentially all of the tests that were available at the time that were believed to indicate possible human health impacts.[17] Although it is clear that Premier was not a safe cigarette, it is also clear that it represented a major effort

[13]For example, Minnesota Trial Exhibit Nos. 2544, 26229, and 12512.
[14]Minnesota Trial Exhibit No. 21951.
[15]The sequence of events regarding the shutdown of the Reynolds research facility is revealed in Minnesota Trial Exhibit Nos. 10257, 2545, 10465, 2548, 2549, 12756, and 12757.
[16]See Minnesota Trial Exhibit Nos. 11523, 11513, 11482, and 11497.
[17]See Minnesota Trial Exhibit No. 12873.

to develop a product that was likely to be safer than existing products, (and to demonstrate that the smoking hazard could be reduced with available methods.)

Premier was a failure in the marketplace. A number of factors seem to have contributed to this failure. First, the Premier smoking experience was a major departure for the smoker. It was difficult to light and keep lit, and it was generally perceived to have an odd taste. Second, Premier was strongly opposed by nonprofit public health groups, which seemed uninterested in affording existing smokers an opportunity to use a potentially safer form of tobacco, arguing that the marketing of a product like Premier would undermine antismoking efforts by suggesting that the hazard could be reduced. At the same time, Reynolds avoided any marketing attempt to utilize the vast array of scientific evidence it had amassed regarding the reduced biological activity of Premier, claiming only that Premier offered a "cleaner" smoke. After the Premier test-marketing was abandoned, evaluations by Reynolds and other companies concluded that Premier's product advantages were not communicated effectively.[18]

It is impossible to know how different the product evolution in this industry would have been if competition with respect to smoking and health had not been restricted by collusive agreement. What is clear is that the aggregate investment in product development efforts have been paltry compared either to the public health stakes or to the companies' own perception of the competitive opportunity. Based on data produced in litigation, the companies' aggregate expenditure on R&D and product development related to the health effects of smoking totaled about $3 billion between 1954 and 1996 (about $2.7 billion of company expenditures and about $.3 billion in funding to the Council for Tobacco Research). Although this may seem like a significant expenditure, it is a small fraction of the almost $50 billion that was spent on advertising and promotion over the same period, and it is a tiny fraction of the almost one-half *trillion* dollars in industry revenues over the same period.

The Development of "Low-Delivery" Products

The primary product response of the manufacturers to consumers' health concerns has been the development of low-tar/low-nicotine ("LTLN") cigarettes, although the companies have consistently denied that these products are designed to reduce the health hazards of smoking. Indeed, they apparently have done no research designed to determine if these products have any reduced health effects. Nonetheless, it is clear that the products are designed to take advantage of the demand for products perceived to be safer, without having to admit that any cigarette products are unsafe.

[18]See Minnesota Trial Exhibit No. 13082, 13481, and 11632.

The market response to products *perceived* to be safer has been clear since the 1950s. This decade saw the introduction and rapid growth of a variety of filter-tipped cigarettes. Filter brands accounted for less than 1 percent of the market in 1952, but had grown to 51 percent by 1959. Viceroy, which received a favorable rating regarding its "tar" delivery from an article in *Readers' Digest,* and Kent, which advertised the superiority of its "micronite" filter, enjoyed rapid share growth. Overall, the sales-weighted average tar delivery has fallen from over 30 mg per cigarette to 12 mg in 1997. Approximately 70 percent of cigarettes sold now have machine-measured tar yields of 15 mg or less.

The trend toward LTLN products was encouraged by the public health authorities, who have suggested since the mid-1960s that reduced deliveries would likely reduce the health risks. It is unclear, however, what, if any, health benefit is actually associated with LTLN products. Reduced delivery of tar and nicotine on a testing machine does not necessarily translate into reduced human intake, largely because of the phenomenon of "compensation." Because people smoke to get nicotine, they take larger and longer puffs to compensate for a cigarette that delivers less nicotine under a standard smoking protocol. Further, some of the technologies used to reduce deliveries, such as perforation of the cigarette paper with tiny holes to draw in additional air, reduce deliveries on smoking machines but are often ineffective in human smoking. As a result, the health benefit associated with the reduction in machine-measured tar and nicotine yields is probably considerably less than would be implied by the average reduction in yields. Some experts have suggested that the compensation phenomenon completely eliminates the potential health benefit of LTLN products.[19]

IV. PERFORMANCE

Market Shares

Firm-level market shares are often considered to be an aspect of industry structure. In the cigarette industry, however, the major realignments that have occurred in market shares suggest that the shares are more a consequence of industry conduct than an aspect of industry structure. Figure 3-5 shows the evolution of firm-level market shares in the industry. The dominant trend is the decline of American Tobacco and Liggett & Myers, and the rise of Philip Morris to almost 50 percent of the market by 1997. Indeed,

[19]See Federal Trade Commission, *Report to Congress for 1997 Pursuant to the Federal Cigarette Labeling and Advertising Act* (1999), and National Cancer Institute, *Smoking and Tobacco Control Monograph 8: Changes in Cigarette-Related Disease Risk and Their Implications for Prevention and Control* (1997).

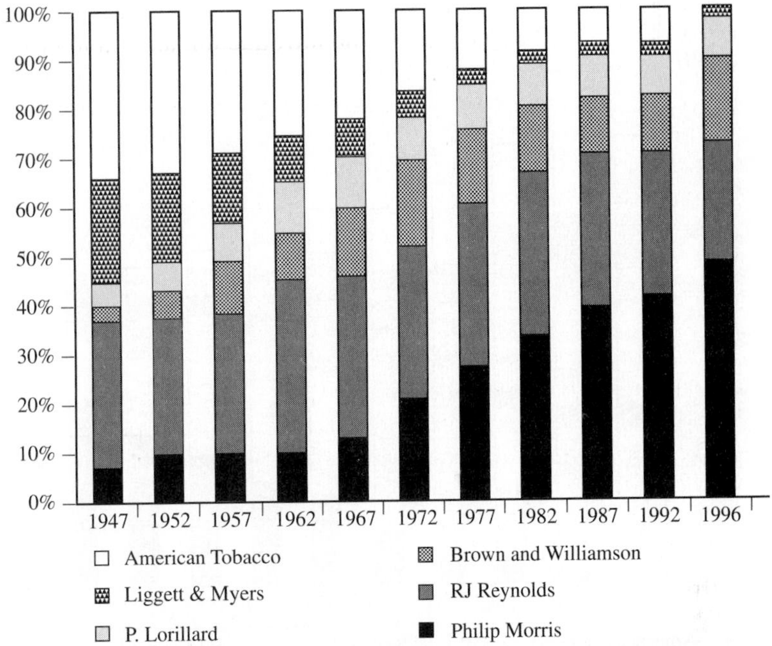

FIGURE 3-5 Cigarette Company Market Shares

Source: Federal Trade Commission, 1997.

American, the company that bore the name of the fabled trust, disappeared from the corporate scene when it was acquired by Brown and Williamson in 1996. Figure 3-6 traces these reversals of fate to the level of particular brands. Chesterfield and Lucky Strike accounted for almost 40 percent of the market in 1950, but had shrunk to insignificance by 1996. Conversely, Marlboro, today's dominant brand with about one-third of all sales, was insignificant in the 1950s.

The growth of Marlboro stands as one of the greatest consumer product successes in recent history; perhaps it is due to the flavor, the package, and the ad campaign. As Marlboro's share was climbing in the late 1960s, Philip Morris's competitors were struggling to understand the sources of its success. They noticed that Philip Morris had begun using ammonia to raise the alkalinity of Marlboro's smoke. Experiments showed that the higher alkalinity of the smoke facilitated the absorption of nicotine, so they speculated that the higher alkalinity improved smoker satisfaction by speeding up the psychopharmacological impact of the nicotine in the smoke. One competitor went so far as to undertake a statistical analysis that suggested a strong correlation between the alkalinity of Marlboro smoke and Marlboro's market share. Many of the other companies

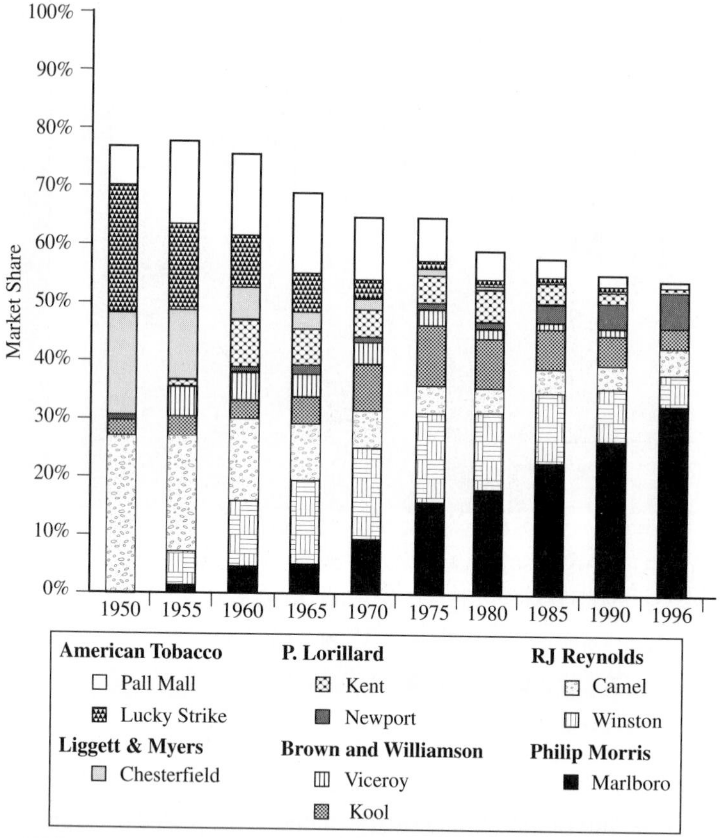

FIGURE 3-6 Leading Brand Sales

Source: Minnesota Trial Exhibit No. 14985; Federal Trade Commission, 1997.

eventually imitated the use of the ammonia technology, and it remains unclear what role smoke alkalinity has played in Marlboro's success.

Profits

Despite the overall decline in industry sales, cigarette manufacture remains one of the most profitable of businesses. Figure 3-7 shows the profits of the major companies. Because the profit margins on premium brands are so much greater than the margins on discount brands, participation in the premium segment is the primary determinant of company profitability. Lorillard and Philip Morris, each of whom have most of their sales in premium brands, have the highest profit rates. Reynolds and Brown and Williamson are intermediate in their reliance on discount sales; Liggett & Myers derives only 25 percent of its sales from premium

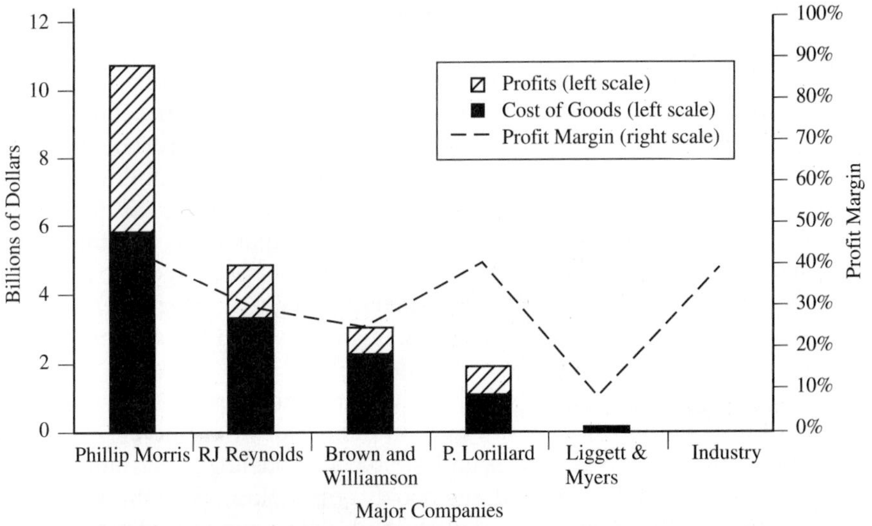

FIGURE 3-7 Profits of Major Cigarette Companies, 1997

Source: Bulow and Klemperer, 1998.

brands. The industry's overall profit margin of 38 percent of sales is one of the highest of any industry[20]

V. PUBLIC POLICY ISSUES

Assessing the performance of the cigarette industry from the perspective of public policy necessitates consideration of the multiple and conflicting policy objectives at issue. First, there is the usual desire related to allocative efficiency that prices approximate competitive levels in order to maximize consumer surplus. Second, there is the government's interest in the tax revenue generated by cigarette sales, and third, is the public interest in reducing the health consequences of smoking.

Exactly what form this concern should take is unclear. One view would be that adult smokers are aware of the health consequences, and choose to smoke because those adverse consequences are more than offset by the benefits they receive from smoking. Under this view, public policy concern would be limited to adverse health consequences that are not born by the smokers themselves. These would include health care

[20]Economic theory suggests that profitability should be compared on the basis of the rate of return on assets, rather than on sales. Census of Manufacturing data indicate that the investment intensity of the industry is not above average, suggesting that the high profit/sales ratio also corresponds to a high rate of return on assets.

expenditures born by insurers or other third-party payers, and health consequences of "second-hand" smoke.

A broader view would be that smokers are addicted to cigarettes and hence incapable of rationally balancing the costs and benefits of the habit. Under this view it should be a goal of public policy to prevent such addictions from forming, and to help those addicted to break the habit. A potential intermediate view would allow adults to make up their own minds, but judge that children are often incapable of well-informed choices about their futures, so that it should be a policy goal to prevent their smoking. Because the overwhelming majority of smokers began smoking before they reached age 18, this view would put a primary policy focus on preventing youth smoking.

These philosophical issues have an important impact on how performance of the industry is assessed. In most industries, the elevation of prices above cost is viewed as undesirable. If we believe that smokers are rationally balancing the risks and benefits of smoking, then this view carries over to the cigarette market, perhaps with a modest adjustment allowing some taxation to compensate for the externalities that smokers impose on others. If, however, we believe that public policy should affirmatively discourage smoking, then high cigarette prices are a good thing, not a bad thing, because they reduce cigarette consumption.

Finally, some might argue that there is a public policy interest in punishing the tobacco companies and their investors for the companies' behavior. Quite apart from the health concerns themselves, companies that engage in fraud and collusion ought to face adverse financial consequences for doing so, in order to create the right incentives in the future for companies to avoid such behavior.

Regulation

Health-related regulation of the cigarette industry dates to the 1950s. At that time, the Federal Trade Commission (FTC) became concerned that the companies were making exaggerated and unsubstantiated claims related to the use of filters to reduce tar deliveries. The FTC promulgated a regulation prohibiting cigarette advertising from making health claims, unless those claims could be scientifically substantiated, and specifically prohibited reference to tar and nicotine deliveries. Because none of the companies were doing the kind of research that could have conceivably substantiated claims for reduced health hazards of particular products, this regulation was interpreted as prohibiting all health claims for cigarettes.

As noted previously, by the mid-1960s the public health community believed that reductions in tar and nicotine yield would probably reduce cigarette health hazards. As a result, the FTC partially reversed itself, allowing the advertising of tar and nicotine yields as determined by a standardized smoking machine. These tar and nicotine ratings were combined with health warnings that were first required in the 1960s and which have been strengthened over time.

The FTC has continued to monitor and regulate cigarette advertising. Tobacco advertising on radio and television was prohibited in 1970. In 1997, the FTC filed a complaint against Reynolds' "Joe Camel" advertising campaign, claiming that it was at least partially targeted at underage smokers. This action was terminated as a result of the litigation settlement discussed later.

Although the FTC regulates cigarette advertising, it has no authority to regulate the cigarettes themselves. The Food and Drug Administration (FDA) has authority under its authorizing legislation to regulate the safety of drugs and drug-delivery devices. In 1996 the FDA determined that cigarettes were drug-delivery devices within the meaning of the law, because they delivered nicotine, which causes psychoactive effects, and is addictive. It also found that the pharmacological effects of smoking were an intentional aspect of product design. It concluded that the most appropriate way to address the adverse consequences of smoking was to prevent minors from smoking. Accordingly, it promulgated regulations designed to prevent the sale of cigarettes to minors, and to restrict advertising that makes cigarette smoking attractive to young people.

The cigarette companies challenged these regulations in federal court. The trial judge upheld the regulations, but was overruled by the court of appeals and the Supreme Court in early 2000. In the meantime, strengthened enforcement of regulations against sale to minors have been allowed to take effect, but the FDA's advertising restrictions have been suspended.

Litigation

The cigarette companies have been the target of litigation seeking recovery of smoking-related health costs for over 3 decades. Until recently, most such suits were on behalf of individual smokers. Until very recently, all such suits were unsuccessful, as juries often concluded that smokers were aware of the harmful effects of smoking and therefore could not blame the manufacturers.[21]

This unsuccessful record led to a new strategy on behalf of plaintiffs' attorneys in the early 1990s. A number of suits were filed on behalf of insurers and state Medicaid programs to recover the expenditures that these entities had made to treat people with smoking-related disease. In

[21] As of this writing in the fall of 1999, there is some evidence that this situation is changing; an individual case in California and a class action on behalf of all smokers in Florida have resulted in initial findings of manufacturer liability for smoking-related health costs.

this way, the issue of smoker responsibility was sidestepped; the smokers may have known that smoking was harmful, but their insurers nonetheless had to bear the costs of treating their illness. The states and insurers argued in various ways that the cigarette companies knowingly sold a dangerous product, that they consciously sought to quiet smokers' fears about health risks, that they suppressed information about the addictiveness of smoking, and that they conspired to suppress competition that otherwise would have led to better information about health consequences and the development of potentially safer cigarette products.

These lawsuits presented the industry with the risk of enormous potential legal liability. Although it remains unclear how they would have come out, the cigarette companies chose to seek an out-of-court settlement. A tentative settlement was reached during the summer of 1997.[22] In return for an initial lump-sum payment of about $10 billion, annual payments tied to cigarette sales that amounted to hundreds of billions more over 25 years, and restrictions on their advertising and promotional activities, the cigarette companies would have received immunity not only from the ongoing cases, but from any class-action lawsuits in the future. In addition, they would have received immunity from the antitrust laws for the purpose of implementing the settlement. Because of these immunity provisions, this initial settlement could only be implemented via a law passed by the Congress. After extensive discussions during the spring of 1998, Congress attempted to pass a bill that would have implemented higher cigarette taxes and marketing restrictions, but not the broad immunity against future suits continued in the original settlement. As a result, the tobacco companies opposed the bill and it was defeated.

As the public debate unfolded, the tobacco companies reached settlements to avoid a trial outcome with the states of Florida, Texas, Mississippi, and Minnesota. An agreement with the remaining states was reached in November 1998. This settlement was constructed to avoid the need for federal legislation; it now appears that it will be implemented by all states. The major features of the settlement are as follows:

- Defendants will make an initial payment of $2.4 billion, with each company's payment based on its market value.
- Defendants will make annual payments in perpetuity that ramp up to $9 billion per year by 2018. These payments will be adjusted for inflation and changes in total sales of cigarettes.
- Restrictions are placed on cigarette marketing, including a ban on the use of cartoon characters, restrictions on sponsorship of

[22]Liggett & Myers, by far the smallest of the major firms, had reached a separate settlement in 1996, in which it agreed to admit publicly that smoking is harmful, and to assist the states in their ongoing suits against the other firms.

sporting events and concerts, a ban on outdoor and transit advertising, a ban on non-tobacco merchandise bearing tobacco-brand names, and limitations on free samples.
- States agree to pass laws imposing similar payment obligations on cigarette sellers not party to the settlement.
- States waive all rights to sue on behalf of state agencies, but no restrictions are placed on suits by others.

It is clear that this settlement achieves only some of the public policy objectives enumerated earlier. It generates significant revenue for the states, some of which will be used for smoking prevention and smoking cessation efforts. The marketing and promotion restrictions that it incorporates will likely have some beneficial effects, but it is difficult to know how large, or whether other forms of restrictions might have been more effective. The primary market consequence of the settlement is that it significantly increases the price of cigarettes to consumers.

What the settlement does not do is punish the tobacco companies for their alleged wrongdoing. The overwhelming majority of the monies that will be paid under the settlement will come from higher cigarette prices. By tying the payments to the quantity of cigarettes sold, the settlement, in effect, converts most of the payments into a cigarette excise tax increase. It was expected that cigarette prices would be increased to cover the cost of the settlement payments, and this has in fact occurred. The payments made by each company in the future will depend on their *future* sales, not on their past sales or any other measure of the harm their actions may have caused.

In contrast, if the companies had lost any of the lawsuits pending against them, the amounts that they would have owed would not have been tied to future cigarette sales. It is far from clear that they could have coordinated price increases designed to recover from consumers the amounts that they were required to pay. Indeed, to the extent that existing prices represented the most profitable price level that could be sustained given the various firms' market positions and competing interests, one could argue that the assessment of lump-sum penalties unconnected to future market performance would not have affected prices, so that all of the cost of such a penalty would be born by company shareholders.

The reality that the payments under the settlement are tax increases rather than damages is further demonstrated by the settlement's treatment of cigarette sellers who were not party to the agreement. This includes Liggett & Myers, existing tiny independents, and also any new entrants into the industry who emerge anytime in the future. Such parties should not be liable for damages based on the settling defendants' alleged past misbehavior, but under the settlement the states agreed to pass laws that would assess charges on new entrants equal to the expected price increases to fund the payments under the settlement.

Thus the end result of litigation with the purported purpose of making the tobacco companies compensate the states and other insurers for health costs that they paid is that future *smokers* will compensate the states instead. This compensation will come, of course, *on top of* existing federal and state excise taxes on cigarettes. Figure 3-8 shows the approximate breakdown of the price of an average pack of cigarettes before the settlement and after it is fully implemented, along with scheduled increases in federal cigarette excise taxes. The estimates in this figure are based on the assumption that the cost of the settlement is passed along to consumers, and that the settlement results in a modest reduction in advertising and promotional expense and a slight reduction in legal costs, and that these savings are also passed through to consumers so that industry profit margins remain unchanged.[23]

Under these assumptions, approximately $1.16 out of the $2.50 retail cost of an average pack of cigarettes in 2004 will go to state and federal excise taxes and the settlement payments. Assuming that consumption will have declined by that point to about 20.3 billion packs per year, consumers will be paying about $23.5 billion dollars to all levels of government for the privilege of smoking, an increase of about 70 percent over the previous combined level of taxation.

The consequences for the tobacco companies, after the initial $2.4 billion lump-sum payment, derive from the reduction in cigarette sales. Considering *both* the settlement payments and the recently enacted federal excise tax increases this reduction can be estimated at about 2.9 billion packs per year. At their estimated gross profit margin of about $.32 per pack, this demand reduction results in a loss of pretax profits of less than $1 billion per year, a reduction of about 12 percent from what they would otherwise have earned. Put differently, once the settlement is fully implemented, the annual cost to the companies will be about one-tenth of its annual cost to smokers.

The only difference between the settlement payments and state excise taxes is that each state's revenues depend on national cigarette sales, not sales in that state. This means that any state that aggressively reduces smoking will not suffer a large revenue reduction as a result; this structure thereby minimizes the awkward incentives that are otherwise created when governments simultaneously try to reduce smoking and collect significant tax revenues from cigarette sales. Of course, the same incentive structure could have been achieved by passing a federal excise tax increase, with the resulting revenues returned to the states.

---

[23]These are the assumptions used by the FTC in its analysis of the earlier proposed settlement (Federal Trade Commission, *Competition and the Financial Impact of the Proposed Tobacco Industry Settlement,* 1997).

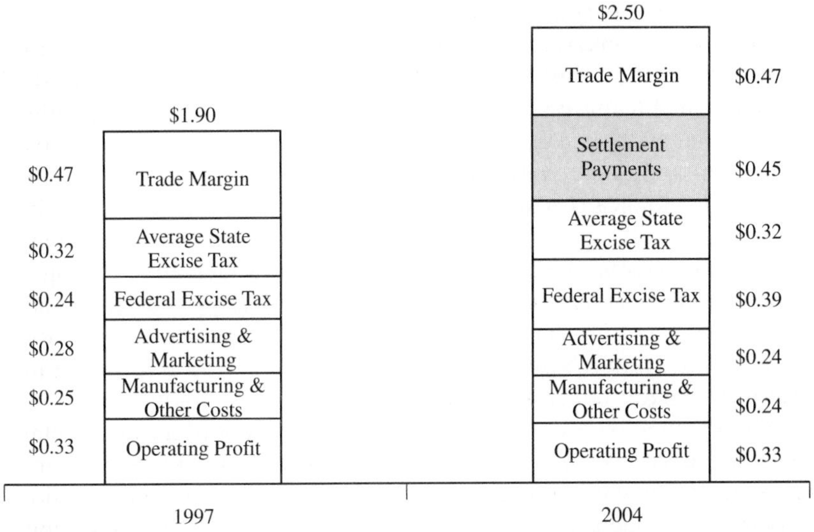

FIGURE 3-8 Estimated Breakdown of Retail Cigarette Price

Source: Author's calculations based on Federal Trade Commission, 1997, and news reports regarding settlement.

The final perverse aspect of the settlement payments is that the states have agreed to pass laws imposing identical payment obligations on cigarette sellers other than the settling firms. This includes Liggett & Myers, that signed its own separate settlement with the states in 1996, tiny independents, and also any potential future entrants. Although the likelihood of such entry is probably remote, it is nonetheless ironic that the settlement of these cases—which were predicated in part on the claim that the firms conspired to suppress the introduction of innovative potentially safer cigarette products—results in a situation where an outside firm, with no history of selling conventional cigarettes and that attempted to develop a new, safer form of cigarettes, would be required in effect to make the same settlement payments as the alleged conspirators.

The only aspect of the settlement that is clearly consistent with public policy objectives is the restrictions that it imposes on marketing and promotion. It is unclear to what extent these restrictions will reduce smoking in general, or youth smoking in particular. The tobacco companies have consistently argued that their promotional efforts are aimed at preserving brand loyalty and inducing smokers of other brands to switch, but are not intended to induce people to smoke. Whatever the intention, if promotional efforts do not affect aggregate sales, then the $5.7 billion of aggregate spending is mutually offsetting, creating no net benefit for the industry. The industry as a whole could enjoy the same sales revenue without this expenditure, so ceasing these efforts would almost double industry profits, yet the industry has always collectively *opposed* restrictions by the government on advertising and promotion. The restrictions in the final settlement are in fact less severe than those in the 1997 proposed settlement and the 1998 federal legislation that failed. Such opposition appears economically irrational if these efforts create no net benefit for the industry.

Public policy has been particularly concerned about the effects of cigarette promotion on youth smoking. The vast majority of all smokers begin smoking before age 18, despite legal restrictions on the sale of cigarettes to minors. Some public health advocates reason from this fact that if youngsters could be prevented from starting smoking, the overall rate of smoking initiation would be dramatically reduced. This conclusion doesn't necessarily follow, because there is no way to know for sure that individuals who choose to start smoking would not make the same decision at a later age if prevented from smoking before 18. It is true, however, that many adult smokers say that they wish they had never started, and that with the greater maturity of a young adult, they might have made different choices. However this might turn out, all parties agree that reducing smoking by minors would be highly desirable.

Despite public positions uniformly opposed to smoking by minors, internal company documents show that the companies historically have paid attention to the use of their brands by minors, and recognized the competitive consequences of brand popularity among underage smokers, given that brand loyalties tend to stick once established. Numerous companies, for example, noted the contribution that Marlboro's popularity among young teens made to the growth over time in the brand's share. The consequences of Reynolds' infamous "Joe Camel" campaign are controversial, but at least one academic study has concluded that the pattern of cigarette advertising spending in relation to readership by young teens is at least consistent with targeting of that advertising to minors.[24]

In addition to the marketing restrictions, some have pointed to the price increases associated with the settlement as an important anti-youth–smoking measure. There have been some studies that suggest that teen smoking is somewhat more price elastic than adult smoking; this is plausible given that young smokers tend to be less addicted, and cigarette expenditures comprise a larger fraction of their disposable income.[25] Finally, part of the revenues from the settlement are being used in at least

[24]Charles King, et al., "Adolescent Exposure to Cigarette Advertising in Magazines," *Journal of the American Medical Association* 279, (1998), pp. 516–520.
[25]FTC (1997). *Op cit.*

some states to fund aggressive counter-marketing measures designed to discourage teen smoking. Unfortunately, no one seems to really understand why teens start smoking well enough to know how much difference any of these measures will make.

VI. CONCLUSION

The history of the cigarette industry presents a unique and complex challenge to students of industrial organization. One of the most concentrated of industries, resting behind apparently significant barriers to entry, it has enjoyed persistently high profits, but also engaged in periodic price wars. The firms spend huge amounts—both absolutely and relative to sales—on advertising and promotion, supposedly in a largely self-defeating effort to steal each others' customers. The industry charges prices that are clearly above competitive levels, but government desire for revenue combined with a belief that high prices will discourage smoking have made increasing rather than decreasing prices the aim of public policy.

A huge legal battle over liability for smoking-related health care costs has strained the legal system and produced a significant effective increase in tobacco taxation without the inconvenience of legislators having to vote for it. The litigation has also brought to light internal company documents that have tarnished the companies' reputations and given a fascinating inside view into competitive (and anticompetitive) behavior. It has also resulted—perhaps much later than anyone in the industry would have guessed 30 years ago—in the companies finally admitting publicly what they all knew privately decades ago, that smoking is a deadly and addictive habit undertaken initially mostly by kids and then continued by adults, most of whom would like to quit.

The next phase in industry evolution is difficult to predict. The significantly higher prices brought about by the settlement will likely slightly accelerate the decline in smoking. If the FDA is ultimately given authority to regulate cigarettes, we could see tighter marketing restrictions, and perhaps eventually limits on permissible levels of tar, nicotine, and other constituents of cigarette smoke, yet the very addiction that makes smoking such a pernicious public policy problem makes it hard to identify good solutions even if legal authority is available. It is clear that there is no political will for another prohibition era. Mandatory reductions in nicotine are unlikely to work for addicted smokers, and could even be counterproductive as smokers smoke more cigarettes to get their desired nicotine level. The technological potential for cigarette-like products that deliver nicotine without other adverse health effects has never been adequately explored, but it is unclear that such products are now being pursued by anyone. It therefore seems likely that the peculiar industrial organization of the cigarette industry will continue for a long time.

Suggested Readings

Adams, Walter, and James Brock, *The Tobacco Wars* (Cincinnati: South-Western College Publishing, 1999).

Bulow, Jeremy, and Paul Klemperer, The Tobacco Deal, *Brookings Papers on Economic Activity: Microeconomics, 1998,* Brookings Institution, pp. 323–394.

Kluger, Richard, *Ashes to Ashes* (New York: Alfred Knopf, 1996).

Tenant, Richard, *The American Cigarette Industry* (New Haven: Yale University Press, 1950).

CHAPTER 4

Beer

—Kenneth G. Elzinga

In 1620, as every youngster knows, the Pilgrims landed at Plymouth Rock. Less commonly known is that the Pilgrims had set sail for Virginia, not Massachusetts. What led them to change their destination? They were running out of beer. One voyager recorded this entry in his diary: "Our victuals are being much spente, especially our beere." We leave to historians the question of how a dwindling beer inventory affected the course of the American nation. We turn to economics for an understanding of the U.S. beer industry today.

Beer is a potable product with four main ingredients:

1. Malt—a grain (usually barley) that has been allowed to germinate in water and then has been dried;
2. Flavoring adjuncts, usually hops and corn or rice—give beer its lightness and provide the starch that the enzymes in the malt convert to sugar;
3. Cultured yeast—ferments the beverage and feeds on the sugar content of the malt to produce alcohol and carbonic acid; and
4. Water—acts as a solvent for the other ingredients.

Because the process of brewing (or boiling) is intrinsic to making beer, the industry often is called the brewing industry.

All beers are not the same. The white beverage (spiced with a little raspberry syrup) favored in Berlin; the warm, dark-colored drink served by the English publican; and the amber liquid kept at near-freezing temperature in the cooler of the American convenience store are all beer. Generically, the term beer means any beverage brewed from a starch (or farinaceous) grain. Because the grain is made into a malt, another term for beer is malt liquor, or malt beverage. In this study, the terms beer, malt liquor, and malt beverage are used interchangeably to include all such products as beer, ale, light beer, dry beer, ice beer, porter, stout, and malt liquor. The factor common to these beverages, and which differentiates them from other alcoholic and nonalcoholic beverages, is the brewing process of fermentation applied to a basic grain ingredient.

Beer's production process is not, however, the key to defining beer as a market for economic analysis. A market is a group of firms (or conceivably one firm) that supplies products that consumers, voting with dollars in the marketplace, perceive as good substitutes. Some avid beer drinkers may prefer light beer over malt liquor at the same price per ounce. But they would prefer either of these over a glass of skim milk. For many consumers, the cross-elasticity of demand between malt beverages is higher than the cross-elasticity of demand between beer and other beverages. The fungibility between malt beverages distinguishes beer as a separate industry. This distinction is supported by the high cross-elasticity of supply between different types of malt beverages and the low cross-elasticity of supply between malt beverages and all other beverages. Among commercial beverages, beer ranks fourth in per capita consumption behind soft drinks, coffee, and milk. Among alcoholic beverages, beer accounts for almost 90 percent of U.S. consumption (by gallons), well ahead of wine and distilled spirits.

I. HISTORY

Beer was a common beverage in England in the 1600s and among the early settlers in America. In 1625, the first recorded public brewery was established in New Amsterdam (now New York City). Other commercial brewing followed, although considerable brewing was done in homes in seventeenth-century America. All that was needed were a few vats for mashing, cooling, and fermenting. The resulting product would not be recognized (or consumed) as beer today. The process was crude, the end result uncertain. Brewing was referred to as "an art and mystery."

Brewing was encouraged in early America. For example, the General Court of Massachusetts passed an act in 1789 to support the brewing of beer "as an important means of preserving the health of the citizens . . . and of preventing the pernicious effects of spiritous liquors." James Oglethorpe, trustee of the colony of Georgia, was even blunter: "Cheap beer is the only means to keep rum out."

The 1840s and 1850s were pivotal decades in the beer industry. The product beer, as it is generally known today, was introduced in the 1840s with the brewing of lager beer. Before this time, malt beverage consumption in America resembled English tastes—oriented toward ale, porter, and stout. Lager beer reflected a German influence on the industry. The influx of German immigrants provided skillful brewers and eager customers for this type of beer. At the start of the decade in 1850, there were 431 brewers in the United States producing 750,000 barrels of beer. By the end of that decade, 1,269 brewers produced more than a million barrels of beer—evidence of the bright future expected by many for this industry.

The latter half of the nineteenth century also saw technological advances in production and marketing. Mechanical refrigeration aided both the brewing and the storage of beer. Prior to this, beer production was partly dependent on the amount of ice that could be cut from lakes and rivers in the winter. Cities such as St. Louis, with its underground caves where beer could be kept cool while aging, lost this (truly natural) advantage with the advent of mechanical refrigeration. Pasteurization, a process originally devised to preserve wine and beer, not milk, was adopted during this period. Beer no longer had to be kept cold; it could be shipped into warm climates and stored without refermenting. Once beer was pasteurized, wide-scale bottling and off-premises consumption became viable. In addition, developments in transportation enabled brewers to sell output beyond their local markets. The twentieth century saw the rise of the national brewer.

The twentieth century also saw beer sales outlawed. The temperance movement, which began by promoting voluntary moderation and abstention from hard liquors, veered toward a goal of universal compulsory abstention from all alcoholic beverages. The beer industry seemed blissfully ignorant of this. Many brewers thought (or hoped) the temperance movement would ban only liquor.

In 1919, 36 states ratified the Eighteenth Amendment to enact the national prohibition of alcoholic beverages. This led many brewers to close up shop; some produced candy and ice cream. Anheuser-Busch and others built a profitable business selling malt syrup, which was used to make "home brew." Because a firm could not state the ultimate purpose of malt syrup, the product was marketed as an ingredient for making baked goods, such as cookies. Prohibition lasted until April 1933, and brewers reopened rapidly after repeal. By June 1933, 31 brewers were in operation; in another year, the number had risen to 756.

In 1948, the demand for beer in the U.S. began a slow decline, from a 1947 record sale of 87.2 million barrels. During this period, per capita consumption of beer fell from 18.5 gallons in 1947 to 15.0 gallons in 1958. It was not until 1959 that sales surpassed the 1947 total. In the 1960s and 1970s, total demand began to grow again at an average rate of better than 3 percent per year. In 1965, for the first time, more than 100 million barrels were sold. Per capita consumption of beer increased from 1958's level of 15 gallons to a level of 24 gallons by the end of the 1970s. The rightward shift in the demand curve for beer was due to the increased number of young people in the United States (the result of the post-World War II baby boom), the lowered age requirements for drinking in many populous states, and the enhanced acceptability of beer among females. Moreover, the number of areas in the United States that were "dry" (i.e., where alcoholic beverages are prohibited) shrank considerably.

In the early 1980s, the market demand for beer stabilized. Demographic patterns reversed themselves as the pool of young people (18 to 34 years of age) declined. Minimum age requirements for the purchase of alcoholic beverages rose to 21 years. Other factors that cut into demand included the pursuit of physical fitness and the increasing concern with alcohol abuse, particularly drunk driving. In some states, laws restraining the use of one-way (nonreturnable) containers also may have reduced consumption. In the latter part of the 1990s, demographics again have begun to favor market growth. From 1998 to 2008, the population in the 21 to 24 age bracket is projected to grow. While this group comprises only 8 percent of the U.S. population, it consumes about 14 percent of all beer. Aggregate consumption should increase moderately as a consequence.

II. STRUCTURE

The most important components in the structure of the brewing industry are the nature of demand, the size distribution of firms and trends in industry concentration, entry conditions, and product differentiation.

Demand

The market demand for beer exhibits seasonal fluctuations as a result of greater thirsts during hot weather. The demand for beer in the United States also varies from region to region and state to state. Adult per capita beer consumption in Utah was 20.9 gallons in 1998, while Nevada led all others with a per capita consumption of 48.8 gallons (the Nevada figure is biased by beer-quaffing tourists). The highest per capita consumption by natives of a state probably occurs in Wisconsin.[1]

Although economists are not able to measure price elasticity infallibly, statistical estimations indicate the market demand for beer is inelastic—in the range of 0.7 to 0.9. Brand loyalty is not so strong as to make the demand for any particular malt beverage inelastic. Indeed, the demand for individual brands of beer appears to be quite elastic. This places an important limitation on the market power of a domestic brewer's attempt to raise prices unilaterally.

Concentration

According to economic theory, consumers facing a monopolist (or tight-knit oligopoly) likely will pay higher prices. For this reason, the size distribution of brewing firms is of economic interest. Is the beer industry unconcentrated, with its customers courted by many firms, or is it highly concentrated, leaving beer drinkers with little choice?

In the post-World War II period, two contrary trends have been at work in the industry. The number of major brewers located in the United

[1]No-alcohol beer is a small component of overall beer sales. Shipments in 1998 were 1.7 million barrels.

States has declined. But the size of the market area served by existing brewers and the volume of beer supplied by importers have increased. Moreover, in recent years, craft brewers (microbrewers, brewpubs, and contract brewers) have grown in number. Craft brewing has caused an explosion in new beer brands and different taste signatures. In 1998, imports held over 8 percent of the U.S. beer market; craft brewers held almost 3 percent.

The Decline in Numbers Craft brewers aside, the decline in the number of individual plants and independent companies in the brewing industry has been dramatic. In 1935, shortly after repeal, 750 brewing plants were operating in the United States. That number dropped to 58 by 1992. Table 4-1 shows the number of beer companies and plants in the period of 1947 to 1998. During 1947 to 1995, the number of beer companies dropped over 90 percent (although beer sales doubled). Few, if any, American industries have undergone a similar structural shakeup. Recently, due to the growth of the craft beer segment, a noticeable increase in the number of new plants and independent companies has occurred—though these new entrants are mostly at the small end of the industry size spectrum.

TABLE 4-1 U.S. Brewing Companies and Plants: 1947–1998*

Year	*Number of Independent Companies*	*Number of Separate Plants*
1947	404	465
1954	262	310
1958	211	252
1963	150	211
1967	124	153
1974	57	107
1978	44	96
1983	35	73
1986	33	67
1989	29	61
1992	29	58
1995	42	77
1997	58	89
1998	89	115

Sources: Adapted from The Institute for Brewing Studies, *Brewers Resource Directory* (various years); and *Modern Brewery Age, Blue Book* (various years).

*Excludes microbreweries of less than 10,000-barrel capacity from 1947 to 1992; excludes microbreweries of less than 15,000-barrel capacity from 1995 to 1998; and excludes all contract brewing companies.

As the number of companies declines, the largest brewers have been increasing their share of the market. As shown in Table 4-2, in 1947, the top five companies accounted for only 19 percent of the industry's barrelage; in 1998, their share was 87 percent. In 1998, three firms met most of the domestic demand: Anheuser-Busch (46.8 percent), Miller (21.2 percent), and Coors (10.2 percent). Another way of summarizing the distribution of firm size is to compute the Herfindahl Hirschman Index (HHI), also shown in Table 4-2. The HHI is each individual seller's market share squared and then added together (its maximum value is 10,000, with one firm in the market). The rising Herfindahl Hirschman Index also testifies to the industry's structural transformation.

The Widening of Markets Even in the days of hundreds of brewing companies, most beer drinkers faced an actual choice of only a few brew-

TABLE 4-2 Concentration of Sales by Top Brewers: 1947–1998

Year	*Five Largest*	*HHI*
1947	19.0%	140
1954	24.9%	240
1958	28.5%	310
1964	39.0%	440
1968	47.6%	690
1974	64.0%	1,080
1978	74.3%	1,292
1981	75.7%	1,545
1984	83.9%	1,898
1987	88.1%	2,267
1990	88.6%	2,555
1992	87.4%	2,574
1993	87.3%	2,603
1994	87.3%	2,637
1995	89.9%	2,659
1996	89.2%	2,732
1997	88.1%	2,729
1998	87.2%	2,789

Source: Based on beer volume. The HHI includes only the top five brewers in that year. Adapted from A. Horowitz and I. Horowitz, "The Beer Industry," Business Horizons, 10:14 (1967), various issues of *Modern Brewery Age,* and *Beer Marketer's Insights 1999 Beer Industry Update.*

ers because most brewers served a small geographic area. Beer is an expensive product to ship, relative to its value, and few brewers could afford to compete in the "home markets" of distant rivals. Thus, at one time, it was very meaningful to speak of local, regional, and national brewers. Of these, the local brewer who brewed for a small market, perhaps smaller than a single state and often only a single metropolitan area, was the most common.[2] The regional brewer was multistate, but usually encompassed no more than two or three states. The national brewers, those selling in all (or almost all) states, were very few. In addition, it was uncommon for a firm to operate more than one plant.

Today, the terms local, regional and national brewers are almost antiquated.[3] The average geographic market served by one brewer from one plant has widened due to the economies of large-scale production and, to some extent, marketing. With the average-size brewing plant much larger today, the brewing company may extend itself geographically to maintain capacity operations. The premier example of this was the Adolph Coors Company, which once reached customers on the Eastern seaboard from its single brewing plant in Colorado. But it did so at a significant transportation cost disadvantage. A second factor extending the reach of large brewers to serve new geographic regions is their propensity to operate more than one plant.

Size of the Market Determining the degree of market concentration in brewing entails knowing how far the geographic markets for beer extend. If there is one national market, then concentration statistics for the entire nation are relevant. But if brewing, like cement or milk, has regional markets, delineating their boundaries is necessary before the industry's structure can be ascertained.

The federal courts have to solve this problem when deciding antimerger cases in the brewing industry. In an early antitrust case involving the merger of two brewers located in Wisconsin, the Antitrust Division asked an eminent economist at Northwestern University to testify in support of the view that the state of Wisconsin alone was a separate market for beer. The economics professor told the government lawyers that such a position was economically untenable. Nevertheless, the lawyers persisted in this view without him and eventually persuaded the Supreme Court that Wisconsin, by itself, is "a distinguishable and economically significant market for the sale of beer."

---

[2]According to Timothy McNulty, Chicago alone had 32 independent breweries in 1937, 10 in 1960, 2 in 1969, and none by 1979.

[3]Robert S. Weinberg bifurcates the contemporary beer market into two broad components: the "core" (the major brands of the large domestic brewers) and the "non-core" (imports and domestic specialty brands).

Although Wisconsin was held to have been a separate market for legal purposes, to single it out as a market in the economic sense is to draw the market boundaries too narrowly (and such a position would not be taken by antitrust authorities today). In 1991, brewers in the state of Wisconsin produced over 17 million barrels of beer; that year, consumers in Wisconsin consumed less than 5 million barrels. Because beer also is "imported" into Wisconsin from brewers in other states, obviously more than two-thirds of Wisconsin beer is "exported" for sale outside the state. To say that Wisconsin is a separate geographic market would be to overlook the impact of most beer production in that state, not to mention the impact on the supply of beer coming into Wisconsin that competes with the beer produced in Wisconsin. In this case, the court erred by singling out Wisconsin as an economically meaningful market. The geographic market for beer is now nationwide.

Reasons for the Decline in the Number of Brewers

In this section, two possible explanations for the decline in the number of brewers are considered: mergers and economies of scale.

Mergers A common explanation for an industry's oligopolization is a merger-acquisition trend among the industry's firms. At first glance, this seems to be the case in brewing. In the period of 1950 to 1983, the beer industry experienced about 170 horizontal mergers. But corporate marriages between rival brewers do not explain the increase in concentration by the largest firms. A review of the merger track record of the top five brewers will prove instructive.

The first antimerger action in the beer industry was taken by the Antitrust Division in 1958 against the industry's leading firm, Anheuser-Busch. Anheuser-Busch had purchased the Miami brewery of American Brewing Company. The government successfully argued that this merger would eliminate American Brewing as an independent brewer and end its rivalry with Anheuser-Busch in Florida. The impact of this early antimerger action was profound. Anheuser- Busch had to sell this brewery and refrain from buying any others without court approval for a period of five years. As a result, Anheuser-Busch forsook acquiring rival brewers and instead began an extensive program of building large, efficient plants in Florida and at other locations. Anheuser-Busch deviated from its internal growth policy in 1980 when it acquired the Baldwinsville, New York, brewing plant of the Schlitz Brewing Company. Schlitz's sales had declined so much that it did not need the brewery; the plant's capacity was so huge that only an industry leader could absorb its output.

The second-largest brewer, Miller, has a very different merger history. Miller purchased brewing plants in Texas and California in 1966 but acquired no other breweries until 1987, when it acquired Leinenkugal, a small family-run operation in Wisconsin. The Miller Brewing Company itself was the subject of a conglomerate acquisition by the Philip Morris tobacco company in 1970. In 1972, Miller acquired three brand names from a bankrupt brewer. Two years later, Miller bought the rights to brew and market Lowenbrau, a leading German beer in the United States. In 1993, Miller acquired the marketing rights in the United States for the brands of Molson, a Canadian brewer.

Third-ranked Coors had a long-time policy to brew its Coors brand in only one location, Golden, Colorado. Later, Coors began shipping the beer in bulk to Elkton, Virginia, where it is bottled and canned for sale in the East. In 1990, Coors acquired the Memphis brewery of Stroh. There, as in Virginia, the company only *packages* the Coors brand (but brews the company's lower priced Keystone brand).

In 1999, the fourth-ranking firm in the beer industry, Stroh, exited the market. Stroh had been a major brewer since 1850 and was, itself, an acquirer until its end. Stroh acquired the F. M. Schaefer Brewing Company in 1980 (Stroh was then the seventh-largest brewer). In 1982, Stroh acquired the downward-spiraling, fourth-largest brewer, the Joseph Schlitz Brewing Company. This acquisition catapulted Stroh to number three in the industry, but it also shackled the firm with debt and set the stage for its demise. In 1996, Stroh made another sizable acquisition: the G. Heileman Brewing Company.

Heileman had been the industry's fifth-ranking firm, as well as the acquirer of over a dozen other companies from 1960 on, notably Wiedemann, Associated Brewing, the Blatz brand, Rainier, Carling, and portions of Pabst. In 1960, before its acquisition strategy began, Heileman was only thirty-first in rank. In 1987, Heileman was acquired by a large Australian brewer and holding corporation, Bond Corp. Holdings. The subsequent collapse of the Bond financial empire put Heileman into bankruptcy. In 1993, Heileman was bought by Hicks, Muse & Co., the turnaround artists who acquired and revived Dr Pepper, 7-Up, and A&W soft drinks but who could not do the same for Heileman.[4]

Most of the mergers in the beer industry did not involve firms of significant stature. Generally, they represented the termination of an inefficient firm that salvaged some remainder of its worth by selling out to

---

[4]In 1981, Heileman was a rejected suitor for Schlitz (just prior to the Stroh-Schlitz amalgamation), and in 1982, it was a rejected suitor for Pabst. The Antitrust Division objected to both mergers. But Pabst and Heileman became substantially intertwined. Pabst, during this time frame, had purchased the Olympia Brewing Company (producer of the Olympia, Lone Star, and Hamm's brands) in a complex exchange that transferred its breweries in Georgia, Texas, and Oregon to rival Heileman, as well as the Lone Star, Red White and Blue, Blitz-Weinhard, and Burgermeister brands; it also entailed the obligation on Heileman's part to brew beer in the Southeast for Pabst at the former Pabst brewery in Perry, Georgia, that Heileman had acquired.

another brewer. The acquiring brewer gained no market power but might have benefitted by securing the barrelage to bring one plant to full capacity or by gaining access to an improved distribution network or new territory. Mergers such as these are not the *cause* of structural change; they are the *effect,* as firms exit or rearrange their assets through the merger route.

In 1999, Miller, Stroh, and Pabst (at the time the number five brewer) consummated a complex acquisition associated with Stroh's exit from the industry. Miller acquired four brands (Henry Weinhard, Mickey's, Hamm's and Olde English 800), and Pabst acquired all the other Stroh brands (including the former Schlitz and Heileman brands[5]). Miller also acquired Pabst's Tumwater, Washington, brewery, and Pabst acquired Stroh's Lehigh Valley, Pennsylvania, brewery. Miller has agreed to meet some of Pabst's expanded demand on a contract brewing basis. Most of the remaining Stroh breweries will be sold as real estate for nonbrewing purposes.[6] Despite the deal's magnitude in terms of brand ownership rearrangement, it resulted in only a small increase in industry concentration and had no antitrust consequence.

Mergers have made an imprint on the structure of the brewing industry, but they have not resulted in market power for merging partners. The most active merging firms, Stroh and Heileman, eventually failed. Much of the increase in concentration in the past three decades was due to the growth of Anheuser-Busch, Miller, and Coors, whose expansion has been largely internal. Indeed, the early enforcement of the antimerger law was somewhat responsible for the emphasis on internal growth by the leading brewers. Later mergers went unchallenged for the most part. The antitrust authorities recognized in the mid-1970s that beer mergers they once would have attacked do not merit challenge, even if the merger involves sizable regional sellers. The trend to concentration in brewing would have occurred even if all mergers had been prohibited. As a consequence, one must look to factors other than mergers to explain the industry's structural shakeup.

Economies of Scale When discussing economies of scale, economists generally plot a smooth, continuous average cost curve that envelopes a series of short-run average cost curves, each representing a different-sized plant. Economies of scale exist if large plants produce at lower unit costs than small ones. What is seldom mentioned in the discussion of these curves, however, is that great confidence cannot be attached to the loca-

---

[5]These would include, in addition to Stroh, Old Milwaukee, Schlitz, Schaefer, Old Style, Schmidt's, Lone Star, Special Export, Schlitz Malt Liquor, and Rainier.

[6]Yuengling acquired Stroh's 1.6-million-barrel capacity Tampa brewery and will use it to meet current demand in the Northeast and for geographic expansion in the Southeast. Stroh's Portland, Oregon, brewery (the former Blitz-Weinhard plant) has ceased operations.

tion of any point on these cost curves, notwithstanding their precise, scientific appearance in the economics literature.

Figure 4-1 is a representation of economies of scale in the brewing industry. It illustrates the fairly sharp decline in long-run unit costs until a plant size of 1.25 million barrels-per-year of capacity is reached. Beyond this capacity, costs continue to decline, but less sharply, until a capacity of 8 million barrels (an enormous brewery) is attained. Only modest cost economies can be exploited in plants with capacity above 8 million barrels.

Table 4-3 shows one method (the survivor test) used by economists to estimate the extent of economies of scale. This test, like all techniques for estimating economies of scale, is not without its difficulties. As its name implies, the survivor test distinguishes those plants that have survived over time. There has been a steady decline (dramatic in some cases) for breweries of under-two-million-barrel capacity and a large increase in breweries of five-million-barrel capacity and above. That large brewing plants not only survived but grew in number is prima facie evidence of their lower unit costs[7]. One can understand much better the concentration statistics in brewing after learning that the 18 plants of industry leaders Anheuser-Busch and Miller in 1998 have an average capacity of slightly over 8.5 million barrels. These are the huge cost-efficient production units for the U.S. market's larger brands. The only exception is the notable jump in small breweries, especially in the 10 to 100,000 barrel capacity range.

FIGURE 4-1 Economies of Scale in Brewing

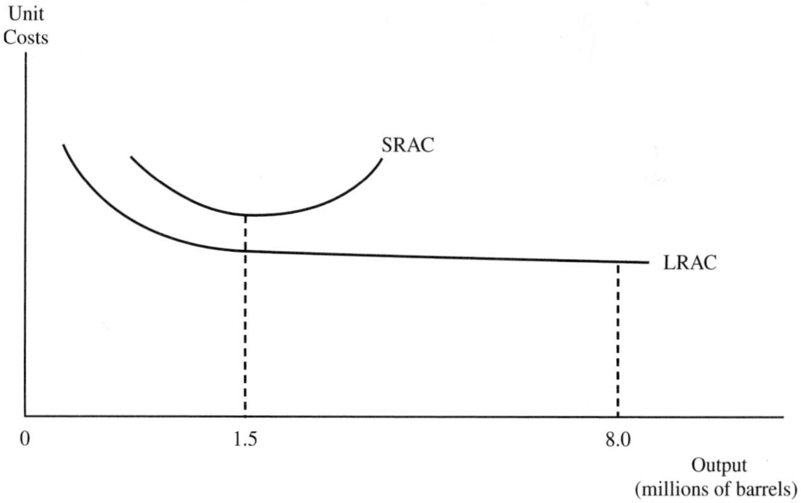

[7]For a sophisticated treatment of cost efficiencies in brewing, see the paper by Joe R. Kerkvliet, William Nebesky, Carol H. Tremblay and Victor J. Tremblay.

TABLE 4-3 Surviving Breweries by Capacity: 1959–1998

Listed Capacity Barrels (Thousands)	*1959*	*1963*	*1967*	*1971*	*1975*	*1979*	*1983*	*1986*	*1989*	*1992*	*1998*
10–100	68	54	36	21	10	10	15	13	8	8	77
101–500	91	72	44	33	19	13	12	8	7	7	19
501–1000	30	33	35	32	13	8	2	3	3	3	1
1001–2000	18	17	18	21	13	11	13	10	5	5	4
2001–4000	8	10	10	12	12	13	9	10	6	6	7
4001+	2	3	4	7	15	20	23	23	20	20	20

Source: Compiled from plant capacity figures listed in the *Modern Brewery Age Blue Book* (various years); Charles W. Parker, "The Domestic Beer Industry" (1984) and industry trade sources. These figures do not include plants listed only on a company consolidated basis (in the case of multiplant firms) or single-plant firms not reporting their capacity and these figures exclude microbreweries of less than 10,000 barrels capacity.

Table 4-3 does not reflect the appearance of very small breweries in the craft beer segment—"microbreweries" or "boutique breweries" or brewpubs (if food is served with on-premises beer consumption). In 1986, there were more than 50 brewers of less than 10,000-barrel capacity; by 1998, more than 175 craft brewers had sales of up to 15,000 barrels. Most are new firms, and some are very small indeed, such as the Little Apple Brewing Co., in Manhattan, Kansas, with 1998 sales of 502 barrels. Microbreweries receive much attention in the business press, in part because there had been, until their arrival, so little *de novo* entry into the beer industry in the post-World War II period; and because they brew beers with a different taste than the mainstream lagers produced by the major domestic brewers. Their owners, who often are also the managers and brewmasters, are portrayed as a new breed of entrepreneur in the beer industry. Craft brewers have their own trade journal, *The New Brewer,* and this segment of the industry is reported on and promoted by the Institute for Brewing Studies.

Figure 4-1 also has a single short-run average cost curve above the long-run average cost curve. A long-run cost curve represents the envelope of different-sized plants, each of which uses the latest production techniques. The short-run average cost curve standing by itself better portrays the situation of many breweries that met their demise in the 1960s and 1970s. These breweries were not only too small to exploit all the economies of scale, but also their capital equipment was of such an outmoded vintage that their costs were elevated even more.

Some of the economies from larger operations come in the packaging of the beer. The newer bottling lines at the Anheuser-Busch Houston brewery have line speeds of 1,100 bottles per minute. Modern canning lines are even faster: 2,000 cans per minute. It takes a brewery of substantial size to utilize such equipment at capacity. Large plants also save on labor costs via the automation of brewing and warehousing and on capital costs as well. Construction cost per barrel is cut by about one-third for a 4.5-million-barrel plant relative to a 1.5-million-barrel capacity plant. However, no significant reduction in production costs was detected in a study of multiplant economies of scale by F. M. Scherer and others.

Cost efficiency relates not only to some finite production capacity but also to management's ability to use the capacity efficiently. Shortly after the repeal of Prohibition in 1933, there was a flood of new entrants into the brewing industry, all expecting to be met by thirsty customers. However, the demand for beer was unexpectedly low after repeal. From a high of 750 brewers operating in 1935, almost 100 were quickly eliminated in but five years. Quite a few of these enterprises had operated before Prohibition, but many were under new management. Some were family-owned firms, and heredity had been cruel to the second or third generations, not endowing them with the brewing and/or managerial capabilities of their fathers or grandfathers. Competitive pressures, with no respect for nepotism, eliminated such breweries.

A small brewer, producing a quality product and marketing it so as to keep transportation costs at a minimum, can survive in today's industry by finding a special niche for itself. This seems to be the status of Wisconsin's Stevens Point Brewery; D. G. Yuengling & Son in Pennsylvania (the nation's oldest brewing firm still in business); and the pioneer craft brewer, San Francisco's Anchor Steam Brewery. However, such cases are exceptions. In brewing—unlike in many other manufacturing industries where optimum-sized plants seem to be getting smaller—large, capital-intensive plants are necessary to exploit economies of scale and survive. In markets where vigorous competitive pressures exist, firms that do not exploit economies of scale or operate with internal efficiency will not survive. This has been the fate of many brewers; they have exited from the industry because of inefficient plants, poor management, or both.

The Condition of Entry

The ease with which newcomers can enter an industry is a structural characteristic of great importance for ensuring competitive performance. If entry is easy, existing firms will be unable to raise prices significantly lest they encourage an outbreak of new competition. On the other hand, if entry is barred, perhaps by a patent or government license, existing firms may be able to garner monopoly gains.

Entry into the beer industry is not hindered by the traditional barriers of patents and exclusive government grants. There are no key inputs whose supply is controlled or limited by existing firms. Nor are economies of scale so important that an efficient entrant would have to supply an enormous share of industry output. However, the expense of entering the beer industry is considerable. The price of constructing a modern four-to-five-million-barrel brewery is some $250 million. Marketing the new brew is costly, too, because entrants must introduce their products to consumers already smitten by the vigorous advertising efforts of competitors.

No top-five firm in the brewing industry has been a new entrant since World War II. *De novo* entry has been from imported beer and craft brewers. In 1998, among the craft-brewing segment, there were more than thirty new entrants (post-1980) producing at least 15,000 barrels annually. The paucity of entry in the core segment is explained by the relatively low profitability of the industry and the ominous fate of so many exiting firms. Moreover, the industry is risky because its plant facilities have few uses other than brewing beer. New entry involves considerable sunk costs.

The eighties and nineties were decades of the market mechanism wringing excess capacity from the industry and not inviting in new firms.

One entrepreneur who recognized the beer industry's excess capacity as a new entry opportunity was Jim Koch of the rapidly growing Boston Brewing Co., the leading craft brewer in the United States. This firm is primarily a contract brewer, having agreements with regional brewers that produce, to Koch's specifications, his firm's Samuel Adams brand. The second-largest craft brewer, Sierra Nevada Brewing Co., has taken a different supply tack. It now owns brewing capacity of 600,000 barrels per year. Presently, the most promising sources of new competition in the market for beer are an established brewer's moving into a new geographic area, a new imported beer, a contract brewer, or the introduction of new product lines by existing brewers. Import competition merits a special mention. Beer imports to the United States, which now come mostly from Mexico, the Netherlands, Canada, and Germany, increased more than eighteen-fold in the period 1970 to 1998. In 1998, imports represented over 8 percent of domestic consumption, up from less than 1 percent in 1970. Imported beer can no longer be discounted as insignificant. In 1998, for the first time, an import (Corona Extra) became a top-ten brand.

Product Differentiation

When consumers find the product of one firm superior to other market alternatives, the favored firm can raise its price somewhat without losing these customers. This phenomenon is called *product differentiation.* Three characteristics of product differentiation in the brewing industry bear mentioning. First, several studies indicate that, under blindfold-test conditions, many beer drinkers cannot distinguish between brands of beer. Second, more expensive brands do not cost proportionately more to produce. Third, considerable talent and resources are devoted to publicizing real or imagined differences in beers, with the hope of producing brand loyalty. Notwithstanding these efforts, product differentiation in the beer industry has not afforded individual brewers market power to a degree that would be a concern of antitrust policy.

The product differentiation of "premium beer" is important to understand. This phenomenon began years ago when a few brewers marketed their beer nationally and added a price premium to offset the additional transportation costs incurred by greater shipping distances. To secure the higher price, their beer was promoted as superior in taste and quality, allegedly because of the brewing expertise found in their locations. At one time, this premium price was absorbed by higher shipping costs. The construction of efficient, regionally dispersed breweries by firms such as Anheuser-Busch and Miller eliminated the transportation disadvantage—but the premium image remained. With transportation costs equalized, and production costs generally lower, these firms could wage vigorous advertising (and price-cutting) campaigns in areas where regional and local brewers were once the largest sellers.[8]

One indicator of an industry's advertising intensity is its ratio of advertising expenditures to sales. For some companies in the soap, cosmetic, and drug industries, this ratio is greater than 10 percent. For the malt beverage industry, the ratio is not trivial but it is less than the ratio for such industries as soft drinks, candy, cigarettes, preserved fruits, and other alcoholic beverages. A significant escalation in beer advertising costs began between 1976 and 1977 and continued until around 1985. According to Jon Nelson's data, total advertising on beer (in real terms) has declined from $917 million in 1985 to $626 million in 1995—a −3.7 annual compound growth rate.

The beer industry is a major buyer of television advertising time. In 1998, Anheuser-Busch, Miller, and Coors spent $3.36, $5.20, and $6.75 per barrel, respectively, on media advertising. Douglas F. Greer, Willard F. Mueller, and others have argued that advertising, particularly television advertising, is a primary cause of increasing concentration in the industry. John Sutton offers a variation on this theme, suggesting that advertising is a sunk cost that protects the leading firms. But the facts do not permit any tidy explanations or conclusions about the consequences of advertising because no hard-and-fast relationship exists between dollars spent on advertising and market share gained.

Miller has long been a heavy advertiser. In the period between 1967 and 1971, Miller generally spent twice as much per barrel as rival brewers. But Miller's market share did not expand then, nor did other firms feel compelled to emulate Miller's sizable promotional outlays. Schlitz spent more on advertising in 1975 and 1976 than either Anheuser-Busch or Miller, and yet sales of the Schlitz brand declined in that very time frame. Coors experienced expanding sales with very small advertising expenditures: in 1968 to 1974, during years of sizable growth, Coors spent an average of only 17 cents per barrel on media advertising. Coors' *growing* use of media occurred when its share position in many states was declining. Miller was not able to secure more than a toehold in the super-premium segment of the market notwithstanding extraordinary advertising expenditures per barrel on Lowenbrau. In 1980, Miller High Life was the most heavily advertised brand of beer in the United States; that was the year its sales slowed down and began declining every year until the brand was repositioned at a lower price point. Anheuser-Busch signifi-

---

[8]The national brewers also have two other advertising advantages: (1) none of their advertising is "wasted," whereas regional brewers do not always find media markets (especially in television) that coincide with their selling territories; and (2) their advertising investment is less likely to be lost when a customer moves to another part of the country.

cantly increased its advertising expenditures on its Budweiser brand—total and per barrel—from 1991 to 1992, but Budweiser's total sales and share of market fell, nevertheless. On the other hand, Natural Light has been one of Anheuser-Busch's steadiest performers even though the company spends less than a nickel per barrel on advertising.

The total amount spent advertising beer is large, and this is not surprising. Brewers want to inform millions of actual and potential beer drinkers about the quality and availability of their products. New beer customers come of age; old customers may need reminding.

Rising per capita income also has contributed modestly to increasing concentration in the beer industry. Premium beer is what economists call a normal good, with a positive income elasticity. The brewers who came to be the major factors in the industry in the 1970s are, essentially, producers of premium brands. Popular-priced brands (now often called the "budget" segment) were once the leading sellers within their home states. No longer. Premium brands (regular and light) now hold about 53 percent of the market; imports and superpremiums have about 12 percent. The loser in the past three decades has been popular-priced beer, dropping from almost 60 percent in 1970 to less than 15 percent in 1998. The traditional domestic superpremium brands (such as Michelob and Lowenbrau) also have faded, replaced by a growing emphasis on craft beers and imports.

Low-calorie beer, virtually nonexistent in 1970, has become the largest market segment with about 41 percent of the total market in 1998—almost all of this being brewed by the top three brewers and much of it selling at premium prices. The decline of once-prominent brewers such as Pabst, Schlitz, and Stroh is explained in part by their lack of success (compared to Anheuser-Busch, Miller, and Coors) in the light-beer segment of the market.

Specialty brands are not just the offspring of microbrewers. Several major brewers have had modest success with specialty brands, usually priced a notch below craft beers and import brands. Coors (Killian Red), Miller (Red Dog), and Genesee (Michael Shea's Amber) are examples of the trend. Product variety generally has a positive income elasticity, and rising income supports greater product variety. Some beverage sector analysts speculate that the beer industry someday will have the same large array of specialty brands one finds now in coffee and wine.

The Philip Morris-Miller Affiliation

In the decade of the 1970s, the most dramatic single factor in the brewing industry's structural change was the rise of the Miller Brewing Company from seventh to second place. Miller's ascent involved far more than a mere shuffling of rank among industry leaders. Its production capacity and marketing methods added a new dimension to the industry that affected the industry's economic behavior throughout the 1980s. Two dates are important in understanding the Miller phenomenon: 1970, when Miller's procurement by the Philip Morris Company was completed, and 1972, when Miller purchased the brand names of Meister Brau, a now-defunct Chicago brewing firm.

The 1970 date initiated the management takeover of Miller by Philip Morris personnel. The new management accomplished three master strokes with the Miller High Life brand. First, it was (in marketing parlance) repositioned to appeal to the blue-collar consumer, who might drink several beers a day. Previously, the brand had been directed toward a group of consumers who rarely consumed more than a single beer at a time. As one Miller advertising executive put it, the strategy was to "... take Miller High Life out of the champagne bucket and put it into the lunch bucket without spilling a drop." Second, Miller improved the quality of its product; any of its beer not sold within 120 days of production was destroyed. Third, the company introduced a 7-ounce (pony) bottle that appealed both to infrequent beer drinkers with small capacities and drinkers who found that the beer remained colder in the small receptacle.

The virtually unnoticed Miller purchase of the three Meister Brau trademarks included one called Lite, a brand of low-calorie beer brewed by the amyloglucosidase process and once marketed locally by Meister Brau to upper-middle-class, weight-conscious consumers. The Miller management noticed that Lite had sold fairly well in Anderson, Indiana, a town with many blue-collar workers. In what is now a marketing classic, Miller zeroed in on "real" beer drinkers, claiming that its low-calorie beer allowed them to drink their beer with even less of a filled-up feeling. The upshot of this marketing campaign was evident to any grocery or convenience-store shelf-stocker at the time: Lite became the most popular new product in the history of the beer industry. Miller failed in its legal campaign to reserve not only Lite but also the term *light* to itself; the courts left the generic word in the public domain allowing other brewers to use it to describe their own low-calorie emulations.

Miller's ascendancy has not been without its brickbats, which come generally in two forms. The first criticism is that Miller changed the process of beer rivalry, with the emphasis no longer on production economies but upon market segmentation and brand proliferation. If "beer is beer," then it is argued that consumers do not truly benefit by the product and packaging differentiation that is now common in the industry. Some economists are concerned that brand proliferation can erect barriers to entry to smaller firms, thereby lessening competition. The contrary argument is that Miller had to bear the financial burden of making low-calorie beer known to consumers; having done this, Miller's rivals have been able to introduce their own light beers more easily.

The second criticism of Miller stems from its conglomerate ownership and the allegation that Philip Morris's "deep pockets" provided unfair advantages to Miller over its rivals. For example, Professor Willard F. Mueller testified before a Senate committee that "Miller's expansion after 1970 was made possible by Philip Morris's financial backing and willingness to engage in deep and sustained subsidization of Miller's operations." Mueller implicitly concluded that Philip Morris's behavior made economic sense only if the goal of its subsidization was a monopoly position for Miller (or shared monopoly with Anheuser-Busch) in the near future.

Mueller's concerns about the Miller-Philip Morris amalgamation have not been borne out, given the sizable rivals remaining in the beer industry, their active rivalry with Miller, and the significant lead that Anheuser-Busch enjoys over Miller. Miller High Life, the company's flagship brand, notwithstanding millions of dollars in advertising expenditures, by 1992 had dropped in sales to 4.5 million barrels from its 1981 peak of 23.5 million, provoking Miller to reposition Miller High Life at a less-than-premium price level in the hope of stemming the brand's free fall. Miller Lite has been passed in sales by Bud Light and is now neck-and-neck with Coors Light for the number two position in the segment it pioneered.

III. CONDUCT

Pricing

Judging from the early records of the pre-Prohibition beer industry, competition in the industry was healthy. Entry was easy; producers were many. Given these two characteristics, economic theory would predict a competitive industry, and the evidence bears this out. In fact, the early beer industry offers a classic example of the predictions of price theory. Because of the market's inelastic demand, brewers saw the obvious advantages of monopolizing the industry, raising prices, and gleaning high profits. Various types of loose and tight-knit cartels were seen as advantageous, but the difficulty of coordinating so many brewers and the lack of barriers to entry prevented these efforts from being successful, at least for long. The degree of competition is evidenced by this turn-of-the-century plea from Adolphus Busch to Captain Pabst:

> I hope also to be able to demonstrate to you that by the present way competition is running we are only hurting each other in a real foolish way. The traveling agents . . . always endeavor to reduce prices and send such reports to their respective home offices as are generally not correct and only tend to bring forth competition that helps to ruin the profits . . . all large manufacturing interests are now working in harmony . . . and only the brewers

> are behind as usual; instead of combining their efforts and securing their own interest, they are fighting each other and running the profits down, so that the pleasures of managing a brewery have been diminished a good deal.

In a free enterprise economy, it is best that rival managers avoid any communications about prices. But if such letters are written, this is the sort of letter market rivalry should provoke.

The beer industry also escaped the horizontal mergers that transformed the structure of so many other industries such as steel, whiskey, petroleum, tobacco products, and farm equipment during the first great merger movement (1880–1904). Attempts were made, mostly by British businessmen, to combine the large brewers during this time. One sought the amalgamation of Pabst, Schlitz, Miller, Anheuser-Busch, and Lemp into one company, a feat that, had it been successful, would have altered the structure and degree of competition in the industry. But the attempt failed, and brewing entered Prohibition with a competitive structure that responded with competitive pricing.

The Pricing Pattern

Beer is generally sold free on board (f.o.b.) the brewery—meaning that brewer's costs end at the loading dock. Customers pay the freight. Some brewers sell on a uniform f.o.b. mill basis, but most vary their prices at times to different customers to reflect localized competitive conditions or to test perceived changes in the marketplace. The present pattern of prices dates back to the start of the twentieth century. For decades, premium beers generally were priced just above the level of popular-priced beers, which in turn were above local (or "price" or "shelf") beer. Because of downward price pressure on premium beer, and the decline of independent brewers producing only popular-priced beer, the marketing segments today often are broken down as premium (regular and light), near premium, and budget. A more contemporary category is the superpremium, a beer selling at a price above premium. A number of major brewers market their own brand of superpremiums, and most imported beers and the output of brewers in the craft segment fall in this price category.

The demarcation between local-popular-premium has become blurred in recent years, not only because of the introduction of the superpremium, but because the price differential between premium and popular-priced brands has narrowed. At the same time, the distinction between local and popular beer on the basis of price has become murky because of pricing specials that regularly appear in either segment of the market. Stagnant market demand in the 1990s also provoked discounting in the beer industry. For example, in 1992, almost 50 percent of the beer sold by Anheuser-Busch, Miller, and Coors included some form of deal: a direct price discount or an advertising/merchandising allowance. Beer price differentials are not fully attributable to some identifiable physical characteristic of the product. In the case of malt beverages, price differences also are the result of customers' tastes, market competition, and history.

Marketing

Although all industries are subject to various federal and state laws that affect the marketing of the industry's product, the brewing industry faces an especially variegated pattern of laws and regulations concerning labeling, advertising, credit, container characteristics, alcohol content, tax rates, and litter assessments. For example, Michigan does not permit a beer label to show alcohol content, while Minnesota requires an accurate statement of alcohol content. In Indiana, advertising is strictly regulated; in Louisiana there are no such regulations. Some states require sales from the brewer to the wholesaler to the retailer to be on a cash-only basis, whereas other states allow credit. Some states stipulate both the maximum and minimum size of containers; Alabama, for example, permits no package-beer containers larger than 16 ounces. States also have varying requirements on the maximum and minimum permissible alcoholic content; in some, alcoholic content is different for different types of outlets.

In the 1970s, beer advertising was criticized because it allegedly could lead to monopoly problems. This turned out to be unfounded. In the 1990s, some beer advertising has been criticized for allegedly leading to underage consumption (the Anheuser-Busch frogs have been compared to tobacco's Joe Camel). At least three federal government agencies [Alcohol, Tobacco & Firearms Agency (ATF), Federal Trade Commission (FTC), and Health & Human Services (HHS)] have been considering advertising and labeling issues that might affect the marketing of malt beverages. The research of Jon Nelson suggests that advertising does not increase market demand but merely rearranges shares among brands. Economists do not always see eye-to-eye. The research of Carol and Victor Tremblay (1995) offers the perspective that, on balance, society might gain from less beer advertising.

Government involvement in the beer industry also includes heavy taxation. The federal tax alone on a barrel of beer is $18.00 and, in 1998, the Treasury Department coffers gathered $3.4 billion in beer taxes. State taxes on beer vary substantially but average $7.37 per barrel. In addition, brewers, wholesalers, and retailers pay federal, state, and sometimes local occupational taxes. Taxes represent the largest single cost item in a glass of beer.

Brewer-Distributor Relations

There is little forward integration by brewing firms into the marketing of beer. In the United States, brewers generally are prohibited by law from owning retail outlets, leaving wholesale distribution as the only legitimate forward vertical integration route.[9] Even wholesaling by brewers is prohibited in some states. The retailing of beer is done through two general types of independent outlets: those for on-premises consumption and those for off-premises consumption.

Most brewers rely on independent distributors to channel their product to retail outlets. A brewer's keen financial interest in the downstream distribution of its beer is self-evident: a disgruntled customer sees the brewer's name on the container, not the name of the wholesaler (or retailer). Therefore, brewers negotiate contracts with wholesalers as to the marketing obligations of each party.

Not all areas of concern to the brewer regarding downstream marketing are open for negotiation. For example, the determination of resale prices is not a matter for private agreement because the antitrust laws limit the contractual opportunities of a brewer in this area. As a consequence, some brewers have introduced *reach back pricing.* Reach back pricing is an attempt by brewers to limit price increases by distributors in response to price increases by the brewer. For example, if a brewer raised its f.o.b. price 15 cents per case, it might expect its distributors to increase their prices to retailers 25 cents per case (and no more), in the hope that the price to the consumer might go up at most 35 cents per case. If a particular distributor increased its price to retailers by, say, 27 cents (more than a dime above the brewer's increase), under reach back pricing the brewer would "reach back" and raise its f.o.b. price 2 cents per case to that particular distributor—to encourage that distributor to cut back by 2 cents its price to retail accounts (whereupon the brewer then would reduce its f.o.b. price by 2 cents). Some distributors dislike reach back pricing and the practice has been challenged by certain state regulatory authorities.

On-premises sales are the leading retail channel (26 percent of U.S. beer volume) followed by convenience stores (20 percent) and supermarkets (19 percent). Some large retail customers, notably chain stores, would prefer to purchase beer directly from brewers, eliminating the wholesale distributor. Or they want to bargain with different distributors of the same brand of beer (possibly purchasing from a price-cutting wholesaler in another area). But brewers almost unanimously market through a three-tier distribution system.

Many brewers have exclusive territories with wholesalers to more efficiently market their beer. Exclusive territories enable brewers to offer incentives to distributors to cultivate their own territory with less fear of free riding. An example of *free riding* would be a distributor who transships dated beer to a territory that has been served by a distributor who,

[9]The exception—sometimes hard-won—has been brewpubs which represent vertical integration from brewing to retailing.

by careful stock rotation, had given that brand a reputation for freshness. Some critics, however, consider exclusive territorial restraints to be anticompetitive. In an important antitrust case against several major brewers, the New York Attorney General challenged the use of exclusive territories. In 1993, the challenge ended when exclusive territories in beer distribution were found, on balance, to be procompetitive.

At one time, beer wholesalers primarily distributed beer in kegs for on-premises draught consumption. In 1935, only 30 percent of beer sales were packaged—that is, in bottles or cans suitable for on- or off-premises consumption. Since that time, there has been a shift to packaged beer relative to draught; by 1998, about 90 percent of beer sales were packaged in cans, one-way bottles, and refillables. The convenience of the can and bottle, and the apparent loss of the "saloon habit" because of Prohibition, mean that the beer distributor today makes more deliveries to grocery and convenience stores than to taverns.

This trend in beer marketing has worked to the disadvantage of the small brewer. When beer sales were primarily by the keg for on-premises consumption, the small brewer could survive by selling to taverns in the immediate area. But packaged beer sales are primarily for off-premises consumption, and the distribution of packaged beer increases the importance of product differentiation and brand emphasis.

Beer and the Global Economy

The United States imports far more beer (16.4 million barrels in 1998) than it exports (5.5 million barrels in 1998). In some situations, the trade asymmetry is stark. For example, in 1998 the Dutch sold about 4 million barrels of beer to the United States and imported about 7,000 barrels of U.S. beer. Mexico, the Netherlands, Canada, and Germany are the main exporters of beer to the United States (in 1998 order of volume). Japan is the number one market for U.S. beer exports, just ahead of Canada.

The U.S. beer industry is a latecomer to the globalization of markets, but the process is underway. For example, in 1993, Anheuser-Busch purchased an 18 percent stake in the largest Mexican brewer (Cerveceria Modelo) and entered into a joint venture with the leading Japanese brewer (Kirin). In 1993, Miller purchased a small stake (8 percent) in the Mexican brewer FEMSA. In 1991, Coors entered into a joint venture with Jinro to build a large brewery in South Korea and signed a license agreement with Scottish & Newcastle in Scotland to brew Coors beer for the European market. In 1992, Pabst dismantled its Fort Wayne, Indiana, brewery, and shipped it to China, where it once again produces Pabst Blue Ribbon beer.

While Anheuser-Busch is the largest brewer of beer in the world, it is not truly a global brewer. Three firms, Heineken (Holland), Carlsberg (Denmark), and Guinness (U.K./Ireland), are considered global brewers.

Each has at least 70 percent of its volume produced outside its home country; each has a marketing presence in at least 150 countries; and each has brands brewed in at least 40 countries. Among U.S. brewers with international aspirations, licensing production in foreign markets has been the favored mode of expansion. The export of product from the United States to foreign markets actually declined in the latter half of the 1990s.

IV. PERFORMANCE

Profits

If an industry is effectively monopolized, one might expect to see this reflected in its profits. This is not necessarily so, since (1) demand may not be sufficiently high to yield profits in spite of monopoly; (2) a monopolist may be inefficient; (3) accounting records often are imperfect measures of economic costs and profits and may not reflect the monopoly gains. In spite of these difficulties, economists regularly look at profit data for some insight into an industry's performance.

On the whole, brewing firms have been less profitable than other average manufacturing firms in the post-World War II period. Profits in the industry were quite modest until 1967. During the three years of 1968 through 1970, the industry's accounting rate of return on net worth after taxes averaged 9.5 percent, compared to the return for all other manufacturing firms of 7.4 percent. However from 1981 to 1985, the beer industry tallied an average return of less than 5 percent—generally below the post-tax return on net worth for other manufacturing firms. In recent years, accounting profits for the industry have increased, averaging 11 percent for the three years 1988 through 1990.

As one might expect from our discussion of economies of scale, the largest brewers have done better than the industry average. Beginning in 1964, the top four companies began to outperform the rest of the brewing industry in terms of profits. Prior to that time, the profit record of the top four brewers approximated that of the rest of the industry and was usually inferior to the firms ranked five through eight.

Externalities

Externalities, or spillover effects, occur when transactions between buyers and sellers have economic consequences on persons not party to the transaction. These spillover effects can be positive or negative. To the extent an industry generates externalities, either in the production process or in the consumption of its product, the social performance of that industry is likely to be affected.

The beer industry is remarkably free of two negative externalities in production often associated with manufacturing enterprises: air and water pollution. Brewing is a very "clean" industry (breweries must be more sanitary than hospitals, in fact), and it is partly for this reason that brewing firms often are courted by areas seeking new industry. But the industry does have two important negative externality problems, and both relate to the consumption of the product: litter and drunk drivers.

Although legislation banning or restricting the sale of beer containers is commonly proposed, only a few states and localities actually have passed such laws. The most restrictive of these laws was enacted in the college town of Oberlin, Ohio, which outlawed the sale or possession of beer in nonreturnable containers. The most well-known of these laws is the Oregon "bottle bill," passed in 1971, which banned all cans with detachable pull tabs and placed a compulsory 5-cent deposit on all kinds of beer and soft drink containers. Because retail stores do not want to handle returned cans, the bill drastically reduced the sale of beverages in cans and encouraged the use of returnable glass containers or on-premises draught consumption. In Oregon and Vermont, mandatory deposit legislation apparently led to reductions of 60 and 80 percent, respectively, in roadside beverage container litter. However, the statewide (or local) approach cannot solve the problem (say, in Vermont) of customers going "over the line" (to New Hampshire) to avoid the deposit requirement and higher prices.

American brewers (with the exception of Coors) historically have opposed all taxes and bans on containers, stressing instead voluntary action and other litter-recovery programs. The latter, if generously financed, could solve the litter problem, but partially at the expense of nonproducers and nonconsumers.

The costly negative externality of driving while under the influence of alcohol was responsible for escalating the minimum drinking age in all states to 21 years of age. But this has had little impact upon drunk driving by young drivers. Economic research suggests that young beer drinkers are sensitive to price increases. Indexing the federal tax on beer to the rate of inflation since 1951 would, by its impact on retail price, have discouraged enough drunk driving by young drivers to save an estimated 5,000 lives in the period of 1982 to 1988 (more than were saved by raising the minimum legal drinking age). As another strategy, the National Highway Safety Administration has endorsed a blood alcohol content (BAC) level of .08 (or above) as a per se driving violation. Most states currently define driving under the influence at a BAC above .08, such as .10. The American Beverage Institute opposes lowering the BAC but supports stiffer penalties for those caught driving while intoxicated. The costs imposed upon third parties by alcohol abuse go beyond automobile injuries and fatalities, and alcohol abuse, of course, is not limited to the consumption of malt beverages.

Competition

In some industries, increasing concentration at the national level coupled with inelastic market demand might raise the specter of tacit or direct collusion. Similarly, with high concentration, the chances may be lessened that smaller firms will follow a truly independent price and production strategy. However, the prospect of joint profit-maximizing behavior in the beer industry is not worrisome for the foreseeable future. Thus far, there is no evidence of price collusion in the industry. Even during the period of increased demand for beer in the 1960s and 1970s, competition forced the exit of marginal firms. Furthermore, competition along nonprice vectors also is robust—such as new product introductions (no-alcohol beer, packaged draught, dry beer), promotional activities, packaging innovations, brand advertising, product freshness, and availability.

One measure of an industry's rivalry is the extent of changes in market share or turnover in the ranking of its sellers. The beer industry exhibits high mobility in this regard. Schlitz, the nation's second-ranking firm in 1976 and the "Beer That Made Milwaukee Famous," no longer is even brewed there. Pabst was the third-leading seller as recently as 1975, ahead of Miller, and the subject of Antitrust Division action. It has become a shell of its former self. In 1998, Pabst sold only 1.8 million barrels of Pabst Blue Ribbon. As a consequence of market forces in the period 1988 to 1998, the once prominent brewing trio of Heileman, Pabst, and Stroh lost over 22 million barrels of sales from their brand portfolios. Miller, number eight in 1968, rose in rank and has been number two since 1977. But Miller, the darling of the industry in the 1970s, experienced an absence of growth in the 1980s and 1990s. Coors once "owned" Oklahoma and California, with 54 percent and 40 percent of the sales in these states. By 1998, these percentages had slipped to 17 and 13 percent.

The one constant in all this has been Anheuser-Busch: number one since 1957. Even more remarkable than its hold on number one has been its relative growth. Throughout the ten year period of 1989 to 1998, Anheuser-Busch's market share has grown almost every year. Several factors contribute to its strong leadership position. All of its breweries are large, low-cost facilities. In addition, most of its output is sold at premium and superpremium prices. Moreover, much of that output takes the form of only two brands, produced primarily in one package format (Budweiser and Bud Light in 12-ounce cans). This means Anheuser-Busch does not often incur the cost of changing brewing formulas or reconstituting packaging lines. Anheuser-Busch's pricing strategy builds on the firm's efficiencies in production. It endeavors to have prices change only in line with production-cost changes and to build overall profits through volume gains. Furthermore, Anheuser-Busch has per-barrel advertising costs significantly below many of its rivals because of its enormous volume—and because its TV ads are acclaimed for their positive recall.[10] Currently, Anheuser-Busch is the price leader in the industry. On the other hand, the company is dependent on the Budweiser brand, whose domestic sales have declined in recent years. Should the bloom ever come off the Bud, Anheuser-Busch's position will become vulnerable.

Rivalry from foreign producers has never been as strong a force in the beer industry as in markets such as consumer electronic products and automobiles. However, the amount of beer imported into the United States has been increasing and provides an important source of rivalry to the high-priced brands. From 1995 to 1998, imports increased 5 million barrels while domestic shipments declined 1 million barrels. The growth in beer consumption in recent years has been significantly import-driven.

Increases in concentration in brewing are neither the result nor the cause of market power. The reasons, rather, are benign: the exploitation of scale economies and the demise of suboptimal capacity; new or superior products; changes in packaging and marketing methods; poor management on the part of some firms; and product differentiation, which, if not unambiguously benign, is outside the pale of traditional antitrust concern.

V. CONCLUSION

The statistics of the structure of the beer industry, the pricing and marketing conduct of its members, and the profits it has received do not mark it as a monopolized industry. Consumers are pursued by price and non-price competition. The changing fortunes of even major brewers indicate that this is no stodgy oligopoly, with firms adopting a live-and-let-live posture toward each other. The extent of exits from brewing in the last three decades indicates this is hardly an industry in which the inefficient producer is protected from the chilling winds of competition.

Suggested Readings

Books, Pamphlets, Monographs, Web Sites

Baron, Stanley Wade. *Brewed in America,* (Boston: Little, Brown and Company, 1962).

Beer Institute, The. *Brewers Almanac.* (Washington, D.C.: The Beer Institute, annual).

Beer Marketer's Insights—Beer Industry Update, (West Nyack, NY: annual).

Beer Marketer's Insights, (West Nyack, NY: published 23 times per year).

Connor, John M.; Richard T. Rogers; Bruce W. Marion; and Willard F. Mueller. *The Food Manufacturing Industries,* (Lexington, MA: Lexington Books, 1985).

---

[10]For example, in 1998, the company's expenditures were about $2.00 per barrel less than Miller's and Coors'.

Freidrich, Manfred, and Donald Bull. *The Register of United States Breweries 1876—1976,* 2 vols. (Stamford, CT: Holly Press, 1976).

North American Brewers Resource Directory, (Boulder, CO: Institute for Brewing Studies, annual).

Modern Brewery Age: Blue Book, (Stamford, CT: Modern Brewery Age Publishing Co., annual).

Modern Brewery Age. (Stamford, CT: weekly news edition and monthly magazine).

The New Brewer. (Boulder, CO: published bi-monthly).

Porter, John. *All About Beer,* (Garden City, NY: Doubleday, 1975).

Robertson, James D. *The Great American Beer Book,* (New York: Warner Books, 1978).

Scherer, F. M., Alan Beckenstein, Erich Kaufer, and R. Dennis Murphy. *The Economics of Multi-Plant Operations,* (Cambridge: Harvard University Press, 1975).

Sutton, John. *Sunk Costs and Market Structure,* (Cambridge: MIT Press, 1991).

Van Munching, Philip. *Beer Blast,* (New York: Random House, 1997).

Vereinsbank, *The Emerging Markets Brewery Fund Factbook,* 1997.

www.beertown.org

Articles

Ackoff, Russell L., and James R. Emshoff. "Advertising Research at Anheuser-Busch, Inc. (1963–1968)." *Sloan Management Review* 16 (Winter 1975).

———. "Advertising Research at Anheuser-Busch, Inc. (1968–74)." *Sloan Management Review* 16 (Spring 1975).

Clements, Kenneth W., and Lester W. Johnson. "The Demand for Beer, Wine and Spirits: A Systemwide Analysis." *Journal of Business* 56 (1983).

Chaloupka, F. J.; M. Grossman; and H. Saffer. "Alcohol Control Policies and Motor Vehicle Fatalities." *Journal of Legal Studies* 22 (1993).

Cockerill, Anthony. "Economies of Scale: Industrial Structure and Efficient Brewing Industry in Nine Nations," in A. T. Jacquemin and H. W. Dejong (eds.), *Welfare Aspects of Industrial Markets,* (Leiden: Martinus Nijhoff, 1977).

Culbertson, W. Patton, and David Bradford. "The price of beer: Some evidence from interstate comparisons." *International Journal of Industrial Organization* 9 (June 1991).

Elzinga, Kenneth G. "The Restructuring of the U.S. Brewing Industry." *Industrial Organization Review* 1 (1973).

Greer, Douglas F. "Beer: Causes of Structural Change," in Larry L. Deutsch (ed.) *Industry Studies,* (Englewood Cliffs, NJ: Prentice-Hall, 1993).

Hogarty, Thomas F., and Kenneth G. Elzinga. "The Demand for Beer." *Review of Economics and Statistics* 54 (May 1972).

Horowitz, Ira, and Ann Horowitz. "Firms in a Declining Market: The Brewing Case." *Journal of Industrial Economics* 13 (March 1965).

———. "The Beer Industry." *Business Horizons* 10 (Spring 1967).

Kerkvliet, Joe R.; William Nebesky; Carol H. Tremblay; and Victor J. Tremblay, "Efficiency and Technological Change in the U.S. Brewing Industry." *Journal of Productivity Analysis* 10 (1998).

Lynk, William J. "Interpreting Rising Concentration: The Case Of Beer." *Journal of Business* 57 (1984).

———. "The Price and Output of Beer Revisited." *Journal of Business* 58 (1985).

McConnell, J. Douglas. "An Experimental Examination of the Price-Quality

Relationship." *Journal of Business* 41 (October 1968).

McGahan, A. M. "The Emergence of the National Brewing Oligopoly: Competition in the American Market, 1933–1958." *Business History Review* 65 (Summer 1991).

McNulty, Timothy J. "Image and Competition Keep Beer Industry Foaming." *Chicago Tribune,* 11 August 1986, p.C1.

Nelson, Jon P. "Broadcast Advertising and U.S. Demand for Alcoholic Beverages." *Southern Economic Journal* 65 (April 1999).

Ornstein, Stanley I. "Antitrust Policy and Market Forces as Determinants of Industry—Structure: Case Histories in Beer and Distilled Spirits." *Antitrust Bulletin* 26 (Summer 1981).

———, and Dominique M. Hanssens. "Alcohol Control Laws and the Consumption of Distilled Spirits and Beer." *Journal of Consumer Research* 12 (September 1985).

Peles, Yoram. "Economies of Scale in Advertising Beer and Cigarettes." *Journal of Business* 44 (January 1971).

Sass, Tim R., and David S. Saurman. "Mandated Exclusive Territories and Economic Efficiency: An Empirical Analysis of the Malt Beverage Industry." *Journal of Law & Economics* 36 (April 1993).

Swaminathan, Anand, and Glenn R. Carroll, "Beer Brewers," in G. R. Carroll and M. T. Hannan, *Organizations in Industry,* (Oxford: Oxford University Press, 1995).

Tremblay, Victor J. "A Reappraisal of Interpreting Rising Concentration: The Case of Beer." *Journal of Business* 58 (1985).

———, and Carol Horton Tremblay, "The Determinants of Horizontal Acquisitions: Evidence from the U.S. Brewing Industry." *Journal of Industrial Economics* 37 (September 1988).

———, "Advertising, Price, and Welfare: Evidence From the U.S. Brewing Industry." *Southern Economic Journal* 62 (October, 1995).

Weinberg, Robert S. "Watching the Market," *Modern Brewery Age,* March 22, 1999, pp. 24–31.

Government Publications

Connor, John M. The U.S. Food and Tobacco Manufacturing Industries, U.S. Department of Agriculture Report No. 451 (March 1980).

Mueller, Willard F. Testimony in Hearings, Mergers and Industrial Concentration, U.S. Senate, Committee on the Judiciary, Subcommittee on Antitrust & Monopoly, 95th Cong., 2nd sess., May 12, 1978.

Staff Report of the Federal Trade Commission Bureau of Economics. *The Brewing Industry.* (December 1978).

CHAPTER 5

Automobiles

—James W. Brock

Three decades ago, a new Buick LeSabre had a sticker price of $3,844. It featured a V-8 engine turning out 220 horsepower; weighed 4,200 pounds; got 12.5 miles to a gallon of gas; and accelerated from 0 to 60 in 14.5 seconds. Thirty years later, a new LeSabre was priced at $23,888. It featured a smaller V-6 engine generating fewer horsepower and was nearly a half ton lighter than its predecessor. But the car's fuel efficiency had nearly doubled (20 miles per gallon), as had its acceleration (0 to 60 in 9 seconds), and it was far safer and environmentally cleaner.

Thirty years ago, General Motors was responsible for 60 percent of all passenger cars produced in the United States. GM officials praised the firm's immense size for providing "economies of scale in individual plant operations, the economies achieved through the carefully designed commonality of certain parts and tooling, the logistic and other benefits resulting from a multi-plant operation, and, most importantly, the management system that exercises overall coordination."[1] Today, however, GM's share of U.S. car production stands at less than a third, and the firm's sub-par performance is considered a classic illustration of the diseconomies of excessive organizational size.

Three decades ago, passenger cars represented 80 percent of new vehicle sales in the United States. Today, however, an explosion of "light" trucks, minivans, and "sport utility vehicles" accounts for nearly half of all new vehicles sold in America.

An examination of the structure, conduct, and performance of this key American industry is essential in analyzing these developments and the contentious public-policy issues swirling around them.

I. HISTORY

The automobile as we know it today first took shape in the 1890s. The early automotive pioneers experimented with gasoline engines, steam engines, and electric motors as sources of propulsion. By 1900, they had sold

[1]Senate Subcommittee on Antitrust and Monopoly, *Hearings: The Industrial Reorganization Act, Part 4, Ground Transportation Industries.* 93d Cong., 2d sess., 1974, 2515.

approximately 4,000 cars. Production expanded rapidly thereafter, reaching 187,000 automobiles by 1910. Entry into the industry was relatively easy, because the manufacturer of automobiles was primarily an assembler of parts produced by others. The new entrepreneur needed only to design a vehicle; contract with machine shops and independent producers for the engines, wheels, bodies, and other components; and announce to the public the car's availability.

The next decade marked the emergence of the Ford Motor Company as the dominant firm. Believing the demand for new cars to be price elastic, Henry Ford's goal was to provide an inexpensive car capable of reaching a large potential market. Standardization, specialization, and mass production, he felt, were the keys to lowering manufacturing costs, and constant price reduction the way to tap successively larger layers of demand. "Every time I reduce the charge for our car by one dollar, I get a thousand new buyers," Ford said. His strategy seemed simple enough: Take lower profits on each vehicle and thereby achieve a larger volume. As Ford saw it, successive "price reductions meant new enlargements of the market, and acceleration of mass production's larger economies, and greater aggregate profits. The company's firm grasp of this principle . . . was its unique element of strength, just as failure to grasp it had been one of the weaknesses of rival car makers. As profits per car had gone down and down, net earnings had gone up and up."[2] By 1921, Ford's Model T, which had remained largely unchanged for 19 years, accounted for more than half the market.

The 1920s witnessed a shift of preeminence from Ford to General Motors, the latter a consolidation of formerly independent firms (Chevrolet, Oldsmobile, Oakland, Cadillac, Buick, Fisher Body, Delco). GM adopted a two-pronged strategy: First, contrary to Ford's emphasis on a single model, GM offered a broad array of products to blanket all market segments. Its motto was "a car for every purse and purpose." Second, again contrary to Ford's strategy, GM elected to modify its cars each year with a combination of engineering advances, convenience improvements, and cosmetic styling changes. GM felt that annual model changes, despite the expense, would stimulate replacement demand and increase sales, and indeed, this strategy catapulted the company into unchallenged industry leadership for a half century. In this era, the groundwork was also laid for the high concentration that became the industry's hallmark for the next 40 years.

Beginning in the mid-1950s, however, successive waves of imports increasingly challenged the domestic oligopoly. By the 1970s, imports had captured more than a quarter of the U.S. market and triggered repeated

---

[2]Ford Allen Nevins, *Ford: The Times, the Man, the Company* (New York: Scribner, 1954), 493.

efforts by the Big Three—in collaboration with the United Auto Workers union—to obtain government protection from foreign competition. In the 1980s, in partial response to the domestic industry's lobbying campaigns, foreign firms (primarily Japanese) began to build production plants in the United States; by 1998, the combined output of these "transplants" reached two million units—a volume equal to GM's total U.S. car production, and greater than the number of passenger cars built in the United States by Ford and Chrysler combined.

II. INDUSTRY STRUCTURE

The most important structural features of the U.S. automobile industry are buyer demand and the nature of the product; the number of rival manufacturers and their relative size (concentration); economies of scale; and barriers to new competition.

Demand and the Nature of the Product

The demand for automobiles is influenced by a variety of factors. First, the demand for new cars is predominantly a replacement demand, and because the purchase of a new car can be postponed, market demand is quite volatile. Second, because the purchase of an automobile constitutes a major investment for the typical household (at an average price of nearly $20,000, currently), the demand for new cars is also highly sensitive to macroeconomic conditions, including unemployment, income and interest rates. Third, a key determinant of demand, of course, is price. Although the demand for new cars generally is slightly price elastic, the demand for particular makes and models is much more price sensitive due to the availability of close substitutes. Also noteworthy in recent years is the revolution in the composition of new "car" demand in favor of light trucks, minivans, and sport utility vehicles (Table 5-1). This fragmentation of demand represents a significant development: Whereas passenger cars accounted for 85 percent of all new consumer vehicles registered in the

TABLE 5-1 Composition of U.S. Demand: 1998 Sales (million vehicles)

New Cars:		8.2
New Light Trucks:		
Minivans and Full-Size Vans	1.6	
Compact and Full-Size Pickups	3.1	
Sport Utility Vehicles	2.8	
Total Light Trucks		7.5

Source: Automotive News, 1999 Market Data Book, pp. 50–51.

U.S. market in 1955, their share has since declined to roughly 50 percent (Figure 5-1).

Industry Concentration

The domestic auto market has long been dominated by a tight triopoly of immense firms. The advent of foreign "transplants" in the 1980s has eroded domestic concentration in production, while the longer-run growth of imports over the past two decades has lessened the Big Three's dominance of U.S. sales. Nonetheless, the Big Three firms remain dominant, while the impact of these procompetitive developments has been attenuated by the Big Three's political success in obtaining government restraints on foreign imports; by a proliferation of joint ventures and "alliances" linking the American oligopoly with its major foreign rivals; and, most recently, by mergers between foreign producers and the Big Three.

Concentration. General Motors remains the largest firm in the industry. Indeed, with assets of $229 billion, annual sales approaching $180 billion, and some 600,000 employees, GM remains the largest industrial concern in the United States and in the world. As Table 5-2 shows, GM's sales are half again greater than either of the two largest Japanese auto producers (Toyota and Nissan). Ford—the second-largest firm in the industry, the nation, and the world—typically has accounted for a quarter

FIGURE 5-1 Market Share by Vehicle Type

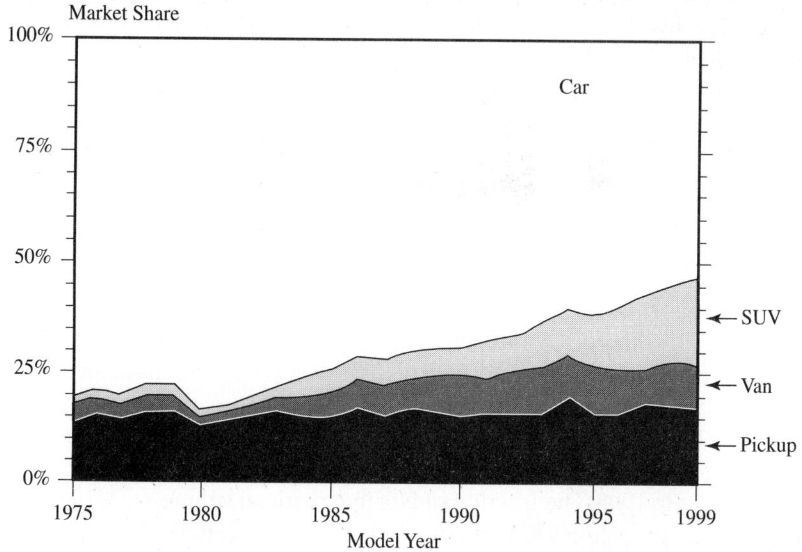

Source: U.S. Environmental Protection Agency, *Light-Duty Automotive Technology and Fuel Economy Trends Through 1999* (September 1999), iii.

TABLE 5-2 World's Top Ten Auto Producers 1998

Rank	*Company*	*Vehicles Produced (millions)*	*Sales Revenues (billions)*
1	General Motors	7.6	$161.3
2	Ford	7.3	144.4
3	Toyota	5.3	99.7
4	Renault/Nissan	4.9	92.9
5	Volkswagen	4.8	76.3
6	DaimlerChrysler	4.4	154.6
7	Fiat	2.7	51.0
8	Honda	2.3	48.7
9	Peugeot	2.3	37.5
10	Suzuki	1.7	11.4

Source: Automotive News, 1999 Market Data Book, 9; *Fortune,* "Global 500".

of the domestic field, while Chrysler traditionally has represented 8 to 10 percent of the market.

The Big Three are globally integrated as well: General Motors is the second-largest automotive firm in Australia, Brazil, and Western Europe generally (including GM's Opel division, the largest German auto company); second-largest in the United Kingdom; third-largest in Spain; and fourth-largest in Italy. Ford is the largest auto concern in the United Kingdom and Australia; second-largest in Argentina, third-largest in Germany and Italy; and the fifth-largest automobile concern in Western Europe generally. Global concentration has accelerated significantly in recent years as a result of cross-national mergers and acquisitions, including General Motors' acquisition of SAAB; Ford's purchase of Jaguar, Rover, and Volvo; Volkswagen's acquisition of Rolls Royce; and Chrysler's merger with Daimler-Benz.

Concentration in U.S. automobile production is depicted in Table 5-3, where the rise and erosion of GM's historical dominance is evident. The deconcentrating effect of foreign-built "transplants" is also clear: Whereas the Big Three's combined share of U.S. production reached a high of 98 percent in the 1966 to 1975 period, their collective share has since fallen to two-thirds. At the same time, the share of U.S. car production accounted for by the transplants (Table 5-4) has risen from less than 1 percent in 1983, to more than one-third, representing a combined output of two million vehicles in 1998. The fraction of North American vehicle sales built in North America includes 82 percent for Honda, 74 percent for Toyota, and 58 percent for Nissan. In fact, Honda recently surpassed Chrysler as America's third-largest *domestic* producer of cars! It is important to note, however,

TABLE 5-3 Concentration of U.S. Domestic Car Production 1913–1998

Year	*General Motors*	*Ford*	*Chrysler*	*Other U.S. Producers*	*Share of Big Three*
1913	12%	40%	*	48%	na
1923	20	46	2%	32	68%
1933	41	21	25	13	87
1946–1955	45	24	19	12	88
1956–1965	51	29	14	6	94
1966–1975	54	27	17	2	98
1976–1985	59	24	13	4	96
1992	42	24	9	25	75
1998	35	22	8	35	65

*Chrysler not yet in existence.
Source: Lawrence J. White, *The Automobile Industry Since 1945,* (Cambridge: Harvard University Press, 1971); *Ward's Automotive Yearbook,* (various years).

that because a number of these transplants are joint ventures involving Big Three firms (i.e., Ford-Mazda, GM-Toyota), or comprise firms which have since merged with one of the Big Three (Daimler-Chrysler), they may not represent genuinely independent competitors.

Concentration within various vehicle segments is shown in Table 5-5, where it can be seen that the Big Three are more dominant in minivans and pickups than in the midrange market for cars, while "others"—imports and the products of U.S. transplants—are relatively more prominent in the various car segments. Despite these variations, the Big Three continue to collectively account for 65 to 70 percent of all new automobiles produced and purchased in the United States.

Foreign Competition. The import share of U.S. auto sales rose from 0.4 percent in the immediate post-World War II decade to 21 percent in the 1976–1983 period. Foreign producers, led by the Japanese, provided a critical, if not the only, source of effective competition for the U.S. oligopoly in the post-World War II era. Initially, foreign firms focused their efforts on the inexpensive small-car segment of the market. Then, beginning in 1981, after the Big Three succeeded in obtaining numerical government restrictions on Japanese imports, Japanese firms moved into the midsize regions of the market—ironically, the mainstay of the domestic oligopoly. Japanese and European producers also began to achieve larger shares of the high-priced luxury end of the market (Lexus, Infiniti, Mercedes-Benz, BMW). In order to circumvent trade restraints, foreign producers—led by the Japanese—also began to construct production facilities in the United States, in which they utilized American labor and

TABLE 5-4 U.S. Transplant Facilities

	Ownership	*Location*	*Vehicles Produced*	*Capacity*
Auto Alliance (1987)	Ford 50% Mazda 50%	Flat Rock, MI	Mazda 626 Cougar	240,000
BMW (1994)	BMW 100%	Spartanburg, SC	Z3	70,000
Honda (1982)	Honda 100%	Marysville, OH East Liberty, OH	Accord Civic Acura	388,000
Mitsubishi (1988)	Mitsubishi	Normal, IL	Eclipse Gallant Chrysler Sebring Dodge Avenger Eagle Talon	240,000
Mercedes-Benz (1997)	Daimler-Benz	Vance, AL	ML320	80,000
New United Motor Mfg (NUMMI) (1984)	GM 50% Toyota 50%	Fremont, CA	Toyota Corolla Toyota Tacoma Chev. Prism	225,000
Nissan (1983)	Nissan 100%	Smyrna, TN	Altima Sentra 200SX Frontier	300,000
Subaru-Isuzu (1989)	Fuji 50% Subaru 50%	Lafayette, IN	Subaru Legacy Isuzu Rodeo Honda Passport	180,000
Toyota (1998)	Toyota 100%	Princeton, IN	T-150	100,000
Toyota (1988)	Toyota 100%	Georgetown, KY	Avalon Camry Sienna	420,000

Source: 1998 Ward's Automotive Yearbook, 107.

TABLE 5-5 Sales Concentration Within Segments 1998

Segment	*General Motors*	*Ford*	*Chrysler*	*Others*	*Share of Big Three*
Cars:					
Small & Budget	37%	17%	11%	35%	65%
Mid-Range	29	19	8	44	56
Specialty & Sporty	19	27	20	34	66
Luxury & Near Luxury	26	14	5	55	45
Light Trucks:					
Minivans	23	20	45	12	88
Pickup	33	38	19	10	90
Sport Utility	26	27	16	31	69
Combined	29	25	16	30	70

Source: Automotive News, 1999 Market Data Book, 50–51.

management to replicate (and even exceed)[3] their initial successes. By 1992, imports comprised 24 percent of U.S. new-car sales. (Although Japanese makers accounted for three-quarters of these, the Big Three at times have been major importers themselves, "re-badging" some 360,000 small cars built by foreign producers in Japan and South Korea, including Ford's Aspire, Chevy's Spectrum, and Dodge's Stealth.) In recent years the import share of U.S. new-car sales has subsided to 17 percent. But the share of new car sales represented by transplants has grown to two million units, or 24 percent, with imports and transplants together achieving a combined 43 percent share of the new-car market.

Needless to say, however, import quotas and the perennial threat of protectionism jeopardize the salutary effect that foreign competition has had in eroding concentration in the American market. As recently as the early 1990s, for example, the domestic oligopoly was lobbying Congress to impose an annual cap of 3.8 million units on Japanese auto sales in the United States—including cars produced in their American transplant facilities! Transnational mergers between the Big Three and major foreign auto producers, of course, can also undermine foreign competition in the American market.

Joint Ventures and Alliances. Also problematic in aggravating concentration is the vast web of "joint ventures" and "alliances" spun among the world's largest automotive producers in recent years: General Motors holds half ownership of the Japanese Isuzu firm; jointly operates New United Motors Manufacturing Incorporated, a California assembly plant, with Toyota; and with Japan's Suzuki, GM jointly owns and operates

[3]See Lindsay Chappell, "Made in America," *Automotive News,* 28 October 1991, 14.

CAMI, a Canadian assembly transplant. Ford has acquired substantial control of Japan's Mazda; is half-owner with Mazda of a transplant facility in Flat Rock, Michigan; holds ownership stakes (with Mazda) in South Korean auto producer Kia (which has supplied Ford with its "Festiva" and "Aspire" small-car models); and has joined with Mazda to produce pickup trucks in Thailand for export to North America. Chrysler originally joined with Mitsubishi to build the "Diamond-Star" transplant assembly operation in Illinois; Diamond-Star has since supplied Chrysler with a number of makes, including Dodge Avengers and Chrysler Sebrings. The Big Three additionally have entered into a number of cross-supply agreements with their foreign rivals for various automotive components (such as engines).

Further tightening these ties among the world's largest auto companies are a raft of rapidly expanding research consortiums in the United States and abroad: The United States Council for Automotive Research (USCAR) combines the Big Three in a dozen different research consortiums (covering materials, air quality, batteries, vehicle recycling, safety, low-emission paint, supercomputer applications, and electronics). USCAR also directs the "Partnership for a New Generation of Vehicles," encompassing a host of additional technology teams composed of Big Three representatives. At the same time, the European Council for Automotive Research and Development (EUCAR), has been established to link European producers in a host of similar research joint ventures.

Alliances and partnership pacts of this magnitude and reach are especially problematic: They conjoin the U.S. oligopoly to each another, as well as to their major foreign rivals. They expand interfirm communication, coordination and cooperation, and thus threaten to undermine independent decision making. They raise the question of whether beyond some point the participants come to view themselves primarily as partners rather than competitors. They thus may raise the effective degree of concentration significantly above the level indicated by market shares alone.

The Question of Economies of Scale

To what extent is high concentration in autos necessitated by economies of large-scale operation? The weight of the evidence suggests that, while substantial, economies of large size are not as extensive as might commonly be assumed, and that they are becoming less so in some important respects.

First, there are definite limits to scale economies in auto production. The Big Three assemble their vehicles at multiple plant locations rather than concentrating the bulk of their production in one or two gigantic plants (Table 5-6). The average capacity of these plants is typically in the range of 200,000 vehicles per year, suggesting this figure as a good estimate of what the firms consider the optimum-sized production facility to be.

TABLE 5-6 Big Three Auto Assembly Plants

	Number of Plants	***Average Annual Capacity (000)***
General Motors:		
U.S.	25	184
Canada	4	229
Mexico	2	152
Ford:		
U.S.	16	219
Canada	3	190
Mexico	3	126
Chrysler:		
U.S.	9	205
Canada	3	251
Mexico	3	129

Source: Automotive News, 1999 Market Data Book, 20.

Second, the Big Three are slashing their vertical scale by divesting their parts- and components-making divisions: General Motors, long the most vertically integrated of the domestic car makers by virtue of producing some 70 percent of its own components, consolidated its major parts-making operations to form the "Delphi" division, which it spun off in 1999 in a move that will reduce the firm's total workforce by fully one-third (200,000 employees). Ford and Chrysler seem to be taking similar steps with their "Visteon" and "Acustar" parts operations. In a related vein, auto companies are increasingly outsourcing the production of entire modules—parts preassembled into complete units, such as a rolling chassis which includes the frame, driveshaft, shocks, wheels and tires—to outside suppliers. They seem to be returning to the turn-of-the-century arrangement in which auto companies design and assemble components produced by others. According to *Fortune,* "Everything from designing cars to building factories will get cheaper as auto companies quit making their own parts and rely more on suppliers."[4]

Third, GM's persistent woes provide further evidence of the diseconomies of excessive scale. General Motors remains the largest automotive firm in the world, yet its vast size and complexity seem to be a daunting liability. Its productivity is perennially the lowest in the American industry: GM requires 43 labor hours on average to produce each vehicle, substantially above the figures for Ford (36) and Chrysler (39), and far worse than smaller transplant facilities operated in the United States by Toyota (31 labor hours), Honda (30), and Nissan (29). To reach the

[4]Alex Taylor, "The Auto Industry Meets the New Economy," *Fortune,* 5 September 1994, 52.

superior efficiency of its smaller rivals, analysts estimate General Motors would need to eliminate at least three assembly plants, slash its assembly plant employment by 20 to 36 percent, and cut another 15 percent from its legions of executives (which currently include 49 vice presidents).[5]

Barriers to Entry

Barriers to the entry of new competition, another important element of market structure, are substantial in the automobile industry.

First, the cost to construct production and assembly plants is daunting: Toyota has invested $4 billion in its Georgetown, Kentucky, transplant facility, while Honda has invested some $2 billion in its Marysville, Ohio, assembly operations.

Second, a new entrant must not only produce and assemble automobiles, it also must market them to consumers—another substantial obstacle to new competition. In 1998, the Big Three ranked as three of the nation's largest advertisers, with combined ad spending of $5 billion ($2.2 billion by GM, $1.4 billion by Chrysler, and $1.1 billion by Ford). On a per-vehicle basis, these amounts represent average advertising expenditures of $412, $501, and $226 for GM, Chrysler and Ford, respectively. The advertising "effort" required by smaller firms is substantially greater: Nissan ($741 in advertising per U.S. vehicle sold), Mazda ($830), Volkswagen ($953), and Isuzu ($1,347).

Finally, in addition to producing and advertising its cars, a new entrant would have to assemble a dealer system for distribution and service. This, too, is a daunting challenge: GM, Ford and Chrysler products are retailed through some 36,000 franchises comprising roughly 17,000 dealerships across the country.

It is not surprising, therefore, that over the post-World War II era, few new firms have commenced domestic production of automobiles, and those that have (the transplants) have been launched by large, established foreign firms.

III. INDUSTRY CONDUCT

Market behavior in the auto industry conforms to what industrial organization theory predicts: The decades of tacit collusion, uniformity of conduct, and noncompetitive parallelism that characterized the Big Three's

---

[5]Harbour and Associates, *The Harbour Report: 1998* (Troy, MI), pp. 171–72, and Stephen J. Girsky, *U.S. Investment Research,* June 26, 1998. For a longer-run perspective, see Harbour and Associates, *Competitive Assessment of the North American Automotive Industry, 1989–1992* (Troy, MI), 1992.

tight reign over the field have been transformed in recent years by the advent of a more competitive, less concentrated industry structure.

Pricing

As the largest seller, General Motors traditionally was the industry's price leader. GM typically initiated general rounds of annual price hikes in the late summer when the industry's new model line-ups were being readied. Ford and Chrysler awaited GM's price disclosures, which they then matched so that the Big Three's prices differed by only a few dollars across their entire range of models. This price interdependence among the firms was captured by the *Wall Street Journal:* "Auto makers can maximize profits because in the oligopolistic domestic auto industry the three major producers tend to copy each other's price moves. One auto executive notes that if one cmpany lowered prices, the others would follow immediately. . . . As a result, price cuts wouldn't increase anybody's market share, and 'everybody would be worse off,' he says."[6]

The advent of foreign competition, however, and the erosion of domestic concentration, has disrupted this noncompetitive pricing behavior. Now, prices are continuously altered through the year. Prices also are more flexible and variable—down as well as up—due to competition that compels the companies to constantly adjust their incentives, lease terms, and interest rates on car loans. Rebates, which are tantamount to price cuts, have reached as high as $1,800 per vehicle in recent years. So dramatic is this change in the industry's pricing behavior that some analysts have dubbed it a new "golden age" of competition in autos.[7]

The critical role of foreign competition in engendering this revolution in pricing conduct is underscored when dollar-yen exchange rates change significantly: When the dollar strengthens against the yen, Japanese firms hold the line on their U.S. prices and compel the Big Three to hold down their prices, too. When the dollar weakens against the yen, however, and Japanese firms raise their prices in the United States, the Big Three are quick to raise their prices, too.

Product Rivalry

A similar revolution has transformed product rivalry in the industry. Decades of tight-knit oligopoly fostered a striking pattern of mutually interdependent behavior which, in turn, generated a bland homogeneity

---

[6] *Wall Street Journal,* 3 August 1983, p. 1.

[7] Gregory L. White, Fara Warner, and Joseph B. White, "Competition Rises, Car Prices Drop: A New Golden Age?" *Wall Street Journal,* 8 January 1999, 1. See also Kathleen Kirwin, "Detroit Finally Gets It," *Business Week,* 25 August 1997, 38; and Ralph Kisiel, "Old Pricing Habits Are Taking A Hike," *Automotive News,* 17 August 1998, 1.

in the product offerings of the Big Three. Primary emphasis was on the superficial (two headlights versus four, recessed door handles versus non-recessed, "fine Corinthian leathers"). Beginning in the mid-1980s, however, and especially by the late 1990s, the impact of serious competition began to unleash a flood of radically new vehicles and designs. An industry habituated to a time scale more familiar to geologists began to operate at a pace more like that of the fashion clothing business. Two specific episodes convey the significance of these developments.

Oligopolistic Restraint: The Case of Small Cars.[8] At the conclusion of World War II, the small, lightweight, inexpensive automobile was seen as a prime means for expanding the postwar market in a manner analogous to Henry Ford's Model T decades earlier. In May 1945, General Motors and Ford disclosed that they were considering the production of small cars; Chrysler announced a similar plan the following year. But the Big Three did not seriously undertake to commercialize such a car until the 1970s, at least in the American market. (A small, lightweight car developed by GM was marketed in Australia in 1948 by a GM subsidiary; Ford's light car appeared the same year in France.) Attempts were made to meet successive import surges in the 1950s and 1960s, but these efforts seemed halfhearted. The consequences of the industry's dilatory response, of course, hit with a vengeance in the 1970s, when oil embargoes and skyrocketing gasoline prices ushered in a flood of Japanese imports which nearly bankrupted the domestic producers.

Lawrence White explains this lethargy in terms of oligopolistic firm behavior: General Motors, Ford, and Chrysler each seemed to recognize that vigorous entry into small cars by any one of them would trigger entry into the field by the others. Believing that the segment was not large enough to profitably support all three firms, and, further, believing that the availability of small cars would undermine high prices and high profits on their large cars, the Big Three refrained from offering the small car as an inexpensive option. Foreign competitors, of course, were not immobilized by such considerations because they had no entrenched oligopoly position to protect. The oil crises of the 1970s provided them a huge entree into the American market. They broke through the logjam of tacit restraint and forced the domestic oligopoly to confront the challenge of building smaller, higher quality, and more fuel-efficient automobiles.

Oligopolistic Restraint Dented: The Chrysler "Minivan".[9] Chrysler's "minivan," introduced in 1983, quickly became one of the most success-

---

[8]This account is adapted from Lawrence J. White, "The American Automobile Industry and the Small Car, 1945–1970," *Journal of Industrial Economics* 20 (1972): 179; and Paul Blumberg, "Snarling Cars," *New Republic,* 24 January 1983, 12–14.

[9]This account is drawn from Alex Taylor, "Iacocca's Minivan," *Fortune,* 30 May 1994, 56–66.

ful automotive products ever built. By the mid-1990s, minivans accounted for more than a quarter of Chrysler's total sales and perhaps as much as two-thirds of its profits.

But pioneering development work on the concept had been done years before at General Motors and Ford. By the late 1970s, in fact, GM designers had built a prototype of what has been described as a "dead ringer" for Chrysler's minivan. Ford designers, too, had developed the concept of a small, radically different front-wheel-drive van. But Ford's top management dismissed the concept, while GM refrained from developing the minivan partly out of fear of cannibalizing its lucrative 40-percent share of station wagon sales.

A renegade band of ex-Ford executives familiar with the minivan concept (led by Lee Iacocca) transferred to Chrysler, however, where they immediately faced disaster: Chrysler had narrowly escaped bankruptcy by virtue of a government bailout in 1979–1980, and it desperately needed a success. The minivan project was quickly seized on because, according to one Chrysler designer, "We didn't have much to lose." Their desperate gamble paid off. Chrysler survived and prospered largely due to the minivan's success and the risk taken in introducing it. Instead of viewing the market as fixed and comprising a few traditional product categories, Chrysler had created an entirely new category of vehicle. Still, it took an extraordinary sense of crisis to overcome the inertia and risk aversion bred by decades of oligopolistic interdependence.

Product Competition Unleashed. The minivan marked a watershed in the onset of genuine product competition in the industry. No longer would the field be rigidly divided between conventional categories of "cars" and "trucks." By the 1990s, structural competition had ignited an explosion of vehicle types and segments: "budget" cars and "midrange" cars; "specialty" and "sporty" cars; "near luxury" and "luxury" cars; "compact" pickups and "full-size" pickups; "compact" sport utility, "small" sport utility, and "full-sized" sport utility; even "crucks" (car-based trucks)—a staggering exfoliation of Amigos, Denalis, RAV4s, and PT Cruisers! Consumers could choose from 260 different makes of cars, trucks, and sport utility models across sixteen vehicle categories, many of which were unimaginable only a few years earlier. More fundamentally, the advent of product competition is transforming autos into a far more fashion-oriented field, in which the premium is on creativity, flexibility, smaller production runs, sensitivity to buyers' shifting preferences, and entrepreneurial risk-taking. In this more competitive milieu, of course, bureaucracy is an even greater disadvantage, which may be an important reason why the companies are concentrating more on design and assembly, vertically dis-integrating themselves, and outsourcing the production of more components, parts, and modules to others.

IV. INDUSTRY PERFORMANCE

For decades, industry defenders insisted that the automobile field's highly concentrated structure was necessitated by the economies of large-scale production, the expenses of modern innovation, and the dictates of effective planning. Testifying before a congressional committee in 1974, GM spokesmen asserted that the firm's "size has been determined by the product itself, the requirements of efficient manufacture, distribution and service, as well as market demand. . . ."[10] In the light of the Big Three's unenviable performance over the ensuing three decades, few today would have the temerity to make such extravagant claims. In fact, the advent of effective competition dramatically revealed how badly the industry's performance had deteriorated during decades of oligopoly dominance.

Production Efficiency

One measure of the degree to which production inefficiency afflicted the Big Three is evident in Table 5-7, depicting long-run labor productivity trends for U.S. and Japanese auto producers. These statistics clearly show that giant firm size is no guarantor of efficiency. They also reveal the degree to which the domestic oligopoly fell behind state-of-the-art manufacturing practices developed by others, especially the Japanese.

Confronted with withering foreign competition, the Big Three struggled through the 1980s to raise their productivity and cut their bloated cost structures. They were forced by competition to redesign their production operations, close antiquated plants, reorganize their management structures, modernize their facilities and purchasing practices, and carve billions of dollars from their costs. And they have recorded dramatic gains as a result: Over the 1979–1998 period, assembly productivity surged 38 percent at GM and Ford, and 45 percent at Chrysler. Overall, the Big Three have narrowed their productivity gap with Japanese car producers by approximately one-half over the past twenty years. Despite these gains, however, General Motors remains the least efficient firm in the industry: While some Ford and Chrysler plants now meet (or exceed) the labor productivity of their Japanese counterparts, GM remains some 50 percent less productive in its use of labor compared to Honda, Nissan and Toyota.[11]

---

[10]Senate Subcommittee on Antitrust and Monopoly, *Hearings: The Industrial Reorganization Act, Part 4, Ground Transportation Industries,* 93d Cong., 2d sess., 1974, 2468.

[11]Productivity statistics calculated from information contained in Harbour and Associates, *The Harbour Report: Competitive Assessment of the North American Automotive Industry, 1989–1992* (Troy, MI, 1992), p. 44; and idem, *The Harbour Report: 1999 North America* (Troy, MI, 1999), pp. 67, 176.

TABLE 5-7 Vehicles Produced Per Worker

	1960	*1983*
General Motors (*)	8	11
Ford (**)	14	15
Chrysler (*)	11	16
Nissan	12	42
Toyota	15	58

*Worldwide
**United States
Source: Michael A. Cusumano, *The Japanese Automobile Industry,* (Cambridge: Harvard University Press, 1985), 187–88.

Dynamic Efficiency

Dynamic efficiency encompasses product innovation, an area in which the domestic industry's performance is marked by four key features:

First, the rate, breadth, and depth of product innovation were great in the era before World War II, when the field was populated by numerous independents. Innovation competition was intense, and new people with new ideas could put their concepts (bad and good alike) into commercial practice.

Second, with the demise of a vibrant independent sector and with the consolidation of the industry into a tight oligopoly, the pace of technological innovation slackened. Innovations like front-wheel drive, disc brakes, fuel injection, fuel-efficient subcompacts, and utilitarian minivans languished in the hands of the Big Three. "Since competition within the industry was mild," David Halberstam summarizes, "there was no impulse to innovate; to the finance people, innovation not only was expensive but seemed unnecessary. . . . Why bother, after all? In America's rush to become a middle-class society, there was an almost insatiable demand for cars. It was impossible not to make money, and there was a conviction that no matter what the sales were this year, they would be even greater the next. So there was little stress on improving the cars. From 1949, when the automatic transmission was introduced, to the late seventies, the cars remained remarkably the same. What innovation there was came almost reluctantly."[12]

Third, while the domestic oligopoly slumbered, foreign producers took the lead in advancing the frontiers of automotive technology. According to veteran industry analyst Brock Yates, foreign firms moved ahead "with fuel injection, disc brakes, rack and pinion steering, radial tires, quartz headlights, ergonomically adjustable bucket seats, five-speed

[12]David Halberstam, *The Reckoning* (New York: Morrow, 1986), 244–45.

manual transmissions, high-efficiency overhead camshaft engines, independently sprung suspensions, advanced shock absorbers, and strict crash-worthiness standards."[13]

Fourth, the injection of competition from abroad has compelled the Big Three to become far more innovative in virtually every aspect of the product—from engines (multi-valves, fuel injection, lightweight ceramic components) and brakes (computer-controlled anti-lock braking), to transmissions (five-speed, six-speed, and recent experimentation with continuously-variable speed), and body styles (sport utility and "retro" vehicles). At the same time, the Big Three have vastly improved the quality of their cars. Chrysler Chairman Lee Iacocca pungently summarized the industry's record in a 1991 advertising campaign, when he said: "All of us—Ford, GM, Chrysler—built a lot of lousy cars in the early 1980s. And we paid the price. We lost a lot of our market to the import competition. But that forced us to wake up and start building better cars."

Nonetheless, years of lethargy have created a chasm that the Big Three must constantly struggle to overcome—a challenge which, once again, elephantine size seems to exacerbate. In the mid-1990s, the average time required to develop a new vehicle from concept to factory production was 29 months for Chrysler, 37 months for Ford, and 46 months for General Motors—rankings inversely correlated with firm size, and all significantly slower than Mazda (21 months) and Mitsubishi (24 months). By the late 1990s, GM had shortened its development-to-production time to 31 months, but Mazda and Nissan had cut their time to 18 to 19 months.[14]

Social Efficiency

Social efficiency addresses how well the industry has served the broader public interest in automotive smog, safety, and fuel consumption. In these areas, the industry's performance has been marked by indifference and denial, followed by resistance and pleas of "technological impossibility."

On the smog front, for example, the industry initially denied the problem: "[W]aste vapors are dissipated in the atmosphere quickly and do not present an air-pollution problem," Ford Motor Company told county supervisors in smog-choked Los Angeles. "The fine automotive powerplants which modern-day engineers design do not 'smoke.'"[15] Later, as

---

[13]Brock Yates, *The Decline and Fall of the American Automobile Industry* (New York: Vintage Books, 1984) 149.

[14]Generally, see Valerie Reitman and Robert L. Simison, "Japanese Car Makers Speed Up Car Making," *Wall Street Journal,* 29 December 1995, B1; Alex Taylor, "GM: Time to Get in Gear," *Fortune,* 28 April 1997, 102; and James B. Treece, "Mazda Claims 18-Month Development Time," *Automotive News,* 17 March 1997, 3.

[15]Senate Subcommittee on Air and Water Pollution, *Hearings: Air Pollution-1967, Part 1,* 90th Cong., 1st sess., 1967, 158. Despite these claims, some of the Big Three were sufficiently concerned about the air pollution problem to begin researching it as early as the

automotive air pollution worsened and as national concern about the problem grew, the Big Three (in the guise of a research "joint venture") conspired to eliminate competition among themselves in developing and commercializing pollution control technology.[16] When the government promulgated auto-emission regulations in the 1970s, the oligopoly insisted that the regulations were impossible to meet, even though some foreign producers introduced innovative engines combining high performance with low exhaust emissions, but without the need for costly catalytic converters (i.e., Honda's Compound Vortex Combustion Chamber, or CVCC, engine). In the 1990s, as California and Northeastern states were implementing tighter, "ultra-low" emission regulations, the Big Three once again decried the standards as unattainable—even though foreign producers (led by Honda) were introducing engine designs capable of meeting the tougher standards while offering more power and acceleration.

On the safety front, patents awarded to the firms in the 1920s and 1930s for such features as padded dashboards and collapsible steering wheels were shelved until their incorporation was mandated by government decree. The industry insisted that safety should be optional, supplied only in response to consumer demand. Yet it refused to make available the safety information and options essential to informed and free consumer decision making. The industry spent millions extolling raw horsepower while hiding behind its slogan "Safety don't sell." Eventually, a decades-long safety battle between government and the industry produced results. The Big Three finally conceded the importance of safety belts, and, in the 1990s—after resisting air bags for two decades and actively discouraging consumers from purchasing them[17]—the oligopoly discovered that "Safety really does sell." It raced to equip its new cars with air bags on the driver side, the passenger side, even in the seats and side door panels. At the close of the decade, however, new safety risks were surfacing as a result of the growth of sport utility sales, which researchers were finding to be significantly more dangerous due to their greater height and stiffer frames—findings which the Big Three have reacted to with an attitude of ignorance and resistance.[18]

In the case of fuel consumption, when asked in 1958 what steps his division was taking in fuel economy, the general manager of GM's Buick

---

1930s. See "Smog Control Antitrust Case," *Congressional Record* (House ed.), 18 May 1971, 15626–27.

[16]"Smog Control Antitrust Case," p. 15627.

[17]See Albert R. Karr and Laurie McGinley, "Auto Shoppers Encounter Stiff Resistance When Seeking Air Bags at Ford Dealers," *Wall Street Journal,* 31 July 1986, p. 23.

[18]See Keith Bradsher, "Further Problems of Safety Found for Light Trucks," *New York Times,* 12 December 1997, p. 1; and Anna Wilde Mathews, "Rollover Rankings Could Shake Auto Makers," *Wall Street Journal,* 24 May 1999, p. B1.

division quipped, "We're helping the gas companies, the same as our competitors."[19] The industry seemed to believe that gasoline would remain forever plentiful at twenty cents a gallon; the fuel efficiency of U.S. automobiles steadily worsened from 1958 to 1973. Only months before the first OPEC oil embargo and gasoline crisis of 1973, when the Big Three's fleet averaged a paltry 13 miles per gallon, GM's chairman suggested faster licensing of nuclear electric power plants as a good way to deal with America's energy problem.[20] Just prior to the nation's second oil crisis in 1979, General Motors declared that auto "fuel-economy standards are not necessary and they are not good for America."[21] In the early 1990s, in the wake of the Persian Gulf War and America's emergency effort to once again secure its foreign oil supplies, the Big Three protested that further gains in fuel economy were infeasible and unnecessary—even as Honda unveiled lean-burning engines able to get 55 miles per gallon. The latter 1990s once again found the Big Three fighting fuel economy standards, this time as a result of their aggressive marketing of gas-guzzling sport utility vehicles, which caused the average fuel economy of their fleets to fall to the lowest level in twenty years.[22] They successfully lobbied Congress to freeze automotive mileage requirements each year between 1995 and 1999. Meanwhile, in 1999, Toyota and Honda were commercially introducing "hybrid" cars (Prius, Insight). These cars have gasoline engines combined with self-charging electric motors to eliminate the need for battery re-charging; achieve 60 miles per gallon or more; generate ultra-low emissions; and are priced at $20,000 or less.

An important explanation for the industry's lackluster performance in these areas once again may stem from the oligopolistic interdependence and mutual restraint that governed the companies' behavior. As former GM president Alfred Sloan once secretly confided, "I feel that General Motors should not adopt safety glass for its cars. I can only see competition being forced into the same position. Our gain would be purely a temporary one and the net results would be that both competition and ourselves would have reduced the return on our capital and the public would have obtained still more value per dollar expended."[23]

---

[19]Quoted in John Keats, *The Insolent Chariots* (New York: Lippincott, 1958), 14.

[20]Senate Committee on Commerce, *Hearing: Automotive Research and Development and Fuel Economy,* 93d Cong., 1st sess., 1973, 564.

[21]Ed Cray, *Chrome Colossus* (New York: McGraw Hill, 1980), 524.

[22]U.S. Environmental Protection Agency, "Light-Duty Automotive Technology and Fuel Economy Trends Through 1999," September 1999.

[23]Quoted in Senate Select Committee on Small Business, *Hearings: Planning, Regulation, and Competition-Automobile Industry,* 90th Cong., 2d sess., 1968, 967.

V. PUBLIC POLICY

Public policy toward the automobile industry can be examined in three main areas: antitrust, protection from foreign competition, and government regulation of automotive smog, safety, and fuel economy.

Antitrust

Most of the antitrust suits in the industry have been tangential and peripheral in nature and have never squarely challenged the industry's concentrated structure. For example, in 1969, the government charged the Big Three with unlawfully conspiring to eliminate competition, but only in the smog-control field. In the early 1970s, the government charged GM and Ford with collusive pricing, but only in the fleet market for new cars sold to businesses and rental car agencies. In the 1990s, the antitrust agencies investigated anticompetitive practices in the industry, but only as they affected supplies of used cars, dealers' use of "no-haggle" pricing, and dealer efforts to impede Internet sales. At the same time, however, antitrust officials have allowed a proliferation of joint ventures to link the domestic oligopoly with its major foreign rivals. And in what might be considered "failing company" antitrust, the government engineered the Chrysler bailout in 1979–80, in part to prevent the American auto industry from becoming even more concentrated.

Protection from Foreign Competition

Mutual oligopolistic interdependence among the Big Three became solidified in the post-World War II era. This, together with the protection afforded by formidable entry barriers, insulated the domestic industry from effective competition. Noncompetitive conduct, including tacit vertical collusion between management and organized labor and steady price-wage-price escalation, flourished in this structural milieu.

Foreign competition eventually began to disturb this oligopolistic bonhomie, inducing the industry to seek government-imposed shelter from imports. Beginning in 1974, management and labor began to lobby for protection. Their efforts succeeded in 1981, when the avowedly free-trade Reagan administration forced "voluntary" quotas on the Japanese. These "temporary" quotas, ostensibly intended to give domestic firms "breathing space," were renewed in 1983 and formally expired in 1985, only to be replaced by a system of manufacturer-specific sales quotas for the U.S. market enforced by the Japanese government through the remainder of the decade.

Predictably, the quotas substantially drove up the price of Japanese imports which, in turn, enabled the domestic oligopoly to push through sizable price boosts of its own. Yet in an ironic twist, these numerical restrictions impelled Japanese firms to take steps to circumvent them, first, by upgrading their offerings and invading the larger midsize and luxury segments of the market, and, second, by building transplant production facilities in the United States. Later, in the early 1990s, the Big Three demanded that the government reimpose quotas on Japanese cars, and that the quotas be expanded to include limits on the number of Japanese cars produced in American transplants. The Big Three's political war against foreign competition continued in 1991, when they demanded that the government restrict imports of minivans—even though the domestic oligopoly accounted for 85 percent of U.S. minivan sales at the time, and even though Chrysler was the country's largest importer of minivans (produced in its Canadian plants). In the mid-1990s, in a variation of the protectionist game, the Big Three lobbied Treasury Secretary Rubin to manipulate the yen-dollar exchange rate in order to force up Japanese auto prices in the United States.

Regulation: Safety, Pollution, and Fuel Economy

Have government attempts to regulate automotive safety, pollution, and fuel consumption been too costly compared with the benefits obtained? Is it true, as the industry has long maintained, that excessive "regulation adds unnecessary costs for consumers, lowers profits, diverts manpower from research and development programs, and reduces productivity—all at a time when our resources are desperately needed to meet the stiff competition from abroad"?[24] Or is it the case, as Henry Ford II once conceded, that "we wouldn't have had the kinds of safety built into automobiles that we have had unless there had been a Federal law. We wouldn't have had the fuel economy unless there had been a Federal law, and there wouldn't have been the emission control unless there had been a Federal law"?[25]

Is it true, as the industry contends, that government auto regulations deny freedom of choice to consumers? Or do the Big Three opportunistically exploit "free consumer choice" only when it suits their purposes, but with no compunction about denying freedom of choice to consumers when it doesn't serve their private interest (by preventing consumers from obtaining imported cars, or safer, less polluting cars)? Is it true, as the industry claims, that government regulations prevent it from obeying consumer sovereignty by supplying the products that car buyers prefer?

---

[24]House Committee on Government Operations, *Hearings: The Administration's Proposals to Help the U.S. Auto Industry,* 97th Cong., 1st sess., 1981, 129.

[25]Senate Subcommittee for Consumers, *Hearings: Costs of Government Regulations to the Consumer,* 95th Cong., 2d sess., 1978, 87.

Or is it the case that if the industry acted more responsibly, it might minimize the need for direct government regulation?

Some economists have contended that less coercive forms of regulation—for example, "incentive-based" measures involving "fees" imposed on the sale of unsafe, polluting, gas-guzzling cars—would be more effective. But is it realistic to assume that government would impose fees if doing so would jeopardize the financial viability of a General Motors, a Ford, or a Chrysler? Would the government seriously consider shutting down GM, for example, if the firm simply refused to pay the "fees"? Conversely, given their size and political clout, would a threat by any of the Big Three to shut down almost inevitably force the government to grant delays, exceptions and exemptions?

VI. CONCLUSION

Perhaps the Big Three will continue to rise to the challenge of competition and close the performance gap with their foreign rivals. Perhaps they will continue cutting their organizational size in order to sharpen their focus, quicken their flexibility, and enhance their efficiency. Perhaps car buying via the Internet, and the formation of "mega-dealers" such as AutoNation and CarMax, will inject new competitive pressures into the industry. More broadly, perhaps declining concentration will also erode the industry's monolithic political clout by inducing individual firms to adopt more divergent positions on major public policy issues.[26] Or, instead, perhaps the domestic oligopoly will subvert competition through joint ventures, transnational mergers, and a resort to government protectionism. These are some of the questions confronting students of this industry as it motors into the twenty-first century.

Suggested Readings

Automotive News, Market Data Book, (Detroit: Automotive News, annual).

Bollier, David, and Joan Claybrook. *Freedom from Harm,* (Washington, D.C.: Public Citizen, 1986).

Crandall, Robert W., et al. *Regulating the Automobile,* (Washington, D.C.: Brookings Institution, 1986).

Cray, Ed. *Chrome Colossus,* (New York: McGraw Hill, 1980).

Dyer, Davis; Malcolm S. Salter; and Alan M. Webber. *Changing Alliances: The Harvard Business School Project on the Auto Industry and the American Economy.* (Boston: Harvard Business School Press, 1987).

Ford, Henry, *My Life and Work,* (New York: Doubleday, 1926).

Halberstam, David. *The Reckoning,* (New York: Morrow, 1986).

[26]See Anna Wilde Mathews, "The Big Two Shift Gears on the Best Way to Reach Washington," *Wall Street Journal,* 27 November 1998, p. 1.

Harbour & Associates. *The Harbour Report.* (Troy, MI: annual).

Iacocca, Lee. *Iacocca,* (New York: Bantam, 1984).

Ingrassia, Paul, and Joseph B. White. *Comeback: The Fall & Rise of the American Automobile Industry,* (New York: Simon & Schuster, 1994).

Koppel, Tom. *Powering the Future: The Ballard Fuel Cell and the Race to Change the World* (New York: Wiley, 1999).

Levin, Doron P. *Irreconcilable Differences: Ross Perot versus General Motors,* (Boston: Little, Brown and Co., 1989).

Luger, Stan. *Corporate Power, American Democracy, and the Automobile,* (New York: Cambridge University Press, 2000).

Madsen, Axel. *The Deal Maker: How William C. Durant Made General Motors,* (New York: John Wiley & Sons, 1999).

MIT International Automobile Program. *The Future of the Automobile,* (Cambridge: MIT Press, 1984).

Porter, Richard C. *Economics at the Wheel: The Costs of Cars and Drivers,* (New York: Academic Press, 1999).

U.S. Congress. Senate. Subcommittee on Antitrust and Monopoly. *Hearings: The Industrial Reorganization Act, Parts 4 and 4A, Ground Transportation Industries,* 93d Cong., 2d sess., 1994.

Ward's Automotive Yearbook. (Detroit, annual).

White, Lawrence J. *The Automobile Industry Since 1945,* (Cambridge: Harvard University Press, 1971).

Womack, James P.; Daniel T. Jones; and Daniel Roos. *The Machine that Changed the World,* (New York: Rawson Associates, 1990).

CHAPTER 6

Computers

—DON E. WALDMAN

The history of the computer industry is closely linked to the history of two firms: International Business Machines (IBM) and Microsoft. The two firms compete in different sectors of the market, but their intertwined histories suggest how quickly economic conditions can change in what might rightfully be called the most rapidly changing, technologically advanced industry in history. For decades, IBM was the firm that stood for high technology and computers, yet today, based on units shipped, it is not the leading manufacturer of personal computers in the United States. IBM's one-time dominance of the entire computer industry has been lost in part to a software manufacturer, Microsoft, and in part to a microprocessor manufacturer, Intel. How did these dramatic changes come about? Furthermore, what lessons can be learned about the relationships among market structure, conduct, and performance through analyzing this rapidly changing industry?

I. HISTORY

A decade ago, IBM produced more than 60 percent of the mainframe computers sold in the world; its annual gross revenues increased every year, peaking at $68.9 billion in 1990; and it employed more than 400,000 people around the world.[1] By 1993, IBM's total world employment had declined by 36.8 percent to 256,000, and the company sustained an $8.1 billion loss! How did this turn of events happen?

Thomas J. Watson, Sr., built IBM by emphasizing to its sales force an understanding and commitment to its customers' needs, and a dedication to quality and to on-time delivery.[2] Watson, Sr., was a salesman, not

[1]For more details of this history, see Don E. Waldman, "IBM," in David I. Rosenbaum, ed., *Market Dominance: How Firms Gain, Hold, or Lose It and the Impact on Economic Performance* (Westport, CT: Praeger, 1998), 131–152.

[2]For more on the life of Thomas Watson Sr., see Thomas G. Belden and Marva R. Belden, *The Lengthening Shadow: The Life of Thomas J. Watson* (Boston: Little, Brown and Company, 1962); Emerson W. Pugh, *Building IBM: Shaping an Industry and Its Technology* (Cambridge: MIT Press, 1995), 29–36; and Robert Sobel, *IBM* vs. *Japan: The Struggle for the Future* (New York: Stein and Day, 1986), 28–34.

a technological genius, and IBM's CEOs for decades to come followed in his footsteps. Watson, Sr., had taken a small firm, The Computing Tabulating Recording Company (name changed to IBM in 1924), specializing in scales and measuring devices, and, by focusing its attention on solving the accounting problems of large corporations, had built up a highly profitable business. Watson, Sr., trained his sales representatives to have one overriding objective—to solve each individual customer's problems with an individual solution. He was convinced that as long as IBM's machines helped its customers' businesses operate more efficiently, IBM would remain the industry's dominant force.[3]

IBM did not start out as the leader in the computer industry. Remington Rand produced the world's first important commercial computer in the late 1940s—the UNIVAC. IBM at that time was concentrating on producing large electronic business calculators that operated on vacuum tubes.[4] By 1952, IBM had succeeded in introducing the IBM 702, an electronic calculator designed to replace its punch-card machines.

When Thomas Watson, Jr., took control of the company from his father, he decided to push IBM into the computer age. IBM moved quickly to gain the lead in transistor technology and by 1957 its sales had reached $1 billion. This was a remarkable achievement considering that in 1946 its sales were a mere $116 million.[5]

Once business firms purchased an IBM computer they quickly became dependent on IBM's software. This phenomenon came to be known as "software lock-in."[6] Up until the point of purchase of a computer system, buyers had a choice regarding what brand to install. After the purchase of an IBM computer, however, the buyer became completely dependent on IBM's software and programming, and the cost of switching to another manufacturer was often prohibitively high. Once a large corporation had paid IBM thousands, or millions, of dollars to install and organize its database, there was little chance it would switch to a new system to save a mere 10 or 15 percent in monthly leasing charges.

By the early 1960s, IBM was firmly established as the computer industry's dominant firm. In 1964, IBM held an 80 percent market share of the "value of installed and on-order data processing equipment." Its profit in 1964 was 19.1 percent of stockholders' equity, making IBM one of the nation's most profitable companies. The maintenance of its dominant position in the 1960s and 1970s was built upon the development of

---

[3]Charles H. Ferguson and Charles R. Morris, *Computer Wars* (New York: Random House, 1993), 3–4.

[4]Ibid., 4.

[5]Pugh, *Building IBM,* 323–324.

[6]Richard T. DeLamarter, *Big Blue: IBM's Use and Abuse of Power* (New York: Dodd, Mead & Company, 1986), 29.

the System 360 series of mainframe computers. At the time of the System 360's development, IBM's market share was being reduced by the inroads of such corporate giants as GE, RCA, Rand, and Control Data. The objective of the System 360 series was to replace all existing computers, including IBM's existing machines.

The idea behind the System 360 was that all of IBM's computers would be compatible because they would all run the same software. Machines that leased for $2,500 a month would run on the same software as machines leased for over $100,000 a month. Furthermore, the 360 could run all the programs that were currently running on IBM's then-leading computer, the IBM 1401. Therefore, the 1401 customers' programs could be transferred directly to the 360. As a customer's needs expanded, IBM would simply add new devices such as a faster processor or more memory. The success of the System 360 established IBM's dominance for 20 years.

Sometime in the mid-1970s, however, IBM began to lose its stranglehold on the industry. Two factors were primarily responsible for this decline: The first was the filing of a government antitrust case against the firm in 1969. The second was the failure of IBM's management to respond to the changing nature of the computer industry as the industry moved rapidly from a world of large mainframe computers to a world of small personal computers.

William Henry Gates III, the world's wealthiest person, was born on October 28, 1955. In 1967, Gates enrolled in the seventh grade at Lakeside, an all boys private preparatory school.[7] Gates was introduced to computers in the spring of 1968 when Lakeside bought a teletype machine. Gates, and his friends Paul Allen, Kent Evans, and Richard Weiland, got their first computer-related job from Computer Center Corporation (CCC). CCC signed an agreement with the newly established "Lakeside Programming Group," giving the boys free computer time in exchange for their finding bugs in CCC's software. The boys spent their evenings and weekends on the computer, carefully documenting each bug. This experience gave Gates a chance to deepen his knowledge of the operation of the minicomputer's hardware and software.

In the fall of 1973, Gates entered Harvard. During the following summer, Allen and Gates worked at Honeywell. It was Paul Allen, however, who pushed Gates to see the vision described by the following scenario:

> Gates and Allen were convinced the computer industry was about to reach critical mass, and when it exploded it would usher in a technological revolution of astounding magnitude. They

---

[7]For more details of this history, see Rochelle Ruffer and Don E. Waldman, "Microsoft," in David I. Rosenbaum, ed., *Market Dominance: How Firms Gain, Hold, or Lose It and the Impact on Economic Performance* (Westport, CT: Praeger, 1998), 153–173.

> were on the threshold of one of those moments when history held its breath . . . and jumped, as it had done with the development of the car and airplane. Computer power was about to come to the masses. Their vision of a computer in every home was no longer a wild dream. "It's going to happen," Allen kept telling his friend. And they could either lead the revolution or be swept along with it.[8]

In December of 1974, the January issue of *Popular Mechanics* featured the Altair 8080—the "World's First Microcomputer Kit to Rival Commercial Models"—as the cover headline. The article was about Ed Roberts of Micro Instrumentation and Telemetry Systems (MITS) who coined the term "personal computer." Gates and Allen promised Roberts a version of an operating system, BASIC, for the Altair and worked solidly for eight weeks to provide it. Allen and Gates recorded Gates' 8,000 lines of machine language code onto punched paper tape because a keyboard had not been planned for the Altair. The program worked, and Microsoft was born.

It was the later development of the MS-DOS operating system that put Microsoft on the path to becoming the dominant firm in the computer industry. IBM initially approached Gates in 1980 to write a version of BASIC for the permanent memory of an 8-bit computer.[9] Gates, however, suggested that IBM meet with Gary Kildall of Digital Research to acquire CP/M as IBM's operating system. Once Gates, Allen, and IBM realized Kildall was not interested, Gates and Allen decided to provide the operating system themselves, but they knew they did not have sufficient time to develop a new system. Instead, they bought a newly developed operating system from Seattle Computer Products, QDOS. Microsoft paid $75,000 for the right to sell QDOS.[10]

Microsoft and IBM signed a contract in late 1980 that prohibited IBM from licensing DOS, but placed no restraints on Microsoft. This stipulation enabled Microsoft to license MS-DOS to clone manufacturers, thereby pushing it as the industry standard. When IBM announced the introduction of its first personal computer on August 12, 1981, the computer included Microsoft's MS-DOS operating system. By 1984, it was clear that MS-DOS was the operating system industry leader. By

---

[8]James Wallace and Jim Erickson, *Hard Drive: Bill Gates and the Making of the Microsoft Empire* (New York: John Wiley & Sons, 1992), 60.

[9]Michael A. Cusumano and Richard W. Selby, *Microsoft Secrets* (New York: Free Press, 1995), 137.

[10]The $75,000 figure is stated in both Cusumano and Selby, *Microsoft Secrets,* 137, and in Ferguson and Morris, *Computer Wars,* 66–67. Daniel Ichbiah and Susan L. Knepper, *The Making of Microsoft: How Bill Gates and his Team Created the World's Most Successful Software Company* (Rocklin, CA: Prima, 1993), 76, state "the exact amount is not clear, but indications are that Microsoft paid less than $100,000 for QDOS."

June of 1986, income from the sale of MS-DOS accounted for half of Microsoft's annual revenues of $60.9 million.[11]

In the 1980s and 1990s, three other important entrepreneurs quietly began to impact the computer industry: Michael Dell, Ted Waitt, and Mike Hammond. Almost simultaneously, they decided that many PC users no longer needed the security of purchasing PCs from a large company such as IBM, Hewlett-Packard, or Compaq. Instead, they believed consumers would purchase custom-made PCs through the mail at relatively low prices. The result was the founding of two small companies: Dell Computer Corporation by Michael Dell in 1984, and Gateway by Ted Waitt and Mike Hammond in 1985.

In recent years, Dell and Gateway have been the most rapidly growing PC manufacturers; others have had to follow their leadership in offering PCs directly through the mail. The result has been a remarkable shift in the market shares of the top PC manufacturers.

II. MARKET STRUCTURE

Market Shares and Concentration

The large number of business contacts that IBM had cultivated through its dominance of the tabulating machine market led to its control of the computer market. By 1956, IBM held approximately 75 percent of the market share of the installed-base of the electronic data-processing market. As Table 6-1 indicates, in 1956, five major firms were competing in this industry: IBM, Sperry Rand (formerly Remington Rand), Burroughs, RCA and NCR. By the end of the 1950s, four additional firms were in the industry: Honeywell, General Electric (GE), Control Data (CDC), and Philco. Other giant firms such as Bendix, Budd, General Mills, ITT, Northrop Aircraft, Sylvania Electric, TRW, and United Aircraft all entered and left the industry prior to 1969. In the early years of the industry, there was certainly no shortage of attempts by major corporations to enter, but ultimately none could compete with IBM.

If "the installed-base of electronic data-processing equipment" is the correct market definition for measuring effective competition in the computer industry, then the figures in Table 6-1 leave little doubt that IBM had a considerable amount of market power. In 1967, despite the protestations of IBM and its lawyers, it may have made some sense to define the industry this way. However, it certainly is inappropriate today. Table 6-2 shows IBM's revenues by market segment for the years 1992–1998. Notice how the importance of the "global services" segment has increased,

[11]Ichbiah and Knepper, *The Making of Microsoft,* 93.

TABLE 6-1 Percentage Shares of the Retail Sales Value of the Installed-Base of Electronic Data-Processing Equipment for the Major Suppliers in the United States (1955-1967)

Year	*IBM*	*Sperry Rand*	*Honeywell*	*RCA*	*NCR*	*Burroughs*	*GE*	*CDC*	*Philco*
1955	56.1	38.5	—	5.1	0.3	—	—	—	—
1956	75.3	18.6	—	1.6	0.1	4.4	—	—	—
1957	78.5	16.3	0.3	0.8	0.1	3.9	—	—	—
1958	77.4	16.3	0.9	1.8	0.1	3.3	0.2	—	—
1959	74.5	17.8	1.2	1.4	0.1	4.2	0.9	—	—
1960	71.6	16.2	0.9	2.4	0.4	3.4	2.8	1.0	1.2
1961	69.3	15.5	2.0	3.0	0.8	2.6	3.4	2.2	1.3
1962	69.9	12.4	2.3	3.5	1.9	2.2	3.7	3.1	1.2
1963	69.8	11.2	1.8	3.5	2.7	2.6	3.5	4.0	1.0
1964	68.3	11.8	2.5	3.0	2.8	3.1	3.3	4.4	0.8
1965	65.3	12.1	3.8	2.8	2.8	3.6	3.3	5.4	0.8
1966	66.2	11.3	5.2	2.7	2.4	3.0	3.5	5.3	0.4
1967	68.1	10.6	4.7	3.2	2.5	2.9	3.0	5.7	0.2

Source: Honeywell, Inc. v. Sperry Rand, Civil Action No. 4-67, Civ. 138 U.S. District Court, 4th Dist. Minn.

while the importance of the hardware segment, which includes both mainframe and PC revenues, has decreased. By 1998, only 43.4 percent of IBM's revenues were generated from hardware. Table 6-2 suggests that IBM is rapidly transforming itself from a computer hardware company into an information technology service company.

Several years ago, the computer magazine *Datamation* began ranking the top 100 "information technology" firms. The definition of "information technology" was quite broad, including everything from computer hardware and software to computer services. The *Datamation 100* list provided insight into the large number of corporations competing in one or more segments of the industry. Unfortunately, 1996 was the last year of the *Datamation 100* list. Table 6-3 identifies the top 20 firms on the 1996 list. The list includes 13 American firms, six Japanese firms and one German firm. The complete list of 100 firms also includes firms from the United Kingdom, France, Italy, the Netherlands, South Korea, Sweden, and Taiwan. The "global information network," is indeed global. While some of the *Datamation 100* firms are exclusively information technology firms, many are highly diversified. Notice that five of the top 20 receive less than 50 percent of their total revenues from information technology markets.

Tables 6-4, 6-5, and 6-6 present more recent market share data for the following information technology segments: high-end servers (including mainframe computers), personal or desktop computers, and software. By 1999, IBM led in only the high-end server market. In software, Microsoft surged past IBM in 1998, and in PCs, IBM ranked only fifth in units shipped for the first three quarters of 1999. With the PC segment growing much more rapidly than the high-end server segment, it is perhaps most revealing that IBM declined from the third-ranked to the fifth-ranked PC supplier in less than two years.

As Tables 6-4 and 6-5 show, the current structure of the computer hardware industry suggests a market that is ripe with competition. Many firms compete effectively in both the high-end and PC markets. The days of complete domination by IBM appear to be long gone. However, lurking behind the figures in Table 6-6 is the fact that in the market for operating systems for "non-Apple PC-computers," Microsoft has a virtual monopoly with approximately a 90 percent market share.

Entry Barriers

Economies of scale exist if the long-run average costs of production decline with output. Economies erect a significant barrier if one optimal size firm produces a significant proportion of relevant market output and if suboptimal firms face significantly higher long-run average costs. According to one engineering study, in 1967, one minimum optimal scale computer plant produced 15 percent of total United States demand for

TABLE 6-2 IBM's Revenues by Source 1992–1998

Revenue Source	***1998***	***1997***	***1996***	***1995***	***1994***	***1993***	***1992***
Hardware Segment	35,419	36,630	36,634	35,600	32,344	30,591	33,755
Global Service Segment	28,916	25,166	22,310	12,714	9,715	9,711	11,103
Software Segment	11,863	11,164	11,426	12,657	11,346	10,953	7,352
Global Financing Segment	2,877	2,806	3,054	7,409	7,222	7,295	7,635
Enterprise Investment Segment/Other	2,592	2,742	2,523	3,560	3,425	4,166	4,678
Totals	81,667	78,508	75,947	71,940	64,052	62,716	64,523

Source: IBM Annual Reports

TABLE 6-3 1996 Datamation Global 100

Rank	*Company*	*Country*	*Total 1996 IT Revenue*	*Total 1996 Net Income*	*Total 1996 Revenue*	*IT Revenue As A % of Total Revenue*
1	IBM	US	75,947	5,400	75,947	100
2	Hewlett Packard	US	31,398	2,708	39,427	80
3	Fujitsu	Japan	29,717	5,300	47,170	63
4	Compaq	US	18,109	1,313	18,109	100
5	Hitachi	Japan	15,242	712	68,735	23
6	NEC	Japan	15,092	841	44,766	34
7	Electronic Data Systems	US	14,441	432	14,441	100
8	Toshiba	Japan	14,050	1,533	58,300	24
9	Digital Equipment	US	13,610	(−343)	13,610	100
10	Microsoft	US	9,435	2,476	9,435	100
11	Siemans Nixdorf	Germany	9,189	20	9,189	100
12	Apple Computer	US	8,914	(−867)	8,914	100
13	Seagate Technology	US	8,500	222	8,500	100
14	Dell Computer	US	7,800	518	7,800	100
15	Packard Bell NEC	US	7,500	N/A	7,500	100
16	Acer	US	7,000	N/A	7,000	100
17	Canon	Japan	6,907	1,000	10,430	51
18	Matsushita	Japan	6,410	(−537)	64,102	10
19	NCR	US	6,403	(−109)	6,960	92
20	Sun Microsystems	US	6,390	447	6,390	100

Source: Datamation, (July 1997).

TABLE 6-4 Worldwide High-End Server Market Share 1998

Company	*1998 Revenues (Billions of Dollars)*	*Market Share*
IBM	6.0	36.8
Fujitsu	1.4	8.6
Hitachi	1.1	6.7
NEC	1.1	6.7
Sun	0.9	5.6
Amdahl	0.7	4.4
Others	16.3	31.1

Source: International Data Corporation.

computers. Furthermore, a plant operating at ⅓ minimum optimal scale had long-run average costs elevated by 8 percent.[12] Those figures suggest substantial production economies of scale existed in 1967. Economies of scale were also associated with research and development expenditures, which totaled several hundred million dollars for the IBM System 360 family of computers.[13] The greater the number of units these R&D expenditures could be amortized over, the lower the average R&D expenditures per machine.

Production and R&D economies of scale were important in the first few decades of the computer industry, but network externalities in combination with these economies were probably more responsible for IBM's market domination. According to Katz and Shapiro, network externalities exist if "the utility that a user derives from consumption of the good increases with the number of other agents consuming the good."[14] For example, the utility that a consumer derives from a telephone is clearly related to the number of other users on the telephone network.

Consider a consumer contemplating the purchase of a computer. If consumers as a group make their purchasing decisions at different times, then each consumer's utility will be affected by the number of consumers already using a given model of computer, and the number of consumers expected to use the system in the future. The more consumers currently using or expected to use the same computer, the greater will be the availability of software applications for that computer, and the greater will be the consumer's expected utility associated with the computer. In addition,

---

[12]William G. Shepherd, *The Economics of Industrial Organization* (Upper Saddle River, NJ: Prentice-Hall, 1997), 182.

[13]Ferguson and Morris, *Computer Wars,* 8.

[14]Michael L. Katz and Carl Shapiro, "Network Externalities, Competition, and Compatibility," *American Economic Review,* 1985, 75(3): 424.

TABLE 6-5 United States PC Shipments (thousands of units)

1999 First 3 Quarters Rank	*Company*	*1999 First 3 Quarters Shipments*	*1999 Market Share*	*1998 Shipments*	*1998 Market Share*	*1997 Shipments*	*1997 Market Share*
1	Dell	5,343	16.5%	4,799	13.2%	2,930	9.3%
2	Compaq	5,251	16.2%	6,052	16.7%	5,316	16.9%
3	Gateway	2,846	8.8%	3,039	8.4%	2,219	7.0%
4	Hewlett-Packard	2,682	8.3%	2,814	7.8%	2,063	6.6%
5	IBM	2,579	8.0%	2,979	8.2%	2,719	8.6%
	Others	13,736	42.3%	16,571	45.7%	16,232	51.6%

Source: International Data Corporation.

TABLE 6-6 Top Software Company Revenues 1996–1998

Company	*1998 Software Revenues (Billions of Dollars)*	*1997 Software Revenues (Billions of Dollars)*	*1996 Software Revenues (Billions of Dollars)*
Microsoft	16.7	12.8	9.2
IBM	13.5	12.8	13.1
Oracle	8.0	4.4	3.6
Computer Associates	5.1	4.5	3.9

Sources: Software Magazine (1996–1997); and International Data Corporation 1998.

the greater the number of current users of a particular computer system, the easier it will be to obtain post-purchase service and technical support. The current demand for a given computer, therefore, is a function of the current installed-base and expected future demand for the computer.

If computers are produced under conditions of economies of scale, then the first firm, in this case IBM, to gain a large installed-base will have significantly lower costs and can charge significantly lower prices. As a result of lower prices and network externalities, the market may be tipped to one dominant product. Once a market is tipped, it may be difficult for competitors to "untip" it.

IBM, as the first mover into the broad-based computer industry, gained an advantage due to network externalities. In addition, as the first mover into a new technologically advanced industry, IBM gained a product differentiation advantage as well.[15] When IBM introduced the System 360, it faced a relatively low demand because few potential buyers were completely informed about the system. Suppose IBM decided to introduce the System 360 at a "low introductory rental rate" to overcome risk aversion and induce consumers to lease the System 360. After the introductory offer ends, consumers who lease the system are much better informed and their demand increases dramatically. As a result, IBM can significantly increase the rental rate to them. The demand by uninformed consumers, however, remains low.

If another company, Firm 2, develops a computer that is more or less identical to IBM's System 360, it faces a serious problem because consumers cannot be certain that Firm 2's computers are as good as IBM's. In fact, consumers cannot even be sure Firm 2's computers are any good. Firm 2's demand thus consists of two separate groups of consumers: Group 1 consists of informed consumers who are already "hooked" on IBM's machines; Group 2 consumers have never tried an IBM machine because even IBM's low introductory rental rate was above the maximum rental rate they were willing to pay. Group 2 consumers, therefore, have a very low demand for computer systems!

Assuming that IBM continues to charge the current rental rate, it will have completely "locked-in" the informed half of the market, and the only group left for Firm 2 are the uninformed consumers. Firm 2 will have to charge a very low rental rate to induce any of the uninformed consumers to lease a computer. This places Firm 2 at a tremendous disadvantage: While IBM continues leasing at a high rental rate, Firm 2 will have to lease at a very low rate to attract any buyers.

---

[15]For a more detailed discussion of this theory, see Don E. Waldman and Elizabeth J. Jensen, *Industrial Organization: Theory and Practice* (Reading, MA: Addison Wesley Longman, 1998), 325–329.

Under these conditions, Firm 2 may find it impossible to enter and earn a profit, particularly if there are significant nonrecoverable fixed costs (sunk costs) associated with entry. Furthermore, in response to entry, IBM is capable of responding aggressively and lowering the rental rate to capture additional uninformed consumers. This serves as an additional deterrent to entry.

Network externalities and the product differentiation advantages of first movers are also critical factors explaining Microsoft's domination of the PC operating systems market. These two structural characteristics, therefore, have played a key role in the computer industry.

III. CONDUCT

As the leading firms in their respective segments of the computer industry, IBM and Microsoft have employed strikingly similar types of strategic behavior to build and maintain their market dominance.

IBM's Early Conduct

Pricing to Educational Institutions Thomas Watson, Sr., realized that the typical business computer user, as distinguished from scientific computer users, lacked any sophisticated knowledge of computer usage. To fill this educational void, and in an effort to tie students to IBM products after graduation, IBM made computers available to schools at huge discounts. This strategy worked extremely well. In the 1960s, an entire first-generation of computer users was trained in college on IBM machines. Upon graduation, these former students thought first to purchase IBM.

Pricing of Service Early computers were constantly breaking down because they were dependent upon vacuum tubes rather than semiconductors. A system "crash" created havoc in a company trying to process its monthly payroll. To avoid this, companies paid premium prices to IBM for access to the company's national service network.[16] IBM covered the nation with service centers to take care of problems, while smaller competitors had far fewer service providers nationwide. This extensive service network meant that customers came to rely on IBM to provide fast, low-cost service.

To further reinforce its service advantage, IBM adopted a pricing policy of tying (or bundling) service with its sale or lease price, so that the marginal cost of an additional service call was zero. This, for a time, prevented the development of an independent service industry to service all brands of computers.

[16]Gerald Brock, *The United States Computer Industry: A Study of Market Power* (Cambridge, MA: Ballinger, 1975), 33–37.

Pre-announcement of the System 360 In the mid-1960s, IBM was concerned that competitors would introduce technically superior machines before IBM could get the System 360 models on the market. One solution to this problem was for IBM to "pre-announce" all five main System 360 models in advance of when most would be ready for delivery. In fact, in April 1964, IBM announced the "forthcoming availability" of five System 360 models even though several were not fully developed and many technical problems remained to be resolved before delivery would be possible.

The decision to pre-announce the System 360 line was a brilliant business strategy. Despite the fact that the first machines were not delivered until April 1965 and that some of the promised models were never developed, the mere announcement of IBM's coming new line prevented buyers from committing to competitors' new machines, some of which were probably technologically superior to the System 360 computers.

Price Discrimination One of the most important strategies was the selective use of price discrimination. Generally, IBM charged much higher list prices than its competitors for individual pieces of equipment. IBM, however, bundled entire systems together and charged one price for the central processing unit (CPU), related software, and maintenance, rather than charging different prices for each component of a system. Through bundling systems, IBM was able to price discriminate between different users because the user did not know what price was being paid for any individual piece of the complete system. A customer who bought from IBM received an entire computer system, and there was no possibility of picking and choosing from other sources.

Pricing in Response to Entry The bundling system worked extremely well for IBM until customers were ready to upgrade their systems in the late 1960s. As previously noted, IBM's list prices for individual pieces of equipment were high compared to those of its competitors. The high costs for replacement equipment were necessary to cover the expenses of providing free service to all customers and free systems to educational institutions.

In November of 1967, the first of many small firms began to sell individual pieces of "plug-compatible IBM equipment," such as tape and disk drives, at prices much lower than IBM's. This market grew rapidly: In 1966, only three manufacturers carried plug-compatible equipment, whereas by 1972 approximately a hundred did.[17] As a result, IBM lost a significant share of the peripheral market.

IBM responded to these inroads with a series of actions. First, it selectively and dramatically reduced the price of peripheral equipment.

[17] *Telex Corporation* v. *IBM Corporation* 510 F.2d 894 (1975).

Next, it redesigned certain equipment so that it could be connected to the IBM central processing unit only through an integrated file adapter, rather than through the traditional external disk control unit. This change made the use of non-IBM equipment much less attractive to users. In 1971, IBM announced a fixed-term leasing plan, which provided for an 8 percent price reduction for users signing a one-year lease on peripheral equipment and a 16 percent price reduction for signers of a two-year lease. Finally, at the same time that IBM announced large price reductions on peripheral equipment, it announced large price increases on its central processing units to recoup lost revenues.

IBM's actions forced the manufacturers of peripheral equipment to cut prices drastically and resulted in several private antitrust actions by those same firms.[18]

One of the unanticipated effects of IBM's new peripheral pricing strategy was to set the price of IBM's mainframe computers (CPUs) high enough to encourage entry. The first major entrant was Amdahl Corporation, founded by Gene Amdahl after he left IBM. In 1975, Amdahl introduced the Amdahl 470, a computer fully compatible with IBM's best System 370 machine (the technologically advanced successor to the System 360), but much faster and priced lower.[19] By 1978, several other firms were producing CPUs to challenge IBM's offerings.[20]

Threatened with a significant decrease in its CPU market share, IBM once again took action. In 1977, it introduced a more powerful computer, the 3033, then reduced prices on its System 370 computers by 20 to 35 percent.[21]

Introduction of the IBM-PC The computer field, as well as the entire world, changed forever in 1971 when Intel developed the first microprocessor, which had an entire computer on a small silicon chip. Continued technological advances in the 1970s led to the first commercially successful personal computer—the Apple, and it was not long before it benefitted from a new independent software market. Once the Apple could be used with both word processing and spreadsheet software, it became a low-priced alternative to expensive computers for small business and educational uses.

As Apple computers became more popular, IBM was left out in the cold. Much of the blame lies with IBM's management, which failed to recognize that the personal computer would one day be something more

---

[18]See for examples, *Telex Corporation* v. *International Business Machines* 510 F.2d 894 (1975); *ILC Peripherals Leasing Company* v. *International Business Machines* 458 F.Supp. 423 (1978); and *Memorex Corporation* v. *International Business Machines* 636 F.2d 1188 (1980).

[19]"A Tyro Challenges IBM in Big Computers," *Business Week,* 12 May 1975, 65–67.

[20]"New Wave of Change Challenging IBM," *Business Week,* 29 May 1978, 92–99.

[21]"I.B.M. Foresees Benefits from Price Cuts," *New York Times,* 26 April 1977, p. 51; and "More Tumult for the Computer Industry," *Business Week,* 30 May 1977, 58–66.

than a home toy. To IBM's senior management in the 1970s and early 1980s, the future was still in mainframes for commercial use. According to one member of the IBM Management Committee, "[t]he general attitude was that you don't have big problems in small markets, and we thought the personal computer was a very small market."[22]

In an almost desperate attempt to catch up in the PC market, IBM broke with all of its corporate traditions and set up an independent development team in Boca Raton, Florida. The team was charged with catching up to Apple *ASAP!* In its rush to catch up, IBM decided to work with an open architecture (as opposed to a proprietary architecture) so that other firms could develop software and peripherals for the IBM-PC. The strategy gave software and peripheral manufacturers a great incentive to produce products for the IBM-PC. It also meant that when IBM's first PC was introduced in 1981, the computer was filled with components and software produced by other companies. As a result, IBM lost proprietary control over the computer industry, which it has yet to win back.

More advanced IBM-PCs were introduced in 1983 and 1984, and IBM earned record profits that peaked at $6.58 billion in 1984. It was at this point that IBM made a series of terrible managerial decisions that set the stage for the company's financial woes in the early 1990s.

Recall that Bill Gates and Paul Allen had turned to a small local firm, Seattle Computing, for help with writing and developing operating systems, and that they subsequently purchased QDOS. In concert with a large group of IBM programmers, Microsoft went to work around the clock to modify QDOS. The result was one of the most significant commercial products of the latter half of the twentieth century—MS-DOS.

IBM management made the first of three major blunders when it failed to secure the rights to the source code for DOS from Bill Gates and Microsoft. Without the code, IBM could not modify DOS and was completely dependent on Microsoft for any improvements.[23]

IBM's second error occurred when it had an opportunity to establish its own operating system in direct competition with MS-DOS. A group of IBM researchers wrote an operating system called CP/X86 for the PC-AT.[24] Later, they expanded the project to include a pictorial program that worked much like Windows. By 1984, the IBM group had developed a product that was clearly superior to DOS. But when management had to decide what operating system would succeed DOS, they chose to develop the OS/2 operating system with Microsoft. Their decision was influenced by Gates' threat that if IBM developed an operating system without

---

[22]Paul Carroll, *Big Blues: The Unmaking of IBM* (New York: Crown Trade Paperbacks, 1994), 18.

[23]Ferguson and Morris, *Computer Wars,* 71.

[24]Ibid., 72.

Microsoft, he would never release the source code for DOS to IBM.[25] This meant that IBM would be on its own with CP/X86, in direct competition with Microsoft's MS-DOS. IBM feared that network externalities would make it difficult to establish CP/X86 as the industry standard.

The OS/2 partnership between IBM and Microsoft was a disaster from the beginning, in large part because OS/2 was tied to a weak Intel microprocessor.[26] By the time the project began, Gates knew that the future was tied to Intel's 386 microprocessor chip, but that IBM management was committed to the 286 chip. Gates thought the 286 chip was "brain dead," but went along with IBM's decision.[27] It has been suggested that Gates went along with the 286 decision in order to sabotage the OS/2 project so that OS/2 would not threaten the pending Microsoft Windows. In any event, OS/2 was a dinosaur when it was introduced along with the Personal System 2 in 1987.[28]

The third error ended any hope IBM may have had of retaining dominance over the computer industry. Because IBM and Microsoft had jointly developed DOS, IBM was in a position to negotiate with Microsoft over how to split the royalties on DOS sales as well as the royalties on any future operating systems that the two firms might develop jointly. In 1985, IBM had one final opportunity to prevent Microsoft from taking control of the personal computer operating system industry. IBM had 80 percent of the PC business, its mainframe revenues were doing extremely well, and it had earned $6.58 billion. IBM's management was convinced that the belief that, "nobody was ever fired for buying from IBM," would continue to keep the company firmly established as the industry leader regardless of future competitive threats.

IBM had one objective in its negotiations with Gates over a royalty split: to pay as low a price as possible for the rights to DOS on IBM machines.[29] Because all other PC producers combined controlled only a 20 percent market share, IBM cared little about royalties on these non-IBM machines. Gates then pulled off a master negotiating stroke: he offered to give DOS to IBM essentially for free. All Microsoft wanted in return was the right to collect the royalties on DOS from clone manufacturers. IBM quickly agreed, and a contract was signed in 1985. Following this third error there would be no more opportunities for IBM to regain control of the operating system market.

Without control over either the operating system or the microprocessor for the IBM-PC, IBM was unable to prevent a flood of low-

[25]Ibid., 74.
[26]Ibid., 76.
[27]Ibid.
[28]Ibid., 80–81.
[29]Carroll, *Big Blues*, 89.

priced clones from capturing a growing share of the personal computer market. Once consumers became aware that the quality of the PC clones was at least equal to the quality of the IBM-PC, buyers bought the cheaper clones in droves. Within a decade, IBM was relegated to being one of the pack in the personal computer market.

Conduct in the Computer Industry Today The elimination of IBM's monopoly in the computer hardware industry has greatly changed industry conduct. Most of the strategic conduct used by IBM to gain control of the computer hardware industry would be impossible today. Consider the following comparisons:

IBM's Conduct	Current Industry Conduct
1. Bundling of custom-made systems that included all hardware software and service.	1. Manufacturers charge for each separate component. "Basic systems" include a microprocessor and an operating system. Buyers pay for extended service contracts or additional upgrades. Buyers pay separately for each upgrade to their systems.
2. Pre-announcing of nonexistent systems.	2. Technological change is so rapid and system upgrades are so easy that buyers would not delay the purchase of a new computer because of the pre-announcement of a nonexistent machine.
3. Price discrimination by charging for a complete system. Educational institutions often received free systems.	3. Firms charge for each component of a system. If a buyer wants another piece of peripheral equipment, i.e., a zip drive or high quality soundboard, the consumer pays separately. Educational institutions pay for equipment, although most companies still offer some grants to schools.

The elimination of IBM's monopoly power in the computer hardware industry has eliminated the monopolistic conduct associated with that power. Today producers of computers quote virtually all buyers identical list prices for a given system or piece of equipment. There are also many producers of peripheral equipment for all types of machines.

Market conduct in the computer hardware industry is now consistent with that of any other competitive industry.

Microsoft

The Pre-announcement of Products In 1990, Digital Research Incorporated (DRI) introduced a new operating system, DR-DOS 5.0, to industry acclaim. Most experts considered DR-DOS to be superior to Microsoft's MS-DOS.[30] DR-DOS began to make significant inroads into MS-DOS's market share; by the end of 1990, DRI had captured a 10 percent market share of new DOS-based operating system shipments.[31]

Within one month of the introduction of DR-DOS, Microsoft announced the "forthcoming" new version of MS-DOS, MS-DOS 5.0. Microsoft's announcement made the introduction of MS-DOS 5.0 appear imminent, but it took Microsoft over a year to market MS-DOS 5.0, which was finally introduced in July of 1991. According to the Federal Trade Commission staff, in the summer of 1990 the new version of MS-DOS 5.0 was nothing more than "vaporware," meaning that Microsoft was not even close to having a marketable product.[32] To make matters worse for DRI, during the year between June 1990 and June 1991, Microsoft continuously announced that its introduction of MS-DOS 5.0 was "imminent." The vaporware strategy worked, and the growth of DR-DOS was stopped. By 1992, Microsoft's share of DOS-based operating systems had increased to 81 percent and DRI's share had shrunk to just 7 percent.

Exclusionary Licenses Typically, a patent license is based on the number of units of the product used by the licensee. Beginning as early as 1983, however, Microsoft negotiated many, but not all, licenses based on the total number of computer processors shipped by an original equipment manufacturer (OEM). Furthermore, every Microsoft license was individually negotiated and an official list price for MS-DOS never existed. The effect was to ensure that Microsoft received a royalty on every computer shipped by an OEM regardless of whether or not the computer had a copy of MS-DOS installed. Licenses based on the total number of computers shipped came to be known as CPU licenses. CPU licenses gained an increasing share of Microsoft's licensing activity over time, increasing from 20 percent of licenses in 1989 to 50 percent by 1992.[33]

[30]Kenneth C. Baseman, Frederick R. Warren-Boulton, and Glenn A. Woroch, "Microsoft Plays Hardball: The Use of Exclusionary Pricing and Technical Incompatibility to Maintain Monopoly Power in Markets for Operating System Software," *Antitrust Bulletin* (Summer 1995): 272.

[31]Ibid.

[32]Ruffer and Waldman, "Microsoft," in David I. Rosenbaum, ed., *Market Dominance,* 165.

[33]*United States* v. *Microsoft,* No. 94-1564 (D.D.C. filed 15 July 1995).

Microsoft's CPU licenses required OEMs to pay for a minimum number of licenses, but this minimum number was typically greater than or equal to the anticipated computer shipments of the OEM. If, for example, an OEM expected to ship 100,000 computers in a year, it would agree to pay a license fee, *f*, on a minimum of 100,000 units. If it shipped machines with a non-Microsoft operating system, say PC-DOS or DR-DOS, it paid a royalty to Microsoft. If it shipped fewer than 100,000 units, it still paid Microsoft for 100,000 licenses. If it shipped more than 100,000 units, the licensee agreed to pay an additional royalty of *f* per unit shipped. Once again, the licensee paid the fee regardless of whether or not the units shipped included MS-DOS. The CPU licenses set the marginal cost of installing additional units of MS-DOS equal to zero up to the minimum number of units agreed to in the license, and then the marginal cost per license jumped to *f* for each CPU shipped beyond the minimum number.

By effectively setting marginal cost equal to zero, the CPU licenses created a system whereby an OEM had to pay double to install a non-Microsoft operating system. Under such a pricing system, buyers would pay for a second system only if the system was technologically superior to MS-DOS. Furthermore, the technological advantage had to be worth the full cost of the second operating system. This is a far more difficult hurdle to overcome for a competitive operating system such as PC-DOS or DR-DOS, than is a simple choice of which operating system to purchase for a given price.

The CPU licenses typically ran for 2 years. Furthermore, Microsoft usually tried to negotiate licenses that set a higher minimum number of units than probably would be shipped by offering a lower per-unit shipped fee. At the end of a year, the licensee typically had a credit for unused licenses, but Microsoft would only permit the licensee to carry the credit forward into the next year. This created an incentive for OEMs to install MS-DOS-based operating systems on next year's machines.

In addition to the implicit penalties associated with the use of a competitor's operating system, Microsoft utilized direct penalties for the installation of non-MS-DOS operating systems. An OEM using large numbers of non-MS-DOS based systems might be prohibited from carrying forward unused credits from previous years, or it might be required to agree to a higher minimum number of licenses in future years. In addition, technical support services might be withheld from firms installing non-Microsoft operating systems. Finally, Microsoft was known to increase the price of Windows for firms installing non-MS-DOS operating systems on their computers.

Creating Technical Incompatibilities It is critical for the developers of alternative operating systems and software to have access to the application programming interfaces (API) for Windows. Without the APIs, coordination between Windows and another operating system or applications software becomes difficult. Microsoft left some of the important APIs undocumented, thus creating problems for the programmers of competitive versions of DOS, and giving Microsoft's application software, such as WORD and EXCEL, an advantage over competitive software such as WordPerfect and Lotus. Even if competitors discovered the necessary APIs, Microsoft could change any undocumented interfaces at a later time to sabotage compatibility.

Because it is to Microsoft's benefit for application developers to produce a variety of software for Microsoft's operating systems, the company makes advance copies of its new or updated systems available to the programmers. The developers then test the compatibility of their software with the new or updated operating system. The compatibility testing procedure is referred to as "beta testing."

In order to create compatibility problems for DR-DOS, Microsoft denied access for beta testing to DRI when Microsoft introduced Windows 3.1 and Windows for Workgroups. In addition, Microsoft's version of Windows for beta testing was programmed to see if the program developers were using DR-DOS. If they were, an error message appeared on the screen asking the programmer to contact Microsoft for a version of MS-DOS or else risk incompatibility with DR-DOS. In reality, there were no incompatibility problems between Windows and DR-DOS, and if the programmer ignored the error message and continued working, everything functioned well. The error message, however, was aimed at creating uncertainty in the minds of the programmers that running Windows with a non-Microsoft operating system would result in serious problems.

Bundling of Products In the applications software market, Microsoft typically competes against companies that produce one major product—for example, WordPerfect in word processing, Lotus in spreadsheets, and Intuit in home financial management. Beginning in 1990, Microsoft began to bundle several pieces of application software together and sell them as an application "suite." Today, the dominant application suite is Microsoft Office. The price of the bundled pieces of software in Office has been greatly discounted: Buyers can purchase the standard version of Office, including Word, Excel, PowerPoint and Access, for about $250 retail. This represents a huge discount compared to the retail list price of about $300 for each individual application. Office has not only resulted in a greatly increased market share for Word and Excel, but has established PowerPoint as a major factor in a market where Microsoft had previously played only a minor role.

Microsoft also now bundles its Internet browsing software, Internet Explorer, with Windows. Microsoft realized that the Internet provided a potential platform for weakening its operating system monopoly. Gates feared that software could be written that would enable PCs to interact directly with the Internet without going through a PC operating system. It was theoretically possible to develop a new operating system that could be downloaded directly from the Internet. Netscape was the first company to produce a high-quality Internet browser, Netscape Navigator, that permitted users to easily surf the Internet, and Navigator quickly became the dominant Internet browser. In 1995, Microsoft recognized Netscape's control of the browser market as a long-term threat to its operating system monopoly. Gates made the strategic decision to gain control of the Internet browser market by bundling Microsoft's Internet Explorer with its Windows operating systems. By controlling this market, Microsoft hoped to control use of the Internet and prevent the development of downloadable alternative PC operating systems.

Although Microsoft may well have used bundling of software applications to gain market share, it is unclear that the net effects on welfare were negative. For one thing, bundling lowered the price of many Microsoft application programs. Furthermore, Microsoft, in some cases, has been unable to gain a large market share when its software is significantly inferior, even when bundling it. For example, Intuit's Quicken continues to dominate the home financial management market, crowding out the inferior Microsoft Money, even though Microsoft has bundled Money with its Works Suite home PC package.

IV. PERFORMANCE

A market is performing well if it is both statically and dynamically efficient. Static efficiency consists of both allocative efficiency (price equals marginal cost), and productive efficiency (average costs are minimized). Dynamic efficiency implies that the rate of technological advance is at a rapid and "optimal" rate.

Static Efficiency Static efficiency is generally achieved in competitive markets because competition rewards firms that produce efficiently and punishes firms that are less efficient. In competitive markets, prices tend to be driven quickly toward the average cost of production.

Little existed in the way of effective competition for IBM in the hardware market until the mid-1980s. Until then, IBM's net income increased every year except for a slight decline in 1979. In 1986, however, net earnings suddenly declined dramatically, and this was only a preview to the early 1990s when the company suffered three consecutive years of staggering losses, culminating with an $8.1 billion loss in fiscal year 1993.

As Table 6-7 indicates, the past decade has seen dramatic swings in the net earnings of all the major desktop computer manufacturers. In

TABLE 6-7 Net Income for the Leading American PC Manufacturers 1990–1998 (millions of dollars)

Year	IBM	Compaq	Dell	Apple	Hewlett-Packard	Gateway
1990	5,967	455	27	475	739	17
1991	−2,861	131	51	310	755	39
1992	−4,965	213	102	530	549	106
1993	−8,101	462	−36	87	1,177	151
1994	3,021	988	149	310	1,599	96
1995	4,178	893	272	424	2,433	173
1996	5,429	1,318	518	−816	2,586	251
1997	6,093	1,855	944	−1,045	3,119	110
1998	6,328	−2,743	1,460	309	2,945	346

Source: Company Annual Reports

1998 Compaq had its net earnings fall by $4.5 billion to a $2.7 billion loss. Gateway's net earnings declined by over 50 percent in 1997. Meanwhile, Apple sustained huge losses in 1996 and 1997, but recovered to earn over $300 million in 1998. Even the Dell miracle suffered a setback in 1993 when the company took a $36 million loss. The emerging picture is of an industry characterized by great volatility in the performance of individual firms from year to year. This is a classic competitive pattern.

The current competitive nature of the hardware industry is further evidenced by the rapid decline in prices in recent years. Consider the following evidence of effective price competition:

1. In July 1997, Compaq reduced the price of its corporate PCs by 22 percent; Hewlett-Packard followed with a 24 percent cut; and Digital Equipment cut prices by 21 percent.[34]
2. In November 1997, IBM introduced its first PC priced under $1,000, the Aptiva E16. That same month, Compaq reduced the prices of eight Presario models by 15 to 25 percent, bringing the price of Compaq's lowest priced model down to $799.[35]
3. In March 1998, Compaq again cut prices by up to 11 percent on some corporate PCs, and IBM responded the next day with price cuts of up to 20 percent on its corporate PCs.
4. In the second quarter of 1998, prices were 10 percent lower than in the first quarter as IBM, Compaq, and Hewlett-Packard all reduced prices.[36]

[34]"Digital Cuts Prices of PCS up to 21%," *Arizona Republic,* 18 July 1997, E2.
[35]"IBM Finally Introduces an under-$1,000 PC," *Ottawa Citizen,* 7 November 1997, F8.
[36]Larry Kaggwa, "Inacom Official Says PC Prices Will Stabilize," *Omaha World-Herald,* 23 July 1998.

5. According to a July 1999 report, "[t]he cost of computers has fallen dramatically in recent years, with the average selling price of a machine down to $1,200 from $1,640 three years ago. . . . That decline accompanies dramatic improvements in processing, speed, storage capacity, and video performance."[37]

Although IBM has struggled through some difficult profit years, Table 6-8 indicates that Microsoft has experienced a series of remarkably strong financial years. Between 1987 and 1999, Microsoft's annual sales increased by 5,607 percent and its net income increased by 10,713 percent! Perhaps even more impressive are the high rates of return on stockholders' equity, ranging from a low of 20.8 percent in 1987 to a high of 34.3 percent in 1991. Microsoft's monopoly power has clearly translated into above-normal economic profits.

Dynamic Efficiency The last column in Table 6-8 shows Microsoft's research and development expenditures as a percentage of sales. The numbers are astounding. Microsoft has consistently spent over 11 percent of its sales on R&D. By comparison, IBM spent $5 billion on R&D in 1998, or 6.2 percent of its net sales. In 1998, Microsoft and IBM together spent $7.9 billion on R&D or 3.6 percent of the nation's total R&D spending; the entire computer industry accounted for $22.5 billion or 10.2 percent of the nation's total R&D spending.[38]

The computer industry, and particularly the personal computer industry, may have experienced the most rapid rate of technological advance of any industry in history. Most of the advances over the last two decades have resulted from Intel's quick development of new microprocessors. Table 6-9 depicts these furious advances. The first microprocessor, the Intel 4004, had only 2,300 transistors, a speed of 108KHz, and 640 bytes of memory; it was good only for powering calculators. By comparison, the Pentium II processor, introduced in 1997, had 7.5 million transistors, speeds over 300 MHz, and 64 gigabytes of memory—while the Pentium III processor operates at speeds of 600 MHz! The power of microprocessors is commonly measured in MIPS, or millions of instructions per second. The Intel 4004 was rated at 0.01 MIPS, while the Pentium II was rated at over 25 MIPS.[39] Intel expects its next processor to be rated at more than 500 MIPS!

The amazing rate of technological advance in the microprocessor industry has given rise to "Moore's Law": Each new chip contains approximately twice as much capacity as the previous chip and new chips come

[37]Nicole Jacoby, "Buying a New Computer," CNN Financial Network, 19 July 1999.
[38]"R&D Continues to Rebound in US—Forecast," *Newsbytes, www.newsbytes.com,* January 4, 1999.
[39]Intel Corporation, Processor Hall of Fame, 1999.

TABLE 6-8 Microsoft's Sales, Profits, and R&D Spending 1987–1999

Year	*Sales (Millions of Dollars)*	*Net Income (Millions of Dollars)*	*Return on Stockholders' Equity*	*R&D Expenditures*	*R&D as a % of Sales*
1987	346	72	20.8%	38	11.0%
1988	591	124	33.0%	70	11.8%
1989	804	171	30.4%	110	13.7%
1990	1,183	279	30.4%	181	15.3%
1991	1,843	463	34.3%	235	12.8%
1992	2,759	709	32.3%	352	12.8%
1993	3,753	953	29.4%	470	12.5%
1994	4,649	1,146	25.8%	610	13.1%
1995	5,937	1,453	27.2%	860	14.5%
1996	8,671	2,195	31.8%	1,432	16.5%
1997	11,963	3,454	32.0%	1,863	15.6%
1998	15,262	4,490	27.0%	2,897	19.0%
1999	19,747	7,785	27.4%	2,970	15.3%

Source: Microsoft's SEC Annual Shareholder's Filings 1987–1999.

TABLE 6-9 Intel's Introduction of New Microprocessors

Intel Processor	Year Introduced	Speed	Bus Width	Number of Transistors	Addressable Memory	Virtual Memory
4004	11/15/71	108 KHz	4 bits	2,300	640 bytes	—
8008	4/1/72	200 KHz	8 bits	3,500	16 Kbytes	—
8080	4/1/74	2 MHz	8 bits	6,000	64 Kbytes	—
8086	6/8/78	10 MHz	16 bits	29,000	1 MB	—
8088	6/1/79	8 MHz	8 bits	29,000	1 MB	—
80286	2/1/82	12.5 MHz	16 bits	134,000	16 MB	1 GB
386 DX	6/17/85	33 MHz	32 bits	275,000	4 GB	64 terabytes
386 SX	6/16/88	33 MHz	16 bits	275,000	16 MB	64 terabytes
486 DX	4/10/89	50 MHz	32 bits	1.2 million	4 GB	64 terabytes
486 SX	4/22/91	33 MHz	32 bits	1.185 million	4 GB	64 terabytes
Pentium	3/22/93	66 MHz	64 bits	3.1 million	4 GB	64 terabytes
Pentium Pro	11/1/95	200 MHz	64 bits	5.5 million	64 GB	64 terabytes
Pentium II	5/7/97	300 MHz	64 bits	7.5 million	64 GB	64 terabytes

Source: Intel Corporation Intel Processor Hall of Fame, 1999.

into production every one to two years. At this pace, computing power rises at an exponential rate over short periods of time.

Until recently, Intel was a virtual monopolist in the market for microprocessors for non-Apple PCs, but two new firms, Advanced Micro Devices (AMD) and National Semiconductors (NSM), have now marketed high-quality chips priced below $1,000. These should compete with Intel for market share in the next few years. All the computer manufacturers have been quick to incorporate the newest microprocessors into their PCs. The rate of diffusion of new technology, therefore, has also been fast.

In terms of both static and dynamic efficiency, the computer hardware industry has performed well in recent years. Most importantly, new technology development and marketing are continuous, and prices based on dollars per MIPS are declining as are the prices of both mainframe and personal computers. But the performance picture is not quite as clear with regard to PC operating systems, where Microsoft has controlled the market with a system that may or may not be the most technologically advanced. Here is where public policy may have a significant role to play in the near future.

V. PUBLIC POLICY ISSUES

Antitrust Policy

IBM Antitrust policy has played an important role in the computer industry since the late 1960s. On the last day of the Johnson Administration, the Justice Department charged IBM with attempting to monopolize the general-purpose electronic digital computer market.[40] The Justice Department measured IBM's market share at approximately 75 percent, based on the lease value of the "installed-base of electronic data-processing equipment." IBM contended that its market share was only 33 percent of the correct relevant market, which it defined as *all* data processing equipment, including computers, programmable hand-held calculators, message-switching equipment, and just about any other piece of equipment imaginable.

The government charged IBM with a series of illegal actions. The complaint alleged that IBM bundled systems together by charging a single price for the central processor, related software, and maintenance. IBM was also accused of introducing new computer lines, particularly the System 360, in ways that were aimed at destroying the sales of machines

[40]For two dramatically different views of the case see Richard T. DeLamarter, *Big Blue;* and Franklin M. Fisher, John J. McGowan, and Joen E. Greenwood, *Folded, Spindled, and Mutilated: Economic Analysis and U.S.* v. *IBM* (Cambridge: MIT Press, 1983).

recently introduced by competitors. In particular, the government cited IBM's practice of announcing the introduction of a new line well in advance of its actual appearance. According to the government, there were also instances when IBM said a machine would be forthcoming even though no such machine existed or was even planned.

On January 8, 1982, the same day it announced that a consent decree had been reached to break up AT&T, the Justice Department dismissed the case against IBM. William Baxter, the assistant attorney general in charge of antitrust, decided that IBM had not committed any major violations of the antitrust laws, and that the case was "without merit." Baxter believed there was little chance of a government victory, and, given court decisions at the time, he was probably right.

One of those decisions involved a private action taken by Telex against IBM. In the late 1960s, Telex was one of many peripheral manufacturers offering IBM plug-compatible peripheral equipment at prices well below IBM's. IBM lost a significant share of the market for IBM peripheral equipment. The company responded with a series of aggressive actions, and Telex sued,[41] claiming that IBM's actions forced it to cut its prices drastically. Despite IBM's price cuts, Telex increased its volume of business between 1970 and 1972, but its profits declined substantially. The District Court ruled in favor of Telex on most issues, and awarded Telex $259.5 million in damages plus $12 million in attorney's fees. The Tenth Circuit Court of Appeals, however, overturned the District Court's decision, arguing that IBM's actions were merely "normal methods of competition."

Microsoft The first government antitrust action against Microsoft was begun by the Federal Trade Commission but concluded by the Department of Justice. This is highly unusual. The FTC staff argued that once Microsoft's basic control over operating systems was established, it continued to maintain power through a variety of illegal practices including the pre-announcement of products, exclusionary per-processor licenses for MS-DOS and Windows, unreasonably long-term licensing agreements, and restrictive nondisclosure agreements.

The FTC staff presented its case to the full Federal Trade Commission, and, in February 1993, the Commission deadlocked 2-2 over whether or not to issue a preliminary injunction against several Microsoft practices.[42] Six months later, the FTC met again and deadlocked for a second time 2-2 on the Microsoft case. This marked the end of the FTC case, but,

---

[41] *Telex Corporation* v. *International Business Machines* 367 F.Supp. 258 (1973); and *Telex Corporation* v. *International Business Machines* 510 F.2d (1975).

[42] *United States* v. *Microsoft Corporation,* No. 94-1564 (D.D.C. filed 15 July 1994). Amended versions filed with the court on 27 July 1994.

in an unprecedented action, the Department of Justice decided to pursue the FTC case against Microsoft.

The Justice Department expanded the investigation, and, on July 15, 1994, it proposed a consent decree.[43] The case then took another bizarre twist—in February of 1995, Federal Judge Sporkin *rejected* the consent decree, fearing that it would not protect the public from Microsoft's monopoly power. The Justice Department and Microsoft filed a joint appeal to Judge Sporkin's decision and the Appeals Court ruled in favor of the Justice Department and Microsoft. The consent decree was finalized.

The major points in the decree were:

1. Microsoft agreed to stop offering large discounts for CPU licenses based on the total number of CPUs shipped instead of the number of copies of MS-DOS actually shipped.
2. Microsoft agreed to end its use of long-term contracts that committed OEMs to purchasing large volumes of software in the future.
3. Microsoft agreed to end its policy of requiring nondisclosure by software developers. This ended Microsoft's practice of requiring beta testers not to disclose details of Microsoft's operating systems for three years after the systems came to market. The nondisclosure requirement had restricted the ability of programmers to move from one company to another, unless the programmer moved from another company *to* Microsoft.

The consent decree did not deal directly with a much more important economic issue—the bundling of Windows with Microsoft's Internet Explorer (IE). The Justice Department believed that the decree banned the tying of the IE browser to Windows and complained to the court that Microsoft was in contempt. On December 11, 1997, the District Court entered a preliminary injunction banning the tying of the Internet Explorer to Windows.[44] Microsoft filed an appeal of this injunction, and, on May 12, 1998, the Court of Appeals granted a stay of the injunction. Six days later, on May 18, 1998, the Justice Department filed a formal antitrust action charging Microsoft with attempting to monopolize the market in Internet browsers by tying the Internet Explorer to Windows.

The trial received great national attention, especially when Bill Gates testified by video deposition. Much of his testimony consisted of the government's attorneys showing Gates e-mail messages that he had either sent or received, with Gates indicating that he had no recollection of the messages.

---

[43]Ibid.

[44]See *United States* v. *Microsoft Corporation,* No. 98-1232 (D.D.C. filed 18 May 1998).

Among the more interesting evidence was a series of 150 e-mails provided by Netscape showing how Microsoft attempted to force users to use Microsoft's IE instead of Netscape's Navigator.[45] For example, in a June 13, 1996, message, a Netscape employee reported that Microsoft had offered a Dutch Internet service provider free browsing software and a $400,000 marketing fund. "This was extended on the understanding that [the service provider] would NOT purchase any s/w [software] from Netscape." In another message, an Internet service company tells a Netscape employee that "we have ceased distribution of Netscape. Your product is excellent but totally lacking in marketing support and we could never justify the $20 setup cost when Microsoft will fly a blimp with our name on it for free." A June 10, 1996, message to Netscape from Kurt Brecheisen, president of a company called Global Telecom, said: "Microsoft gave me a deal I couldn't refuse. Free dialer, browser, developer kit, freely distributable, etc. I know Netscape is better, but $0 vs $18K is impossible to beat."

On November 5, 1999, District Judge Thomas Penfield Jackson issued his findings of fact in the case: that Microsoft was a monopolist in the market for Intel-compatible PC operating systems and that the company had used its monopoly power to restrict competition and harm consumers. Judge Jackson concluded:

> Most harmful of all is the message that Microsoft's actions have conveyed to every enterprise with the potential to innovate in the computer industry. Through its conduct toward Netscape, IBM, Compaq, Intel, and others, Microsoft has demonstrated that it will use its prodigious market power and immense profits to harm any firm that insists on pursuing initiatives that could intensify competition against one of Microsoft's core products. Microsoft's past success in hurting such companies and stifling innovation deters investment in technologies and businesses that exhibit the potential to threaten Microsoft. The ultimate result is that some innovations that would truly benefit consumers never occur for the sole reason that they do not coincide with Microsoft's self-interest.[46]

On April 13, 2000, Judge Jackson issued his final verdict, holding that Microsoft had illegally monopolized trade, put its "oppressive thumb on the scale of competitive fortune," and "trammeled the competitive process through which the computer software industry generally stimulates innovation and conduces to the optimum benefit of consumers." Microsoft vowed to appeal the decision as a tragic miscarriage of justice.

---

[45] "U.S. Releases E-Mail to Back Up Testimony," *Washington Post,* 24 October 1998, D4.

[46] *United States* v. *Microsoft Corporation,* Civil Action No. 98-1232 5 November 1999, District Court for the District of Columbia.

Copyright Protection for Software

A very important issue affecting the rate of technological advance in the computer industry is the attitude of the federal courts toward copyright protection in the software industry. Some issues are straightforward. For example, a firm cannot purchase a license for 100 copies of Microsoft Windows and then make 200 illegal copies to be placed on employees' computers.

Most issues, however, are complex. The copyright law with regard to computer software presents a dilemma for policymakers and the courts. If the courts take a tough stand against the infringement of copyrighted software, they will be further solidifying the monopoly power of software manufacturers. However, such a tough position would create an increased incentive for other firms to invent around copyrighted materials. Alternatively, the courts might liberalize the definition of "fair use" with regard to computer software and reduce the software manufacturers' short-run monopoly power. Such a policy, though, might create an environment that would be less conducive to technological change in the future because there would be less incentive to invest in new product development.

Several important cases have occurred in recent years, none watched with more interest than the battle between Lotus and Borland. Lotus 1-2-3 was the first commercially successful spreadsheet software for business accounting on PCs. When Borland developed a competing product, Quatro Pro, it admitted that it copied the basic menu commands from Lotus 1-2-3. In July 1992, the District Court ruled that Borland had infringed on Lotus' copyrights.[47] However, on March 9, 1995, the First Circuit Court of Appeals reversed.[48]

Borland's defense was based on the company's belief that the menu structure of Lotus 1-2-3 was a "system" or "method of operation," and, as such, was not protected by copyright law. The federal copyright laws, in fact, expressly state that "systems" and "methods of operation" cannot be protected. The Appeals Court ruled that the menu displays of *Lotus 1-2-3* were a "method of operation," comparing them to the buttons on a VCR, and therefore, the menu structure could not be legally copyrighted. This was the first time a federal court had taken such a broad interpretation of the "fair use" doctrine with regard to computer software.

Borland appealed the ruling to the Supreme Court and the Court agreed to hear the case. However, on January 16, 1996, the Supreme Court, by a 4-4 tie vote (Justice Stevens not participating), let stand the

---

[47] *Lotus* v. *Borland,* 788 F.Supp. 78 (D. Mass. 1992); and *Lotus* v. *Borland,* 799 F.Supp. 203 (D. Mass. 1992).

[48] *Lotus* v. *Borland,* 49 F.3d 807 (1st Cir. 1995).

First District Court's ruling.[49] The decision could create a much more open environment for the software industry.

Another important court battle took place between Apple and Microsoft over Microsoft's introduction of Windows. Apple claimed that Windows infringed on Apple's copyrights in 189 different ways. Microsoft's defense was based primarily on a 1985 licensing agreement between Apple and Microsoft. In 1992, the District Court ruled in favor of Microsoft.[50] The Judge found that of the 189 claimed infringement violations, 179 were clearly protected by the licensing agreement. Of the remaining 10 claimed violations, the Judge ruled that the ideas were not original to Apple, and therefore, could not be protected. Apple appealed this decision to the Appeals Court, but the Court affirmed the decision.[51] Apple then appealed to the Supreme Court, which denied the appeal.

VI. CONCLUSION

The performance of the computer industry will continue to be crucial to the growth of the United States economy. It will probably remain a market where giant firms and small entrepreneurs compete to be the first to develop and commercialize major new technologies. Where all of this competition will lead is impossible to predict.

Managerial risk-taking will continue to be an important means to success. By boldly undertaking risks, Thomas Watson, Jr., recognized long before others that high-technology electronics would rule the end of the twentieth century. Much like Bill Gates after him, Tom Watson, Jr., saw the future and moved to gain control of it. Thirty years later, however, IBM's management had become ossified and was unable to stay ahead of its smaller, quicker competitors. The lesson is clear: In this rapidly changing industry, only those best able to see into the future will survive in the long run.

Even today's most powerful firm, Microsoft, finds itself facing serious challenges, not only from a potentially devastating antitrust ruling, but in the marketplace as well. Given the reliance of Microsoft on Bill Gates, one has to wonder what will happen to Microsoft once Gates relinquishes control. Even as large and dominant as Microsoft has become, Gates still plays the leading role in Microsoft's strategic decisions as well as its product strategy.[52] Gates is expected to head Microsoft for the next ten years before assuming a smaller role in the company.[53] This raises additional

[49] *Lotus* v. *Borland,* 516 US 233 (1996).
[50] *Apple* v. *Microsoft,* 799 F.Supp. 1006 (N.D. Cal. 1992).
[51] *Apple* v. *Microsoft,* 35 F.3d 1435 (9th Cir. 1994).
[52] Cusumano and Selby, *Microsoft Secrets,* 418.
[53] Ibid., 419.

uncertainty about Microsoft's future. Consider, for example, that few would have predicted in the late 1970s IBM's $8.1 billion loss in 1993. Just as it would have been impossible to predict the future of IBM in the 1970s, it is impossible to predict what the future holds for Microsoft and the entire computer industry.

Suggested Reading

Belden, Thomas G., and Marva R. Belden. *The Lengthening Shadow: The Life of Thomas J. Watson,* (Boston: Little, Brown and Company, 1962).

Brock, Gerald. *The United States Computer Industry: A Study of Market Power,* (Cambridge, MA: Ballinger, 1975).

Carroll, Paul. *Big Blues: The Unmaking of IBM,* (New York: Crown Trade Paperbacks, 1994).

Cusumano, Michael A., and Richard W. Selby, *Microsoft Secrets,* (New York: Free Press, 1995).

DeLamarter, Richard T. *Big Blue: IBM's Use and Abuse of Power,* (New York: Dodd, Mead & Company, 1986).

Dorfman, Nancy. *Innovation and Market Structure: Lessons from the Computer and Semiconductor Industies,* (Cambridge, MA: Ballinger, 1987).

Feruson, Charles H., and Charles R. Morris, *Computer Wars,* (New York: Random House, 1993).

Fisher, Franklin M., John J. McGowan, and Joen E. Greenwood, *Folded, Spindled, and Mutilated: Economic Analysis and U.S.* v. *IBM,* (Cambridge: MIT Press, 1983).

Flamm, Kenneth. *Targeting the Computer: Government Support and International Competition,* (Washington DC: Brookings, 1987).

Ichbiah, Daniel, and Susan L. Knepper, *The Making of Microsoft: How Bill Gates and his Team Created the World's Most Successful Software Company,* (Rocklin, CA: Prima,1993).

Manes, Stephen, and Paul Andrews. *How Microsoft's Mogul Reinvented an Industry—and Made Himself the Richest Man in America,* (New York: Doubleday, 1993).

Pugh, Emerson W. *Building IBM: Shaping an Industry and Its Technology,* (Cambridge: MIT Press, 1995).

Sobel, Robert. *IBM* vs. *Japan: The Struggle for the Future,* (New York: Stein and Day, 1986).

Wallace, James, and Jim Erickson, *Hard Drive: Bill Gates and the Making of the Microsoft Empire,* (New York: John Wiley & Sons, 1992).

CHAPTER 7

Motion Picture Entertainment

—Barry R. Litman*

The motion picture entertainment industry will be one of the most fascinating and dynamic industries of the twenty-first century. Awash in a whirlwind of merger activity involving domestic and international communication conglomerates and intricately linked to new telecommunication and computer technologies, even now it hardly resembles that quaint, turn-of-the-century invention of Thomas Edison that would fulfill the master inventor's dream of "doing for the eye what the phonograph does for the ear." Rather, it is at the center of the information and communication revolution that has transformed modern society over the last quarter-century and will shortly bring hundreds of channels of entertainment and information into the household through a fiberoptic cable.

Indeed, the motion picture is one of America's most treasured art forms, more popular than ever, here and abroad. As an industry, it has met the test of time, enduring and adapting in the midst of continual competitive threats from new media. The major studios no longer fear new competition from any source; rather, they embrace it and use it to expand their overall business enterprise, both domestically and internationally. No longer reliant on theatrical attendance, motion pictures can be viewed by consumers through an expanding panoply of exhibition "windows," including broadcast television, cable and pay television, and the videocassette recorder. The traditional order has been completely upset as historic business relationships and lines of demarcation have become intertwined and blurred. It is now proper to refer to this broadened landscape as encompassing a motion picture "megaentertainment" industry.

To gain insight into the breathtaking developments that have transformed the industry, it is important to begin with a historical perspective. The past is, indeed, prologue to the present, since attempts to control content and exhibition windows are rooted in a hundred years of industry history.

---

*With assistance of Kuo-Feng Tseng.

I. HISTORY

Shortly after receiving his patent for the motion picture camera and its viewing machine in 1894, Edison introduced motion pictures to an unbelieving public.[1] These early peephole-viewers (kinetoscopes), with their continually rotating 50-foot strips of celluloid film, were an instantaneous success.

The arrival of the nickelodeon theater in 1905 provided the nascent industry with its first opportunity to stand on its own as an entertainment medium. Later on, one-reelers gave way to two-reelers and then to full-length feature films. Finally, the nickelodeon was replaced by first-class and then deluxe movie houses. Thus, motion pictures developed as a mass medium in a series of cycles, each with some driving force that further cultivated a mass audience with the moviegoing habit. Each new invention and quality improvement propelled the industry through a ratchet-type effect to a new, higher equilibrium.

The Search for Market Power

Concomitant with the development of motion pictures as a cultural medium was the continual attempt by a small cadre of companies to acquire monopoly power. In the early years, Edison and a few other inventors tried to dominate the market by exploiting their patents on cameras, projectors, film, and other integrated components. After a cycle of costly patent infringement suits threatened the stability of the industry, a truce was called in 1909 among the 16 key patent holders, including Edison, Biograph, Armat, and Eastman-Kodak. They created a collusive patent-pooling arrangement that was implemented through the Motion Picture Patents Company. By cornering the market on equipment and offering top-quality productions, the trust believed that it could monopolize the industry and exclude independents at all access points. The trust ran into trouble, however, when it was unable to prevent maverick exchanges and nickelodeons from dealing with independents for additional needed product. This instability was alleviated through integration into the distribution stage. The General Film subsidiary of the trust acquired almost every licensed exchange, thereby creating monopoly control over every stage of production, save exhibition, during the first few years of the industry's existence.

With the rise of feature films through independents, a new distribution organization was needed to handle this different species of film. Un-

---

[1]The sources for our discussion of the industry's history are A. R. Fulton, *Motion Picture: The Development of an Art from Silent Films to the Age of Television* (Norman: University of Oklahoma Press, 1960); and the contributions by Tino Balio, et al., in *The American Film Industry,* Tino Balio, ed., Rev. ed. (Madison: University of Wisconsin Press, 1985).

der the leadership of Adolph Zukor, the head of Famous Players, an exclusive alliance was formed in 1914 with an association of state's-rights distributors (known as Paramount) to distribute feature films. Within two years, Zukor assumed control and merged his Famous Players company with Paramount, beginning a trend toward the vertical integration of the production/distribution sectors that continues to this day.

When Paramount's terms became too expensive, the largest first-run exhibitors integrated backward into production to supply their own needs and circumvent the power of the Zukor organization. A merger race ensued as the large companies in each stage of the industry sought partners to guarantee either an assured supply of films or access at reasonable terms. By 1925, there were only a handful of giant vertically integrated firms remaining in the industry.

The arrival of sound occurred in the mid-1920s at precisely the time when something new and exciting was once again needed to stimulate movie attendance and compete with radio. During the slump of the Depression years, the industry solicited new business by appealing to more salacious themes as well as by introducing the double feature. Most important, it crafted the Code of Fair Competition under the National Industrial Recovery Act of 1933 to protect itself against the ravages of unbridled competition. The code regulated various trade practices and was administered by the Motion Picture Producers and Distributors of America, the industry's trade association. Such trade practices as block booking and blind selling, which severely disadvantaged independent theater owners, were now legally sanctioned and enforceable in a court of law.[2] Within 2 years, the National Industrial Recovery Act was declared illegal and the code was discontinued, but the industry had learned an important lesson: the beneficence of mutual cooperation. From now on, it would follow a policy of tacit collusion—a form of shared monopoly[3]—that yielded handsome rewards over the years.

The Paramount Case

During the late 1930s, the five fully integrated firms ("the majors") deliberately sought to eliminate the remaining independents. Since none of the majors individually possessed enough of the highly desirable first-run

[2]Block booking is the forced licensing of a package of feature films, tying together high- and low-quality films and offering them on an all-or-nothing basis. Blind selling is the forced licensing of a film before it is made available to the theaters for commercial preview. For more details, see Balio, ed., *The American Film Industry,* pt. III.

[3]For the export market, the Webb-Pomerene Act permitted the industry to establish an export cartel known as the Motion Picture Export Association (MPEA), which could establish common policies and negotiate on behalf of its members. The MPEA continues to dominate the world markets, even though the Webb-Pomerene Act was finally repealed over a decade ago.

theaters or produced enough A-quality feature films to be self-sufficient, they needed one another. Acting in concert, they had enough first-run theaters to provide a nationwide exhibition showcase for their films, and their combined production efforts (in association with three minor distributors) were sufficient to supply an entire year's schedule of films.[4] Achieving near 100 percent self-sufficiency severely restricted the freedom of the independent producers, distributors, and exhibitors to gain access at any one stage in the vertical chain. At the exhibition level, the Big Five collectively operated 70 percent of the all-important first-run theaters in the 92 cities with a population of 100,000 or more and 60 percent in those cities with a population of between 25,000 and 100,000.

Beginning in 1938, this pattern of vertical organization and accompanying price fixing was attacked by the Antitrust Division of the Justice Department. The ultimate outcome of the decade-long case was a court order mandating a structural solution—vertical divestiture of the exhibition level from the production/distribution level and, furthermore, requiring that those theaters illegally acquired or used as part of the conspiracy be sold off by the newly reconfigured exhibition circuits. For the most part, the divested chains of theaters could not acquire new theaters without specific court approval, and none of the affected parties could reintegrate (either forward or backward). In addition, competitive bidding was suggested (but not mandated) as a way of further ensuring that decentralization of power and open access would prevail at the exhibition level.

The Advent of Television

The motion picture industry initially ridiculed the early television programming of its new rival, comparing it with the B films of the 1940 era. Nevertheless, as TV penetration increased and Americans stayed at home rather than going to movie theaters, the industry soon understood the enormity of the situation. Its initial strategy was to boycott television by refusing to permit its creative personnel (primarily actors) to appear on television programs, produce television series, or license films for television exhibition. It also sought to counter the inroads of television by introducing a number of product innovations, including Cinerama, three-dimension movies, drive-ins, and big-budget films with lavish production values.[5]

After recognizing the revenue-generating capability of television production, though, Warner Brothers became the first major to break the

---

[4]The five majors were Twentieth-Century Fox, Loews, RKO, Paramount, and Warner Brothers. The three minor distributors were United Artists, Columbia, and Universal. None of the latter companies officially owned theaters, although United Artists had interlocking directorships with a major chain.

[5]See Balio, ed., *The American Film Industry,* "Introduction," pt. IV.

boycott in 1955 by agreeing to produce a weekly series. Shortly thereafter, the rest of the majors hitched their wagons to television's rising star rather than retain their purity in films. They also realized that the television networks (and, later, the television stations) could become subsidiary markets for licensing theatrical films once those films had played out their theatrical run. The temporal price-discrimination pattern of multiple theatrical runs that had worked so well when only theaters were involved could now accommodate the new television technology. Therefore, what had begun as a major confrontation between two entertainment media gradually evolved into a pattern of stability, mutual interdependence, and economic symbiosis.[6] This stable business relationship continues and has been extended to the newest technologies of cable, videocassettes, and fiber-optic telephone systems—all of which have been folded into the distribution price-discrimination process.

II. MARKET STRUCTURE

Because of the various subsidiary markets and the historical pattern of vertical integration, the structure of the motion picture entertainment industry is extremely complex.

Distribution

The distribution stage remains under the control of a handful of major companies, although a few names have changed since the Paramount divestiture.[7] In terms of the majors, RKO has left the scene; in 1983, MGM took over distribution for United Artists and eight years later acquired the company completely. Monogram became Allied Artists and was later purchased by Lorimar, which in turn was acquired by Warner Brothers.[8] Another independent, Embassy, was sold in 1985 to Columbia and then resold that same year to Dino DeLaurentis and was eventually reacquired by Columbia and now Sony. American International was sold to Filmways in 1979, and its name was changed to Orion in 1980. Another key player is Tri-Star. Formed in 1983 as a joint venture of Columbia, HBO, and CBS, it was purchased late in 1987 (including its theater circuit)

---

[6]Barry R. Litman, "Decision Making in the Film Industry: The Influence of the TV Market," *Journal of Communication* (Summer 1982): 33–52.

[7]For a good overall account of the various mergers, see Michael Conant, "The Decrees Reconsidered," in *The American Film Industry,* T. Balio, ed., (Madison: University of Wisconsin Press, 1985) chap. 20; Thomas Guback, "The Theatrical Film," in *Who Owns the Media? Concentration of Ownership in the Mass Communications Industry,* Benjamin Compaine, ed., 2nd ed. (White Plains, NY: Knowledge Industries, 1982), chap. 5; and end-of-year roundups in *Variety,* annual editions, January, various years.

[8]*Multichannel News,* 16 May 1988, p. 1, and June 20, 1988, p. 40.

by Columbia, folded into the new Columbia Entertainment Division, and sold to Sony.[9] Finally, the latent Disney studio was reorganized in the mid-1980s, shed its exclusive family orientation, and established itself as an industry leader.

The market shares of the leading distributors are given in Table 7-1. The familiar majors still collectively account for three-fourths of the total industry, even though their stranglehold on industry power has slipped somewhat over the last decade[10] owing to the entry of significant newcomers such as Tri-Star and the intensified competition provided by Disney, Orion, and independents such as Cannon and New Line. The four-firm concentration level increased from 59 percent in 1990 to 66 percent in 1998, while the eight-firm concentration is consistently over 90 percent for the past few years. (The Herfindahl-Hirschman Index rose correspondingly from 1264 in 1990 to 1532 in 1997 and then fell back to 1348 in 1998.) These numbers still indicate considerable oligopoly power remaining in this sector of the industry. Interestingly, market shares and industry leadership seem very volatile, often influenced by having one or two box office smashes in any given year.

Barriers to Entry

It is not surprising that the distribution level is highly concentrated. This is a characteristic common to all the mass media and is due to economies of scale that accompany the national distribution of the entertainment product. To service the 34,000 North American movie screens and exploit the foreign market potential, a distributor must have a vast worldwide network of offices. Furthermore, if the other subsidiary markets are to be efficiently tapped, additional bureaucratic layers must be created. Focusing on the domestic distribution of motion pictures, a major company needs 20 to 30 regional offices and a sizable sales and marketing force. It also needs a steady stream of features released throughout the year so that these offices can work at full capacity.

Although some critics argue that ownership of studios and back lots is an albatross around the necks of the major distributors (because it drives up overhead costs), there still may be some strategic advantage that accrues to those so situated, especially during a production boom. There also must be a corresponding level of demand to justify such a large enterprise and to use the capacity most efficiently. Here is where product ideas, differentiation, and managerial skill play such an important role. The studio must consistently make correct decisions concerning the

---

[9] *Variety,* 15 January 1988.

[10] The aggregate market share of the Big Six Paramount majors and minors fell from 89 percent in 1982 to 77 percent in 1992.

TABLE 7-1 Market Shares for North American Film Distributors,[1] 1990–1998

Company	1998 %	1997 %	1996 %	1995 %	1994 %	1993 %	1992 %	1991 %	1990 %
Disney	21	21	25	23	24	17	19	14	16
Paramount	16	12	13	10	14	10	10	12	15
Warner Brothers	18	17	16	17	16	19	20	14	13
Sony	11	20	11	13	9	18	19	20	14
Twentieth-Century Fox	11	10	13	8	9	11	14	11	14
Universal	7	10	8	13	13	14	11	11	14
New Line[2]	—	—	5	6	7	4	2	4	4
MGM-UA	6	3	5	6	3	2	1	2	3
Miramax[3]	—	—	—	—	—	3	1	1	1
Others	10	7	4	4	5	2	5	11	6
Total	100	100	100	100	100	100	100	100	100
CR4	66	70	67	66	67	68	72	60	59
CR8	90	90	96	96	92	96	94	88	93
H-H	1348	1532	1470	1408	1442	1408	1544	1199	1264
Instability[4]		24	30	20	16	36	19	26	24

[1]Market Shares = percentage of annual film rentals to distributors.
[2]Merged with Warner Brothers in 1997.
[3]Merged with Disney in 1994.
[4]Instability = $\Sigma S_t - S_{t-1}$.
Source: Variety; annual editions.

composition of its product. Unlike a modern industrial enterprise, in which automobiles are turned out in large quantities over long manufacturing runs, each film is handcrafted, with a very short product life and only occasional opportunities for reusing the creative inputs. The successful studio requires a continual stream of new ideas.

Given the escalating production and advertising costs of recent years, the average release by a major distributor runs more than $35 million plus at least half that amount to give it a national day-and-date launch. Understanding these economic risks and the fact that they have a portfolio of such projects at different stages in the 2-year cycle, the major distributors and their corporate parents tend to act rather conservatively, seeking to minimize their financial risks by searching for a formula such as that of their television counterparts. This formula may take the form of employing bankable movie stars, top directors, and writers who at some point have touched the magic of a box office smash, or else spreading the risk through co-production with foreign investors.[11] Alternatively, they may repeat ideas, themes, or characters that worked well in the past, thus generating the ever-present sequel.[12]

Vertical Integration and Conglomeration

Part of the risk can also be lessened if distributors have vertical integration or deep corporate pockets. Even though the Paramount decrees forbade reintegration between the distribution and exhibition levels, as time has passed, the original companies have been resold or absorbed into larger conglomerate corporations. Furthermore, entry has occurred at both levels, introducing new companies that are not covered by the original decrees. Most important, new subsidiary exhibition markets have opened up, reducing the fears of an earlier era, and the antitrust-tolerant Department of Justice has not opposed reintegration by the original Paramount defendants.

There currently exists a significant degree of forward integration by the leading distributors into theatrical exhibition. The advantages of vertical integration are numerous—greater distributor control over admission prices, release patterns, and the avoidance of anti-blind-bidding statutes. This permits all the box office dollars to remain with the distributor rather than sharing them with exhibitors.

---

[11]Gorham Kindem, "Hollywood's Movie Star System: A Historical Overview," in *The American Movie Industry: The Business of Motion Pictures,* Gorham Kindem, ed., (Carbondale: Southern Illinois University Press, 1982), chap. 4.

[12]Thomas Simonet, "Conglomerate and Content Remakes, Sequels and Series in the New Hollywood," in *Current Research in Film: Audiences, Economics and Law,* Bruce A. Austin ed., (Norwood, NJ: Ablex, 1987), vol. 3, chap. 10.

The biggest players have been MCA (Universal) and Paramount; Disney, Fox, and MGM-UA have diversified into other sectors. In 1986, MCA acquired a 50 percent interest in Cineplex-Odeon, the second-largest theater circuit in North America. Similarly, Paramount has roughly 470 domestic and 433 Canadian theaters, making it a large North American circuit. It also is a partner with MCA in the 76-screen circuit in Europe, known as Cinema International Corporation.[13] In late 1987, Columbia Entertainment acquired Tri-Star, including its circuit of 310 theaters (the former Loews circuit). In early 1988, the Loews' subsidiary acquired the USA circuit, adding another 317 screens to Columbia's holdings. Meanwhile, Cannon, which had a 525-screen circuit in Europe, bought the domestic Commonwealth circuit in 1986, with its 432 screens.

Most interesting is the position of one of the top five industry leaders, United Artists Theater Circuit. It has aggressively sought merger partners and embraced new theater construction programs, and at one point was controlled by Tele-Communications, Inc. (TCI), the dominant multiple-system cable television operator. Given this strong position across multiple exhibition windows and with vertical integration into the distribution arena through such cable networks as Turner Broadcasting Systems (CNN, WTBS, TNT), Black Entertainment Network, and American Movie Classics, we may be witnessing a vertical chain of control never dreamed of by the Paramount conspirators. TCI's blockbuster $48 billion merger with AT&T in 1999 suggests even greater size across many different communication technologies and services.

In terms of conglomeration, the major motion picture companies are subsidiaries of large communication corporations or other conglomerates. As these major distributors rely on the resources of their parents for production loans or capital expansion, this further enhances the barriers to entry and widens the historic gap between the majors and independents.

Table 7-2 gives a brief synopsis of each parent company and the percentage of its 1998 revenues that came from filmed entertainment. Columbia, Disney, Universal, Twentieth-Century Fox, and Warner Brothers are subsidiaries of very large corporate giants and consequently account for a rather small percentage of the parent company's operations. These parents have their businesses based in either electronic equipment (Sony) or other mass media or entertainment properties (Time Warner, News Corporation, Viacom, and Walt Disney). Smaller production companies, such as Carolco, Savoy, or Orion, have no significant family ties and hence have low diversification percentages. These may be termed pure motion picture companies.

---

[13]Thomas Guback, "The Evolution of the Motion Picture Theater Business in the 1980s," *Journal of Communications* (Spring 1987): 60–77.

TABLE 7-2 1998 Diversification Ratios for Selected Film Distributors

	*(A) Total Corporate Revenues**	*(B) Total Communication Revenues**	*(C) = B/A Communication Total (%)*	*(D) Filmed Entertainment Revenues*	*(E) = D/A Diversification (%)*
Sony (Columbia + Tri-Star)	61.48	10.83	17.6	4.50	7.3
Walt Disney (Disney-Buena Vista)	22.98	17.44	75.9	10.30	44.8
Viacom (Paramount)	12.10	12.10	100.0	8.65	71.5
News Corporation (Twentieth-Century Fox)	18.95	18.12	95.6	5.90	31.1
Time Warner (Warner Brothers)	26.83	26.83	100.0	12.10	45.1
Seagram (Universal)	6.40	5.40	84.4	3.90	60.9
MGM-UA	0.83	0.83	100.0	0.83	100.0
Carolco	0.054	0.054	100.0	0.054	100.0
Savoy	0.023	0.023	100.0	0.023	100.0
Orion	0.011	0.011	100.0	0.11	100.0

*Revenues are stated in billions of dollars.

Source: Calculation from various company 1998 annual reports.

Exhibition

The days of the stand-alone theater owner or other media enterprise are fast diminishing. Chain ownership yields efficiencies in spreading managerial (such as motion picture booking) and legal expertise, as well as advertising and marketing costs, across a large number of outlets; yet it has the potential for raising entry barriers and enhancing market power.

The indices given in Table 7-3 indicate only a moderate degree of national concentration in theater ownership, but the recent trend is definitely on the rise.[14] Since 1990, the four-firm concentration index has increased by 5 points while the eight-firm index has risen by 12 points. The current industry leaders—Regal, Loews, Carmike, and American Multi-Cinema (AMC)—have more than doubled their theater holdings over the last few years. Regal has risen to first by merging with Act III and by adding over 1,500 screens, while Loews leaped over long-time industry leaders Carmike and AMC by merging with Cineplex-Odeon. It should be noted that the expansion of circuit size is not limited to the acquisition route: nearly 11,000 new screens have also been built. Interestingly, the theater circuits originally divested by Paramount have been absorbed by other equally large circuits.

Nonetheless, it would be wrong to examine only national concentration, because movie theaters are local retail outlets. In local markets, the trend toward concentration of ownership repeats itself with a rotation of leadership among the top national chains and the occasional appearance of a smaller regional chain. In most localities, therefore, the consumer is faced with a handful of oligopolists.

New Developments

Between 1985 and 1991, five of the seven Hollywood majors either were acquisition targets or were involved in mergers, signaling the beginning of a new conglomerate firm era for Hollywood. These changes included News Corporation buying Twentieth-Century Fox, Sony acquiring Columbia, Time and Warner Brothers merging, Pathe buying MGM/UA, Viacom acquiring Paramount, and Matsushita acquiring MCA. All were predicated on the belief that to survive in the new global media environment, companies must become large and take advantage of the potential for hardware/software efficiencies and synergies between in-house units. Such efficiencies include the ability to produce and distribute major motion pictures through all the new video windows that new technology is creating. After these initial consolidations, only Disney remained as an unattached major, and is acquisition-minded itself. The only

[14]Regrettably, the number of screens rather than box office admissions is the only available measure of assessing market shares.

TABLE 7-3 Market Concentration of Top Ten U.S. Theater Circuits, 1998–1990

Circuit	*1998* # *Screens (%)*	*1997* # *Screens (%)*	*1995* # *Screens (%)*	*1994* # *Screens (%)*	*1993* # *Screens (%)*	*1990* # *Screens (%)*
Regal[1]	3672 (11)	2393 (8)	861 (3)	454 (2)	—	—
Loews[2]	2764 (8)	917 (3)	946 (3)	904 (3)	885 (3)	837 (4)
Carmike	2750 (8)	2721 (9)	2037 (7)	1735 (7)	1570 (6)	813 (3)
AMC	2644 (8)	2406 (8)	1632 (6)	1603 (6)	1628 (6)	1649 (7)
United Artists	2210 (7)	2191 (7)	2295 (8)	2237 (8)	2310 (9)	2699 (11)
Cineplex Odeon	—	1710 (5)	1056 (4)	1055 (4)	1039 (4)	1365 (6)
Cinemark	2180 (6)	1652 (5)	1224 (4)	1149 (4)	1059 (4)	645 (3)
General Cinema	1288 (4)	1170 (4)	1202 (4)	1268 (5)	1355 (5)	1444 (6)
National Amusements	1063 (3)	978 (3)	870 (3)	840 (3)	780 (3)	625 (3)
Act III	—	836 (3)	575 (2)	568 (2)	544 (2)	486 (2)
Total						
(Indoor & Drive-in)	34,168	31,865	27,843	26,689	25,626	23,814
CR4	34.6%	30.5%	25.8%	25.6%	26.8%	30.1%
CR8	54.4%	47.8%	40.4%	40.4%	41.5%	42.3%
H-H	<1000	<1000	<500	<500	<1000	<1000

[1]Regal Cinemas on May 27, 1998, was purchased by investment firms Hicks, Muse, Tate & Furst and Kohlberg Kravis Roverts & Co. The chain was merged with the KKR-owned Act III circuit.

[2]Loews Theatres Exhibition Group and Cineplex Odeon on May 14, 1998, announced that they had completed a merger of the two companies to form Loews Cineplex Entertainment Corp.

Source: Data from *Encyclopedia of Exhibition,* annual editions; company annual reports.

other alternative was to build a major Hollywood studio from scratch, a path followed by Penta (Italy) and Polygram (Netherlands).

On a parallel path, media firms began to realize that no one firm had all the financial and technological resources to fully exploit a media environment consisting of digital compression, computers, and interactive services. With such uncertainty and huge capital risks involved, a mind-set developed that it was better to engage in joint ventures and alliances with other firms than to shoulder the whole risk and cost alone.

Both trends—globalization through the acquisition of Hollywood studios and entrance into the media technologies of the future through alliances and joint ventures—continue. Examples include Bell Atlantic's attempted buyout of TCI (and indirectly QVC's attempt to acquire Paramount), the recent Viacom-Paramount-CBS network merger, Turner's acquisition of Castle Rock and New Line and its subsequent integration into Time Warner, and Disney's buyout of Miramax and Capital Cities/ABC network. Warner Brothers and Paramount established fifth and sixth television networks.

The most recent interesting development was the effort by Bell Atlantic to take over TCI. The significance of the transaction for the motion picture industry is that both are leading "exhibition" firms in their respective industries. In a deal valued at $26 billion, Bell Atlantic would have obtained access to 42 percent of American homes and the capability of developing a superhighway for informational and entertainment digital services. Among the purported rationales for the merger were the potential economies of scale in digital technologies and the synergies that may come from marrying the fiber optics, programming, and interactive expertise of TCI with the switching and computer technology of Bell Atlantic.[15] The development of these superhighways to the home would offer revolutionary new approaches to consuming motion pictures, no longer confined to the theater setting; they would create almost an instant supermarket for consumer choice.

A second key development is the recent merger of Viacom and Paramount. Viacom, valued at $8 billion, and Paramount, valued at $10 billion, came under the control of the former, making the new entity a conglomerate giant on a par with Time Warner. This vertical merger brings together Paramount's movie and television studios with Viacom's cable networks (for example, MTV and Showtime), local television stations, and cable systems. In addition, Viacom's presence in overseas markets (MTV is strong in Europe and Latin America) will create additional distribution outlets for Paramount products. Thus, there is a strong programming/distribution fit in the merger that will give Viacom an assured

[15]Geraldine Fabrikant, "$23 Billion Media Acquisition Reported to Be Near Completion," *New York Times,* 13 October 1993, p. A1.

flow of programming to accompany its move into interactive media, in association with AT&T and Sony.[16] In September 1999, Viacom struck the biggest media deal yet by agreeing to pay $36 billion in stock for CBS. The mammoth merger, the latest in a series of deals that are transforming the face of entertainment, broadcasting, and communications, will turn Viacom into an $80 billion power with assets in broadcast and cable TV, movies, radio, theme parks, Internet sites, home video, publishing, and billboards. Its name brands will include CBS, UPN, Paramount Pictures, MTV, Nickelodeon, Blockbuster, and Simon & Schuster.[17]

Finally, in January 2000, America Online (AOL) and Time Warner disclosed plans to combine in a record-shattering $165 billion merger which, if permitted by the antitrust agencies, will vastly extend Time Warner's grasp on the Internet as perhaps a new, vast "pipeline" for video distribution and exhibition.

In fact, the long run raises the specter of the pre-Paramount days, especially if several telephone-cable-film-broadcast giants are formed in the next few years: Although no single company would be strong enough individually to monopolize the mass media industries, it could do so in concert with others and realize the benefits of cooperation and reciprocity. There could evolve a system of arrangements with the power to regiment or control competition at virtually all access points in the media industry. Such a scenario necessitates a watchful eye by government regulators as they monitor for potential antitrust violations.

Finally, this possibility of monopoly further heightens the importance of the Hollywood studios. Each of these new distribution channels will need programming, and those media conglomerates that have established some measure of control over film production and distribution will find themselves in a better long-run competitive position than those that have not. As long as this remains true, Hollywood will continue to remain at the epicenter of the new global media environment.

Only weeks before the Viacom-Paramount announcement, Ted Turner made another foray into Hollywood. Previously, Turner had acquired the rights to the MGM film library by buying the studio and then selling it back without the film library. With a vast library of film classics in hand, TNT was created, which was followed by the later acquisition of the Hanna Barbara cartoon library and the founding of the Cartoon channel. In his most recent Hollywood dealings, Turner acquired the rights to 300 Paramount films to use as the backbone of his new Turner Classic Movies (TCM) channel. Not content with film libraries, Turner Broadcasting has now taken the plunge into Hollywood studio ownership

---

[16]"Viacom-Paramount Merger in Works," *Broadcasting and Cable,* 13 September 1993, 10.
[17]"David Lieberman, "CBS to join Viacom: empire Deal would create new $80 billion giant" *USA Today,* 8 September 1999.

by acquiring New Line Cinema and Castle Rock Entertainment, moderately successful independent production companies. Such purchases should put Turner Broadcasting in a better position to ensure a steady flow of theatrical products and stabilize its future.[18]

Until recently, only Disney remained as an unacquired Hollywood major. Disney's expansion plans (beyond film-related growth such as EuroDisney) involved Miramax, a successful independent film producer. This acquisition gives Disney a larger presence in film production, creating a fourth movie label to go with Walt Disney Pictures, Touchstone, and Hollywood Pictures. In addition to the merger of production, on July 31, 1995, Disney purchased Capital Cities/ABC for $18.5 billion. With the acquisition of the ABC network and stations, Disney created what may become the model for vertically integrated media companies—able not only to produce shows but also to deliver them all the way to America's living rooms. Disney was enticed by the endless promotional and marketing opportunities, heralded by the company as an innovative way to save money and get more Disney-owned shows on ABC's prime-time schedule. The economic benefits of the Disney-ABC merger, however, have been disappointing, with infighting between the two sides frequent. Disney's version of "synergy" since acquiring Capital Cities/ABC in February 1996 appears to have little more depth than the facades along Disneyland's "Main Street USA." Disney's wave of cross-promotions with ABC have had little effect. The entertainment giant has so far failed to pull off an effective melding of these two immense firms.[19]

These developments in the mass media industries are a sign of increased competition across multiple venues, at least in the short run, until positions of dominance can be established. At the same time, however, the competitive viability of unaffiliated, nonintegrated independents may once again be in jeopardy.

III. CONDUCT

The process of product pricing and revenue sharing has changed very little since the Paramount restructuring. At the exhibition level, theaters will either bid for upcoming features or individually negotiate the contract. The Paramount decrees suggested that motion pictures be contracted for

---

[18]Rich Brown, "Turner Signs Paramount Titles for $30m," *Broadcasting and Cable,* 16 August 1993, 12; and "Kudos for Turner's Hollywood Deals," *Broadcasting and Cable,* 23 August 1993, 17.

[19]"The Week of Mega-Deals," *Broadcasting and Cable,* 8 July 1996; Bruce Orwall and Kyle Pope, "Relativity: Disney, ABC Promised 'Synergy' in Merger; So, What Happened?" *Wall Street Journal,* 16 May 1997; Bruce Orwall and Kyle Pope, "Merger of Disney's Production Studio With ABC TV Network Sparks Unrest," *Wall Street Journal,* 25 August 1999.

picture-by-picture at the local rather than the chain level so that all theaters have an equal competitive opportunity to bid. The contract generally has standard provisions with respect to admission prices, beginning date, length of run, minimum guarantee, dollar advance, terms for extended runs and early cancellation, and, most critical, rental terms. "Rental terms" refer to the percentage split of box office dollars between the exhibitor and the distributor. The industry standard is a 90-10 split in favor of the distributor after the house expenses are deducted. This small profit margin for theater owners demonstrates the bargaining power of the distributors in relation to the exhibitors.

Price Discrimination

With the arrival of television and other subsidiary markets, the theatrical tiering system of runs and clearances was replaced by the sequencing of exhibition "windows." Both systems represent forms of second-degree price discrimination: charging different prices to classes of customers who place different utility valuations on the product. With motion pictures, these groups cluster according to the time dimension. Avid moviegoers who absolutely must be the first to see newly released films are willing to pay the highest price per ticket.[20] Those willing to wait until the second theatrical run or until the movies appear in the video stores or on cable pay lower prices, and those with even less interest may wait several years until the film's appearance on network or local television or on video at the library.

Formulating the optimal time sequencing of exhibition windows maximizes profits for those distributors who have obtained rights across all these windows, provided that everyone follows the same pattern and there is no significant leakage or resale between the windows.

Exhibition Conduct

The process of downsizing theater size and building multiple-screen auditoriums illustrates a different profit-maximization approach by the theater owners. This permits a more cost-efficient utilization of seat capacity than was possible in the old single-auditorium theaters. With six to eight screens or more per site, a theater owner can manage a portfolio of different pictures with confidence that at least one or two of the screens will have a hit and that the others will do moderate business until their run is

[20]David Waterman, "Prerecorded Home Video and the Distribution of Theatrical Feature Films," in *Video Media Competition Regulation, Economics and Technology,* Eli Noam, ed., (New York: Columbia University Press, 1985), chap. 7. If the movie theaters were to vary their prices according to how long the film had been at the particular location, a certain group would undoubtedly pay premium prices to see certain highly publicized movies their first night or opening week.

over. In this way, average load factors can be increased, in contrast with the hit-and-miss strategy associated with having a single screen.

The multiple-screen concept is also tied to the shopping-mall phenomenon.[21] The movie theater complex is an integral part of the modern shopping mall, since it generates a lot of foot traffic for other store owners. If one looked only at theaters in isolation, given the stagnant demand for admissions due to the VCR and pay-cable alternatives, one could not explain the addition of 500 to 1,000 new screens per year. Theater construction can be justified only as part of the profit-maximizing calculus of building a successful shopping mall.

The theater concession stand also fits into this traffic-flow analysis and multiple-screen concept. Because the theater retains 100 percent of all concession revenues (which have an extremely high markup) yet makes only about 10 percent profits from box office gross, any strategy that maintains a high load factor can be very profitable.

The theaters can further minimize their excess seat capacity by negotiating escape clauses in their contracts that permit shortened runs for unpopular films and lengthened runs, additional screens, and move-overs (to a larger auditorium) for films that prove unexpectedly popular. Although theaters seldom charge differential prices based on the perceived quality or popularity of the individual film, they do practice discounting for off-peak time periods (such as matinees, twilight, and, occasionally, certain weekdays) and for customers with elastic demands (such as children and senior citizens). Once again, this brings more customers into the theaters and sells more popcorn.

The Television Network Market

The major movie distributors have maintained an extraordinary presence in the market for regularly scheduled prime-time programs, collectively averaging in excess of 40 percent of regular series since the mid-1960s. The networks themselves produce a small but now increasing percentage of their programming needs, concentrating primarily on news, sports, soap operas, and specials rather than entertainment series.[22] Prime-time series are also produced by independent production houses, many of whom have market shares comparable to those of the major studios. The majors have no economic advantage in this programming area because of a well-developed rental market for inputs, minimal economies of scale, and easy entry.[23]

---

[21]This section draws heavily on Guback, "Evolution of the Motion Picture Theater Business in the 1980s."

[22]Until the judicial review is complete, the networks are still prohibited by the FCC's Financial Interest and Syndication Rules from coventuring prime-time programs with outside sources, and they are barred under consent decrees from producing themselves more than two-and-one-half hours of prime-time programming per week.

[23]Bruce Owen, Jack H. Beebe, and Willard G. Manning, *Television Economics* (Lexington, MA: Lexington Books, 1974), chap. 2.

Given such competitive conditions, the program supply industry has been unable to countervail the coordinated buying power of the Big Three networks. The networks understand that their bargaining advantage is greatest in the initial developmental stages, when the quality of the scripts and pilots is unknown and the future success of the programs is uncertain. At this stage, venture capital is scarce because of the financial risk. Once a show becomes a hit, its true value is known, and it can command a high price on the open market.

Motion pictures, by contrast, represent a different species of network programming because of prior knowledge about their value in the theatrical market, and each movie is a uniquely crafted entity. The known quality of the movies reduces the risk to the networks and enables the movie companies to demand prices reflecting the marginal worth of their pictures.

The movie majors initially received high and increasing prices for their films. Prices for theatrical movies have always been two to three times higher (per hour) than the prices of regularly scheduled programs of comparable quality. To countervail the studios' bargaining power in this market and stabilize licensing prices, the networks took a number of steps. In the mid-1960s, they began commissioning made-for-television movies that were a substitute for theatrical movies and could be produced at significant cost savings. Second, ABC and CBS entered directly into motion picture production. This vertical integration into production resulted in some 80 theatrical movies between 1967 and 1971 and 40 to 50 percent of their annual requirements of made-for-television movies. Private and public antitrust litigation ensued.[24] Distributors charged that the television networks were violating the Paramount decrees, since they had set up a fully integrated market chain through network distribution, ownership, and affiliation with broadcast exhibition outlets and now production of theatrical movies. The case ended with a consent decree that basically ratified the FCC's rules and limited the networks' ability to produce in-house television series. (Paradoxically, the decrees did not forbid the networks from producing movies or from broadcasting them on their own network after the theatrical run.[25])

The Pay-Television Market

The development of the pay-television market filled a void created by the scarcity of space in the electromagnetic spectrum that limited the number

---

[24] *Columbia Pictures* v. *ABC and CBS,* U.S. District Court, Southern District of New York,1972; *U.S.* v. *CBS, NBC, and ABC,* U.S. District Court, Central District of California, 1974.

[25] For more details about these decrees see FCC Network Inquiry Special Staff, An Analysis of Television Program Production, Acquisition and Distribution (Washington, D.C.: U.S. Government Printing Office, 1980), chap. 8.

of available very high frequency (VHF) stations in any local market. Given the powerful economic incentive to share programming expenses through networking, and the necessity for networks to have local affiliates to transmit their programs, there was room for only three national TV networks. With only three network signals and the incentive to maximize ratings by seeking the lowest common denominator of programming, many program forms were not used, even though public broadcasting sought to bridge the cultural programming gap.

Proponents of pay TV argued that direct consumer payment would make programming more sensitive to viewers' preferences than would the advertiser-supported system of "free television."[26] With the development of cable television during the 1960s, a collection mechanism was now in place for excluding free riders—the basic market failure problem associated with over-the-air broadcasting.

After the broadcast interests lobbied to forbid pay TV from gaining a foothold, the issue was resolved with a series of FCC rules that permitted pay TV to exist but restricted its programming to those types that were not available from commercial broadcasting (for example, recent theatrical movies that had not yet appeared on network television). In 1972, Home Box Office initiated a pay-cable program service consisting of recent uncut, uninterrupted movies, Las Vegas night club acts, and special sporting events. This channel of programming was sold on a monthly subscription basis to those areas already wired for cable. Yet, its nationwide expansion would not come until a new cost-effective satellite-to-dish transmission system replaced microwave and until the U.S. Court of Appeals, in 1977, declared null and void all programming limitations imposed by the FCC on pay-cable networks. This provided a lift for pay-cable networks, since they could now become full competitors to the three commercial networks. (Cable television now penetrates more than two-thirds of all U.S. households.)

Such movie-driven premium networks as the Movie Channel and Showtime joined HBO, the industry leader, to exploit this new market.[27] In recent years, other specialty networks have entered, differentiating their product in other dimensions (for example, Disney, Playboy, and American Film Classics) rather than offering a full range of motion pictures and entertainment specials.

Ironically, in these pre-VCR days, consumers appeared willing to subscribe to several redundant networks to gain more viewing flexibility, and

---

[26]This section is based largely on Barry R. Litman and Suzannah Eun. "The Emerging Oligopoly of Pay TV in the USA," *Telecommunication Policy,* June 1981, 121–135.

[27]A corollary market of advertiser-supported cable networks, such as USA, ESPN, CNN, MTV, and several superstations, emerged and was packaged together by local cable systems and sold as "basic" cable service. The premium channels just mentioned have always been sold separately.

soon most cable systems began offering multiple networks. For example, HBO set up a second service, Cinemax, to try to capture the extra business, but the genie could not be put back in the bottle, and competition through differentiation became the new reality. At first the networks continued licensing box office hits on a nonexclusive basis and licensed exclusively the less successful movies (sports and specials) and all-time classics. By 1981, exclusive rights were obtained for all movies (just as the commercial TV networks had done). Throughout this period, HBO/Cinemax collectively dominated this market, with a combined market share of nearly 60 percent, over twice that of Showtime. HBO used its monopsony power to reduce the license prices to the motion picture distributors, paying on a flat rental, take-it-or-leave-it basis rather than the customary per-subscriber method. Nevertheless, this represented additional revenue for the motion picture distributors.

Various attempts by the major motion picture studios to establish their own distribution networks for this important subsidiary market, and thereby circumvent HBO, did not withstand antitrust scrutiny or were short-lived in nature. Nevertheless, HBO had learned an important lesson: Lacking an assured source of films, it was vulnerable to such an "end around." It thus decided to become vertically integrated through ownership and long-term contracts to avoid future problems. It established a production subsidiary called Silver Screens, joined CBS and Columbia in launching a new mini-major company called Tri-Star, and signed long-term exclusive contracts for the full line of theatrical films of Columbia, Orion, and CBS.

To counteract this move, in 1983, the owners of Showtime and the Movie Channel (numbers two and three, respectively) in conjunction with Warner Brothers, Universal, and Paramount, announced a new joint venture. Even though the principals claimed that these networks would continue to be run separately, the Justice Department believed otherwise.[28] Upon the withdrawal of the major distributors, Showtime and the Movie Channel were permitted to merge. The premium pay-cable industry would now be restructured as a duopoly under the control of subsidiaries of Time Warner (HBO) and Viacom (Showtime and The Movie Channel).

Although some large studios have not signed long-term agreements and prefer to negotiate cable rights picture by picture, a significant share of the supply industry has been committed to a form of vertical tying arrangement that severely limits the ability of a potential pay-cable distributor from obtaining hit movies to compete with HBO or Showtime.

---

[28]Lawrence White, "Antitrust and Video Markets: The Merger of Showtime and the Movie Channel," in *Video Media Competition,* E. Noam, ed. chap. 11.

The Videocassette Market

Of even greater importance to the motion picture industry than cable has been the videocassette revolution of the past decade. VCR penetration, at nearly 90 percent, now exceeds cable penetration by nearly 20 percent and has surpassed the theatrical box office in revenues generated.[29] It soon may be considered the main reason for a universal service, on a par with telephones and over-the-air broadcasting. The popularity of the VCR is its versatility; it permits viewers to time-shift programming; it allows playback of family home video photography; and, finally, it allows consumers to access, through purchase or lease, a wide array of prerecorded videocassettes.

Unlike the television and cable markets, the major studios act as VCR distributors themselves rather than relying on specialized distributors. In fact, VCR distribution is very much like that of magazines, paperback books, and records, with retail establishments acting as the point of sale to consumers. The market shares for VCR distributors are similar to those given in Table 7-1. It is clear that the major studio distributors have transplanted their power into this market, although their dominance in VCR software is much smaller than in the traditional theatrical market.[30] The VCR market is consequently a substantial source of revenue for the motion picture distributors and has moved toward the front of the line of exhibition windows. There is a constant potential threat of pay-per-view services displacing VCRs in the windowing process, but this has not yet materialized.

The International Market

Historically, the second most important exhibition window has been the international market, an aggregation of some 80 or more trading partners of the United States. As far back as World War I, American film distributors have dominated this world market for film, later extended to television and most recently to videocassettes.[31] In fact, American control has been so pervasive that charges of media imperialism have frequently been leveled.

The reason for this dominance rests primarily on the enormous size and strength of the American market compared with those of other countries (see Table 7-4). American producer-distributors can recoup a

---

[29]Ibid.

[30]If one defined the market narrowly as theatrical videos, their control would be approximately equal to that of the theatrical movie market. However, just as movies on television must compete with other entertainment and information programming, so must videocassette recordings.

[31]This section draws heavily on Guback, "Hollywood's International Market," in *The American Film Industry,* Balio, ed., chap. 17.

TABLE 7-4 The Major Export Markets for Major U.S. Distributors (Theatrical Film Rentals to Members of the MPEA, $ Millions)

Country	*1998*	*1996*	*1994*	*1992*	*1990*
Japan	377	270	242	165	237
Germany	335	310	264	162	175
U.K./Ireland	246	168	155	127	144
France	236	187	182	141	164
Canada[1]	—	147	127	130	148
Spain	176	164	130	123	110
Italy	160	135	99	65	117
Australia	128	153	105	67	70
Brazil	121	86	53	23	48
Mexico	84	53	—	40	23
Taiwan	73	80	50	22	27
Top 4 Markets (%)	44.2%	43.3%	47.4%	41.5%	43.9%
Top 8 Markets (%)	65.9%	71.2%	73.3%	68.1%	70.6%
Total Exports	2,700	2,150	1,780	1,440	1,650
United States only	3,000	2,750	2,320	2,000	1,626
Total World	5,700	4,900	4,100	3,440	3,276
Domestic (%)	52.6%	56.1%	56.5%	58.1%	49.6%

[1] The 1998 theatrical film rental of Canada was included in United States.

Sources: Compiled from *Variety,* 28 June 1993, 11; *Hollywood Reporter,* 25 November 1997, and 26 August 1999. Revenues are film rentals from theatrical release, not the box office revenues from which the rentals were paid as exhibitor license fees. These rentals include theatrical license fees from films released in all or some areas by the MPEA members, including films that were released only in certain export areas. Furthermore, these rental figures include some modest revenues from foreign sales of advertising-publicity accessories for the promotion of the feature.

greater percentage of their production costs from the domestic market alone, and, given that the greatest expense is the first-copy production cost, distribution prices to foreign lands need cover only the incremental expenses. This pricing practice is often mislabeled as "dumping." Since prices are based mainly on the strength of a country's demand, the richer and more populous countries pay higher prices for the same video product. For example, a theatrical movie currently distributed in France would yield $30,000 to $150,000 in rentals; $60,000 to $200,000 in Japan; and only $3,500 to $7,000 in Norway or Denmark.[32]

The major American distributors also have bolstered their economic advantage by developing far-flung distribution networks throughout the world, including significant ownership of foreign theaters!

[32] *Variety,* 7 October 1991, M-84.

The protectionist response of foreign countries to American dominance has been the erection of trade barriers, including import quotas, tariffs, strict licensing procedures, limitations on the percentage of screen time for imported films (and TV programs), and measures preventing local currencies from leaving the country. In addition, foreign governments have encouraged indigenous producers through subsidies, prizes, tax breaks, or loans at favorable (or zero) interest rates.

In general, one should expect that the foreign markets for U.S. films will increase in importance in the foreseeable future, owing to developments such as "Europe 1992," the opening of Central and Eastern Europe, cataclysmic changes in the former Soviet Union, the international multiplexing phenomenon, and an increased scrutiny of piracy in Asia.

IV. PERFORMANCE

If an industry has a concentrated market structure, tries to coordinate pricing behavior, and has significant barriers to entry and an inelastic demand, the end result should be high prices for the consumer and excess profits for the companies. But, according to a study by Veronis and Suhler that separated motion picture entertainment from the other product lines, the average operating-income margin (on sales) for 41 companies from 1990 to 1994 was 9.16 percent, and the cash-flow margin was 12.18 percent. For the 420 companies occupying all 10 communication industry segments, the corresponding margins were 13.44 percent and 20.44 percent, respectively.[33]

It seems that the motion picture distributors have not been able to exert as significant a degree of market control in their own industry segment as have some other communication distribution companies; yet, compared with a broader grouping of leisure and service companies throughout the economy, they have done relatively well. This internal failure is undoubtedly due to the vast degree of differentiation accompanying the motion picture product, the unpredictability of consumer tastes, and the instability of market shares from one year to the next. This is compounded by the fact that industry leadership rotates among the top firms and that market shares are more evenly dispersed than in other industries with comparable concentration ratios. It may also reflect the fact that there is now a plethora of different media through which consumers can obtain their entertainment.

What about the impact of this market structure on the public? One way to answer this question is to examine inflationary trends in motion picture

[33]Veronis, Suhler, and Associates, *Ninth Annual Communications Industry Report* (New York: Veronis, Suhler, and Associates, 1994). Another good source for financial information is Harold L. Vogel, *Entertainment Industry Economics: A Guide for Financial Analysis* (Cambridge: Cambridge University Press, 1998), especially chaps. 2–4.

admission prices compared with other products and services in the economy at large. Using 1982–1984 as a common base period, movie admission prices rose by just over 50 percent during the 1980s and 1990s; the CPI category of entertainment products and services climbed by 60 percent for the same period; while the category of "all goods and services" climbed by 63.0 percent. Hence, admission price inflation has risen at roughly the same rate as these other categories. The evidence is consistent with the profitability data and implies that the full force of the concentrated market structure is not inflicting cruel and unusual pain on consumer pocketbooks.

Diversity

Because the motion picture industry produces cultural products, a critical question is whether concentration of control adversely affects product diversity for the American people. Various studies of other mass media all have reached the same conclusion: Without the spur of competition, oligopoly firms with diversified parents tend to lead a quiet, imitative, unimaginative life rather than engage in costly product experimentation and new ideas.

The incentive for the studios may be to stress the bottom line rather than worry about the impact of motion pictures as an art or cultural form. This would lead the studios on a constant search for formulaic content that reduces risks for a motion picture as it winds through all the subsidiary markets. This might mean a reliance on sequels that have a built-in recognition factor or extravagant spectacles with universal themes and international stars who appeal to international audiences. In either case, the end result is the homogenization of content. In recent studies, Dominick, Litman and Kohl, and Sochay documented the strong correlation between the concentration of control and the lack of content diversity.[34]

V. PUBLIC POLICY

For a century, vertical market power has perennially occupied the center stage of public policy in the video entertainment field. As each new technology and distribution channel for movie fare has appeared on the scene (broadcast television, cable and pay TV, direct satellite broadcasting), concerns about vertical integration and vertical market power have soon followed.[35]

[34]Joseph Dominick, "Film Economics and Film Content: 1964–83," in *Current Research in Film,* ed. Bruce Austin, chap. 9; Barry R. Litman and Linda Kohl, "Predicting Financial Success of Motion Pictures: The 80s Experience," *Journal of Media Economics,* (Fall 1989): 35–50; and Scott Sochay, "Predicting the Performance of Motion Pictures," unpublished paper, Michigan State University, 1993.

[35]Generally, see Walter Adams and James W. Brock, "Vertical Integration, Monopoly Power, and Antitrust Policy: A Case Study of Video Entertainment," *Wayne Law Review,* 36 (1989), 51–92.

We have seen how the Antitrust Division and the courts attacked the vertical integration of the major movie firms in the Paramount cases a half-century ago. This massive antitrust battle was launched in the 1930s, fought all the way up to the Supreme Court and back, and finally culminated in the late-1950s with court orders requiring the majors to divest their vast theater operations.

In the 1960s, 1970s and 1980s, following the advent of television as a new major medium, antitrust action shifted to this field. By vertically integrating into the production of their own TV fare, it was charged, the three major broadcast organizations were leveraging their dominance of broadcasting into the production field and foreclosing motion picture companies from competing to supply broadcast programming. The motion picture industry had never complained in the past about the networks' production of their own television programs because the networks did so little of it, limiting themselves to news, sports, daytime, late night, and only a few prime-time series. In fact, the major movie companies supplied the majority of prime-time entertainment programming, although they complained they had to suffer production deficits for the initial work-run. What triggered their complaints this time, however, was the entry of CBS and ABC into feature-film production as a means of reducing the license prices paid for network broadcast of studio feature films, and also the increasing use of made-for-television movies as a substitute for theatrical films. The studios saw these actions as a means for shrinking the market for television exhibition of feature films and reducing access if the networks favored their own theatrical product over that of the studios.

In response to these complaints, the Federal Communications Commission (which regulates broadcasting) promulgated its "Financial Interest and Syndication Rules" in the early 1970s, in order to remove the networks from active participation in the syndication industry and prevent them from obtaining equity consideration (profit shares) in the programming they obtained from independent suppliers. To solidify these vertical proscriptions, the Justice Department filed parallel antitrust suits against ABC, CBS and NBC challenging these same practices—antitrust actions that were contested throughout the 1970s, and, finally, were settled by 1980 in "consent decrees" agreed to among the networks, the Antitrust Division, and the courts.

However, the FCC's "fin-syn" rules were repealed in 1995, and, in conjunction with the expiration of the consent decrees, the broadcast network in-house production units began producing an increasing proportion of network programs as part of their desire for greater self-sufficiency. There are now powerful incentives for networks to increase their own production of content: By adopting such an integration strategy, networks can rein in program costs and utilize their existing distribution outlets as "launch pads" for their own content to be sold in aftermarkets.

The revenues from sales of these other broadcast rights should be sufficient to induce networks to produce more programs—or to take a financial interest in more of the programs carried on their networks. On the other hand, their need for theatrical movie product has significantly diminished as new exhibition windows such as VCR, pay-per-view, and pay cable have become the primary outlets by which viewers watch movies on television.[36]

During the industry-friendly Reagan and Bush administrations of the 1990s, the old Paramount decrees were also abandoned, leading to the return of studio-owned theaters. However, in February 1999, the Justice Department once again began investigating the issue of whether the massive vertical reintegration campaign conducted by the majors in acquiring theaters was undermining competition at the exhibition level. Two issues once more were preeminent among the Antitrust Division's concerns: The first is the practice of "block booking," in which studios force theater chains to take other movies, often less popular, in order to get the rights to show a very popular one. The second is the practice of "clearances" that give a theater exclusive rights to a film in a particular area.[37] At the same time, the FCC and a number of congressional committees have become increasingly attuned to potential antitrust problems posed by the increasing vertical integration of the nation's largest cable operators into programming and production, as well as by immense corporate consolidations combining vertical operations across all the major media channels of distribution (such as the Time-Warner-AOL, Disney-ABC, and Viacom-Paramount-CBS mergers). Once again, charges are being levelled that these new media-motion picture giants are exploiting their vertical power to subvert competition within and across the industry's major stages.

Clearly, vertical integration and vertical market power remain a pivotal concern for public policy in this field. Whether resurgent scrutiny by antitrust agencies, regulatory commissions, and congressional oversight committees will induce firms to curb their vertical leverage rather than suffer a new round of costly antitrust litigation remains to be seen.

VI. CONCLUSION

The American people's love affair with motion pictures has lasted for a century. Although production budgets have skyrocketed since the days of the one-reelers, and the space-age and computer technologies have opened

[36]B. R. Litman, *The Motion Picture Mega-Industry* (New York: Allyn & Bacon Publishers, 1998), 68–69.

[37]"U.S. Starts Inquiry on Movie Distribution," *New York Times,* 9 February 1999.

up many new points of competitive access, the motion picture industry remains a cherished institution on the American landscape, as venerable as the automobile. The basic structure of this industry was forged in the 1920s and continues largely intact except for the growth of subsidiary markets to replace the traditional system of theatrical runs. The concentration of market power, which had its roots in economies of scale and a vertically interlocking, self-sufficient system of arrangements, was decimated by the Paramount consent decrees but has regrouped and refocused at the distribution stage. Throughout all of the technological innovations, the resilience and adaptive capability of the industry have been truly remarkable. As distributors and circuits seek new merger partners and form strategic alliances with hardware and other diversified conglomerates under the more laissez-faire attitude of the antitrust authorities, the historic dangers of expanding market control may resurface and even take on global proportions. In this regard, most dangerous and hence most important is the kind of multimedia acquisition strategy of companies such as AT&T/TCI and Time-Warner-AOL which seek dominance of multiple exhibition markets. Constant antitrust vigilance is required lest the type of vertical market control—originally confined to the motion picture industry alone—spreads across the entire entertainment landscape, extinguishing the competitive fires that have brought so many benefits to consumers in recent years.

Finally, in the coming information superhighway age, with the progress of new communication technologies, digitized movies will be transmitted through high-speed, fiber-optic networks or satellite directly to movie theaters. Customers may be more satisfied by pay-per-view or video-on-demand services showing on their high-definition television sets. Animated and computer-aided technology will be used more often in most movies to create "reality." The future global high-speed Internet network will generate movie audiences without the space and time boundary. All exhibitors, distributors, and producers of motion pictures must reconsider their competitive strategies to survive in the new digital millennium.

Suggested Readings

Books

Balio, T., ed. *The American Film Industry,* 1st and 2d eds., (Madison: University of Wisconsin Press, 1976, 1985).

Compaine, B. M. *Who Owns the Media? Concentration of Ownership in the Mass Communications Industry,* 2d ed., (White Plains, NY: Knowledge Industries, 1982).

Fulton, A. R. *Motion Pictures: The Development of an Art from Silent Films to the Age of Television,* (Norman: University of Oklahoma Press, 1960).

Gregory, M. *Making Films Your Business,* (New York: Schocken Books, 1979).

Guback, T. *The International Film Industry: Western Europe and American Since 1945,* (Bloomington: Indiana University Press, 1969).

Hampton, B. *History of the American Film Industry from Its Beginnings to 1931,* (New York: Dover, 1970).

Kindem, G., ed. *The American Movie Industry: The Business of Motion Pictures,* (Carbondale: Southern Illinois University Press, 1985).

Litman, B. R. *The Motion Picture Mega-Industry,* (New York: Allyn & Bacon Publishers, 1998).

Noam, E., ed. *Video Media Competition,* (New York: Columbia University Press, 1985).

Vogel, H. L. *Entertainment Industry Economics: A Guide for Financial Analysis,* 4th ed., (Cambridge, England: Cambridge University Press, 1998).

Wildman, S. S. *International Trade in Films and Television Programs,* (Cambridge, MA: Ballinger, 1988).

Articles

Crandall, R. W. "The Post-War Performance of the Motion Picture Industry," *Antitrust Bulletin,* (Spring 1975).

Gomery, D. "The Contemporary American Movie Business." In *Media Economics Theory and Practice,* edited by A. Allison, et al., (Hillsdale, IL: Erlbaum, 1993).

Helliman, H., and M. Soramaki. "Economlc Concentration of the Videocassette Industry: A Cultural Comparison." *Journal of Communication,* (Summer 1985).

Litman, B. R. "Decision Making in Film Industry: The Influence of the TV Market." *Journal of Communication,* (Summer 1982).

———. "The Economics of the Television Market for Theatrical Movies." *Journal of Communication,* (Autumn 1979).

———, and S. Eun. "The Emerging Oligopoly of Pay TV in the USA." *Telecommunication Policy,* (June 1981).

CHAPTER 8

Airlines

—William G. Shepherd[1]

The airline industry offers a dramatic story about deregulation and its complicated aftermath. The struggle to free U.S. airlines from government controls was waged between 1977 and 1978 over huge stakes, with complicated ramifications, and controversial consequences that are still playing out.

For 40 years, a handful of airlines dominated the industry, under benign supervision by the Civil Aeronautics Board (CAB). During 1978 to 1983, however, the CAB was abolished, thereby liberating the carriers and exposing them to tough competition.[2] Three phases followed: turbulent competition during 1978 to 1983, a restoration of market power during 1984 to 1988, and increasing pockets of more potent monopoly during the 1990s.

Airline deregulation has been hotly debated from the start. Its advocates praise deregulation as a brilliant success, yielding lower prices and a freer, more efficient industry.[3] Others are less impressed or are highly critical, pointing to a rise in many indicators of monopoly power and numerous areas in which passenger service has deteriorated.[4]

In the 1990s, market power actually seemed to rise further in several venues: higher airline concentration, sharp ticket-pricing tactics, and high

---

[1]I am indebted to James W. Brock, who co-authored this chapter in the previous edition of this book. The chapter also draws on his "Industry Update—Airlines," *Review of Industrial Organization* 16 (February 2000).

[2]The actual abolition of the CAB was led by Alfred E. Kahn, a brilliant, witty economics professor from Cornell University. President Jimmy Carter appointed him to head the Civil Aeronautics Board for the purpose of eliminating it.

[3]Including Steven A. Morrison and Clifford Winston, *The Evolution of the Airline Industry* (Washington, D.C.: Brookings Institution, 1995); John R. Meyer and Clint V. Oster, *Deregulation and the Future of Intercity Passenger Travel* (Cambridge: MIT Press, 1987); and Elizabeth E. Bailey, David R. Graham, and Daniel P. Kaplan, *Deregulating the Airlines* (Cambridge: MIT Press, 1985);

See also Alfred E. Kahn, "Surprises of Airline Deregulation" *American Economic Review* (May 1988): 316–22; and Kahn, "Airline Deregulation—A Mixed Bag but a Clear Success Nevertheless" *Transportation Law Journal* 16 (1988): 229–52.

[4]See, for example, James W. Brock, "Industry Update: Airlines" *Review of Industrial Organization,* 16 (February 2000). The business press also contains many critical articles, some of them cited in this chapter. They point out in detail the monopoly impacts of many airline actions.

airline profit rates. And service quality has eroded to yield long lines of passengers, crowded aircraft, and frequent flight delays. The glamour of being a "jet-setter" has vanished for many passengers.

I. HISTORY

Self-powered human flight began with the Wright brothers' first demonstration on the beach at Kitty Hawk, North Carolina, in 1903. After a decade of fitful progress, World War I brought rapid advances and growing practical uses. The U.S. air transport industry featured mainly a lot of derring-do up to about 1925, led by death-defying barnstormers and loop-the-loop entertainers. The U.S. government began sponsoring air mail postal service in the 1920s, however, and that opened the door to air passenger service in the 1930s.

By 1938, the industry had vigorous competition among a dozen leading airlines, some national, some regional. Price cutting was often sharp, and the airlines complained that competition was "excessive," "unstable," "cut-throat," and "destructive." They lobbied intensively for the creation of a regulatory body, both to solidify their own positions and to block out new competitors. The new CAB froze the industry's structure, with the leading carriers holding favored positions on city-pair routes throughout the country. Some 90 percent of these routes, with 60 percent of all air passenger travel, were essentially monopolies. Most of the important routes had just two or three airlines, competing moderately rather than intensely.

The CAB barred the entry of new airlines almost completely over the 1940–1960 period, despite massive growth in traffic, ample profits, and changing conditions as the industry developed. Thus protected, the major carriers functioned much like a market-rigging cartel, usually agreeing on fare rises and then submitting them to the CAB for approval and enforcement. On the whole, the CAB did not apply ceilings to fares to protect customers. Instead it placed floors under fares in order to minimize price competition.

By the 1960s, as new jet-powered aircraft flooded into the industry and made competition much more tempting, the CAB was still blocking out new competition from virtually all of the hundreds of city-pair routes throughout the United States. And the CAB's handling of airline fares remained hostile to competitive price cutting. The urge for rivalry was artificially channeled into nonprice directions, such as airplane decor, youthful female cabin attendants, sumptuous meals, and a high frequency of flights. The result was too many planes in the air, typically only half full; they were often stacked up and delayed trying to take off or land. Attractive meals were served, but ticket prices were much higher. Economists developed a research consensus that costs were raised by as much as 50 percent.[5] The CAB had prevented the flexible, competitive pricing and route adjustments that would have expanded the market to the populace at lower prices.

The CAB's policies were increasingly recognized to be unwise and economically indefensible. Its policies stirred resentment among possible new competitors, while high profits enticed them to try to enter the industry somehow. By the early 1970s, strong pressures were beginning to favor abolishing the airlines' shelter for their lucrative, privileged positions.

The case for deregulating the industry reached sufficient "political mass" by the 1970s. Bolstered by economic studies showing that CAB regulation prevented competition, caused inefficiency, and raised air fares by some 50 percent, airline deregulation's appeal began to reach across the political spectrum. By 1975, both free-market Republicans and consumer-oriented Democrats supported deregulation and its promise to reduce airfares, improve consumer choice, enhance efficiency and productivity, and "get government out of the marketplace."

The CAB's chairman Alfred E. Kahn, along with member Elizabeth E. Bailey, began removing regulatory restrictions during 1977, even before the Airline Deregulation Act was passed in 1978.[6] The Act provided for completely free entry by 1980 and free pricing by 1983, though the CAB moved immediately to allow freer pricing. The incumbent carriers quickly began adjusting their routes, while a number of regional airlines (US Air, Piedmont, Delta) vigorously expanded and merged toward nationwide operations.

More than 60 new, maverick carriers entered the industry by 1983—including People Express, Southwest, New York Air, and World Airways—cutting fares by 20 to 40 percent and offering "few-frills" service. Airfares started to drop.

These changes triggered sharp debate. With the spread of hub airports and airline mergers, there was still much monopoly, despite intensive price discounting. Was deregulation really beneficial, or was it just an exposure of customers—now unprotected by government regulation—to serious exploitation?

The new competition soon encountered trouble. The largest airlines developed "hub-and-spoke" patterns after 1978 in order to organize their flight patterns. Many long, direct flights were replaced by two-part trips: first to the hub airport, next to a change of planes, and then out to

---

[5]The study by Theodore Keeler was especially complete and accurate in estimating the enhancement of costs.

[6]Both Kahn and Bailey have published later, favorable views about how well deregulation has worked. See Kahn, "Surprises of Airline Deregulation," *American Economic Review* (May 1988), 316–22; and "Airline Deregulation—A Mixed Bag but a Clear Success Nevertheless" *Transportation Law Journal,* 16 (1988): 229–52. And see Elizabeth E. Bailey, David R. Graham, and Daniel P. Kaplan, *Deregulating the Airlines,* (Cambridge: MIT Press, 1985).

the destination. This hub system yielded some efficiency, but it was not so easy for passengers. It also allowed more control by the major airlines. The larger airports quickly became dominated by just one or two of the old, entrenched carriers.

To "rationalize" the turbulent discount pricing, American Airlines installed in 1984 a rigid, comprehensive structure for fare discounts. It limited discounts to trips over Saturday night, required advance booking, disallowed changes in plans, and prohibited refunds. All the major carriers adopted this set of rules, and discounting became tightly structured.

The industry's two new major computer-reservation systems (CRSs)—created by American Airlines and United Airlines after 1978—raised efficiency. But they also developed quickly into powerful systems for applying price discrimination. Those two airlines also brazenly exploited their CRSs so as to channel passengers their way.[7] Though that biasing of sales caused severe complaints, the bias was not fully reduced until about 1990, and traces of it still linger.

From 1985 to 1988, the leading airlines also made a series of blockbuster mergers, which raised concentration even higher than it had been before 1978. The mergers intensified dominance at fortress hubs. Officials at the Department of Transportation allowed them despite opposition by antitrust agencies and intense public condemnation.

The 1990s brought new entry by a number of small carriers, along with vigorous expansion by Southwest Airlines from its regional base into eastern markets. But Southwest concentrated on leisure-travel passengers at secondary airports. It did not challenge the leaders for business passengers at major hub airports. So it and the new small competitors mostly were confined to the fringes of the main markets.

The major airlines have fought back against the entrants with fare cuts, which sometimes have forced the newcomers to surrender. These retaliations have drawn severe criticism for being "predatory," and some antitrust lawsuits and official actions have followed.

II. STRUCTURE OF THE INDUSTRY AND ITS MARKETS

The deregulation theory was straightforward: New airlines would crowd in quickly, erode the leaders' dominance, and create fluid competition among swarms of competitors. Most markets would have many rivals. Even if some markets had few rivals or just one, the threat of entry would keep those airlines from raising prices.

---

[7]The airlines' own flights were placed at the top on the travel agents' computer screens, ahead of other airlines' flights. That tilted the agents' choices to favor those first-listed flights.

Lively entry and competition did prevail for a few years during the brief "Golden Era" of deregulation. But then concentration returned by 1988, and the current monopoly patchwork became firmly set. To understand this troublesome mix of competition and monopoly, we first define the nature of airline markets and consider their structure.

Defining the Markets

An economic market is a zone of consumer choice, containing closely substitutable goods.[8] Rather than sharp, bright lines, the edges of most markets are shaded and blurred. Every market has two main dimensions: the product types and the geographic area.

The Product Dimension The literature agrees that airline transportation is a distinct product type: At distances over 150 miles, it is so much faster than automobile, bus or train travel that there is no close substitute for it. Therefore, the great majority of air travel is a distinct market. For shorter trips, however, there is more similarity in speed and cost among the alternative modes of travel.

There also are some significant differences between full-size jet aircraft and small commuter aircraft. The small planes are usually much wobblier, louder, slower, lacking in food, and less comfortable. For many travelers, the small craft are not closely substitutable; many passengers would pay significantly more to be on the larger planes. Economically, this suggests that small aircraft may operate in distinctly different economic markets.

The Geographic Dimension The geographic edges of airline markets are more complicated. Each pair of cities can be a distinct market; there is usually no reasonable substitute for getting exactly from your starting place to your destination. Yet many parallel city-pair routes overlap, partly or totally. For example, the New-York-to-Denver route is overlapped by the New-York-to-Chicago-to-Denver route, and by New-York-to-Pittsburgh-to-Denver, New-York-to-St.Louis-to-Denver, and even by the New-York-to-Atlanta-to-Denver route. Though physically different in their layouts, these routes may be close economic substitutes in their service (getting from New York to Denver) and in price. In general, some of the flights between big cities afford a choice among routes, but most of the small-volume, city-pair routes do not (for example, Chicago-to-Des Moines, Iowa, and Denver-to-Billings, Montana). And the major hub airports themselves are often regarded as forming meaningful local markets

---

[8]Standard methods of defining markets are discussed in William G. Shepherd, *The Economics of Industrial Organization,* 4th ed. (Upper Saddle River, NJ: Prentice-Hall, 1997); and F. M. Scherer and David Ross, *Industrial Market Structure and Economic Performance,* 3d ed. (Boston: Houghton Mifflin, 1991).

of their own. The airlines that dominate those hubs control access along their spoke routes, which radiate out of the hub airports.

So the economics of defining markets in this industry are intriguing: Many markets are shaded and blurred, but many city-pairs are quite distinct markets. And many hub cities are seen as meaningful markets or as the cores of regional air-travel markets.

Concentration

Deregulation first caused a drop in concentration, both industry-wide and on individual city-pair routes. Not only did dozens of new airlines enter, but the leading carriers also moved freely into routes that previously had been served by only one or two airlines.

But in 1985 the largest airlines engaged in a binge of mergers, with little resistance from the Department of Transportation (DOT), which now had jurisdiction. Some "end-to-end" mergers did not reduce competition directly; they merely combined airlines from different regions. But several other mergers did directly eliminate competition from scores of markets by uniting large, overlapping airlines.

The "abysmal dereliction" of DOT officials in permitting these mergers, as Kahn called it, harmed deregulation by raising concentration even higher than before 1978. The largest eight airlines' shares of passenger traffic rose sharply, as shown in Figure 8-1, from 73 percent in 1986 to 92 percent in 1988. That was a 10 percent rise from 1978 to 1988, and now there was no public regulation to protect consumers.[9] Because of the DOT's failure to stop anticompetitive mergers, Congress took away its merger jurisdiction and gave it to the Antitrust Division of the Justice Department. But the Justice Department too has not been strict toward airline mergers.

Many regional feeder airlines existed before 1978 or were formed between 1978 and 1985. But they, too, were soon absorbed or tied as ancillaries to the big airlines. In short, deregulation's Golden Era of 1978 to 1984 was followed by a period of careless, laissez-faire policy during 1984 to 1988. The old airlines were permitted to nullify much of the beneficial initial effects of deregulation.

American, United, and Delta emerged as the "big three" in size and financial strength, as Table 8-1 indicates. Northwest and US Airways have been moderately strong.[10] Continental and TWA, on the other hand, have suffered through bankruptcy.

---

[9]See also A. S. Leahy, "Concentration in the U.S. Airline Industry," *International Journal of Transportation Economics,* 21 (June 1994), 209–15.

[10]But Northwest Airlines was harmed by a takeover in the early 1990s that led to unwise cutbacks in staffing, operating efficiency, and service quality. See Michelle Conlin, "Northworst," *Forbes,* 30 November 1998, 105.

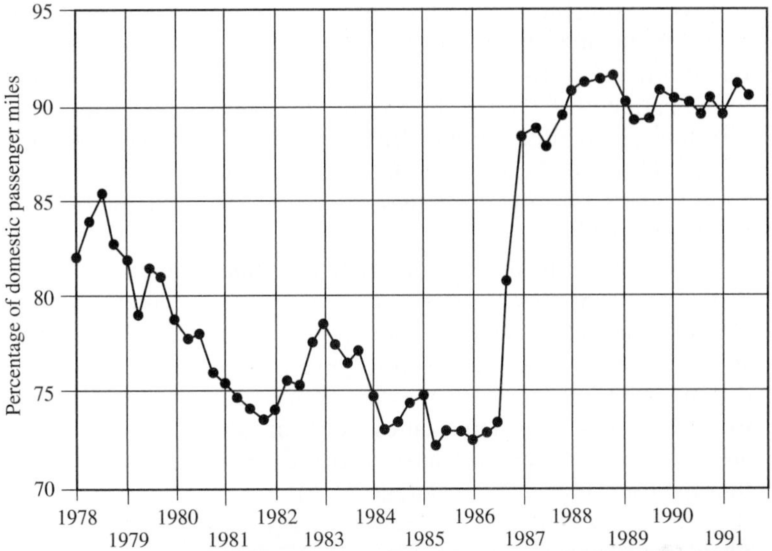

FIGURE 8-1 Percentage of U.S. Air Passenger Miles Controlled by the Eight Largest Carriers

Source: Steven A. Morrison and Clifford Winston, *The Evolution of the Airline Industry* (Washington D.C.: Brookings Institution, 1994).

TABLE 8-1 Leading Airlines in the United States, 1997

	Passenger Revenue		
	Amount ($ billion)	***Share (%)***	***Aircraft***
United Air Lines	$15.1	19.0	571
American Airlines	$14.3	18.0	641
Delta	$12.8	16.1	559
Northwest	$8.7	10.9	405
US Airways	$7.1	8.0	376
Continental	$5.7	7.2	388
Southwest	$3.6	4.5	261
Trans World	$2.9	3.6	184
America West	$1.8	2.3	103
Alaska	$1.3	1.6	78
Industry Total	$79.5	100.0	
Largest 4		64.0	
Largest 6		79.2	

Source: Air Transport Association, *Annual Report,* 1998.

As a result, the average level of concentration in city-pair routes rose substantially after 1986. The average number of "effective competitors" on all routes had risen before 1986, but it decreased from 2.5 in 1986 to just 2.2 after 1993. On the short routes (below 500 miles), the number of effective competitors shrank from 2.0 to just 1.6 after 1995. On long routes (over 2,000 miles), the numbers declined over the same period from 3.5 to 3.4.[11] In general, these numbers have remained low in more recent years.

The decline in competition occurred despite the efforts of independents such as Southwest and other new carriers to enter markets in the 1990s. The newcomers did obtain 12 percent of all U.S. passenger miles by 1996; Southwest alone had almost 5 percent. Though the shares of the independents rose after 1986, they have been fragile, subject to reversal in total, as well as on certain, routes. Many of the entrants are confined to lesser routes between middle-sized cities, which are less profitable than the best routes between the largest cities.

Hub Dominance

Single-carrier dominance at major airports has been high for 15 years and may still be increasing rather than receding.[12] Table 8-2 shows the leading examples of high market shares.

TABLE 8-2 Leading Instances of Hub Dominance, 1998

Airport	*Primary Airline*	*Share of Seats*
Cincinnati	Delta	90.8%
Pittsburgh	US Airways	87.6
Minneapolis-St. Paul	Northwest	82.0
Houston	Continental	79.3
Detroit	Northwest	78.4
Atlanta	Delta	77.9
Denver	United	72.4
Dallas-Ft. Worth	American	69.5
Newark	Continental	55.8

Source: Laurence Zuckerman, "Firing on Fortress Northwest," *New York Times,* 25 August 1999, C1, C17.

[11]See for example Steven A. Morrison, "Airline Service: The Evolution of Competition Since Deregulation," in Larry L. Deutsch, ed., *Industry Studies,* 2d ed. (Armonk, NY: M. E. Sharpe, 1998).

[12]See Alfred E. Kahn, "The Competitive Consequences of Hub Dominance: A Case Study," *Review of Industrial Organization,* 8 (August 1993): 381–406.

The same kinds of fortress hubs are common in big European airports too, thanks to the longstanding role of state-owned monopoly airlines. And they have the same monopoly implications: "The sad truth is that, despite deregulation and the growth of low-cost carriers in Europe on many important routes, travelers still do not have a lot of options because European airports are running out of room."[13]

Alliances among Airlines

Airline alliances began in the 1960s, as commuter carriers adopted the codes of major airlines so as to enlarge their listings and ticketing opportunities. This has spread as commuter carriers typically share the colors, insignia, and names of their parent carriers.

Alliances really are semimergers, which give marketing and operating advantages but also add more market power. By 1998, they had expanded to include proposed alliances even among the six biggest airlines, as Table 8-3 shows. Alliances have also intensified the role of hub dominance. The airlines claim that code-sharing alliances—which involve the sharing of flights, planning, and other resources—will provide better efficiency, but those gains might be minor compared to the suppression of competition.

Some antitrust-agency resistance to alliances has recently emerged, setting some limits on existing and new alliances but not removing them.

Alliances are international as well, linking many of the world's largest airlines, as Table 8-4 shows. These global groupings reduce the possibilities of foreign airline competition in U.S. markets by linking important foreign carriers (which might otherwise invade U.S. markets) with the dominant American lines.

TABLE 8-3 Proposed Alliances among Leading U.S. Airlines Announced in 1998

Alliance	*Combined Share of U.S. Passenger Revenues*
Delta/United	35.1%
American/US Airways	26.0%
Northwest/Continental	18.1%
Total	79.2%

Source: Table 1.

[13]See for example Janet Guyon, "British Airways Takes a Flier," *Fortune* magazine, 27 September 1999, 220.

TABLE 8-4 U.S. Airlines' Participation in Global Airline Alliances, 1999

American Airlines:	
"Oneworld" Alliance	British Airways, Cathay Pacific, Qantas Airways, Canadian Airlines
Other Partners	Alitalia, British Midland, Gulf Air, LOT (Poland), Singapore, South African Airways
Proposed Other Partners	Aerolineas Argentina, Air Liberte, Asiana (South Korea), Avianca (Columbia), China Airlines (Taiwan), El Al, Iberia, LanChile, Philippine Air, TACA International (the six Central American countries), TAM Lineas Aereas del Mercosur.
United Airlines:	
"Star" Alliance	Air Canada, Lufthansa, SAS
Code Sharing Partners	Thai International, Varig (Brazil)
Delta Air Lines:	
"Atlantic Excellence" Alliance	Air France, Austrian Airlines, Sabena, Swissair
Code Sharing Partners	Aer Lingus, Aeromexico, Air Jamaica, Finnair, Korean Air, Malev, TAP Air Portugal, Transbrasil
Northwest Airlines and Continental Airlines:	
Alliances and Code-Sharing Partners	KLM, Air U.K., Alitalia, Eurowings (Germany), Pacific Aviation
Proposed Partners	Air China, Garuda (Indonesia), JAS (Japan)

Source: Adapted from James W. Brock, "Industry Update—Airlines," *Review of Industrial Organization,* 16 (February 2000), Table 5; and Daniel Michaels, "British Midland Tries to Make Its 'Slots' Count," *Wall Street Journal,* 30 September 1999, A21.

The leading grouping has been the 1997 "Oneworld" alliance, which unites American Airlines and British Airways (BA), Cathay Pacific Airways of Hong Kong, Qantas Airways of Australia and Canadian Airlines, plus Finnair (Finland) and Iberia (Spain).[14] U.S. officials offered little response to Oneworld at first, but when European Union (EU) officials objected and threatened to block it, U.S. officials finally took steps to deny

[14]"Announced in June, 1996, the deal set off alarms because the airlines would control almost 60% of the U.S.-Britain market." David Leonhardt and William Echikson, "Taking a Whack at Airline Alliances," *Business Week,* 16 March 1998, 106D-106G. That was one purpose of the alliance: to increase the two airlines' control on such major routes.

antitrust immunity (a denial that continues).[15] Other airlines have criticized the AA-BA alliance strongly, because they are "frozen out of the key Heathrow hub."[16] In 1999, BA temporarily suspended its role in the alliance because EU regulators insisted that BA give up more than 300 take-off and landing slots at Heathrow and Gatwick, the two London airports.

Next biggest is the Star alliance (formed in May 1997) which includes United, Lufthansa, Air Canada, Scandinavian Airlines, Thai Airways, Ansett Australia and Air New Zealand. All Nippon Airways of Japan joined in 1999, with plans for Mexicana and Singapore Airlines in 2000. A third major alliance is Delta Air Lines, Austrian Airlines, Sabena, Swissair and Air France, which is also in the process of adding AeroMexico.[17]

The anticompetitive potential is clear: "Global airline alliances are seen as strategic weapons to boost traffic and market share, just as hub airports emerged as strategic weapons for airlines in the 1980s."[18] Indeed, since 1992, "Major carriers have synchronized schedules, combined frequent-flier programs, and promised seamless service between hundreds of cities around the globe—all without investing in planes or hubs. The result: hundreds of millions of dollars of extra profit each year."[19]

Entry Conditions

It would be extremely procompetitive if entry by new airlines into air-travel markets were easy and quick. If it were, the fear of that new competition might keep monopoly airlines from raising fares, and high concentration would be irrelevant, at least in theory.

That was a leading hope of deregulation: Free entry would guarantee competitive results. In its more ambitious form, this was the theory of perfectly "contestable" markets, as Baumol and his co-authors offered it.[20]

"Competing alliances, including pacts between Northwest Airlines and KLM Royal Dutch Airlines, and UAL Corp.'s United Airlines and Lufthansa, have antitrust immunity and can code share, which allows them to operate on a quasi-merged basis. They are also allowed to share vital business data such as prices, strategic plans and capacity. With such close ties, the airlines can cut overhead and redeploy resources, such as eliminating competing flights on the same routes and creating additional shared flights to new destinations." (*Ibid.*)

[15] Christopher J. Chipello and Susan Carey, "Fight for Canadian Carriers Threatens Alliances," *Wall Street Journal,* 26 August 1999, A3.

[16] See Anna Wilde Mathews and Daniel Michaels, "Regulators Foil American-British Air Pact," *Wall Street Journal,* 29 July 1999, A4.

[17] Martha Brannigan, "AeroMexico To Join Alliance of Two Carriers," *Wall Street Journal,* 13 September 1999, A12.

[18] Christopher J. Chipello and Susan Carey, "Fight for Canadian Carriers Threatens Alliances," *Wall Street Journal,* 26 August 1999, A3, A10.

[19] David Leonhardt and William Echikson, "Taking a Whack at Airline Alliances," *Business Week,* 16 March 1998, 106D-106G.

[20] See especially William J. Baumol, John C. Panzar and Robert D. Willig, *Contestable Markets and the Theory of Industry Structure,* (New York: Harcourt Brace Jovanovich, 1982).

They claimed that high market shares—even complete monopolies—on major city-pair routes or at fortress hubs would be nullified by the power of ultrafree entry and exit. The fear of powerful, instantaneous new entry would compel the existing quasimonopolies to keep their prices down at competitive levels.

But Baumol soon admitted that the leading airports were not "contestable" (that is, easily entered) after all; nor were many of the routes linked to fortress-hub airports.[21] In fact, entry into those airports and routes was well-nigh impossible, unless the incumbent airlines voluntarily chose to let new competitors in. And they have rarely done that.

Access to terminal gates and time slots for takeoffs and landings is a crucial bottleneck at the crowded hub airports. The airlines that hold the gates and slots can fly in and out, but others are blocked out. Most of these rights were retained by the dominant carriers, who had obtained them decades earlier during regulation.[22] In many cases, the dominant airlines effectively "own" their hub airports. They hold leases, often of very long durations; they may retain unused gates without letting others use them; and they often hold veto rights over expansion projects that might let in new competitors. In addition, dominant hub carriers may control critical ground-handling and baggage services, and they usually charge smaller lines prohibitively high prices for using them.

There are various proposals for overcoming these bottlenecks. Some remedies would price the gates and slots so that they could be traded in ways which would promote competition.[23] But the dominant airlines oppose those methods and have prevented progress, so far.

Therefore, new entry into many of the most lucrative markets—the fortress hubs—is virtually blocked. That is why Southwest and other independent airlines have had to try secondary airports at smaller cities. And that is why entry is not a serious force for reducing market power in hundreds of airline markets.

---

[21]That admission is in Elizabeth E. Bailey and William J. Baumol, "Deregulation and the Theory of Contestable Markets," *Yale Journal on Regulation,* 1 (1984): 111–37. For other criticisms of the idea, see William G. Shepherd, "'Contestability' versus Competition," *American Economic Review,* 74 (September 1984): 572–87; and Shepherd, "Contestability vs. Competition—Once More," *Land Economics,* 71 (August 1995): 299–309.

[22]Slot controls were first imposed in the 1960s, before slots became a major bottleneck against competition. Dominant airlines have been permitted to continue hoarding them, despite the obvious anticompetitive effect of that control. See the Transportation Research Board, *Special Report 255.* "Entry and Competition in the U.S. Airline Industry: Issues and Opportunities" (Washington, D.C.: National Academy Press, 1999).

[23]See Chapter 3 of the Transport Research Board, *Special Report 255;* "Entry and Competition in the U.S. Airline Industry: Issues and Opportunities" (Washington, D.C.: National Academy Press, 1999) and Steven A. Morrison and Clifford Winston, "Enhancing the Performance of the Deregulated Air Transportation System," *Brooking Papers: Microeconomics 1989* (Washington, D.C.: Brookings Institution, 1989).

Frequent-Flyer Bonus Plans

The barriers posed by fortress hubs are reinforced by frequent-flyer bonus plans. When airlines give mileage bonuses for tickets it not only builds loyalty to the airline—it also ties the travelers to their local hub-dominant airlines. Travelers living near the hub naturally build up bonus holdings in the dominant airline. This raises entry barriers even further: Any new competitor must overcome the loyalty of these bonuses. So, frequent-flyer bonus plans block entry, even if entrants could obtain airport gates and slots.

Economies of Scale and Scope

Before 1960, a common belief was that the economies of scale were large, making large airlines more efficient. But by 1970, the consensus was shifted by a series of economic studies. Economies in airline operation were reached at a relatively small scale; large airlines did not enjoy significant cost advantages. The emergence of smaller airlines during 1978 to 1983 and during the 1990s has shown that a wide range of airline sizes have comparable costs. In short, the industry's technology makes it naturally competitive; there is ample room for many efficient airlines to coexist and compete.

"Economies of scope" is a recent name for what has long been known as "network effects." Once an airline operates in a network of city-pair routes, the marginal costs of adding new routes are low. Economies of scope are gained by adding flights between cities that the airlines already reach by other routes. Those economies could make it easier for carriers to enter many routes and might raise the degree of competition.

Yet recent evidence suggests that these economies are finite, perhaps even small in many cases. Hub operations are costly to create and maintain, so some airlines are reducing their reliance on large hubs in favor of a wider variety of flight patterns and smaller hubs. Rather than offering powerful competition, economies of scope remain highly dependent on specific conditions in each area.

III. BEHAVIOR

The behavior of the airlines poses two main problems for analysis: possible collusion on ticket price levels by the largest carriers; and extraordinarily refined price discrimination among passengers.

Basic Conditions of Demand and Cost

Consider first the basic conditions under which ticket prices are determined. One set of conditions involves the "fewness" of the rivals. When two or three airlines have competing flights, there are strong incentives to cooperate in setting high prices along classic oligopoly lines. The airlines deny any such tendencies, but they may occur.

Cost conditions are also important, and they are highly unusual. Each city-pair route has distinctive cost conditions, and each airline has an enormous array of costs within its system. In addition, the actual costs of each flight will vary according to timing and fluctuations between peak loads and off-peak times. These cost differences have three main causes: the season, day of the week, and exact time of day; the date when the flyer bought the ticket (e.g., well ahead of the flight or at the last moment); and the nature of the service (e.g., varying from last-minute, stand-by seating to fully guaranteed seats).

Demand, too, is diverse among types of customers and specific markets. The group exhibiting highly elastic demand is leisure travelers. These consumers can make arrangements well in advance, can be flexible in arranging their schedules, and are often thrifty and have limited incomes. This group is very sensitive to prices. Business travelers, on the other hand, exhibit highly *in*elastic demand. They often must get urgent flights on short notice, cannot stay over weekends, and their tickets are usually paid for by their companies. Business travelers are traditionally quite insensitive to prices.

In addition to this deep division, there are endless varieties of demand among individual travelers within each group. Some are more or less urgent, others have more or less money to spend, and still others have varying abilities to plan ahead by a few hours, a few days, or a few weeks or months.

Possible Collusion

Little direct collusion has been observed in the industry, despite the widespread tight-oligopoly conditions both across the industry generally and within hundreds of specific markets. (The CEO of American Airlines did, however, place a telephone call in 1982 to his chief Dallas rival—who secretly recorded the call—urging that the two airlines collude to raise their prices.)

But when the airlines do raise their fares, the sequence of events often suggests a degree of implicit cooperation among the leaders. In 1998 and 1999, for example, the leading carriers tried repeatedly to raise fares. Several times, the first airline's price hike was immediately matched by the others—but not always. In those cases, the initial fare increase was withdrawn.

This quick-response action could be interpreted as merely normal competitive behavior. But, it could instead be seen as joint behavior in a tight oligopoly, with a high degree of shared understanding about the conditions favoring price rises.

In the 1980s, the airlines developed a common practice of listing discount fares with termination dates signalling to competitors when the discounts would end, thereby helping rivals coordinate their pricing decisions. Challenged by the antitrust agencies, this tactic was abandoned by the airlines during 1992–1993.

Price Discrimination

Price discrimination occurs when customers can be separated into groups with low- versus high-demand elasticities. The seller sets higher prices—compared to cost—for inelastic-demand customers and lower prices for elastic-demand customers.

The price-sensitive, low-fare customers must be prevented from reselling their tickets to the inelastic-demand, price-insensitive customers. Airlines achieve this by selling tickets to only specifically named customers.[24] That rigid rule is found in no other important industry; elsewhere, consumers own what they buy and may do with it what they wish.

All these favorable conditions have enabled the airlines to create a vast array of price discrimination, going well beyond any other industry's patterns. The explosion of price discrimination since 1980 has been intensified by the growth of elaborate computer reservation systems, which instantly manage many thousands of fares.

The disparity among fares is deep and pervasive. Figure 8-2 illustrates the variety of fares for a typical flight. The highest price may be more than eight times greater than the lowest fare. The contrasts are created by the airlines' huge and relentless system of discounting. Each major carrier has hundreds of skilled "yield managers," working to adjust—often hour by hour—the number of seats in each discount category.[25] This extremely thorough price discrimination extracts every dollar possible from customers.

Business passengers encounter the greatest overcharging, and the resulting profits are the main source of airline profitability—and of business complaints.[26]

---

[24]In the mid-1990s, the FAA imposed extra "safety" requirements, which required travelers to show their identification to the check-in agent. That may improve safety. But its more important effect has been to prevent any possible re-selling of tickets. Requiring identification is a perfect device to promote the airlines' self-interest in maximizing the use of price discrimination.

[25]For example, American Airlines' yield managers "monitor and adjust the fare mixes on 1,600 daily flights as well as 538,000 future flights involving nearly 50 million passengers." "The Art of Devising Air Fares," *New York Times,* 4 March 1987, D1.

[26]See for example Nancy Keates, "As Air Fares Soar, More Companies Cancel Trips," *Wall Street Journal,* 3 December 1997, B1; David Leonhardt, "Business Is In a Flying Rage," *Business Week,* 13 October 1997, 38; and Scott McCartney, "Business Fares Increase Even as Leisure Travel Keeps Getting Cheaper," *Wall Street Journal,* 3 November 1997, A1.

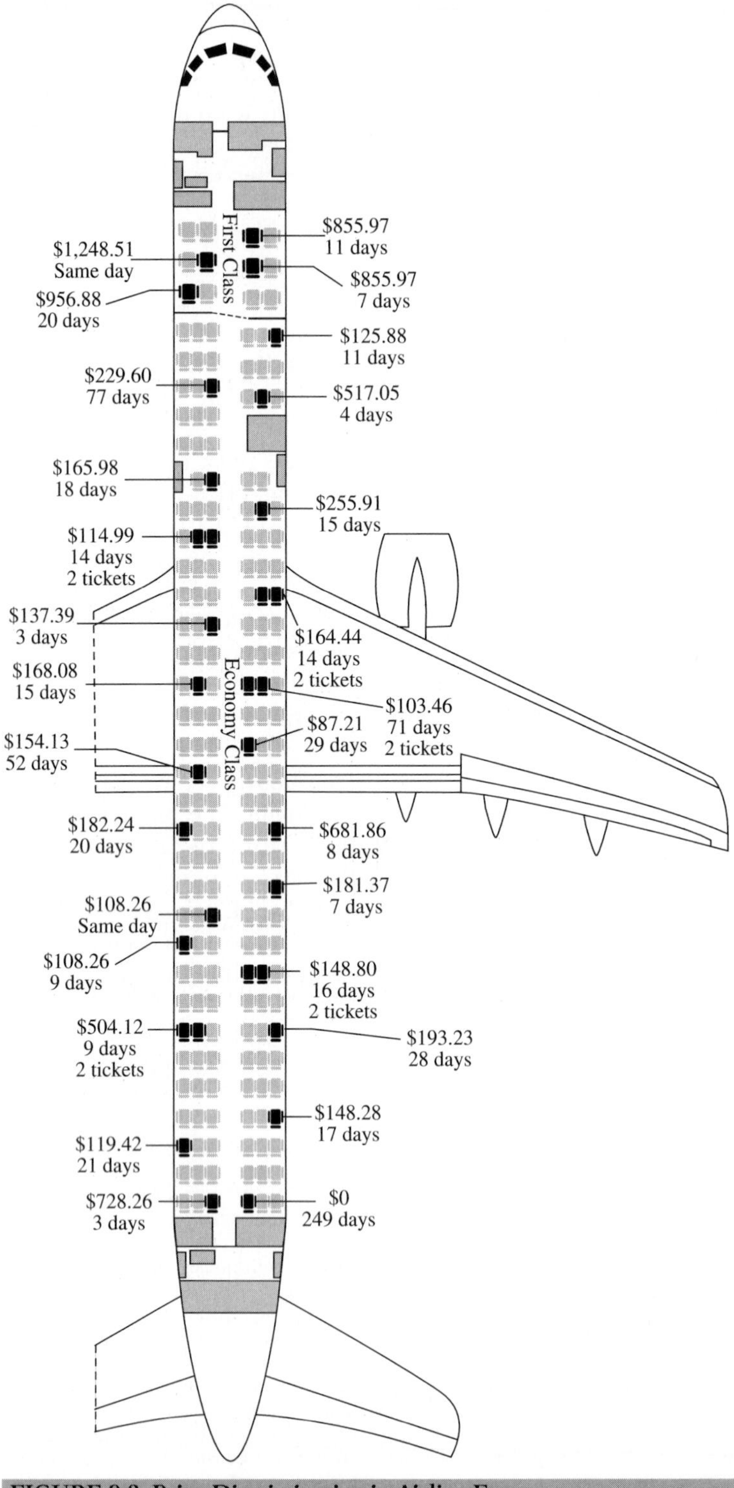

FIGURE 8-2 Price Discrimination in Airline Fares

Source: Adapted from the *New York Times,* 12 April 1998, Section 4, p. 2.

During 1978 to 1984, airline price discrimination was fluid, chaotic, and extremely effective as a competitive device. But then American Airlines set tight patterns for the discounting, which cut out most of its competitive force. Discounts were limited to trips arranged at least two weeks in advance and that included Saturday night. That blocked out virtually all business customers, leaving them captive to high prices.

Anticompetitive Pricing to Block New Entry?

The airlines have also used fare cuts to fight the entry of new airlines on specific routes. These are the alleged "predatory" incidents, when retaliation against newcomers is so sharp that it eliminates the entrants. The usual question is whether the dominant airline's price is cut below costs.

Seven such disputed cases from 1993 to 1999 are summarized in Table 8-5. The initial high prices, the deep price cutting, the exit of some of the entrants, and the later boost in fares strongly suggest the effects of eliminating competition.[27]

The dominant carriers claim that they merely respond to new competition, and that their prices are not cut too low. That claim has some merit, but it ignores the fact that established airlines usually have superior experience and equipment and better reputations for reliability and amenities. Their "equal" fares are, in fact, substantially lower, given the quality differences. Often, too, the incumbent airlines add capacity so as to increase sales by taking away the newcomers' passengers.

Major airlines fit the standard definition of "predatory pricing," when they cut price below the costs of providing the service. Below-cost prices have handsome payoffs when stopping one new rival signals other possible competitors that they, too, will be pummelled if they attempt to enter. This "signalling" may multiply the benefits of predation and make the strategy economically worthwhile.

During 1993 to 1999, there were 32 complaints of unfair practices in the field.[28] Half involved fare cutting, increased flights, and increased capacity on the entered routes. The others alleged slot and gate restrictions, manipulation of travel agents, and other exclusionary tactics. Entry usually caused fares to fall, but the retaliation removed the entrant in half of the cases. The strongest blow to competition occurred when the dominant airline added new flights that directly "overlaid" the entrant's flights.

---

[27]Anna Wilde Mathews, "DOT Task Force Will Urge Airports to Stop Anticompetitive Moves at Hubs," *Wall Street Journal,* 14 September 1999, A4; Anne Wilde Mathews and Scott McCartney, "U.S. Sues American Air in Antitrust Case," *Wall Street Journal,* 14 May 1999, A3, A6; and Wendy Lellner, "How Northwest Gives Competition a Bad Name," *Business Week,* 16 March 1998, 34.

[28]Transportation Research Board, *Special Report 255,* chapter 4. "Entry and Competition in the U.S. Airline Industry: Issues and Opportunities" (Washington, D.C.: National Academy Press, 1999).

TABLE 8-5 Some Examples of Price Retaliation to Defeat Entrants into Fortress Hubs

			Quarter Before Entry				*Second Quarter After Entry*				*Eighth Quarter After Entry*[1]				
Entry Year, QTR	*City-Pair*		*Average Fare*	*Seats Avail-able*	*Flights*	*Avg. Load Factor*	*Average Fare*	*Seats Avail-able*	*Flights*	*Avg. Load Factor*	*Average Fare*	*Seats Avail-able*	*Flights*	*Avg. Load Factor*	*Status of New Entrant*
Complaints received by DOT															
1996-2	DTW-BOS	Incumbent	$257	227,400	648	57%	$ 99	306,700	832	82%	$232	273,800	675	71%	
		New Entrant	—	—	—	—	$ 70	12,400	71	27%	—	—	—	—	exited
1996-1	ATL-MOB	Incumbent	$186	202,900	700	73%	$112	207,000	725	70%	$ 88	209,800	712	70%	
		New Entrant	—	—	—	—	$ 42	17,000	75	51%	$ 54	45,000	205	34%	competing
1995-2	MSP-MCI	Incumbent	$201	92,800	407	52%	$ 69	141,700	603	70%	$ 78	150,300	676	75%	
		New Entrant	—	—	—	—	$ 43	11,300	30	NA	$ 60	43,000	160	55%	competing
1995-2	DFW-ICT	Incumbent 1	$111	27,300	430	46%	$ 65	47,900	820	58%	$ 89	54,200	673	68%	
		Incumbent 2	$126	22,100	482	32%	$126	18,200	510	41%	$100	15,700	525	66%	
		New Entrant	—	—	—	—	$ 44	24,300	189	60%	—	—	—	—	exited
1996-1	ATL-PIT	Incumbent 1	$168	153,600	538	59%	$ 93	147,000	544	77%	$217	144,100	530	58%	
		Incumbent 2	$161	90,300	434	59%	$ 86	121,100	520	61%	$203	87,800	395	58%	
		New Entrant	—	—	—	—	$ 79	40,900	181	50%	—	—	—	—	exited[2]
1995-1	ATL-DTW	Incumbent 1	$184	165,600	493	67%	$108	204,209	515	64%	$111	238,400	630	75%	
		Incumbent 2	$177	131,900	527	57%	$ 93	172,600	694	68%	$ 95	173,900	697	71%	
		New Entrant	—	—	—	—	$ 86	53,000	237	50%	$ 99	31,100	143	55%	competing

NA = information is not available due to lack of reporting.
[1]Most recent quarter if 8 quarters have not elapsed.
[2]New entrant (ValuJet) permanently exited market following suspension of operation in 2nd quarter 1996.
Note: See Appendix D for airport codes.

Source: Transport Research Board, *Special Report 255*, "Entry and Competition in the U.S. Airline Industry: Issues and Opportunities," 1999, Table 2-6.

IV. PERFORMANCE

At first, deregulation and strong competition generated good performance results from 1978 to 1984: It moved fares below their natural downtrend, it enhanced growth, and it raised load factors while keeping profits normal. But from 1984 to 1988, the rise of concentration and hub dominance arrested the decline of prices, eliminated many new competitors, and reduced the flexibility of routes. During the 1990s, pockets of market power tended to deepen, and monopoly effects on prices and efficiency increased.

Prices Some deregulation enthusiasts estimate that new competition pushed fares 30 percent below the ongoing trends and specific cost factors (higher fuel prices and wages). Figure 8-3 shows the changes. After 1994, fares went up, so the lasting price effects of deregulation are debatable.

FIGURE 8-3 Fares Stopped Declining after 1994, Apparently Reflecting Market Power of the Large Airlines

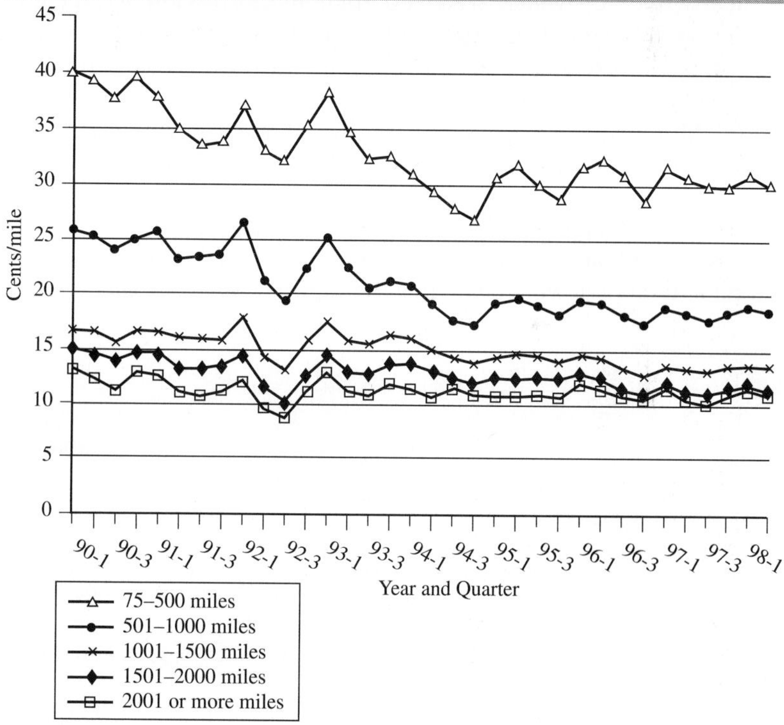

Note: Average yield per passenger trip (average fare/miles flown) was calculated using the DOT 10 percent ticket sample accessed through Database Products. Figures were adjusted using the GDP price deflator. Trips with zero fares were excluded.

Source: Transport Research Board, *Special Report 255,* "Entry and Competition in the U.S. Airline Industry: Issues and Opportunities," 1999, Figure 1-1.

Business fares rose steeply in the 1990s, as price discrimination sharpened. On the whole, events since deregulation have made inelastic-demand travelers worse off in terms of higher real prices and lower service quality.

Fortress hubs have played a significant role in raising fares by at least 20 percent and in many cases by as much as 40 percent.[29] Dominance on specific city-pair routes also has raised ticket prices significantly. This can be seen each time Southwest Airlines enters a market. As Table 8-6 shows, Southwest's entry has driven fares lower in scores of markets.

Quality of Service The quality of service has fallen for all passengers. The time required for trips (including time for arriving early to cope with airport congestion, time spent at airport check-in counters, and time taken to break trips in half for transfers between flights at hubs) has risen greatly. There is a substantial risk of missing flights at hubs (from flight delays or cancellation of flights for revenue reasons), and there is crowding in long lines at virtually every stage of a trip. Most aircraft now fly nearly filled up, which makes boarding more stressful and the crowding during the flight even more unpleasant. Some airlines have continued to reduce the size and spacing of aircraft seats to (and perhaps below) the absolute limits of tolerance.

Moreover, most discounts can be obtained only by warping trips to fit tight restrictions and by planning weeks ahead of the trip, with no chance for refunds if conditions change. Even the spread of Internet ticketing has created new burdens: Instead of having convenient help from travel agents, many travelers must now spend their scarce time and effort doing their own work searching the Internet for discounts.

TABLE 8-6 Change in Average Yield and Traffic in Markets Entered by Southwest Airlines*

	1990	*1997–98*	*Percent Change*
Passenger Trips	12,170,210	33,372,310	174%
Average Yield (cents/mi)	32.40	14.80	−54%

*Includes only markets that Southwest did not serve in 1990 but where it accounted for 10 percent or more of total market passenger trips in the full year from 1997 3rd Quarter to 1998 2nd Quarter. The GDP price deflator was used to adjust for inflation.

Source: Transport Research Board, *Special Report 255,* "Entry and Competition in the U.S. Airline Industry: Issues and Opportunities," 1999, Table 1-5.

[29]See Department of Transportation, Office of Aviation and International Economics, "The Low Cost Airline Service Revolution," Washington, D.C., April 1996; and Department of Transportation, "Proposed Statement of Enforcement Policy Regarding Unfair Exclusionary Conduct," Docket No. OST-98-3713, April 1998.

All this adds up to a substantial degradation of quality, which, for many air travelers, offsets any reductions in ticket prices.

Profits The large airlines' profits were generally normal from 1978 to 1988, then dipped low during 1989 to 1994 as net profit margins were actually negative during 1990 to 1994.[30] But, profits have been substantial and rising since 1995. The industry's operating profit was at historic highs in 1997 ($8.6 billion) and has been above that more recently. Stockholders in the airlines have done well, especially since 1996.

Efficiency Surprisingly, the big airlines have continued to exhibit higher costs than necessary. This partly reflects higher wages, especially for unionized pilots and other employees. Southwest and other no-frills airlines have shown that staffing, worker incentives, and aircraft management can be much improved. But large airlines have changed little. They have increased their load factors, partly by using extreme price discrimination in "yield management" in order to pack in more passengers. The rise in load factors would seem to suggest more efficiency in the use of aircraft. Yet load factors as high as 75 percent in the 1990s also involve crowding of passengers and low service quality (contributing, perhaps, to increasing incidents of "sky rage").

Innovation Early competition generated the creation of computer reservation systems, as well as the hub-and-spoke system. Many airlines have become nimble and "innovative" in adjusting routes and fares. The greater use of small and mid-sized aircraft can also be considered an innovation.

But the large airlines have not noticeably been more innovative in deploying equipment or creating new services. Southwest Airlines has created innovations in service, speedier equipment handling, and pricing, but it is not a dominant carrier. Airline competition may have stirred innovation, but monopoly conditions retard it, as economic theory predicts.

V. PUBLIC POLICY

Before 1978, the CAB froze routes rather than applying classic rate-of-return regulation of prices and profits. That was dysfunctional: It blocked out new competition, encouraged collusion on prices and discouraged price cutting, and promoted inefficiency in airline costs.

Deregulation worked well because it was *not* premature. It removed the CAB's controls only after competition was bursting to begin in a naturally competitive industry. But after five years, patches of monopoly

[30]See Air Transport Association, *Annual Report, 1998,* Washington, D.C.: 1998, 3.

began growing. Fortress hubs, megamergers, and rigid pricing patterns to contain discounting had, by 1988, restored strong pockets of market power. Since then, monopoly effects have grown.

What Failed in Deregulation?

Contestability Relying on free entry failed to check market power because fortress hubs blocked entry.

Lax Policies toward Mergers and Alliances DOT officials permitted important anticompetitive mergers during 1985 to 1988. More recently, antitrust officials have permitted major alliances that reduce competition even further.

Failing to Increase Airport Capacity or Liberalize Slot Controls These have strengthened hub dominance at major airports throughout the United States.

Scarcity of Air Traffic Controllers The firing of traffic controllers in 1981—plus the bizarre perpetual prohibition on rehiring any of them—reduced the system's capacity and intensified the other causes of monopoly effects.

Tolerance of Predatory Pricing Severe price discrimination has helped drive small competitors from the market.

What Policies Are Needed?

Altogether, these mistakes have increased monopoly power in scores of routes and hubs and throughout the industry. Though it is too late to reverse their past effects, some policy changes would improve future chances for competition.

Reducing Hub Dominance One important and immediate improvement would be to set a cap on the market share that any airline could hold at a hub airport. A 35 percent cap, for example, would guarantee at least three airlines at every airport. It would permit adequate hub efficiencies because hub operations could still be substantial. Hub shares over 35 percent could be freely sold for reasonable asset values. Only the monopoly-based value of the excess dominant share would be removed, as it should be.

A recent proposal is to eliminate slot controls entirely, replacing them with pricing and other market-based methods for allocating landing and take-off slots.[31] Other proposals are less promising because they rely

[31]It is urged in the Transportation Research Board *Special Report 255*. "Entry and Competition in the U.S. Airline Industry: Issues and Opportunities" (Washington, D.C.: 1999).

on the voluntary cooperation of the very carriers whose market power and profits they seek to lessen.[32]

Enlarging Airport Capacity Airport capacity has remained surprisingly meager, despite the massive growth in traffic. The tight capacity has fortified hub dominance against entry by new airlines and against price cutting by smaller rivals. In order to raise traffic volume (and the scope for competition), the FAA has tried to fit more traffic into the airports' capacity.[33] But the effort has been controversial because it may also raise the risk of collisions. There is an added need to guide the construction of new capacity so as to expand newcomers' access.[34]

Enlarging FAA Capacity The FAA has been given skimpy resources that limit the industry's capacity. Superb aircraft and rising traffic volumes are forced to rely on antiquated traffic controls and constricted airport capacity. (The FAA's starved funding, which is favorable to the largest carriers, suggests that the latter may not entirely resent this situation.) A procompetitive policy would give the FAA greater resources and rapidly replace its obsolete technology. Doing that and enlarging many airports without further delay are necessary, minimal steps toward making competition effective.

Preventing Predatory Actions Antitrust officials announced in 1998 a stricter policy against anticompetitive price cutting.[35] It would prohibit a dominant airline from cutting fares below cost *and* simultaneously adding capacity to increase its traffic on the route. This rule has been criticized for being difficult to apply, but it does warn dominant airlines to avoid blatant actions that block competition.

VI. CONCLUSION

Passenger air travel evolved from a rugged early period into 40 years of growth under CAB controls against competition. The 1978 to 1984 "Golden Era" of deregulation was followed by mergers, structured

[32]The Task Force also urged other ways of loosening controls, including making slots and gates subject to flexible free-market pricing rather than permanent control by dominant airlines.

[33]See William M. Carley, "FAA Sparks Criticism With Efforts to Speed Traffic at Airports," *Wall Street Journal,* 9 September 1999, A1, A8. The changes include closer spacing for aircraft on flight paths and during landing.

[34]See the Transport Research Board, *Special Report 255;* "Entry and Competition in the U.S. Airline Industry: Issues and Opportunities" (Washington, D.C.: 1999); see also Anna Wilde Mathews, "DOT Task Force Will Urge Airports to Stop Anticompetitive Moves at Hubs," *Wall Street Journal,* 14 September 1999, A4.

[35]Department of Transportation, Office of the Secretary, "Statement of Enforcement Policy Regarding Unfair Exclusionary Conduct," Docket No. OST-98-3713, Notice 98-16, April 1998.

controls on fare discounts, hub dominance, and high degrees of market power on hundreds of city-pair routes. The industry's complicated patchwork of competition and monopoly has been only moderately softened by some new entry in the 1990s. Future events may concentrate the industry further, with mergers and even greater dominance in many places. Alternatively, market dominance may be weakened via greater entry by more low-cost carriers. How this will play out depends on public officials who can protect and expand competition, or who will permit it to continue to be eroded and subverted.

Suggested Readings

Books

Bailey, Elizabeth E., David R. Graham, and Daniel P. Kaplan. *Deregulating the Airlines,* (Cambridge: MIT Press, 1985).

Baumol, William J., John C. Panzar, and Robert D. Willig. *Contestable Markets and the Theory of Industry Structure,* (San Diego: Harcourt Brace Jovanovich, 1982).

Caves, Richard E., *Air Transport and Its Regulators: An Industry Study,* (Cambridge: Harvard University Press, 1962).

Douglas, George and James Miller. *Economic Regulation of Domestic Air Transport: Theory and Policy,* (Washington, D.C.: Brookings Institution, 1974).

Jordan, William A. *Airline Regulation in America: Effects and Imperfections,* (Baltimore: Johns Hopkins University Press, 1970).

Meyer, John R., and Clint V. Oster. *Deregulation and the Future of Intercity Passenger Travel,* (Cambridge: MIT Press, 1987).

Morrison, Steven A., and Clifford Winston. *The Evolution of the Airline Industry,* (Washington, D.C.: Brookings Institution, 1995).

Articles

AuBuchon, M. J. "Testing the Limits of Federal Tolerance: Strategic Alliances in the Airline Industry," *Transportation Law Journal* 26, no. 2 (Spring 1994): 219–46.

Bailey, Elizabeth E., and William J. Baumol. "Deregulation and the Theory of Contestable Markets," *Yale Journal on Regulation* 1 (1984): 111–37.

Borenstein, Severin. "Hubs and High Fares: Dominance and Market Power in the U.S. Airline Industry," *RAND Journal of Economics* 20 (Autumn 1989): 344–65.

———. "The Evolution of U.S. Airline Competition," *Economic Perspectives* (Spring 1992): 45–73.

Brock, James W. "Industry Update: Airlines," *Review of Industrial Organization* 16 (February 2000).

Evans, William N., and Ioannis Kessides, "Structure, Conduct and Performance in the Deregulated Airline Industry," *Southern Economic Journal* (January 1993): 450–67.

Kahn, Alfred E. "Surprises of Airline Deregulation," *American Economic Review* (May 1988): 316–22.

———. "Airline Deregulation—A Mixed Bag but a Clear Success Nevertheless," *Transportation Law Journal* 16 (1988): 229–52.

———. "The Competitive Consequences of Hub Dominance: A Case Study," *Review of Industrial Organization* 8 (August 1993): 381–406.

Keeler, Theodore E. "Airline Regulation and Market Performance," *Bell Journal of Economics* (Autumn 1972): 399–424.

Levine, Michael E. "Is Regulation Necessary? California Air Transportation and National Regulatory Policy," *Yale Law Journal* 74 (July 1965): 1416–47.

Morrison, Steven A. "Airline Service: The Evolution of Competition Since Deregulation." In *Industry Studies,* 2d ed., edited by Larry L. Deutsch. (Armonk, NY: M. E. Sharpe, 1998).

Morrison, Steven A., and Clifford Winston. "Enhancing the Performance of the Deregulated Air Transportation System," *Brooking Papers: Microeconomics 1989,* (Washington, D.C.: Brookings Institution, 1989).

Review of Industrial Organization, August 1993 8, 4 (Special Issue devoted to articles assessing airline deregulation).

Saunders, Lisa M., and William G. Shepherd, "Airlines: Setting Constraints on Hub Dominance," *Logistics and Transportation Review* (September 1993): 201–20.

Zuckerman, Laurence "Firing on Fortress Northwest," *New York Times,* 25 August 1999, C1, C17.

Government and Other Reports

Air Transport Association. *Annual Report 1998,* (Washington, D.C.: 1998).

Craun, J. M., and R. Bennet. *The Airline Deregulation Evolution Continues: The Southwest Effect,* (Office of Aviation Analysis, Department of Transportation, 1993).

Transportation Research Council. Committee for a Study of Competition in the U.S. Airline Industry. *Entry and Competition in the U.S. Airline Industry: Issues and Opportunities.* Washington Special Report 255, National Research Council, National Academy of Sciences, July 1999.

U.S. General Accounting Office. *Airline Competition: Higher Fares and Less Competition Continue at Concentrated Airports.* Washington: Report GAO/RCED-93-171. July 1993.

U.S. General Accounting Office. *Airline Deregulation: Barriers to Entry Continue to Limit Competition in Several Key Domestic Markets.* Washington: Report GAO/RECD-97-4. October 1996.

U.S. General Accounting Office. *Airline Deregulation: Changes in Airfares, Service, and Safety at Small, Medium-Sized, and Large Communities.* Washington: Report RCED-96-79. 1996.

U.S. General Accounting Office. *Aviation Competition: Effects on Consumers From Domestic Airline Alliances Vary.* Washington: Report GAO/RCED-99-37. January 1999.

U.S. Department of Transportation. Office of Aviation and International Economics. *The Low Cost Airline Service Revolution.* Washington: 1996.

U.S. Department of Transportation. Office of the Secretary. "Statement of Enforcement Policy Regarding Unfair Exclusionary Conduct." Washington: Docket No. OST-98-3713, Notice 98-16. April 1998.

CHAPTER 9

Commercial Banking

—Steven J. Pilloff*

The commercial banking industry provides financial services to a substantial portion of firms and households in the United States and is one of the largest, most important sectors of the nation's economy. Banks provide a wide range of financial products and services, but their traditional activities fall into two basic areas: They offer customers safe, liquid, and convenient deposit products; and they lend deposited funds to consumers, governments, and businesses that need to borrow money. Typically, banks pay interest to depositors and collect interest from borrowers. A large portion of their profits comes from the difference between interest received from loans and interest paid on deposits. Therefore, high loan rates and low deposit rates are associated with high profitability.

The industry is made up of commercial banking institutions chartered either by the national bank regulator (the Office of the Comptroller of the Currency) or by the state bank regulator in the bank's home state. Some institutions operate as independent banks; others operate as part of a bank holding company—a company that owns one or more banking institutions and may also own nonbank subsidiaries such as data processing, specialty lending, and venture capital firms. Excluded from this definition of the commercial banking industry are nonbank depository institutions (savings banks, savings and loan associations, and credit unions) and nonbank, nondepository firms (e.g., mortgage companies, consumer finance firms, and mutual fund organizations). Also excluded are nonbank subsidiaries of bank holding companies.

Throughout this chapter, the terms "bank" and "banking organization" are used to refer to an independent bank or to the aggregate of all bank subsidiaries owned by the same bank holding company. The term "banking institution" refers to an entity that has its own bank charter—an independent bank or an individual bank subsidiary of a bank holding company.

---

*The views expressed in this chapter are those of the author and do not necessarily reflect those of the Board of Governors or its staff. I would like to thank Beth Kiser, Steve Rhoades, and Sherrell Varner for helpful comments and suggestions. I also want to thank Paul Tan and Onka Tenkean for excellent research assistance.

The description of bank activities as collecting deposits and extending loans overly simplifies commercial banking. For one thing, banks also provide financial services in numerous other areas—trust, investment advisory, and cash management, for example. Moreover, the deposit and loan options available to customers are numerous and varied. Banks typically offer many types of deposit accounts—savings, demand deposit (checking), money market deposit, and certificates of deposits—each with different features such as rate and fee schedules, minimum balance requirements, and withdrawal restrictions. A key feature of bank deposits is that they are federally insured up to $100,000 and provide a level of safety that cannot be matched by nondepository firms.[1] The credit services offered by banks are also varied and include, for example, automobile, residential mortgage, and consumer loans and commercial and home equity lines of credit.

Each product and service offered by banks could potentially be analyzed as a separate market. Each has unique characteristics, is offered by a different (though often overlapping) set of firms, and is demanded by a different (though again often overlapping) set of customers. For example, mortgage loans, automobile loans, checking accounts, and cash management services could all be considered distinct product markets. Nonetheless, commercial banks are the only firms that provide the broad range of financial services that are commonly thought of as "commercial banking." As a result, banks may have the unique ability to form long-term customer relationships that have a special economic importance beyond the actual products and services being offered. Customers of financial services frequently view a commercial bank as their primary provider and typically obtain multiple financial services from that institution.[2]

In this chapter, commercial banking is considered to involve two distinct markets—retail banking and corporate banking—each of which consists of the set of traditional deposit, loan, and other financial services that are provided by banks to a particular type of customer. The retail segment of commercial banking consists of financial services offered to households and small businesses. Not only does nearly every bank engage in retail banking, but most banks engage exclusively in retail banking. The

---

[1]The $100,000 federal protection, provided by the Federal Deposit Insurance Corporation (FDIC), applies to each separate account registered at a given institution. Therefore, a household or company can fully protect deposits above $100,000 by (a) maintaining several accounts, each with less than $100,000, at an institution under different account holders, or (b) maintaining multiple accounts, each with less than $100,000, under the same account holder at different institutions. Deposits held at savings banks and savings and loan associations are protected by the same insurance, and deposits held at credit unions receive similar protection.

[2]These and other findings from the Federal Reserve Board's 1993 Survey of Small Business Finances and 1992 Survey of Consumer Finances are discussed in Myron L. Kwast, Martha Starr-McCluer, and John D. Wolken, "Market Definition and the Analysis of Antitrust in Banking," *The Antitrust Bulletin,* Winter 1997, 973–995.

relevant geographic market for retail banking is local. On the demand side, retail customers strongly prefer to bank locally, so they usually seek their financial services from a bank near their home or office. On the supply side, it is relatively costly for banks to provide retail services to customers not living or working close to a bank office because retail accounts typically involve small amounts of money.

Corporate banking involves providing financial services to large businesses—commercial deposit and loan products, as well as sophisticated financial services such as foreign exchange. A relatively small number of large banks are involved in corporate banking. The geographic market for corporate banking is regional, national, or even international. Because corporate accounts typically involve large sums of money, large firms have a sizable financial incentive to look throughout a wide location for their best alternative; they are also likely to have the resources and expertise to engage in such a search. And because the potential profits associated with serving large business customers are substantial, banks are likely to search widely in their pursuit of corporate banking business.

Although both retail and corporate banking are important components of the commercial banking industry, this chapter focuses on retail banking, which is much better suited for an analysis within the structure-conduct-performance framework. Retail banking has received a good bit of attention from antitrust authorities because retail customers are more geographically limited and retail markets are smaller. As a result, extensive research has been done on the proper definition of retail markets and the relationships among market structure, bank performance, and, to a lesser extent, bank conduct. Corporate banking raises fewer competitive concerns, and few studies have been directed at this segment of the industry.

I. HISTORY

For much of its history, the U.S. commercial banking industry has been made up mainly of a large number of small, local organizations. Federal and state legal restrictions on bank activities have been a major reason for the development of this structure. Restrictions on branching and interstate banking, which limited the ability of both state-chartered and federally chartered banks to grow large and operate over sizable geographic areas, have been particularly influential.

Essentially, all banks operate a head office where deposits are accepted and loans are originated.[3] Most banks also maintain branch of-

[3]The only exceptions are a small number of recently established "Internet" banks, which conduct all business without any physical offices. These banks constitute an extremely small segment of the industry, but their importance may increase in time as Internet commerce grows.

fices. For many years, state-chartered banks were prohibited from operating branches outside their home state. In fact, in many states, state-chartered banks were permitted to operate branches only in a limited portion of the state, such as the bank's home county or its home and contiguous counties; in other states, branching was completely prohibited. A bank that wanted to operate in an area of the state in which it was prohibited from branching needed to form a bank holding company and establish (or purchase) a separate bank subsidiary with its own charter and head office.

Before 1927, federally chartered banks were prohibited from branching at all. The McFadden Act of 1927 gave national banks some expanded branching rights but still limited them to the same branching restrictions imposed on state-chartered institutions. National banks were essentially prohibited from interstate branching, and, in many cases, were limited in their extent of intrastate branching.

Although no banks could branch across state lines, a loophole in the McFadden Act made it possible for a bank holding company to conduct interstate banking by purchasing a banking institution operating in a state different from the acquiring holding company's headquarters state. However, the Douglas Amendment to the Bank Holding Company Act of 1956 prohibited such interstate acquisitions unless the state legislature of the target institution's home state expressly permitted such acquisitions. For many years, no states passed laws permitting interstate acquisitions.

The banking industry also faced other restrictions—most notably the Glass-Steagall Act of 1933, which mandated that commercial banking (gathering deposits and making loans) and investment banking (underwriting securities) remain separate activities. Although these other restrictions greatly affected the structure of the banking industry, restrictions on branching and interstate banking had the greatest influence.[4]

In recent years, many restrictions on interstate banking have been lifted. In 1975, Maine's state legislature passed a law allowing bank holding companies headquartered in other states to make acquisitions in Maine. Other states have followed that lead. By year-end 1984, eight states had enacted enabling legislation, and by year-end 1995, every state had passed legislation allowing some interstate banking. Restrictions on branching have also been relaxed. Many states have liberalized their branching rules, so it has become easier for banks to expand their operations within their home state. At year-end 1994, statewide branching was prohibited in only two states.

---

[4]Although the Glass-Steagall Act separated commercial and investment banking, regulatory decisions have blurred the line. For example, the Federal Reserve Board has determined that under section 20 of the Bank Holding Company Act, bank holding companies may form subsidiaries that engage in a limited amount of certain underwriting activities.

In 1985, the Office of the Comptroller of the Currency also began to facilitate interstate branching for national banks under an existing rule referred to as the "thirty-mile rule." The rule allowed a national bank to relocate its head office anywhere within thirty miles, even if it meant moving the office into a different state. Following the move, the original head office could be operated as a branch. Banks used this type of expansion to enter new states, and many bank holding companies used it to consolidate subsidiaries.

The Riegle-Neal Interstate Banking and Branching Efficiency Act, enacted in 1994, removed many of the remaining limitations on interstate banking and branching. Interstate banking was facilitated as bank holding companies could purchase banking institutions in any state. Riegle-Neal also removed restrictions on interstate branching: A banking institution in one state could merge with an institution in another state, creating a single institution with branches in multiple states. Such mergers could take place among affiliated (owned by the same holding company) or unaffiliated banks. States were given the opportunity to "opt out" of interstate branching by merger by June 1, 1997, but only two, Texas and Montana, elected to do so. The prohibition on interstate branching expired in Texas in 1999 and will expire in Montana in 2001. In those states that explicitly authorize such entry, banks may also establish new interstate branches. By August 1998, fewer than half of the states had elected to permit such branching.

II. STRUCTURE

The structure of the commercial banking industry changed markedly in the 1980s and 1990s, largely as a result of extensive consolidation. The number of banks has declined and concentration at the national level has risen; interestingly, average concentration at the local level has not changed nearly as much. The number and size of very large banks has also increased, a development with potentially important consequences for the industry.

Mergers

Historically, the banking industry has consisted of a large number of small, locally oriented organizations. Although the industry continues to exhibit this basic structure, it has changed dramatically over the past 20 years. Much of the change is attributable to the extensive merger and acquisition activity that has taken place since the early 1980s.[5]

---

[5]The terms merger and acquisition are used interchangeably throughout this chapter.

Merger Activity From 1980 to 1998, more than 6,100 bank mergers involving nearly $2.3 trillion in acquired assets were completed in the United States (Table 9-1). Although the intensity of activity has varied over the period, the number of mergers has been consistently high, with at least 200 mergers in all years but one after 1980.[6] The greatest number took place in the 1980s, but activity remained strong throughout the 1990s, especially in terms of bank assets acquired. The merger wave is expected to continue.[7]

A small proportion of the deals has accounted for a large share of the total acquired assets. These mergers, involving an acquirer and a target with substantial assets, have become more common over time. Deals in

TABLE 9-1 Bank Mergers and Acquisitions (1980–1998)

Year	Number	Bank Assets Acquired ($ Billion)	Pct of Total Industry Assets[1]	Mergers with Acquired Assets Greater than $1 Billion	$10 Billion	$50 Billion
1980	178	10.4	0.7	0	0	0
1981	328	34.6	2.1	4	0	0
1982	370	43.8	2.4	6	0	0
1983	362	61.0	3.0	13	0	0
1984	337	69.1	3.2	15	0	0
1985	390	67.0	2.8	11	0	0
1986	487	95.9	3.7	16	1	0
1987	378	123.4	4.8	16	3	0
1988	354	91.8	3.3	14	2	0
1989	308	43.5	1.5	9	0	0
1990	322	43.4	1.4	6	0	0
1991	253	149.2	4.9	13	4	0
1992	302	167.1	5.3	25	2	1
1993	347	103.7	3.2	18	2	0
1994	341	107.9	3.1	14	2	0
1995	285	181.0	4.9	15	3	0
1996	221	220.6	5.7	11	6	2
1997	216	144.6	3.4	13	4	0
1998	344	501.6	10.7	23	7	2
Total	6,123	2,259.6	—	242	36	5

[1]Total industry assets measured as of December 31.

Sources: Federal Reserve Board and Reports of Condition and Income (Call Report).

[6]The merger year is the year that the relevant federal regulator approved the merger.

[7]Tania Padgett, "New Merger Wave Seen Under Way," *American Banker,* 1 June 1999, 20–21.

which both organizations had total assets of at least $1 billion were infrequent in the early 1980s but became more common in the years following. Only about 4 percent of all deals between 1980 and 1998 involved two banks with at least $1 billion, but these transactions accounted for more than three-quarters of all acquired assets. The number of deals in which the acquirer and the target had total assets of at least $10 billion were rare before 1991 but occurred more often in the last half of the decade.

In 1998, merger activity reached an unprecedented level, when several of the largest bank deals in history took place (NationsBank-BankAmerica; Banc One-First Chicago NBD; and Norwest-Wells Fargo). Several other sizable, and many smaller, deals also took place. More than 10 percent of industry assets were acquired. In addition, The Travelers Group, a large, diversified nonbank financial services firm with extensive insurance and investment banking activities, and Citicorp, a large banking organization, merged to form the largest banking organization in the United States.[8]

Merger Motivations The gradual removal of geographic restrictions on branching and interstate banking made consolidation in the commercial banking industry possible but does not explain why the merger wave developed. The extensive acquisition activity has been driven by the belief of bankers that substantial gains can be achieved by acquiring other organizations.

A key and commonly cited source of anticipated gains is reduced costs resulting from economies of scale.[9] Economies of scale exist when average costs decline as firm size increases. If scale economies exist in the banking industry, then larger banks would have lower average costs than smaller banks. As a result, they would be able to earn greater profits, either by lowering their prices (raising deposit rates, lowering loan rates, or lowering fees) to attract more customers or by increasing their profit margins (by maintaining prices and enjoying a greater spread between income and expenses) or through some combination of the two tactics.

In the commercial banking industry, economies of scale may derive from several sources. Technology is a particularly important potential source. Banks rely heavily on extensive computer systems, which involve

---

[8]Although this deal may appear to violate the Glass-Steagall restrictions on combining commercial banking and investment banking, as well as other restrictions on the insurance activities of commercial banks, the Federal Reserve Board, which approved the case, may allow the combined firm to operate for as long as five years before requiring that certain activities be divested.

[9]A somewhat related, although less relevant, concept in a discussion of retail commercial banking is economies of scope. Scope economies occur when it is less expensive to jointly produce multiple outputs than to produce them separately. Scope economies are more relevant in the context of combining commercial banking with other financial service activities such as investment banking or insurance.

substantial fixed costs and more limited variable costs. Because their total computing and maintenance costs increase relatively little as transaction volume increases, banks may benefit from operations that generate a large number of transactions.

Greater size also enables banks to increase employee specialization, possibly resulting in more effective and more efficient operations. Another source of economies of scale is advertising. It may be efficient for large banks, which operate over wide geographic regions, to advertise through radio, television, and large newspapers, which reach broad areas. In contrast, advertising by small banks through those media may reach many individuals who, being outside the banks' service areas, are not potential customers.

Mergers may enable banks to benefit from some sources of economies of scale by eliminating redundancies. Many back-office functions that are performed separately by two independent banks may possibly be performed at lower cost by one consolidated bank. For example, following a merger, it may be possible to eliminate one bank's check-processing facility or payroll department. Likewise, when both the acquiring and the target banks operate branches in the same neighborhood, branches can often be closed without greatly inconveniencing customers.

Consolidation may also result in greater market power, that is, a greater ability to sustain prices (service levels) above (below) competitive levels without being forced by market pressures to lower (raise) them. If two banks competing in the same market merge and form a bank with a high market share, then (assuming that the postmerger market is sufficiently concentrated) the resulting banking organization may be able to exercise market power. Customers of the consolidated bank may be more willing to accept higher prices because no alternatives may be more attractive than maintaining their existing banking relationship. If smaller banks in the market recognize that higher prices do not necessarily result in numerous customer defections, they may follow the market leader and also raise prices. In the premerger, less concentrated market, neither merging party may have been able to sustain high prices because customers of each partner may have viewed the other partner as a convenient alternative and would have transferred their business if prices were raised.

Similarly, the merger of two banks that are not direct competitors often results in substantial resources, or "deep pockets," which allow them more flexibility in pricing strategies. For example, a large bank may decide to set its prices above the competitive level in a market. Smaller banks in that market might try to undercut those prices to attract customers. The large bank could retaliate by lowering prices to the point at which it would incur losses. Because of its greater financial resources, the large bank would be able to sustain losses for a longer time than the small banks. Knowledge that this sequence of events might take place could be sufficient to dissuade small banks from undercutting the prices charged by the large bank. They may elect to be price followers because failure to do so could invite so-called "pricing discipline." Extensive financial resources may enable large banks to exercise market power by exerting price leadership.[10]

A large bank may increase its market power after a merger if it is able to strengthen its brand identity. Because large banks may advertise more frequently, maintain more offices, and have a more prominent profile as a result of involvement in public activities such as sponsoring a local sports team, customers may develop a stronger familiarity with their brand. This familiarity may lead customers to have greater trust in a recognized bank and be willing to pay higher prices for that bank's products and services.

Finally, mergers may benefit banks by reducing risk through diversification. With limited exposure to any particular geographic region, industry, or product type, a large and diversified bank is less vulnerable to problems in any one area. Greater diversification may also make large banks better equipped to take advantage of emerging profit opportunities. In particular, geographically diverse organizations are likely to be better suited to allocating resources to new opportunities because they can easily transfer resources from less profitable to more profitable markets. Smaller, more locally oriented banks do not have similar outside resources to draw on to take advantage of such opportunities.

Failures and New Bank Formations

Although mergers and acquisitions were the dominant force driving changes in the structure of the banking industry in the 1980s and 1990s, the failure and formation of banking institutions also played a role. More than 1,500 banking institutions, with total assets of $235 billion, failed between 1980 and 1998 (Table 9-2).[11] Failures were rare in the early 1980s but grew more common through the decade until peaking in 1988. Many of the failures in the latter part of the decade were a result of problems in the oil and real estate industries in Texas and other southwestern states. Starting in 1989, the number of failures diminished, and by 1995, fewer than 10 banks were failing each year. This trend of increasing health in the banking industry is attributable to the economic recovery in the south-

---

[10]Large banks may benefit from economies of scale, if they exist, in a similar manner as from deep pockets. Moreover, according to Bernard Shull, being "too-big-to-fail" may provide large banks more freedom to exert an anticompetitive influence in markets in which they operate. Because the potential failure of a very large bank poses substantial risk to the entire financial system, investors and analysts generally believe that regulators will not permit them to fail.

[11]In addition, about 1,400 thrift institutions (savings banks and savings and loan associations) with total assets of nearly $700 billion failed.

TABLE 9-2 Bank Failures and Formations (1980–1998)

	Failures		*Formations*
Year	***Number***	***Assets ($ Billions)***	***Number***
1980	11	8.2	206
1981	7	0.1	199
1982	35	2.5	316
1983	46	4.6	366
1984	79	42.7	400
1985	118	3.3	318
1986	144	8.0	248
1987	201	7.7	212
1988	280	53.9	228
1989	206	28.1	201
1990	159	10.7	175
1991	108	44.0	107
1992	100	15.6	73
1993	40	2.9	59
1994	11	0.9	48
1995	6	0.8	110
1996	5	0.2	148
1997	1	0.0	207
1998	3	0.3	193
Total	1,560	234.5	3,814

Sources: Failure data come from the Federal Deposit Insurance Corporation Web site: (*http://www2.fdic.gov/hsob/*). Formation data come from various issues of the *Annual Statistical Digest* and *Annual Report* published by the Federal Reserve Board.

western United States and the strong overall expansion of the U.S. economy during most of the decade. The decline in failures is also attributable to falling interest rates: Banks have not faced the difficult situation in which their fixed-rate assets are not generating sufficient funds to meet obligations on deposits, for which rates adjust frequently.

During the period when more than 1,500 banking institutions failed, more than twice as many new banking institutions were formed (Table 9-2). However, the large number of new formations overstates their importance to the industry. New institutions start out small and remain that way for years. Also, many of the institutions classified as "new" were formed by established bank holding companies, so they were actually expansions of existing firms. In general, the number of formations rose in the early 1980s, declined for about 10 years, and then began increasing in 1995.

The number of start-ups has been limited by various barriers to entry into the industry. One barrier has been legal restrictions limiting the parties that are allowed to open a banking institution. For example, investment banks and insurance companies, firms that are already prominent financial services providers, are prohibited from operating commercial banks. Nonfinancial firms are prohibited as well.

Even as legal barriers to entry erode, others not attributable to legal restrictions will continue to exist—barriers that discourage not only the formation of start-up banks but also the opening of branches in new markets by existing banks. A lack of accurate and comprehensive information is the source of one of these nonstatutory barriers. Operating a bank, particulary extending credit, requires extensive knowledge of market conditions. Although profitable banking opportunities may exist in a given community, a party that is unfamiliar with local businesses and residents may be unable to exploit those opportunities. Evaluating credit risks involves a great deal of uncertainty, and making bad loans can result in unprofitability and possibly failure. Prospective bankers may be hesitant to begin operating in a market with which they are unfamiliar, even if the market offers potentially profitable opportunities.

Another entry barrier not related to legal restrictions is that attracting customers to a new bank may be difficult. Customers face substantial switching costs when they change from one bank to another. Such tasks as opening and closing accounts and arranging for direct deposits and automatic bill payments can be aggravating and time-consuming. Many customers are likely to stay with their current bank, even if another bank offers better prices or service.

Number of Organizations

A key development in the U.S. commercial banking industry has been a decline in the total number of organizations. Between 1980 and 1998, the number fell almost 45 percent from more than 12,300 to fewer than 6,900 (Table 9-3). The decline is expected to continue, with many additional firms leaving the industry through merger. However, the common view is that the industry will always have a large number of organizations.

A major consequence of the consolidation-driven decrease in the number of organizations has been a rise in the number of very large banks, particularly in the latter years of the 1990s. At year-end 1998, seven banks had at least $100 billion in domestic banking assets, including one with assets of more than $250 billion. Before 1991, only one bank had assets exceeding $100 million, and before 1997, none had assets of $250 million. Although consolidation has resulted in many banks exiting the industry, it has resulted in a rise in the number of moderately large banks, especially in the 1980s. More banks with assets above the $1 billion, $10 billion, $25 billion, and $50 billion thresholds have been created by mergers than have been eliminated.

TABLE 9-3 Banking Organizations (1980–1998)

		Number with Domestic Banking Assets Greater than					
Year	***Total***	***$1 Bil***	***$10 Bil***	***$25 Bil***	***$50 Bil***	***$100 Bil***	***$250 Bil***
1980	12,332	206	19	8	1	0	0
1981	12,176	223	23	8	1	0	0
1982	11,930	239	24	10	2	0	0
1983	11,673	252	28	10	2	0	0
1984	11,347	258	31	10	2	0	0
1985	11,015	264	40	10	3	0	0
1986	10,501	269	48	15	3	1	0
1987	10,097	263	52	18	4	0	0
1988	9,715	261	55	23	7	1	0
1989	9,451	264	60	24	7	1	0
1990	9,217	268	59	26	7	0	0
1991	9,003	262	54	25	7	3	0
1992	8,722	247	55	27	10	3	0
1993	8,318	240	56	30	10	3	0
1994	7,891	242	60	31	12	4	0
1995	7,564	249	63	30	15	4	0
1996	7,304	245	56	29	16	7	0
1997	7,112	264	58	33	18	7	1
1998	6,831	270	58	33	15	7	1

Sources: Federal Reserve Board and Reports of Condition and Income (Call Report). Data are as of December 31.

The number of very large banks is likely to continue to increase in the immediate future, but, at some point, that growth is likely to level off. The Riegle-Neal Act of 1994 placed a cap of 10 percent on the share of total insured deposits that a banking organization would be allowed to control as a result of an interstate acquisition. The largest banks will reach a point where extensive additional growth will be legally constrained. In fact, a few banks are already approaching the limit: At year-end 1998, BankAmerica Corporation controlled about 8 percent of U.S. insured deposits. However, merger-related growth may not ultimately be limited to 10 percent because Congress may raise the cap.

Industry and Market Concentration

As consolidation has progressed and the number of moderately large and very large banking organizations has increased, fewer banks now account for a greater proportion of industry deposits (Table 9-4). However, the class of large banks that have accounted for that rise has varied over time.

TABLE 9-4 Concentration of the U.S. Banking Industry (1980–1998)

	Percentage of Total Domestic Deposits Held By the			
Year	*10 Largest Banks*	*25 Largest Banks*	*50 Largest Banks*	*100 Largest Banks*
1980	18.8	29.1	37.1	46.4
1981	18.9	29.8	37.7	47.2
1982	17.9	28.9	37.2	47.1
1983	17.9	28.7	37.8	48.4
1984	16.8	27.3	37.2	48.7
1985	16.7	27.6	38.3	49.9
1986	17.4	28.8	40.9	53.1
1987	18.1	30.6	43.3	56.3
1988	18.4	32.0	46.5	59.1
1989	19.1	32.9	46.5	59.2
1990	20.0	34.3	48.2	60.6
1991	19.5	34.0	47.0	60.0
1992	23.3	36.8	48.6	60.3
1993	22.9	37.1	49.7	60.8
1994	24.4	40.4	53.3	64.5
1995	24.6	40.8	54.4	66.0
1996	29.6	46.2	58.2	67.9
1997	29.6	46.0	58.6	68.5
1998	31.9	48.2	60.6	69.6
1998[1]	36.9	51.2	61.9	70.1

[1]Data reflect the effects of five large mergers completed during the second half of 1998: NationsBank-BankAmerica; Banc One-First Chicago NBD; Norwest-Wells Fargo; SunTrust-Crestar; and Firstar-Star.

Source: Summary of Deposits, Federal Deposit Insurance Corporation. Data are as of June 30.

The early years of the consolidation wave involved banks that were large, but not among the largest in the industry. Mergers enabled these banks to expand their presence within their home state or into neighboring states. Between mid-year 1980 and mid-year 1990, the 100 largest organizations increased the share of deposits under their control from 46.4 percent to 60.6 percent, but most of the increase was attributable to a greater share among banks ranked 11 through 100, especially banks ranked 11 through 50. The share controlled by the 10 largest firms increased only slightly.

As banking organizations increased their presence throughout their home and immediately surrounding states, and as restrictions on interstate banking were relaxed, banks began to expand more aggressively. Deals through which large banks moved into chunks of new territory became more common in the 1990s, increasing the prominence of leading banks. Between 1990 and 1998, the share of deposits under the control of the 10 largest banks grew almost 12 percentage points (60 percent), from 20.0 to 31.9. Over this period, the share controlled by banks ranked 11 through 25 showed a modest increase of 2.0 percentage points, and that of banks ranked 26 through 100 dropped by nearly 5 points.

When 1998 data are adjusted to account for five large mergers that were completed in 1998, but after June 30—the date on which the deposit data were reported—the numbers are even more striking.[12] The 10 largest banks in 1998 accounted for 36.9 percent of deposits nationwide, about 17 percentage points greater than in 1990 and 5 percentage points greater than June 30, 1998. Moreover, the share controlled by the 10 largest banks was approximately the same share that was controlled by the 25 largest just a few years earlier in 1992.

Although concentration at the national level provides information about the relative roles of large and small firms in the banking industry, that measure does not provide information on the structure of markets that are most relevant for conduct and performance in retail banking. Concentration at the local level provides this information because banking markets for retail services tend to be local. Urban (defined here as metropolitan statistical areas—MSAs) and rural (non-MSA counties) local areas are analyzed separately here because the two markets differ in key ways, particularly in physical size and density of population and commercial activity. These differences may influence competitive interactions among banks.

Concentration at the local level can be measured in several ways. The number of banks provides a simple measure of the number of choices customers have. In markets with fewer banks, customers are likely to have fewer convenient choices, and banks are more likely to be able to exercise market power. The three-firm concentration ratio (CR3)—the aggregate share of deposits controlled by the three banks with the greatest individual market shares—provides a measure of the prominence of the leading firms. The Herfindahl-Hirschman Index (HHI) takes into account the market shares of all banks in the market. It is computed as the sum of the squared market shares of every bank in the market and ranges from 10,000 for a monopoly to nearly 0 for a market with numerous competitors, each with a small market share. In markets having a high HHI, the leading banks have a substantial market share, and in markets having a low HHI, no single bank has a sizable market share. Therefore, the ability to exercise market power should be positively related to the HHI.

Concentration in urban markets remained stable in the 1980s and 1990s (Table 9-5). The median number of banks per urban market was

[12]The five large mergers were NationsBank Corporation-BankAmerica Corporation; Banc One Corporation-First Chicago NBD Corporation; Norwest Corporation-Wells Fargo & Company; SunTrust Banks, Inc.-Crestar Financial Corporation; and Firstar Holdings Corporation-Star Banc Corporation.

TABLE 9-5 Concentration of Urban and Rural U.S. Banking Markets (1980–1998)

	Urban Banking Markets (MSAs)			*Rural Banking Markets (Non-MSA Counties)*		
Year	*Number of Banks*	*CR3*	*HHI*	*Number of Banks*	*CR3*	*HHI*
1980	21.9	66.0	1953	4.0	90.0	4451
	(14)	(67.4)	(1852)	(3)	(100.0)	(3757)
1982	21.9	65.5	1935	4.1	89.7	4397
	(14)	(66.2)	(1855)	(3)	(100.0)	(3710)
1984	21.8	65.8	1930	4.1	89.8	4397
	(14)	(65.7)	(1843)	(3)	(100.0)	(3730)
1986	22.6	67.1	1995	4.1	89.8	4386
	(14)	(67.9)	(1935)	(4)	(100.0)	(3694)
1988	21.7	67.5	2002	4.0	90.0	4354
	(13)	(68.2)	(1962)	(3)	(100.0)	(3704)
1990	21.3	67.2	1990	4.1	90.0	4330
	(14)	(67.2)	(1868)	(4)	(99.6)	(3688)
1992	20.8	67.1	2000	4.1	89.6	4263
	(14)	(67.4)	(1865)	(4)	(96.8)	(3633)
1994	19.6	66.8	1980	4.2	89.2	4210
	(13)	(66.8)	(1852)	(4)	(95.6)	(3588)
1996	19.1	67.0	1997	4.3	88.8	4146
	(13)	(66.9)	(1854)	(4)	(94.9)	(3534)
1998	19.8	65.8	1975	4.5	88.0	4090
	(14)	(65.4)	(1822)	(4)	(93.2)	(3474)

Source: Summary of Deposits, Federal Deposit Insurance Corporation. Data are as of June 30. CR3 is the three-firm concentration ratio and HHI is the Herfindahl-Hirschman Index. The top figure in each cell is the mean and the figure in parentheses is the median.

13 or 14 throughout the period; the mean number fluctuated more, varying between 19 and 23 and decreased slightly over the period. The average HHI fluctuated little, remaining near 2000 throughout the period. Using the Department of Justice's definition of a highly concentrated market as one having an HHI above 1800, urban markets, on average, have been somewhat highly concentrated. CR3 has also remained steady over the period: The average CR3 for urban markets fluctuated within the tight range of about 65 to 68 percent.

Concentration in rural markets was much higher and did not show the same degree of consistency. That concentration was greater is not surprising: Because they are smaller than urban markets, rural markets can profitably support fewer banks. Banks cannot operate in a rural market with a small market share because they cannot generate sufficient revenues to cover their costs. A small share of an urban market involves more activity, so it is easier to earn sufficient revenue to cover costs. Both the median and mean number of banks operating in rural markets was around four throughout the 1980s and 1990s.

The average HHI in rural markets during the period was above 4000, or about twice the average HHI for urban markets, and well above the 1800 level used by the Department of Justice to define a highly concentrated market. Moreover, the three leading banks have tended to control all, or at least much, of their rural markets, although concentration decreased steadily from 1980 to 1998: The average HHI decreased about 360 points, the mean CR3 fell about 2 percentage points, and the average number of firms in a market increased by one-half.[13]

Although average concentration in rural and urban banking markets has decreased or remained stable over time, levels have varied considerably from market to market (Table 9-6). For example, in 1998, half the urban markets had 10 to 22 banks and half had an HHI of 1460 to 2260; for each measure, the other half was outside these ranges. Although rural markets showed less dispersion in the number of banks (at least half had three to six banks), they showed considerable dispersion in HHI levels (the middle half had HHIs in the broad range between 2500 and 5000).

TABLE 9-6 Variation in Concentration of Urban and Rural U.S. Banking Markets (1998)

	Urban Banking Markets (MSAs)			*Rural Banking Markets (Non-MSA Counties)*		
	Number of Banks	*CR3*	*HHI*	*Number of Banks*	*CR3*	*HHI*
Minimum	3	32.6	730	1	32.7	856
25th percentile	10	56.8	1457	3	78.0	2478
Median	14	65.4	1822	4	93.2	3474
75th percentile	22	73.2	2259	6	100.0	5044
Maximum	199	100.0	7785	18	100.0	10000

Source: Summary of Deposits, Federal Deposit Insurance Corporation. Data are as of June 30. CR3 is the three-firm concentration ratio and HHI is the Herfindahl-Hirschman Index.

[13]Measures of local concentration cited in the text and tables include only commercial banks. When analyzing proposed bank mergers, antitrust authorities often include, on a partial basis, savings banks and savings and loan associations. When measures are computed with thrift institutions receiving at least partial weight, a somewhat different picture of local concentration emerges. For example, computing the HHI with the deposits of thrift institutions included at 50 percent, as is typically done by the Federal Reserve Board in its competitive analysis, yields lower average levels (below 1800 in urban markets and below 4000 in rural markets), but those levels have increased over time in urban areas and remained stable in rural areas.

The substantial changes in concentration in the commercial banking industry at the national level during the 1980s and 1990s and the more modest average changes at the local level reflect the influence of consolidation. Mergers have enabled banks to increase in size by enhancing their presence within states and across large regions of the country. However, mergers have not resulted in banks greatly increasing their presence in local markets. These patterns are a direct reflection of antitrust policy in banking. Mergers between banks that do not compete with each other in local markets do not raise serious antitrust concerns, and few limits other than interstate banking restrictions have been placed on so-called "market-extension" mergers. In contrast, mergers between banks that operate in the same local markets do raise antitrust concerns, especially when one or both have a large presence. Antitrust authorities seek to limit the amount of change in the HHI, the postmerger level of the HHI, and the level of the consolidated bank's postmerger market share resulting from so-called "in-market" mergers. Banking antitrust policy has restricted in-market mergers, and most of the consolidation activity in the industry has involved market-extension mergers.

Relevant Market Definition

A key issue in applying the structure-conduct-performance framework to an analysis of the commercial banking industry is determining the relevant market. This task involves defining both the product and geographic markets. As previously discussed, the relevant product market is ambiguous, as commercial banking encompasses numerous financial services, many of which might be considered a unique product. For this analysis, the relevant product market is assumed to be the group of financial products and services constituting retail banking.

The relevant geographic market in retail banking is the area from which banks can attract customers and within which customers can find banks. Surveys show that most retail customers establish relationships with banking organizations that have a physical presence close to where they live or work (in the case of households) or close to where they are located (in the case of small businesses). For this analysis, the relevant geographic market is local. Such an approach is consistent with most research and is the approach taken by antitrust authorities.

In the future, expansion of the geographic market may be warranted. Recent technologies, such as telephone banking, ATMs, personal computers, and the Internet, may enable banks lacking a physical presence in a geographic region to provide convenient financial services to customers therein. These technology-based delivery systems allow customers to make deposits, apply for loans, discuss financial needs, and obtain updated account information without having to visit a traditional bank office or, in some cases, interact with a bank representative. Although many nontraditional delivery systems are already available, consumer and small business surveys suggest that they are not yet widely accepted. Most customers still prefer that their bank have a local physical presence. Nonetheless, the increasing influence of technological advances suggests that the relevant geographic size of retail banking markets should be reassessed regularly.

Role of Nonbank Firms

Commercial banks are the largest, most prevalent, and most diversified group of depository institutions operating in the United States, but they are not the only depository institutions. Thrift institutions (savings banks and savings and loan associations) and credit unions also provide depository services, including insured deposit accounts. Thrifts held total assets of $1.1 trillion and credit unions had $400 billion at the end of 1998, compared with domestic assets of $4.7 trillion for commercial banks. In addition, nonbank, nondepository firms provide some of the same financial services as commercial banks.

Thrift Institutions Thrift institutions raise funds primarily by collecting consumer deposits and investing them in mortgage and other consumer loans. Thrift deposits are protected up to $100,000 by the same federal deposit insurance that covers bank deposits. For many years, thrifts provided a limited set of consumer-oriented financial services because they were restricted in the types of accounts they could offer and loans they could make. Of particular importance, they were restricted from originating commercial loans. Beginning in the early 1980s, restrictions on their activities, including commercial lending, were relaxed. Few thrifts have taken full advantage of expanded powers.

Although many thrift institutions engage in some commercial lending, few engage in more than limited activity.[14] At year-end 1997, more than 75 percent of savings banks and 50 percent of savings and loan associations held at least some commercial loans, but fewer than 14 percent of savings banks and only about 4 percent of savings and loans held at least 5 percent of their assets in such loans. In contrast, nearly all commercial banks made some commercial loans and about 75 percent had at least 5 percent of their assets in these loans. Because a large proportion of commercial loans are extended to small businesses, the limited involvement of thrifts in commercial lending suggests that they do not provide much competition to banks in at least one important retail banking product—small business lending.

---

[14]Steven J. Pilloff and Robin A. Prager, "Thrift Involvement in Commercial and Industrial Lending," *Federal Reserve Bulletin,* December 1998, 1025–1037, discusses the involvement of thrifts in commercial lending and clearly illustrates that the large majority are much less active in such lending than commercial banks.

The lack of full competition from thrifts in retail banking is recognized by antitrust authorities. In the competitive analysis of proposed bank mergers, thrifts are regarded as market competitors, but their role is viewed as limited. However, antitrust authorities often treat thrifts that provide a full set of bank products and services, including commercial loans, as full members of the commercial banking industry. In this chapter, thrifts are not included in the analysis. As a result, measures of concentration may be somewhat overstated, especially in markets having a large thrift presence.

Credit Unions Credit unions are nonprofit, cooperative financial institutions that collect deposits from and make loans to members. Deposits at credit unions are protected up to $100,000 by federal insurance, which is administered by the National Credit Union Administration. For each credit union, members must share a "common bond" such as belonging to the same organization or being employed by the same company. This requirement greatly limits the competitive importance of credit unions because they are unable to gather deposits from or make loans to many potential customers.

Also hurting the competitive importance of credit unions is their limitation by regulation of the range of products and services they may offer. Too, many credit unions are very small and cannot efficiently provide more than basic deposit and loan products.

Other Nonbank Firms The financial services industry has many specialized firms that compete in certain respects with commercial banks. This competition is limited, however, because specialized firms do not offer as full a complement of financial services as banks provide. For example, mortgage originators compete with banks for residential mortgages but not for other loan products, and certainly not for federally insured deposit products. Likewise, many consumer finance companies specialize in lending to consumers but offer no credit services to businesses and no deposit products to anyone. On the deposit side, money market mutual funds, which are not federally insured, offer some competition to bank deposit products, but none to loan products. Because nonbank institutions offer a limited set of products and services, they are less likely to form the special type of customer relationship that is formed with banks.

III. CONDUCT

According to the structure-conduct-performance model, market structure affects bank performance by influencing bank conduct, that is, the ways in which banks compete with each other and the intensity of that competition. Like firms in other industries, banks engage in price competition. Unlike prices in many other industries, however, bank prices can be ambiguous, making price comparisons difficult for customers. Banks also compete with each other in several ways unrelated to price. This section discusses the ways banks compete with each other and the unique roles large banks play in that competition.

Price Competition

Banks engage in price competition. However, that competition is not nearly as straightforward as in other industries because the price of bank products is not always obvious. First, the price of many financial services involves both an interest rate and fees. Banks charge a variety of fees payable under widely varying circumstances. Some fees, such as for monthly accounts, are assessed regularly; others are assessed only when a specific service, such as an ATM, is used; still others are charged only when some condition, such as a minimum balance requirement, is not satisfied. Therefore, two customers having the same type of account at the same institution could pay very different prices if their banking practices differed greatly.

Adding to customers' difficulty in evaluating the price of bank products is the nature of the business. Commercial banking is marked by customers maintaining a multiproduct relationship with a primary organization, and the most meaningful price for retail banking services is likely to be a composite price of a set of products and services. Such a composite price may be difficult for customers to calculate. Moreover, the products and services included in the set (as well as the weight assigned to each) may differ from customer to customer depending on individual banking needs. Despite these problems, price competition among banks may be driven by a desire by banks to establish and maintain customer relationships. As such, banks may establish a pricing schedule designed to attract and retain a particular customer base.

Nonprice Competition

Banks also compete in ways unrelated to price. The location of branch offices (and more recently, the location of ATMs) is an important form of nonprice competition. Another is customer service. Length of operating hours, length of waiting times for tellers, loan officers, and customer service representatives, and access to senior personnel are just a few of the elements banks can control that determine the level of service they provide. Banks compete, too, in their provision of services through alternative delivery channels—such as dial-up computer networks, the Internet, and the telephone—that may be more convenient than traditional "brick and mortar" offices for some customers.

The set of products offered is another dimension along which banks compete. Product variety directly influences a bank's ability to meet customer needs. Some banks offer many different products to appeal to a broad cross-section of customers; others offer a small set of highly specialized products.

Brand recognition is an important component of competition among banks. Through advertising and involvement in community activities banks attempt to establish an institutional image such as "integral part of the community" or "trustworthy" or "knowledgeable." Much brand imaging in the retail banking industry revolves around the fundamental differences between small and large banks. Small banks emphasize their local ownership and management and their ability to provide personalized service. Large banks emphasize their wide product offerings, extensive experience, and vast resources as tools to help customers in an increasingly complex financial world.

Relationship Competition

Banks compete in developing customer relationships so as to enhance their prospects for cross-selling. Cross-selling—selling additional products and services to existing bank customers—can be a lucrative and efficient means of expanding business. For example, a bank may encourage its checking account customers to take out a home equity loan, or a bank holding company may try to sell the products of its nonbank subsidiaries, such as an insurance or investment product, to its banking customers.

In attempting to sell additional products, a customer's existing bank or bank holding company has several advantages over other banks. First, because it regularly interacts with customers as they do business it has many opportunities to cross-sell. Customers may be more responsive to this approach than to more impersonal or intrusive methods such as advertising, direct mail, and telephone solicitations from other banks. Another advantage for an existing bank holding company is the information it has on its customers. Such information may enable a bank to identify those products most likely to be desired by particular segments of its customer base, allowing it to focus its marketing and cross-selling efforts. A third advantage is the trust that an established relationship may engender between a customer and a bank; customers may be more likely to place their confidence in a bank with whom they already do business.

Cross-selling is such an important aspect of competition that many banks actively seek to expand their opportunities. In fact, the potential for cross-selling was a primary motivation for the 1998 merger of Citicorp and Travelers. As relaxation of restrictions on the activities of banks and bank holding companies continues—so that additional investment and insurance products can be sold—cross-selling is sure to become an even more critical part of competition.

Influence of Entry Barriers on Competition

Bank conduct, or competition, is sometimes influenced by the numerous barriers that make it difficult for both new and existing organizations to enter new markets. These barriers—including customer switching costs, a lack of clear information about market conditions, and legal restrictions on who is allowed to operate a bank and where it may be operated—give incumbent firms advantages that can affect their conduct and facilitate the exercise of market power. If entry barriers are sufficiently high, a bank (or potential banker) may still be deterred from entry, even if existing firms in the market are charging high prices and earning high profits.

Special Issues Related to Large Banks

An important development that may influence conduct in the banking industry is the increased prominence of large banks. Large banks may behave differently than smaller banks and may exert a unique effect on competition. In fact, the mere presence of a large bank in a market may affect competition indirectly by influencing the conduct of smaller rivals.

As discussed earlier, large banks having access to considerable resources may be able to sustain market prices above competitive levels. If they benefit from economies of scale, they may also be able to charge lower prices or offer superior service relative to smaller banks. Moreover, if large banks are diversified, they may be more easily able to reallocate their resources to profitable opportunities.

Large banks may also have a negative influence on competition as a result of multimarket contact. Multimarket contact occurs when two or more banks compete with each other in several geographic areas, or markets. Consolidation has resulted in increased contact of this nature. Specifically, a bank may not act aggressively in a market in which its rivals in other markets operate because those rivals could retaliate in their other markets. If a bank competes with other banks that it does not encounter elsewhere, then it may feel more willing to exploit competitive advantages without fear of retaliation.

Large banks, particularly those with a small share of a local market, may also increase competition because they can easily draw on out-of-market resources to exploit profitable opportunities. This ability may restrain other banks, with large shares of the market, from exercising market power. If locally dominant banks attempt to raise prices, the large bank may bring in resources from elsewhere to exploit the opportunity.

Such a response would eventually drive prices down toward their competitive level. Anticipation that large banks might respond to high prices in this way is likely to discourage locally dominant banks from trying to sustain high prices in the first place.[15]

IV. PERFORMANCE

The structure-conduct-performance paradigm asserts that market structure influences bank conduct which, in turn, affects performance. Because direct observation and measurement of bank conduct is difficult, research generally focuses on the relationship between structure and performance.

Influence of Market Structure on Performance

Prices In unconcentrated banking markets, consumers are likely to have numerous convenient banking alternatives. If any single bank attempts to charge excessively high prices, its customers can turn to another bank. For this reason, high prices are less sustainable in unconcentrated markets. In more concentrated markets, higher prices may be easier to sustain. Fewer banks operate and market shares are larger, so customers have fewer convenient alternatives. They may accept higher prices or poorer service if going to a rival bank that charges lower prices or offers better service is too inconvenient. If all banks in the market know that high prices can be sustained, then all banks are likely to charge high prices.

Empirical research shows that market structure is related to bank prices in a way that suggests that the exercise of market power increases with concentration. Many studies have found that loan rates rise and deposit rates fall as local market concentration increases.[16] No significant relationship between market concentration and bank fees has been identified in the limited research that has been conducted on that subject.[17]

Efficiency The market structure in which a bank operates may influence bank incentives for and managerial dedication to cost savings. In less concentrated, more competitive markets, market forces exert pressure on managers to maximize profits, making efficient operations a top

---

[15]See William M. Landes and Richard A. Posner, "Market Power in Antitrust Cases," *Harvard Law Review* 94, March 1981, 937–996, for a thorough discussion of this hypothesis.

[16]For example, Timothy H. Hannan, "Market Share Inequality, the Number of Competitors, and the HHI: An Examination of Bank Pricing," *Review of Industrial Organization,* February 1997, 25–35; Anthony W. Cyrnak and Timothy H. Hannan, "Is the Cluster Still Valid in Defining Banking Markets? Evidence from a New Data Source," *The Antitrust Bulletin,* Summer 1999, 313–331.

[17]Timothy H. Hannan, "Bank Fees and Their Variation across Banks and Locations," working paper, Board of Governors of the Federal Reserve System, December 1996.

priority. If managers are unable to maximize profits, returns are low and they may be relieved of their duties or forced to sell the bank to a more profitable rival. In the worst case, an inefficient bank could become insolvent and fail.

In more concentrated markets, competition is less intense, so banks can sustain prices at levels that generate sizable profits. Managers may intentionally operate inefficiently either for their own or the bank's benefit. For instance, a manager may direct costly resources toward preserving the existing market structure or pursuing additional market share so that large profits continue or are increased. Or a manager may prefer to sacrifice some firm profits in order to live a "quiet life" or to enjoy costly perks such as a large staff or a luxurious office. The additional profit generated by greater efficiency may not, in the manager's opinion, be worth the additional effort. Even if they operate their banks at inefficient levels, above-competitive pricing may make it possible for managers to earn returns for shareholders that compare favorably with other investment alternatives. Finally, managers may operate less efficiently in more concentrated markets because they lack ability—although not seriously enough to be forced to exit banking; high profits generated from above-competitive prices may mask a lack of managerial skill.

Empirical analysis indicates that bank efficiency is negatively related to concentration.[18] Managers of banks in markets that are less concentrated and governed more strictly by competitive pressures are more effective at operating efficiently than managers of banks in more concentrated, less competitive markets.

Profitability Because greater market concentration is associated with higher prices—higher loan rates and lower deposit rates—greater concentration might be expected to lead to a greater net interest margin (the difference between interest income and expenses) and a corresponding rise in bank profitability. However, research shows that, as concentration increases, efficiency drops—in which case greater concentration might be expected to lead to a decline in bank profitability.

Studies of bank profits and market structure indicate that the concentration-pricing relationship is stronger than, and is only partially offset by, the concentration-efficiency relationship.[19] Banks operating in

---

[18]For example, Allen N. Berger and Timothy H. Hannan, "Using Efficiency Measures to Distinguish Among Alternative Explanations of the Structure-Performance Relationship in Banking," *Managerial Finance,* 1991, 6–31; Allen N. Berger and Timothy H. Hannan, "The Efficiency Cost of market Power in the Banking Industry: A Test of the 'Quiet Life' and Related Hypotheses," *Review of Economics and Statistics,* August 1998, 454–465.

[19]For example, Steven J. Pilloff "Multimarket Contact in Banking," *Review of Industrial Organization,* March 1999, 163–182; Stephen A. Rhoades "Market Share Inequality, the HHI, and Other Risk Measures of the Firm-Composition of a Market," *Review of Industrial Organization,* December 1995, 657–674.

more concentrated markets earn higher profits than banks operating in less concentrated markets.

Influence of Size on Performance

Their size may enable large banks to operate more efficiently and more profitably than their smaller rivals and to exert a unique influence on market competition. The trend in the 1980s and 1990s of ever-larger banks controlling ever-larger shares of the industry may have affected the performance of both large banks and their smaller rivals.

Performance of Large Banks Data for commercial banks of various sizes indicate that small banks are clearly less profitable than large banks but that the largest banks are not more profitable than smaller banks that may still be considered large (Table 9-7). For 1998, the smallest banks (assets of up to $50 million) were the least profitable, as measured by an average return on assets (net income divided by average assets), of nearly 1 percent. Average profitability increased for groups of progressively larger banks up to those with assets of $50 billion. Beyond that level of assets, increasing size was associated with slightly lower profitability. Greater profitability among large banks relative to small banks may reflect superior operating performance or the effect of off-balance-sheet activities, which are more common at large banks and affect the income statement (net income) but not the balance sheet (total assets).

Evidence on the relationship between bank pricing and bank size is mixed. Strong evidence suggests that larger banks charge higher fees than smaller banks.[20] For example, one study found that in 1997, banks with

TABLE 9-7 Profitability and Efficiency of U.S. Banks By Size Class (1998)

Asset Size ($ Millions)	*Mean Return on Assets*	*Mean Efficiency Ratio*
≤50	0.99%	68.7%
51–100	1.14	63.8
101–500	1.21	62.1
501–1000	1.28	60.8
1001–10,000	1.42	59.0
10,001–50,000	1.50	60.7
≥50,000	1.40	62.0

Source: Reports of Condition and Income (Call Report).

[20]Summary statistics of survey data on bank fees are reported in the Board of Governors of the Federal Reserve System's 1998 *Annual Report to the Congress on Retail Fees and Services of Depository Institutions.*

assets of more than $1 billion charged an average fee of nearly $19 for a stop-payment order compared with less than $13 for institutions with assets of less than $100 million; similarly, large banks charged $21 on average for a bounced check while small banks charged about $15. Because the study summarized fee data for all banks with assets of more than $1 billion, it is unclear how fees charged by the largest banks differ from those charged by other banks. Study of the relationship between bank size and loan rates provides weak evidence suggesting that large banks charge lower prices than their smaller rivals. For example, recent research found a significant negative relationship between bank size and the rate charged on secured, variable-rate, commercial loans.[21] However, since loan rates are frequently set to reflect the expected risk of a loan, differences in rates between large and small banks may reflect differences in the types of loans made and the types of businesses served, rather than a difference in prices for a uniform product. In summary, large banks clearly charge higher fees, but whether they charge higher prices overall is unclear. Moreover, it is unclear whether the fees charged by the largest banks differ from those charged by institutions of other sizes.

Although economies of scale have been found for smaller banks, there is little evidence that scale economies extend to the largest banks. The precise point at which scale economies disappear is unclear; studies have found benefits from increased size for banks with assets of $100 million to $10 billion or $25 billion.[22] Regardless of where in this range economies of scale cease to exist, the efficiency gains from economies of scale are more likely and larger for the smaller banks in the range than for the larger ones. Economies of scale are unlikely beyond the upper end of the range. Banks that have been most active in the merger movement and have used acquisitions to grow substantially are unlikely to derive benefits from scale economies.

Average efficiency ratios calculated from 1998 commercial bank data likewise indicate that the largest banks do not experience economies of scale (Table 9-7). The efficiency ratio, a measure commonly used by bankers and financial analysts, is calculated as total noninterest expense divided by the sum of net interest income (interest revenue less interest expense) and noninterest revenue. A lower ratio corresponds to greater efficiency.

---

[21]Anthony W. Cyrnak and Timothy H. Hannan, "Is the Cluster Still Valid in Defining Banking Markets? Evidence from a New Data Source," *The Antitrust Bulletin,* Summer 1999, 313–331.

[22]For example, Allen N. Berger and Loretta J. Mester, "Inside the Black Box: What Explains Differences in the Efficiencies of Financial Institutions?" *Journal of Banking and Finance,* 1997, 895–947; David B. Humphrey, "Why Do Estimates of Bank Scale Economies Differ?" *Federal Reserve Bank of Richmond Economic Review,* September-October 1990, 38–50.

The smallest banks are the least efficient and could benefit the most from increasing their size, all else equal. The average ratio for that group (total banking assets of $50 million or less) was 68.7 percent, compared with 63.8 percent for banks in the next-larger size group (assets of $50 million to $100 million). Average efficiency ratios decrease slightly over the next several size ranges, and then begin to increase with size, suggesting that scale economies are unlikely to provide the industry's largest banks impressive cost advantages relative to most other banks in the industry.

Finally, large banks appear to be no better than, and possibly inferior to, smaller banks at attracting and retaining customers. One study found that, from 1990 to 1996, the average market share of the 50 largest banks in the industry declined in markets in which they had engaged in no mergers or acquisitions.[23] The pattern of declining market share was particularly pronounced in rural areas, but even in urban areas, where large banks maintained constant market shares, the large banks demonstrated no special ability to attract customers. These results are consistent with those of other studies, which have shown that large banks are not especially successful at grabbing and holding onto market share.[24]

In summary, there is no clear evidence that large banks behave or perform much differently than their smaller rivals. Although large banks are more profitable than small banks, the largest banks are not the most profitable, as average return on asset levels tend to decrease slightly for banks with assets greater than $50 billion. Bank efficiency ratios show a similar pattern with average efficiency decreasing for the largest banks. The evidence on pricing is mixed: Large banks charge higher fees, but some evidence suggests that small banks charge higher rates on loans; moreover, it is unclear whether the fees charged by the largest banks differ from those charged by banks of other sizes. Finally, the inability of large banks to grow their share of deposits in local markets suggests that large banks do not have sizable competitive advantages over smaller rivals that enable them to attract and retain customers.

Performance of Other Banks Facing Large Banks If large banks have some unique influence on competition, then the presence of a large bank in a market may influence the competitive environment, which may, in turn, affect the performance of smaller, local banks that also operate in that market. Several studies suggest that large banks may lower the level of competition in markets in which they operate.

23Steven J. Pilloff and Stephen A. Rhoades, "Do Large, Diversified Banking Organizations Have Competitive Advantages?" *Review of Industrial Organization,* forthcoming.

24For example, John T. Rose and John D. Wolken, "Geographic Diversification in Banking, Market Share Changes, and the Viability of Small, Independent Banks," *Journal of Financial Services Research,* March 1990, 5–20.

One study found that the profitability (as measured by return on assets) of small banks that operate in a single rural market in which a large bank also operates is higher than that of comparable small banks that do not compete with a large bank.[25] This finding supports the idea that large banks exert a special anticompetitive influence on the market, such as disciplinary pricing. It does not support the idea that large banks with small or moderate market shares procompetitively prevent the exercise of market power by smaller banks with large market shares.

Another study found that multimarket contact—the extent to which banks in a given market also compete with each other in other markets—is positively related to the profitability of all banks in the market.[26] This result suggests that when banks compete with each other in several markets, they may be unwilling to compete aggressively in any particular market out of fear of retaliation in the other common markets. This lack of vigorous competition appears to influence all the banks in a market, large and small. However, large banks are more likely to be strongly influenced by multimarket contact because they have extensive operations in many markets and are more likely to encounter each other frequently. Competition in markets in which large banks operate is most likely to be strongly affected by multimarket contact.

V. PUBLIC POLICY

Current antitrust policy toward the U.S. commercial banking industry is concerned primarily with mergers, particularly with whether proposed transactions violate antitrust standards. The basic goal is to limit the concentration of the set, or "cluster," of bank products and services, as measured by total deposits, in banking markets that are defined to be local in scope. The discussion in this chapter suggests that this approach is appropriate. High local levels of concentration are associated with higher prices, higher profits, and lower efficiency. Prohibiting transactions that would result in high levels of concentration is an effective way of maintaining competitive markets that offer customers adequate choices and prevent banks from sustaining extremely high prices.

One issue that merits scrutiny but is not incorporated in current policy, or is only minimally incorporated, is whether very large banks have a

[25]Steven J. Pilloff "Does the Presence of Big Banks Influence Competition in Local Markets?" *Journal of Financial Services Research,* 199, 159–177. Also, see John D. Wolken and John T. Rose. "Dominant Banks, Market Power, and Out-of-Market Productive Capacity," *Journal of Economics and Business,* August 1991, 214–229.

[26]Steven J. Pilloff "Multimarket Contact in Banking," *Review of Industrial Organization,* March 1999, 163–182. Also, see Gary W. Whalen, "Nonlocal Concentration, Multimarket Linkages, and Interstate Banking," *The Antitrust Bulletin,* Summer 1996, 365–397.

unique effect on competition independent of their prominence in a local banking market. Key differences may exist among banks of different sizes in their behavior, performance, and effect on rivals. The issue is important because the dichotomy between the largest organizations in the industry and the many community banks is increasing as mergers create larger and larger banking firms that have substantial resources and operate over extensive geographic areas. Understanding such issues as whether large banks have unique sources of market power and whether banks of different sizes differ substantially in their ability to operate efficiently and meet customer needs is critical in designing and implementing an effective antitrust policy.

Another issue that warrants continued examination is the size of the market that should be used when looking at concentration. The relevant geographic market, at least for retail banking, is assumed to be local. Changing this assumption to expand the geographic scope of the relevant market might seem appropriate because, with increased use of the Internet and other advanced technologies, banks may be able to serve customers without having a physical presence. If customers can complete all banking transactions through alternative delivery channels and are comfortable doing so, then retail banking markets may not be limited to a local area. However, until customers feel more comfortable about establishing and maintaining a relationship with a bank that does not have a nearby physical presence, technological advances will not effectively extend the borders of retail banking markets. Determining the appropriate size of banking markets is an important issue that could have a substantial effect on antitrust policy because, if markets were enlarged, fewer mergers would likely raise serious competitive concerns.

Finally, one of the most controversial issues in banking involves the ATM surcharge fee, which is imposed when a customer of a given bank uses an ATM that is not owned by that bank. The fee is levied by the ATM owner and is charged directly to the ATM user in addition to any other fees imposed by the ATM user's bank. Paying this fee leads many consumers to feel that they are being gouged by ATM operators and forced to pay for access to their own money. Public outrage has been so vehement that some areas, including San Francisco, have banned banks from imposing ATM surcharges. Banks contend that they are charging a fair price for providing consumers access to their deposits and that consumers who do not want to pay a surcharge can avoid it by accessing their accounts through a different channel. The ATM surcharge fee also raises antitrust issues. In particular, large banks, which tend to own numerous ATMs over an extensive area, may be able to use surcharge fees to encourage customers of small banks to switch to larger banks. One way that small bank customers can avoid surcharges is to switch to a larger bank with more widely distributed ATMs—increasing the likelihood that an ATM owned by their bank will be conveniently located.

VI. CONCLUSION

Commercial banking is one of the largest and most important industries in the United States. A substantial portion of businesses and households rely on commercial banks as their primary source of credit and as a safe and convenient place to keep cash. In the 1980s and 1990s, the commercial banking industry was affected by developments—mainly mergers and acquisitions but, to a lesser extent, failures and new formations—that transformed the industry, but that did not substantially affect competition. Although the industry has experienced a large decline in the number of banks and an associated emergence of larger banks that control more of the industry, the evidence is mixed regarding whether size enables large banks to influence competition. Moreover, although competition may be affected by increased market concentration at the local level, changes in (and levels of) average concentration during the 1980s and 1990s did not indicate that mergers resulted in much less competition.[27]

In future years, banks should continue to be the primary providers of financial services to many American households and businesses. Moreover, the industry is likely to experience further structural change as consolidation, regulatory reforms, and technological developments take place at a rapid pace. Therefore, identifying relevant markets and understanding the key factors that influence competition in those markets will continue to be an important challenge for effective public policy.

Suggested Readings

Amel, Dean F. "Trends in the Structure of Federally Insured Depository Institutions, 1984–94," *Federal Reserve Bulletin,* January 1996, 1–15.

Berger, Allen N., Rebecca S. Demsetz, and Philip E. Strahan. "The Consolidation of the Financial Services Industry: Causes, Consequences, and

[27]Bank-only measures of concentration have remained stable in urban markets and decreased somewhat in rural markets between 1980 and 1998. When deposits of thrift institutions are included on a partial basis in concentration measures, the concentration of urban markets has risen during the 1980s and 1990s. However, the average level of the HHI in urban markets, with thrifts included at 50 percent, has remained less than 1800 during the period, suggesting that many urban markets have not become highly concentrated and that competition has remained strong. In rural markets, concentration measures that include thrift institutions have remained constant over time.

Implications for the Future," *Journal of Banking and Finance,* 1999, 135–194. This paper is in a special edition of the journal in which many other interesting articles on the consolidation of the financial services industry appear.

Edwards, Corwin D. "Conglomerate Bigness as a Source of Market Power." In *Business Concentration and Price Policy,* (Princeton, NJ: Princeton University Press, 1955), 331–359.

Hanweck, Gerald A., and Bernard Shull. "The Bank Merger Movement: Efficiency, Stability, and Competitive Policy Concerns," *The Antitrust Bulletin,* Summer 1999, 251–284.

Rhoades, Stephen A. "Retail Commercial Banking: An Industry in Transition." In Larry L. Deutsch ed., *Industry Studies,* (Armonk, NY: M.E. Sharpe, 1998), 176–199.

———. "Commercial Banking: Two Industries, a Laboratory for Research." In Larry L. Duetsch ed., *Industry Studies,* (Upper Saddle River, NJ: Prentice Hall, 1993), 271–305.

Rose, Peter S. *Banking Across State Lines,* (Westport, CT: Quorum Books, 1997).

Shull, Bernard. "The Origins of Antitrust in Banking: An Historical Perspective," *The Antitrust Bulletin,* Summer 1996, 255–288.

Sinkey, Joseph F. *Commercial Bank Financial Management,* (Upper Saddle River, NJ: Prentice Hall, 1998). Chapter 19 provides a nice discussion on consolidation.

Thomas, Lloyd B. *Money, Banking, and Financial Markets,* (New York: McGraw-Hill, 1997).

CHAPTER 10

Health Care

—JOHN GODDEERIS

Health care is, in important ways, our largest industry. Currently, national health expenditures account for 13.5 percent of gross domestic product. In other words, more than one in every seven dollars spent on final goods and services produced in the United States is devoted to health. Collectively, we spend over $1 trillion, and, on a per capita basis, nearly $4,000 for every man, woman, and child in America.

This vast total includes a tremendous variety of goods and services: An expectant mother's visit to her doctor for a routine prenatal checkup; a pair of contact lenses; a surgical operation to replace a failing hip; or the drug "cocktail" that keeps a potential AIDS patient relatively symptom-free are all included as outputs of the health care sector. Figure 10-1 shows the major components of national health expenditures, as defined by the U.S. Health Care Financing Administration (HCFA). The largest categories, in order, are hospital care, physicians' services, nursing home care, and prescription drugs. The "other" category encompasses a wide range of goods and services, such as dental care; home health care; the services of other professionals such as chiropractors and optometrists; over-the-counter medications; durable medical equipment such as eyeglasses, hearing aids and wheelchairs; the costs of administering government health programs and private health insurance; and government-funded public health services and medical research.

The sheer size of the health care sector makes it a key component of the U.S. economy. Some of our most intense policy debates revolve around health care issues. When President Clinton took office in 1993, he made health care reform a centerpiece of his first 2 years. His effort to reshape the health care system and guarantee insurance coverage for all received enormous attention in Congress and the national media, and, though it ultimately failed, reform in various guises has remained on the national agenda. For example, the future of the huge and rapidly growing Medicare program features prominently in discussions of federal budget policy, and the emerging dominance of "managed care" health insurance plans has raised many questions. Regulation of managed care has been hotly debated in Congress and in state legislatures over the last several years. The health care industry is a fascinating one for students of industrial organization to examine, as traditional relationships between patients, doctors,

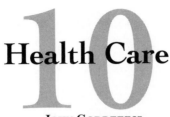

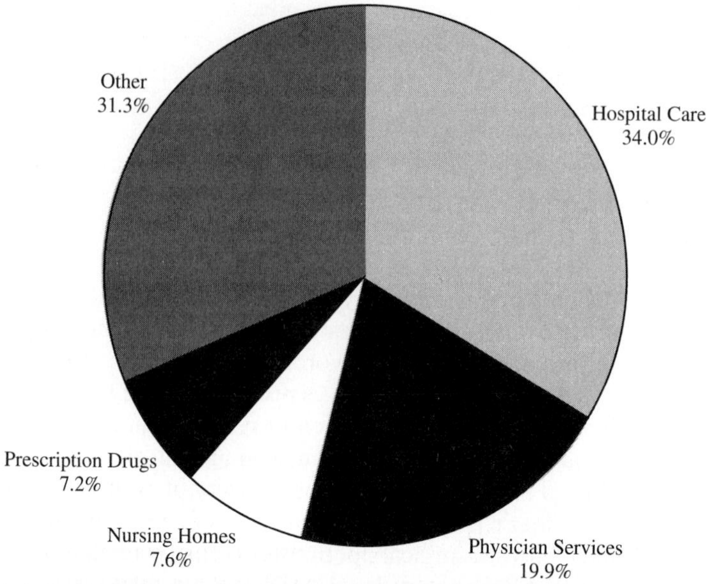

FIGURE 10-1 National Health Expenditures, 1997 By Type of Service

Source: U.S. Health Care Financing Administration, National Health Expenditures 1997, *www.hcfa.gov/stats/nhe-oact/tables/chart.htm.*

health insurers, hospitals, and other suppliers of care have undergone much change in the last 15 years, with nothing approaching a long-run equilibrium configuration yet in sight.

I. HISTORY

Today, we take it for granted that medical care is expensive, but that it also can be very powerful. A typical day in the hospital cost about $1,200 in 1997, and several times as much for intensive care. Modern hospital care, however, can often save the lives of heart attack victims or those suffering from severe burns or the trauma of an automobile accident. It is generally agreed that people need a mechanism, either private insurance or support through public programs, to enable them to obtain care without suffering staggering financial losses. The fact that 44 million Americans (16.3 percent of the population) are uninsured and lack such a formal mechanism is widely viewed as a serious public policy problem, the failure of the Clinton health care plan notwithstanding.

To gain some perspective, we should remember that things were not always as they are today. One hundred years ago, medical care was not very expensive, and medical insurance was virtually nonexistent in the

United States. The workers' compensation system was developing in the early twentieth century, making employers responsible for the costs of work-related injuries, but workers were much more concerned about income losses from lost work time than about the costs of medical care.

By 1929, the first year for which we have reasonably good data on national health expenditures, health spending was only about 3.5 percent of GDP. One important reason that the health care industry was much smaller is that the capabilities of medicine at the time were quite limited. In 1976, the President's Biomedical Research Panel would write "Fifty years ago the term technology, and for that matter science, would have seemed incongruous in a discussion of medical practice. The highly skilled practitioner was a master of diagnostic medicine, but the ultimate intentions of his skill were limited to the identification of the particular illness, the prediction of the likely outcome, and then the guidance of the patient and his family while the illness ran its full, natural course."[1]

That situation gradually changed. As technology improved, hospitals began to evolve from charitable institutions utilized only by the poor to facilities for the treatment of serious illness or injury. In 1929, the first prototype for a Blue Cross plan was developed at Baylor University, enabling subscribers to pay a little each month to avoid large bills when hospital care was needed. The idea spread, backed by groups of hospitals which saw it as a way to increase the certainty of revenue during the Great Depression. Blue Shield plans, organized by doctors as a mechanism for prepaying for physician care, began to emerge about a decade later.

Still, by 1940 only about 9 percent of the American public had any private health insurance, and national health expenditures stood at about 4.1 percent of GDP. A remarkable transformation was beginning, however. During World War II, a time of tight labor markets at home, employee fringe benefits—including health insurance—were exempted from wage-price controls and became an important tool for attracting and retaining workers. The fact that the cost of health insurance to the employer was not counted as part of the employee's taxable income made insurance a preferred form of compensation even after the war ended. At the same time, advances in surgery and increases in the cost of hospital care increased the financial risks associated with not having insurance coverage.

This combination of circumstances led to a rapid spread of health insurance. By 1950, over half the population had some private coverage. The numbers continued to grow, reaching over 82 percent of the population by 1975, although they have since declined.[2] Private insurance has

---

[1]President's Biomedical Research Panel, *Report of the President's Biomedical Research Panel* (Washington, D.C.: GPO, 1976).

[2]Health Insurance Association of America, *Source Book of Health Insurance Data, 1990* (Washington, D.C.: Health Insurance Association of America, 1990).

remained closely tied to employment. In 1998, about 88 percent of those with private insurance got it through their own job or that of a family member (usually a parent or spouse).[3] For a variety of reasons, health insurance is less expensive if purchased by large groups than if purchased directly by individuals, and place of employment is one natural basis for grouping. The favorable tax treatment of employer-provided health insurance has also encouraged the link between insurance and jobs.

In the era of the War on Poverty and President Johnson's Great Society, there was also interest in extending coverage through government programs to groups that had difficulty obtaining it. Medicare and Medicaid were enacted in 1966 and grew rapidly. Medicare is a federal program that provides substantial, though incomplete, health insurance coverage to nearly all of those aged 65 and over. Medicaid is a federal-state matching program aimed at providing coverage for the poor, though in practice it reaches far from all of them and there is a good deal of variability across states. Both programs made significant contributions to reducing the residual number of Americans with no source of insurance.

Although the overall trend in the last 50 years has certainly been toward expanding insurance coverage, it should be noted that in recent years private insurance coverage has eroded somewhat and the share of the population without either public or private coverage has increased. The most widely accepted estimates show that 86.1 percent of the population had health insurance in 1990, with 73.2 percent having some private coverage, but that the shares had fallen to 83.7 and 70.2 percent respectively by 1998.[4]

Even more striking than the spread of public and private insurance has been the growth of health care spending in the post-World War II era. Between 1950 and 1997, health care spending per capita went from about $469 (in 1997 dollars, using the consumer price index to adjust for changes in the price level) to about $3,613, an increase of 670 percent over and above the general increase in prices.[5] For comparison purposes, GDP per capita deflated by the CPI grew by about 135 percent over the same period. Figure 10-2 displays the growth of health care spending since 1960 in a slightly different way. It shows for each year the percentage increase over the previous year in per capita spending on health care, after adjusting for the change in the CPI. Over the entire period, health care

---

[3]Jennifer A. Campbell, "Health Insurance Coverage: 1998," *Current Population Reports* (Washington, D.C.: U.S. Census Bureau, October 1999), 60–208.

[4]Campbell, "Health Insurance Coverage, 1998," and *Statistical Abstract of the United States: 1998* (Washington: U.S. Census Bureau, 1998) Table 10-181.

[5]Health care spending is measured here by "personal health care expenditures," which is national health expenditures minus administration costs, public health spending, and spending on research and construction of new facilities.

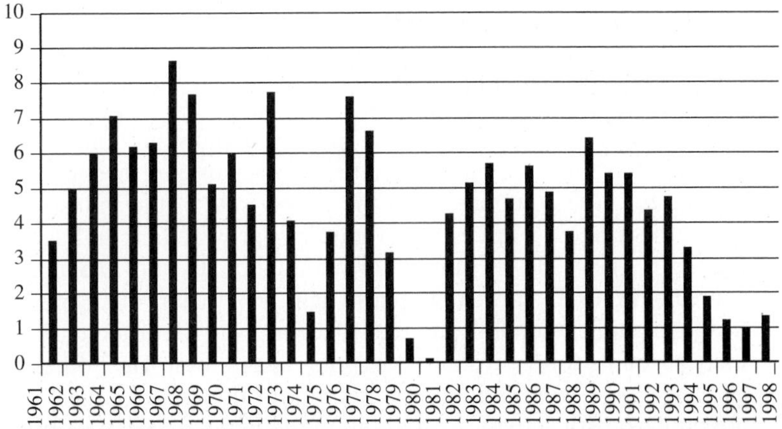

FIGURE 10-2 Annual Percentage Increases in Real Health Spending per Capita

Sources: Author's calculations from U.S. Health Care Financing Administration, *National Health Expenditures 1997, www.hcfa.gov/stats/nhe-oact/tables/chart.htm;* U.S. Bureau of the Census, *Total U.S. Population;* U.S. Bureau of Labor Statistics, *Consumer Price Index.*

spending per capita never increased more slowly than the general price level in any year, and in 30 of the 37 years, it increased at least 3 percentage points faster. The average of the annual changes over the period is 4.6 percentage points more than the CPI. The years of relatively slow growth are the most recent 4, suggesting that the shift to managed care may have slowed the growth of spending, at least temporarily. But many observers warn that a return to more rapid spending growth is on the near horizon.

What can account for such dramatic growth of spending, sustained over such a long period? Surely several factors have contributed, but most economic experts have stressed that the growth of insurance and spending are closely entwined, each feeding on the other, along with a third factor, the advance of knowledge, which creates new capabilities for diagnoses and treatments, often at high cost.[6] The health care financing system in place for most of the second half of the twentieth century, increasingly dominated by third party payment as time went on, imposed little restraint on the adoption and application of innovations in health care, however costly, that offered some hope of medical benefit.

---

[6]Joseph Newhouse, "An Iconoclastic View of Health Cost Containment," *Health Affairs* 12 (Supplement 1993): 152–171; and Burton A. Weisbrod, "The Health Care Quadrilemma: An Essay on Technological Change, Insurance, Quality of Care, and Cost Containment," *Journal of Economic Literature* 29 (June 1991): 523–552.

II. INDUSTRY STRUCTURE

Space does not permit an in-depth discussion of the structure of all aspects of the vast and varied health care industry. We will focus primarily on three key components: health insurance (now predominantly provided in the form of managed care), physicians, and hospitals. Before turning to these components of the supply side of the industry, a brief look at its current sources of revenue will provide helpful background. Figure 10-3 gives HCFA's breakdown for national health expenditures by source of funds. It shows that nearly half (46 percent) of all spending on health is publicly funded, and that Medicare and Medicaid each individually accounts for a substantial fraction of the total. The "other public" category includes spending on a number of things, the largest of which are public health activities, programs of the Veterans Administration and the Department of Defense (including health care coverage for the dependents of armed services personnel), state and local government hospitals, and medical research. On the private side, we see that payments by way of private insurance are nearly twice as great as those that come directly from consumers out-of-pocket. The small "other private" share

FIGURE 10-3 National Health Expenditures, 1997 By Source of Funds

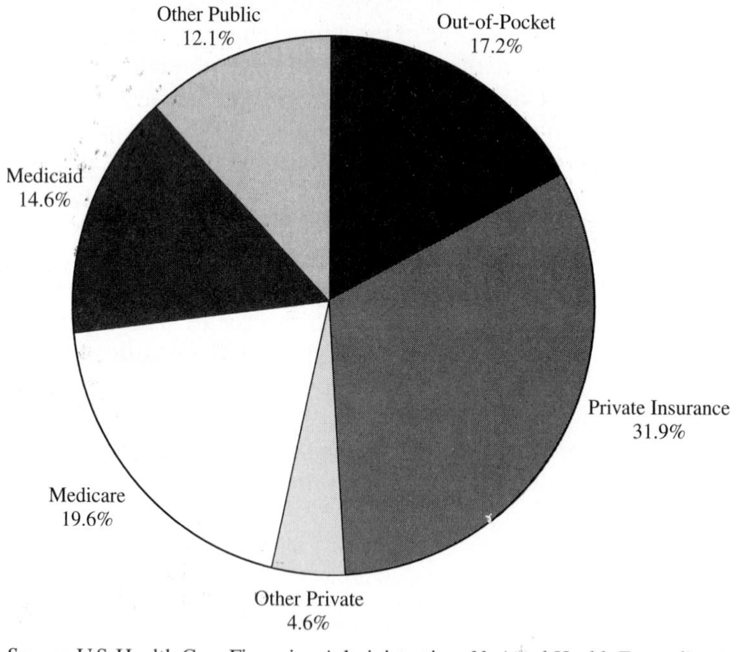

Source: U.S. Health Care Financing Administration, *National Health Expenditures 1997, www.hcfa.gov/stats/nhe-oact/tables/chart.htm.*

includes some nonpatient revenues of health care institutions, such as hospital revenues from parking lots and cafeterias, as well as philanthropic contributions.

The breakdown in Figure 10-3 is true on average, but as Table 10-1 shows, sources of revenue vary a good deal by type of service. For hospital care, for example, the out-of-pocket share is much smaller than the overall average at about 3 percent, while Medicare alone accounts for one-third of revenues. Medicaid is especially important for nursing homes, accounting for nearly 48 percent of their revenues, while private insurance accounts for only 5 percent. The absence of an outpatient prescription drug benefit in Medicare and relatively incomplete private insurance coverage for drugs leaves a relatively high share of those expenses paid directly out-of-pocket.

Health Insurance and Managed Care

Health insurance is the point of contact for access to most health care services for most of the population, and a good place to start examining the structure of the health care industry. To oversimplify slightly, most health insurers in the United States prior to the mid-1980s played a passive role with regard to the provision of health care. The insurance contract defined the financial terms of the policy, including the premium, scope of services covered, and cost-sharing arrangements for the enrollee. Decisions about what services to provide were left to the enrollee and his or her doctor. The enrollee's choice of doctor was also unrestricted by the insurance plan.

Health insurance was at first dominated by Blue Cross and Blue Shield plans, nonprofit organizations set up by hospital and doctors' associations. Later, companies operating in other lines of insurance, so-called commercial insurers such as Aetna, Travelers, New York Life, and Prudential, entered the market, and, by the early 1950s, had as a group surpassed Blue Cross-Blue Shield in total number of people covered.

TABLE 10-1 Sources of Revenue By Type of Service, 1997

	Hospital Care	*Physicians Services*	*Nursing Homes*	*Prescription Drugs*
Out-of-Pocket	3.3%	15.7%	31.1%	29.2%
Private Insurance	30.5%	50.2%	4.9%	48.2%
Other Private	4.6%	2.0%	1.9%	0.0%
Total Public	61.6%	32.2%	62.2%	20.2%
Medicare	33.3%	21.3%	12.3%	1.2%
Medicaid	15.5%	7.2%	47.6%	16.8%

Source: U.S. Health Care Financing Administration, *National Health Expenditures, 1997*, *http://www.hcfa.gov/stats/nhe-oact/nhe.htm.*

For policies written by commercial insurers, sometimes called indemnity policies, the doctors, hospitals, and other providers of covered services would bill the enrollee, who would pay the bill and then recover the insured amount from the insurer. In the case of policies written by Blue Cross and Blue Shield, as well as for individuals covered by Medicare and Medicaid, coverage was more commonly in the form of "service benefits." The insurer agreed to cover a specified set of services when needed, with perhaps some cost-sharing on the part of the enrollee. Providers would be paid (or "reimbursed" in the typical language) directly by the insurer. For doctors, this usually meant they were paid according to what they charged for services, with some screens applied to assure that a doctor's charge was not far out of line with what was customary in the community. Hospitals and other providers were usually reimbursed for costs incurred. Regardless of whether the indemnity or service benefit approach was used, the insurer took little active role in treatment decisions.

In the last 15 years, the health insurer's role has shifted dramatically, in the direction of managed care. Managed care is an amorphous concept, encompassing a broad range of organizational forms and management tools. What its various forms have in common is at least some attempt to go beyond consumer cost-sharing and benefit package design in influencing the nature of the care that an enrollee receives.

At the extreme is the staff model health maintenance organization (HMO). In a staff model HMO the doctors caring for the enrollees are employees, or part owners, of the organization providing health insurance. Because the HMO agrees to provide care to its enrollees for a fixed premium, the organization has an incentive to minimize the cost of providing that care. Given that additional services do not generate additional revenue (except consumer cost-sharing payments, if any are used), each additional dollar of cost reduces the organization's net profits. If the organization's incentive to minimize cost can be translated to its medical staff, then the staff may be expected to manage the care of enrollees in a cost-conscious way.

The concept of the staff model HMO has been around a long time. The term "health maintenance organization" was coined in the early 1970s, but the most successful example of the staff model, the Kaiser Health Plan, dates back to the collaborative efforts of medical entrepreneur Dr. Sydney Garfield and the industrialist Henry Kaiser in the 1930s.[7] The Kaiser Plan grew to over 1 million enrollees by 1962, and over 2.5 million by 1972. Another early example of this model, which used to be called

---

[7]Paul Starr, *The Social Transformation of American Medicine* (New York: Basic Books, 1982). The Kaiser Plan is technically a "group model" rather than a staff model HMO. Rather than employing its doctors, the health plan contracts in each region that it operates with a single medical group, who serve only Kaiser patients.

prepaid group practice, is the Group Health Cooperative of Puget Sound, founded in 1947, and today serving about one-half million enrollees in the state of Washington.

Other types of HMOs contract nonexclusively with groups of doctors or Independent Practice Associations (IPAs) of individual doctors. This form integrates the insurance plan less tightly with physicians than the staff model, as the same doctors might contract with several other HMOs and also see patients not affiliated with any HMO. The insurer, however, can still attempt to influence the provision of care by a variety of methods, including monitoring the use of services (e.g., requiring preapproval of nonemergency hospital admissions, concurrently reviewing length of hospital stay), requiring that enrollees be approved for specialty care by a "gatekeeper" primary care physician, selectively contracting with doctors and hospitals rather than allowing enrollees unrestricted choice, or using payment methods other than straight fee-for-service to influence provider incentives. For prescription drug coverage, the set of drugs covered and the manner in which they can be obtained may also be limited.

Other forms of managed care use some or all of these tools, in various forms and combinations, and the lines between different types of organizations are increasingly blurry. In a preferred provider organization (PPO), the insurer contracts selectively with a preferred set of providers at discounted rates and creates incentives in the form of reduced cost-sharing for enrollees to use those providers. Typically, PPOs also use some forms of utilization management. Many HMOs now also include a point-of-service (POS) option, which allows enrollees to see providers outside the regular network, usually with considerably higher cost-sharing by the enrollee.

Figure 10-4 shows the rapid shift in health plan enrollments from unmanaged to managed care. In 1980, managed care meant only HMOs, which had less than 10 percent of health insurance enrollment nationally. The rest were in more traditional health insurance plans, referred to in the figure as "unmanaged fee-for-service." By 1992, POS and PPO variants had emerged, and the traditional fee-for-service plans had mostly adopted at least some utilization management tools. By 1996, there had been further movement away from fee-for-service toward managed care. The less restrictive forms of managed care have shown the most growth recently, however. Within the HMO sector, growth since 1992 has been strongest in the IPA segment and in point-of-service plans.

The use of managed care has also increased dramatically in the publicly funded Medicare and Medicaid programs. Since 1985, Medicare has been willing to contract with HMOs on a "risk-contract" basis, paying a fixed amount per enrollee, often referred to as a "capitation" (per head) payment, and letting the HMO manage the risk that the enrollee's expenditures might be higher or lower than the capitation amount. Medicare

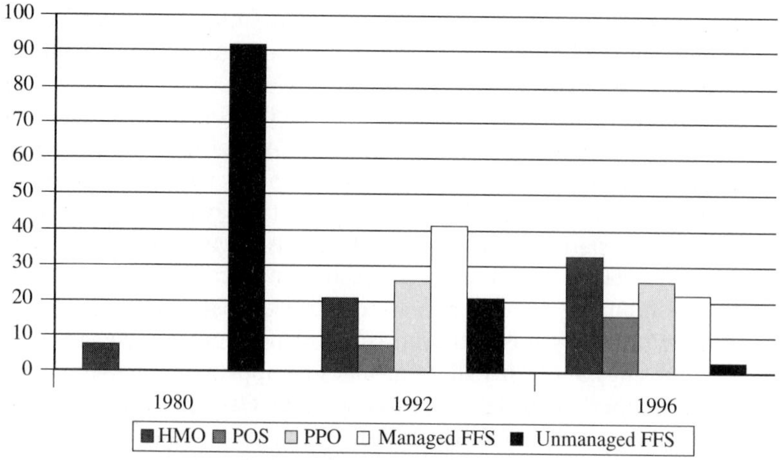

FIGURE 10-4 The Shift to Managed Care in Private Insurance

HMO = Health Maintenance Organization, POS = Point-of-Service, PPO = Preferred Provider Organization, FFS = Fee-for-Service

Source: David M. Cutler and Richard J. Zeckhauser, "The Anatomy of Health Insurance," National Bureau of Economic Research Working Paper 7176, June 1999.

paid HMOs 95 percent of the average of what it spent on fee-for-service Medicare enrollees in the same geographic area. The number of enrollees participating in risk contracts grew slowly. About 1 million participated in 1987, at that time about 3 percent of Medicare enrollees. By the end of 1995, the number was about 3.1 million, and by the end of 1998 about 6 million, or about 15.5 percent of enrollees.[8]

While Medicare has thus far made managed care participation a matter of enrollee choice, many states now require that their Medicaid beneficiaries enroll with a managed care plan. Initially, federal law prohibited states from restricting the choice of medical providers for Medicaid beneficiaries (though the low payment rates characteristic of Medicaid often made it difficult for beneficiaries to find doctors willing to see them). The law changed in 1981, allowing states to experiment with managed care and other innovative approaches. Managed care participation was still low going into the 1990s, but has expanded very rapidly since then.[9] In 1991, less than 10 percent of Medicaid beneficiaries were in managed care. By 1995, the number had grown to nearly 30 percent, and by 1998 to

[8]Data are taken from *Medicare + Choice: Changes for the Year 2000,* available at the U.S. Health Care Financing Administration (HCFA) web site at *http://www.hcfa.gov/medicare/mgdcar1.htm.*

[9]Data are taken from the U.S. Health Care Financing Administration web site, at http://www.hcfa.gov/medicaid/mcaidsad.htm.

nearly 54 percent, which included about 16.6 million enrollees. Some of this enrollment is in a mild form of managed care called "primary care case management," in which a primary care doctor agrees to manage the care of a set of enrollees but is not at risk for the cost of hospital and specialty care. But this model has been shrinking in importance relative to capitated models, in which the managed care organization is at risk for the costs of all covered services. Primary care case management accounted for 30 percent of Medicaid managed care enrollment in 1996 but only 24 percent in 1998.

There has also been some movement toward consolidation in the managed care industry, at least when the national market is viewed as a single entity. Health care is largely a locally delivered service, and many HMOs operate in a single local market area, frequently organized around a single hospital or group of hospitals. However, some large HMOs operate health plans in a number of markets, and mergers and acquisitions have produced an increase in the national market share of the largest of these. Table 10-2 shows an analysis of the market share of the top national HMO firms from 1994 to 1997, from the work of Feldman, Wholey, and Christianson.[10] The table shows that while the number of local HMOs unaffiliated with a national firm increased over the period, the national market share of the top five firms also increased. A substantial increase in this share happened in 1997, owing largely to the merger of Aetna and U.S.

TABLE 10-2 Market Share of Top National HMO Firms, 1994–1997

Firm	1994	1995	1996	1997
Blue Cross/Blue Shield	16.42%	16.82%	17.78%	19.60%
Kaiser Foundation Health Plans	14.32	12.39	11.67	11.96
United HealthCare Corp.	4.79	4.75	6.69	6.34
PruCare/Prudential Health Care Plans	3.86	4.05	3.92	—[1]
U.S. Healthcare Systems	3.82	3.79	3.92	—[1]
Aetna Healthcare Programs	—[1]	—[1]	—[1]	6.21
CIGNA Health Plan	—[1]	—[1]	—[1]	5.30
Top 5 Total Share	43.21	41.80	43.98	49.91
Top 10 Total Share	58.31	56.81	58.82	67.15
Total Number of HMOs	519	564	595	608
Total Number of Local HMOs	171	184	213	240

[1]HMO was not one of top five in this year.

Source: Roger Feldman, Douglas Wholey and Jon Christianson, "HMO Consolidations: How National Mergers Affect Local Markets," *Health Affairs* 18 (July-August 1999).

[10]"HMO Consolidations: How National Mergers Affect Local Markets," *Health Affairs* 18 (July-August 1999): 96–104.

Healthcare occurring in that year. In 1999, Aetna also acquired Prudential Health Care Plans, which will further increase concentration. Except for Aetna and CIGNA, the large commercial insurers have now generally exited the health insurance market.

Another trend among HMOs and health insurers is a movement away from nonprofit organizational forms toward entities organized as for-profit businesses. Early HMOs were predominantly organized as nonprofits, which were the only type eligible for federal subsidies under the HMO Act of 1973. When direct federal subsidies ended in the early 1980s, market share began to swing heavily toward for-profits, partly as a result of entry of new for-profit HMOs and their growth, but also from conversion of nonprofit HMOs to the for-profit form. From 1981 to 1995, the percentage of HMOs organized as nonprofits plummeted from 82 percent (accounting for 88 percent of enrollees) to 29 percent (41 percent of enrollees).[11] In 1994, the national Blue Cross and Blue Shield Association decided for the first time that for-profit firms could affiliate with the organization, paving the way for a number of regional Blue Cross plans to convert to for-profits.

Before leaving the subject of the structure of health insurance markets, some mention should be made of the role of employers, who often arrange for health coverage for their employees, and the phenomenon of self-insurance. The purchase of insurance is fundamentally a way of transferring risk from an individual or group to an insurer, who, by virtue of pooling together large numbers of enrollees with largely independent risks, is better able to accept it. For large employers, those with 500 employees or more, pooling within the firm accomplishes much of what an insurer could provide in this regard. Many large employers find it attractive to "self-insure," that is, bear the risks associated with random year-to-year fluctuations in health care utilization, to escape some state and federal regulations associated with purchased health insurance, and perhaps to gain more control over the insurance they provide and how it is administered. A recent survey of employers in seven states found that 55 percent of employees with insurance coverage in firms with 500 or more workers were in self-insured plans.[12]

In most cases, self-insuring employers still rely on insurance companies or HMOs to provide administrative functions and management of care, but sometimes individual employers or groups of employers are playing a more active role. For example, the Pacific Business Group on Health negotiates rates with 12 HMOs for 21 companies and 400,000

---

[11]Gary Claxton, Judith Feder, David Schactman, and Stuart Altman, "Public Policy Issues in Nonprofit Conversions," *Health Affairs* Mar./Apr. 1997, 16 no. 2, 9–28.

[12]M. Susan Marquis and Stephen H. Long, "Recent Trends in Self-Insured Employer Health Plans," *Health Affairs* 18 (May-June 1999): 161–166.

beneficiaries in California using a standard benefit package, and the Buyers Health Care Action Group has developed a uniform benefit package and self-insured PPO product for 132,000 enrollees in Minneapolis.[13]

Physicians

In his influential 1974 book on health care and economics, *Who Shall Live?,* Victor Fuchs called the physician the "captain of the team" in health care. While managed care has challenged the physician's preeminent position, Fuchs's characterization remains largely accurate. In addition to the medical and surgical services they provide directly, physicians admit and discharge patients from hospitals, order diagnostic tests, and prescribe drugs, although these tasks are increasingly scrutinized by insurance providers. About 581,000 medical doctors were active in patient care in 1996, according to American Medical Association data. Fuchs notes that a century ago, two out of three persons employed in health care were doctors. As the health care system developed, with the rise of the modern hospital and the nursing home industry, and the introduction of a broad variety of other types of specialized services such as physical therapy and respiratory therapy, employment opportunities vastly expanded for other workers without the breadth and depth of training of an M.D. The number of nonphysician health care workers has risen much faster than the number of doctors, to the point where the ratio is now more than 15 to 1.[14]

Doctors spend more years in training than almost any other workers. Medical school generally requires 4 additional years after a bachelor's degree, and this is usually followed by at least 3 additional years in a hospital-based residency program in order to become board certified as a specialist or as a generalist family practitioner. The need to be accepted by a medical school and then complete this long training period is clearly an important barrier to entry into the medical profession. Some economists have argued that the control exerted by the AMA over the number of medical school slots available and the length of the training period has helped keep doctors' incomes artificially high. The counter argument in favor of supply restrictions and extensive training has been that they promote quality of care, which consumers would find difficult to evaluate in the absence of professional certification.

It is true that most doctors have been and continue to be near the top of the income distribution. According to AMA survey data, median physician income in 1997 was $164,000. An important question for public

---

[13]James C. Robinson, "The Future of Managed Care Organization," *Health Affairs* 18 (March/April 1999): 7–24.

[14]*Statistical Abstract of the United States: 1998* (Washington: U.S. Census Bureau, 1998), Table 189.

policy is whether this level is "artificially high" given the amount of time invested in training, the level of ability, and the level of work effort exerted by the typical doctor (the AMA also reports that average work hours for doctors are about 55 per week). Several studies (none of them, unfortunately, very recent) have addressed this question by asking whether the rate of return on the investment in a medical education is unusually high compared with alternatives.[15] An important component of the investment costs are the opportunity costs of foregone earnings during the long training period. The weight of the evidence for the postwar period through about 1985, when the published studies end, suggests that a medical degree has been an economically attractive investment, with rates of return usually estimated at 13 percent or higher, even after accounting for the high costs of acquiring one.

Table 10-3 shows the number of medical doctors involved in patient care from 1970 to 1996, and the breakdown by type of practice. The number of doctors increased substantially over this period, the result primarily of a buildup in medical school capacity that began in the late 1960s. For most physicians, the base of practice is in an office rather than in a hospital, and the fraction of doctors who are office-based has increased since 1970. About 15 percent of doctors are in residency or other training programs, usually hospital-based, and another smaller fraction are employed as full-time hospital staff. Most of the small fraction of physicians who are federally employed are hospital-based.

Traditionally, most doctors have been self-employed or partners in small groups. Table 10-4 summarizes data on changes over time in the distribution of office-based physicians by style and size of group. In 1969, the majority of office-based physicians, 78 percent, was in individual practice, which the AMA defines to include offices with one or two physicians. By 1995, those in individual practice were still in the majority, but barely so. Both single-specialty and multispecialty group practices had grown considerably as a share of all physicians, and, within each type, the average group size increased. Within physicians' offices has also been a trend toward larger numbers of aides per physician. The number of aides per physician in office-based practice was 1.54 in 1970 and had grown to 2.54 by 1995.[16]

The trend toward larger groups suggests that some real economic advantages to group practice have probably increased over time. Some economies of scale exist in production, particularly in the way physicians delegate tasks to allied health workers and use other inputs to production. A group of physicians may be able to fully utilize a certain type of aide or piece of equipment where a solo practitioner could not. Consumers may

[15]See Paul Feldstein, *Health Care Economics,* 5th ed. (Albany, NY: Delmar), 1999, 363–64 for a summary and references.

[16]Feldstein, *Health Care Economics,* 246.

TABLE 10-3 Doctors in Patient Care By Type of Practice

	1970		1980		1990		1996	
	Total (1,000s)	%	***Total (1,000s)***	%	***Total (1,000s)***	%	***Total (1,000s)***	%
Total	278.5		379.7		508.3		601.1	
Nonfederal								
Office-Based	188.9	67.8%	271.3	71.5%	359.9	70.8%	445.8	74.2%
Residency or Other Training	45.8	16.4%	59.6	15.7%	89.9	17.7%	90.6	15.1%
Hospital Staff	20.3	7.3%	31	8.2%	38	7.5%	44.3	7.4%
Federal	23.5	8.4%	17.8	4.7%	20.5	4.0%	20.4	3.4%

Source: U.S. Census Bureau, *Statistical Abstract of the United States: 1998,* and earlier years.

TABLE 10-4 Trends in Distribution of Office-Based Physicians, By Group Affiliation

	% Distribution of Physicians			Average Size of Group		
	1969	*1980*	*1995*	*1969*	*1980*	*1995*
Individual Practice	78.3	67.2	51.9			
Group Practice	21.7	32.8	48.1	6.2	8.2	10.5
Single-Specialty	7.1	10.9	20.1	4.1	4.8	6.2
Multispecialty	13.2	20.1	25.8	10.1	15.2	25.4
Family or General Practice	1.5	1.8	2.1	3.5	4.5	5.6

Source: Adapted from Paul J. Feldstein, *Health Care Economics,* 5th ed., 1999, Table 10.2, 247.

also prefer to deal with groups for convenience in getting appointments, and because a group can develop a kind of "brand name" image for quality which the consumer would have more difficulty in assessing at the individual-doctor level. Several physicians who share a practice are also likely to experience less variability in workload and income at the individual level than would a solo practitioner, and this risk-spreading feature of groups is valuable to risk-averse doctors. Still, there are disadvantages to increasing group size. For example, if a group of doctors shares the costs of a set of inputs, individual incentives to economize in the use of those inputs are blunted. The distribution of physician group size reflects a balancing at the margin of those forces that push in the direction of larger and smaller size, as well as differences in size of market (a small town cannot accommodate a large multispecialty group) and in preferences of doctors and consumers concerning style of practice.

Another reason for doctors to form into larger groups is to position themselves to be responsible for managing all of the health care—or some well-defined subset of it—for a defined population of enrollees, and to accept payment on a capitation basis. Accepting capitation payments is, in effect, acting like a health insurer. The advantage of capitation from the group's point of view is that it has a greater incentive to manage the total costs of care and can profit from doing so effectively. Capitation is risky for an individual doctor or a small group, however, because the patient population the group can handle may be too small to predict accurately the level of costs that will be incurred, even if care is managed efficiently. Increasing group size can reduce that risk. In some parts of the country, large groups, sometimes numbering in the hundreds of doctors, contract with managed care plans and sometimes directly with employers on a capitation basis.[17] Changes in Medicare incorporated in the Bal-

[17]James C. Robinson and Lawrence P. Casalino, "The Growth of Medical Groups Paid Through Capitation in California," *JAMA* 333 (21 December 1995), 1684–87.

anced Budget Act of 1997 were designed to make it easier for Provider-Sponsored Organizations (PSOs) to contract directly with Medicare (rather than through HMOs) to provide care on a capitation basis, although physician groups have so far not been quick to respond.

The growth of managed care has spurred more affiliations of physician practices with hospitals, insurers, or physician practice management companies (PPMCs), although some of those affiliations are proving to be short-lived. Doctors or groups that had been in independent practice have sometimes sold the physical assets of their practices to a hospital or managed care organization, and accepted salaried compensation. Frequently, however, the buyers became dissatisfied with the performance of salaried physicians and have found it more advantageous to contract with independent groups. PPMCs, a relatively new phenomenon, sometimes buy the assets of groups of doctors, and then negotiate contracts with managed care organizations and provide certain management services to the groups, in return for a share of net revenues after practice expenses have been paid. A few publicly traded PPMCs grew very rapidly in the mid-1990s but seemed to overemphasize expansion at the expense of good management, and just as quickly went into decline. MedPartners, which became the largest PPMC, and, at its peak, managed the practices of more than 10,000 doctors, has exited the market. FPA Medical, another large and fast-growing PPMC, has gone into bankruptcy.

Despite the growth of a variety of business models under which physician practice is organized, most physicians continue to view themselves as independent professionals, not as employees, and some form of fee-for-service is the predominant method by which they are paid. In the AMA survey of physicians for 1998, 64 percent of physicians identified themselves as self-employed or as independent contractors, with only 36 percent calling themselves employees, down from 39 percent the year before.[18] At least as of 1995, capitation payments at the level of the individual physician accounted for only a small share of total physician revenues.[19] While 84 percent of doctors in the AMA survey reported that they had at least some managed care contracts (with the percentage varying between 80 and 90 across the nine census regions), on average, only 36 percent of revenues were from managed care. Only 32.5 percent of physicians nationally reported having any capitated contracts, and for those with such contracts, only 19 percent of revenues, on average, came from capitation. Multiplication of those two percentages suggests that

---

[18]Mary C. Jaklevic, "AMA Survey: Median Doc Income Down," *Modern Healthcare,* 17 May 1999, 6.

[19]Numbers are reported in Carol J. Simon and David W. Emmons, "Physician Earnings at Risk: An Examination of Capitated Contracts," *Health Affairs,* 16 (May/June 1997): 120–126. The sample consists of physicians active in patient care and does not include those in residency training.

capitation may have accounted for only about 6 percent of revenues for nonresident physicians in patient care in 1995.

Hospitals

Hospitals are unusual economic entities. Most are organized as nonprofit firms. In 1995, about 70 percent of short-term general hospital beds were in private nonprofit entities, another 18 percent in hospitals run by state or local governments, and 12 percent in for-profit firms. Like any such firm, the nonprofit hospital is not owned by individuals, so no one has a claim to any profits that might accrue to it. While the administrators are responsible to the hospital's board of trustees, the trustees do not represent ownership in the same way that a private corporation's board of directors does. In addition, decisions about how a hospital's resources—its beds, employed staff, and equipment—are utilized are made to a large extent by its medical staff—doctors who practice in the hospital but generally are not its employees.

Table 10-5 provides data on the evolution of community hospitals since 1946, the year of the passage of the Hill-Burton Act, which subsidized the construction and expansion of hospitals. "Community hospitals" is a broad classification used by the American Hospital Association. It includes 81 percent of all hospital beds, excluding only 7 percent that are in federal hospitals and 12 percent in long-term hospitals of various types. The table shows strong expansion in number of hospitals continuing until about 1970, and even stronger growth in number of beds, which continued until about 1985. Hospital admissions grew much faster than the population from 1946 to about 1980, but began to decline thereafter. Average length of hospital stay (not shown in the table) began to decline even earlier, as can be inferred from the fact that admissions per bed grew in the 1970s, but occupancy levels declined. Optimal occupancy levels for hospitals are a good deal less than 100 percent, as the need for beds fluctuates and it is important to hold some reserve capacity to accommodate periods of peak demand. However, nationwide occupancy levels of well under 70 percent, as have existed since the mid-1980s, are surely indicative of a substantial amount of excess bed capacity in the industry.

Accompanying the decline in inpatient hospital usage during the 1980s and 1990s has been rapid growth in the number of outpatient visits. This movement toward shorter hospital stays and substitution of outpatient for inpatient care has resulted in part from technological changes, such as the development of less invasive laser-assisted surgical techniques, as well as from changing attitudes about the benefits of prolonged hospitalization. It has also been spurred by cost containment efforts by managed care organizations, and earlier by Medicare, that focused heavily on the reduction of inpatient care. Inpatient care was undoubtedly overused in the 1960s and 1970s, as there was little incentive for doctors

TABLE 10-5 Selected Statistics for Community Hospitals

Year	*Hospitals*	*Beds (1,000s)*	*Admissions (1,000s)*	*Occupancy*	*Outpatient Visits (1,000s)*
1946	4,444	473	13,655	0.72	n.a.
1950	5,031	505	16,663	0.74	n.a.
1960	5,407	639	22,970	0.75	n.a.
1970	5,859	848	29,252	0.78	133,545
1980	5,830	988	36,143	0.76	202,310
1985	5,732	1,001	33,449	0.65	218,716
1990	5,384	927	31,181	0.67	301,329
1996	5,194	862	31,099	0.62	439,863

Source: American Hospital Association, *Hospital Statistics.* For 1946–1970, the data are for non-federal short-term general and other special hospitals, which include a small number of hospital units in other institutions.
n.a.: not available.

or their well-insured patients to weigh costs against potential benefits. The pendulum may have swung too far, however, in the direction of shorter stays. In the quest to reduce hospital usage because the *average* cost per patient day is very high, the fact that *marginal* cost near the end of a stay may be much lower is often insufficiently appreciated.[20] If a bed would otherwise be unoccupied, the incremental cost of extending the stay of a patient needing relatively little care is modest.

Hospitals are multiproduct firms. For inpatient care alone, the Medicare program now recognizes for payment purposes 495 diagnosis-related groups (DRGs), classifications of patients based on their medical problems. Even this large number of categories lumps together patients with widely varying severity of illness and needs for care. Differences across hospitals in average cost per admission are strongly related to differences in the mix of diagnoses among the patients that they treat. Holding patient mix constant, research studies do not indicate substantial economies of scale beyond very small-sized hospitals, and any economies are probably exhausted at a size between 200 and 300 beds. In 1997, about 71 percent of community hospitals had fewer than 200 beds. The 29 percent of hospitals that were larger, however, accounted for about 68 percent of admissions.

An important phenomenon in health care industry structure has been the development of Integrated Delivery Systems (IDSs). These are vertically integrated organizations that combine some or all of the inputs

[20]Uwe E. Reinhardt, "Our Obsessive Quest to Gut the Hospital," *Health Affairs* 15 (Summer 1996), 145–154.

needed to provide the full range of medical services that an individual might require; hospitals, physicians, outpatient clinics, home health care agencies, nursing homes, and so forth. A group or staff model HMO with its own hospitals (Kaiser is the outstanding example) is one form of IDS. Many other IDSs have formed with a hospital or group of hospitals at the center. The hospital affiliates with physician groups, sometimes hiring doctors on a salaried basis, and with other elements of the "continuum of care." Some hospital-based IDSs have met the necessary legal requirements and have become HMOs. IDSs might also contract with HMOs, or directly with purchasers of care. As noted earlier, recent changes make it easier for provider-sponsored IDSs to contract directly with Medicare on a capitation basis.

At first blush, it seems sensible that an organization taking on the financial risk of providing a complete package of medical services would want the capability of providing most of those services "in-house." At least at its top level, such an integrated organization has incentives to be conscious of the costs of the resources it uses—substituting, for example, outpatient for inpatient care, or preventive for acute care where appropriate. But it may be difficult to transmit those top-level incentives to decision makers in other parts of the organization. The success of the organization may depend heavily on the behavior of its affiliated physicians, but if a large part of their compensation is in guaranteed salary, for example, their incentives to work hard and direct the use of other inputs optimally are attenuated.

A vertically integrated organization is in competition to satisfy purchasers of care who are concerned about the cost and quality of the package. It is not obvious that such an organization will out-compete one that purchases most of its inputs through market transactions (e.g., an IPA HMO) and that relies on a combination of incentive contracts and regulatory tools to achieve its goals. Indeed, recent trends suggest that less tightly integrated organizations are competing more successfully. Nonetheless, many successful HMOs have their roots in hospital-based IDSs. It is too early to be confident about what forms of organization will win out in competition among managed care plans; it may well be that different types of organizations will best satisfy the preferences of different types of consumers.

III. CONDUCT

Premanaged Care

Physicians In the postwar, premanaged-care period, markets for physician and hospital care were not characterized by overt price competition. The majority of doctors practiced on a fee-for-service basis. In the early 1960s, before the introduction of Medicare and Medicaid, about 60 percent of payments for physicians' services still came directly from consumer pockets, so, in setting fees, doctors were, to some degree, subject to the usual restraint of consumer demand. But obtaining relevant information was difficult for consumers because of the complexity of the set of services that doctors provide and the difficulty of judging quality. It was made more difficult by prohibitions against advertising, which were supported by the AMA and often legally enforced. (Advertising by doctors is no longer prohibited, according to a 1982 Supreme Court ruling.) Thus, even though a large number of doctors practiced in a typical metropolitan area, each individual enjoyed some degree of local monopoly power.

By 1975, the share of physician revenues directly from consumers was down to 37 percent, with 35 percent coming from private insurers and 28 percent from public programs. Payments for services were, by then, heavily influenced by the policies of insurers and government payers. Medicare and most insurers adopted the "usual, customary, and reasonable" approach to reimbursement, which paid what the doctor charged unless it was found to be out of line with what that doctor "usually" charged for the same service, or what was "customary" for other doctors in the same community (the "customary" screen was often set at the 75th or 80th percentile of charges in the community). Such an approach is sensible for an insurer who is a small part of the market and is simply trying to match market rates. As the market becomes dominated by insurers paying in this way, however, the approach tends to freeze in place existing differences in fees across doctors, locations, and types of services, and to encourage continued upward drift of charges.

Health economists have devoted a great deal of attention to the question of how much control physicians have over the demand for their own services.[21] This question has important implications for the effect of an increase in physician supply, such as the one the United States has experienced since the late 1960s (see Table 10-3). Standard economic analysis would say that an increase in physician supply leads to lower fees and doctors' incomes as the supply curve shifts out against a downward-sloping demand curve. But because patients rely so heavily on them for advice, might not doctors who find themselves less busy when the number of competitors rises simply find more services to recommend, in effect, shifting the demand curve outward to match the increase in supply?

While it strikes most people (especially noneconomists!) as plausible that doctors can influence demand for their services, the importance of the "demand-inducement" phenomenon has eluded precise quantification. Evidence suggesting that inducement exists, such as the common

---

[21]The Feldstein, Phelps, and Folland, Goodman, and Stano textbooks cited in the Suggested Readings all have extensive discussions of this issue with references to the literature.

finding that doctors' fees are higher in places where physicians are more densely located, may have alternative explanations. Perhaps, for example, consumers are willing to pay more when physicians are more numerous because of greater convenience and shorter waits for services, and perhaps even more attention from the doctor. While the extent of doctors' power to induce demand remains unsettled, the subject gets less attention in the managed-care era. Today, doctors' financial incentives are often to deliver fewer rather than more services, and insurers also seek to manage utilization more directly.

Hospitals In the early 1960s only about 20 percent of hospital revenues came directly from consumers, according to HCFA data on national health expenditures. By 1969, that share had fallen to under 10 percent, with 56 percent accounted for by public sources and 20 percent by Medicare alone. Medicare and most private insurers also gave consumers little or no financial incentive to choose less costly over more costly hospitals. What the consumer paid out-of-pocket for a hospital stay, if anything, was often the same regardless of the hospital chosen.

A number of theories have been suggested for understanding the behavior of nonprofit hospitals. Some of them depict the hospital's administration as seeking to maximize some combination of quantity and quality of care. Another model views the hospital as being run in the interest of its staff physicians. Both types of model are broadly consistent with the behavior of hospitals during this period. Hospitals needed physicians to bring in patients, so they made the work environment attractive to the doctors by providing support staff, including interns and residents, and adding the latest facilities and services. In addition to satisfying the medical staff, these types of actions signaled that the administrators were running a high-quality institution that the trustees and the community could take pride in. The accommodating payment system of the time, along with advancing technology, provided the other ingredients for increases in expenditures. Spending growth was even faster for hospitals than for the health care industry as a whole. On average, over the entire period from 1960 to 1979, expenditures in community hospitals rose about 8 percentage points per year in excess of the increase in the consumer price index.

Such increases were, by no means, unnoticed even at the time. The states, the federal government, and, to some extent, Blue Cross plans explored a number of regulatory approaches to restraining expenditure growth in hospitals. Certificate-of-Need (CON) regulation is an attempt to control capital investment by requiring that a hospital (or other entity) demonstrate that a need exists in the area before investing in new beds or expensive equipment. This approach was tried in most states, with the earliest adopting it in the 1960s, and it was supported for a time by federal law. Economic studies of CON are uniform in affirming its ineffectiveness in reducing the growth of total hospital spending. Any expenditure-reducing effects it may have had through reductions in the number of beds appear to be offset by higher spending in other areas. Some economists have argued that a regulatory process of this kind is likely to be "captured" by existing hospitals, which have advantages in political clout and control of information, and may be a barrier to potentially valuable innovation.

A number of states also experimented with regulation of the rates at which hospitals were paid for services. The weight of the evidence on rate regulation, from studies that compare hospital spending increases in states that adopted regulation with states that did not, suggests that in some cases it was at least modestly effective in slowing spending growth. Nonetheless, hospital rate regulation has largely been abandoned in the managed-care era.

A development of great importance to hospitals was Medicare's change in its method of paying for inpatient care, beginning in 1983. At that time, Medicare accounted for 28 percent of all hospital revenues, and an even higher share in the typical community hospital. The program shifted from reimbursing hospitals on an actual cost basis to paying pre-determined rates based on the patient's diagnosis. The new system creates a clear incentive to reduce lengths of stay, as additional days of care add costs but generate no additional revenue. Hospitals responded strongly to this incentive. Lengths of stay for Medicare patients, which had been falling slowly for some time, dropped rapidly in the first few years of the Prospective Payment System (PPS). Average length of stay had dropped from 11.2 days in 1975 to 10.3 in 1982, a little less than a day over 7 years, but then it fell an additional 1.7 days over the next 3 years as PPS took effect.

The response to the new system showed that an incentive directed at hospitals could affect their resource use, despite the fact that doctors make the decisions about discharging patients. Medicare remains very important for hospitals, accounting for a third of all hospital revenues in 1997. Hospitals respond to the incentives Medicare creates, which, however well-intentioned, are sometimes perverse. For example, after the PPS began paying hospitals for inpatient care at a fixed rate per case regardless of length of stay, reimbursement for care provided after discharge in other settings was still done on a cost basis. This created incentives for hospitals to provide skilled nursing care and home care, to discharge patients as early as feasible (sometimes to a different bed in the same facility), and to collect additional revenue from the provision of "post-acute" care, incidentally shifting costs as much as possible to the cost-reimbursed sector. Medicare expenses on skilled nursing care and home care soared and Congress attempted to address the problem in the Balanced Budget Act of 1997—but getting the incentives right while protecting the access of seniors to important medical services is no easy matter.

Health Insurers As discussed earlier, health insurers in this period often left the organization and delivery of care to the providers. Commercial insurers did compete with Blue Cross and Blue Shield to sell plans to employers. They made significant inroads, surpassing the Blue plans in total enrollees from the early 1950s onward, despite certain advantages held by the Blues. The Blues were organized as nonprofits and, as such, enjoyed some federal and state tax advantages over for-profit plans. As plans originally organized by hospital associations and medical societies, they also had some advantages in dealing with providers. For example, in some states, Blue Cross received significant discounts on hospital care compared to what was charged to commercial insurers.

Commercial insurers competed by offering an insurance package different from that of the Blues, and pricing it differently. The Blues emphasized service benefits and "first dollar" coverage for hospital care (meaning that individuals faced no copayments or deductibles for inpatient care), but placed limits on the total number of days covered. These limits left the individual facing large risks in the case of long stays. The commercial insurers offered "major medical insurance," covering a wide range of services, with deductibles, copayments, and better coverage for extremely high-cost events. The philosophy of the Blues was also to practice "community rating," to set premiums equally across a community in order to spread risks broadly. The problem with community rating in a competitive market for insurance is that groups that expect their health care costs to be lower than the community-wide average have an incentive to split themselves off. Large employers who believed that they had relatively healthy workers turned to commercial insurers to get premiums based on their own experience rather than community rates. As time went on, the Blues responded to competition by behaving more like the commercial insurers, including the use of experience rating for large groups.

Managed Care and Conduct

An important contributing factor in the transformation of the health insurance market to managed care in the 1980s and 1990s was the growing concern on the part of employers, especially large ones, with the costs of the insurance. The HMO Act of 1973 promoted HMO growth to some degree, and enrollment grew rapidly—from a small base—in the 1970s. By the 1980s, the idea of managed care was becoming more familiar, and employers began to look to insurers for ways to gain control over rising premiums, even if it meant placing some restrictions on enrollees' choice of medical providers and access to services. The PPO concept also emerged in the early 1980s as a less restrictive form of managed care, and a more palatable one to many employees. Pressured by employers, health insurers began to compete in new ways, including selectively contracting with hospitals and doctors, negotiating with them for lower payment rates, and implementing other tools of utilization management.

As Figure 10-4 suggests, most health insurance in most parts of the country now incorporates managed-care techniques in at least their milder forms. There is still wide variation across geographic areas in the degree of market penetration of managed-care plans, the aggressiveness of price competition among plans, and the extent to which plans have put pressure on providers.

Especially in those places where managed care is most aggressive, providers feel pressured to change their behavior or risk being left out of managed-care networks, which may considerably reduce demand for their services. Some of their responses involve banding together to become actively engaged in managing care. As discussed earlier, some large physician groups—especially in California—have accepted capitation payments and taken responsibility for all, or a defined subset of, their enrollees' health care. Many hospitals or groups of hospitals throughout the country have been instrumental in developing Integrated Delivery Systems, which may also provide comprehensive care in return for capitation payments. Frequently, however, managed-care organizations purchase services from providers using some form of fee-for-service, with the organizations themselves taking much of the responsibility for managing utilization. Rather than being reimbursed for what they consider reasonable costs or charges, as they were in the past, hospitals and doctors now often find that payment rates are determined by what the market will bear. They thus find themselves in price competition with their peers to a degree not previously experienced. Predictably, both hospitals and doctors are showing more interest in horizontal combinations (mergers of hospitals or affiliation with larger groups for doctors) to gain bargaining leverage with insurers. At the AMA's annual meeting in June 1999, delegates voted for the first time to support both unionization of employed physicians and changes in federal law that would allow collective bargaining groups to represent independent doctors.

Managed care may be changing the way hospitals compete. Formerly, hospital competition focused on quality to attract doctors and patients. Markets with more hospitals might, therefore, have greater duplication of services and higher unit costs. Recent evidence, mostly from California, suggests that when managed care dominates insurance markets, prices of hospital services are lower where competition is more intense, as traditional industrial organization theory predicts.[22]

---

[22]David Dranove and William D. White, "Recent Theory and Evidence on Competition in Hospital Markets," *Journal of Economics and Management Strategy,* 3 (Spring 1994): 169–209, and Emmett B. Keeler, Glenn Melnick, and Jack Zwanziger, "The Changing Effects of Competition on Non-Profit and For-Profit Hospital Pricing Behavior," *Journal of Health Economics* 18 (1999): 69–86.

IV. PERFORMANCE

Concerns about American Health Care

How are we to assess the performance of our health care industry? Can we point to deficiencies, and are they the kinds of problems that managed care seems well-suited to address? Rising expenditures, as summarized in Figure 10-2, have been a cause for concern as well as a driving force behind recent structural changes in the industry. By increasing labor costs, higher health insurance premiums surely spurred employers' interest in managed care. Cost growth in Medicaid and the pressure it placed on state government budgets drove the states in the same direction.

Rising expenditure on a group of products does not necessarily imply that the associated industry is performing poorly. For example, if *prices* fall due to cost-reducing innovations, as with personal computers, an increase in *spending* will follow naturally if demand is elastic. Total spending could also rise if new, higher quality but more costly products replace older ones—a more likely scenario for health care. A recent study looking at the treatment of heart attacks between 1983 and 1994 found that while the spending per case was rising, the quality-adjusted price was actually falling about 1 percent per year if improvements in survival were accounted for in a reasonable way.[23] Still, there is a strong suspicion that in the premanaged-care era, health spending was "too high" and rose "too rapidly." The suspicion stems partly from beliefs about the financing system in place at the time. Providers of care and well-insured consumers had incentives to expand services as long as the expected benefits were positive, with little regard for costs. The creation of managed-care organizations as a countervailing force with incentives for cost-conscious behavior thus held some promise of better results.

American health care needs improvement in areas other than spending growth, too. Comparisons of health care data across countries, for example, are not particularly flattering to the U.S. system. The United States ranks first by a wide margin in amounts spent, but is much further down the list in most indicators of population health.

Table 10-6 provides comparative data on a few countries, along with median values for a set of 29 (mostly high-income) countries surveyed by the Organization for Economic Cooperation and Development. On a per capita basis, with due allowance for differences in national currencies, the United States spent almost three times as much on health as the United Kingdom, more than twice as much as Japan, and 54 percent more than the second-highest country, Switzerland. While there is a strong positive

[23]David M. Cutler et al., "Are Medical Prices Declining?" *Quarterly Journal of Economics* (November 1998): 991–1024.

TABLE 10-6 Health Care Spending and Health in Selected Countries

	Spending, 1997		*Health, 1996*	
	Per Capita	*% of GDP*	*Infant Mortality*	*Female Life Expectancy at 65*
United States	$3,925	13.5	7.8	18.9
Canada	$2,095	9.0	6.0	20.2
Germany	$2,339	10.4	5.0	18.6
Japan	$1,741	7.3	3.8	21.5
United Kingdom	$1,347	6.7	6.1	18.4
OECD median	$1,728	7.5	5.8	18.9

Source: Gerard F. Anderson and Jean-Pierre Poulier, "Health Spending, Access and Outcomes: Trends in Industrial Countries," *Health Affairs* 18 (May/June 1999).

correlation between health care spending and income across countries, this factor alone cannot account for America's position as an outlier in health spending. Comparing health spending as a share of GDP is a crude way of standardizing for differences in economic productivity. Here, also, the United States leads all other developed countries by a large margin, with Germany a rather distant second. We fare much worse in comparisons of the most common measures of population health, such as infant mortality and life expectancy. The United States ranks among the worst of the OECD countries in infant mortality, and below other wealthy countries in life expectancy at birth (not shown in the table). We do somewhat better in life expectancy at older ages, but, as the information on female life expectancy at age 65 suggests, still trail a number of other countries.

We should be cautious about condemning the United States health care industry based on data such as that in Table 10-6. Aggregate measures of population health are influenced in important ways by factors over which the health care system has no direct control. For example, greater income inequality and relatively high poverty rates in the United States, as compared with other developed countries, likely contribute to high infant mortality. Lower mortality, though relatively easy to measure, is also not the only health system output of importance. Alleviation of pain and anxiety and improvements in physical and mental functioning are among other outputs that should count. Perhaps if we could reliably measure these forms of value added the relative standing of the United States would improve. Still, it is natural to look at the Table 10-6 data and wonder whether the incremental spending in the United States, as compared with other countries, brings with it commensurate benefits.

Another phenomenon that indicates room for improvement in the American health industry (and probably elsewhere in the world) is the existence of substantial variation across geographic areas in the use of particular types of medical procedures, from relatively simple ones like hernia repair to very expensive surgeries such as coronary bypass and total hip replacement.[24] Variations in use rates are too large to explain by chance or by variation in illness across areas. While these variations are not well understood, they seem to indicate that different standards of appropriate treatment somehow get established in different communities, which reflects considerable uncertainty among doctors about the effectiveness of care in many circumstances. The social payoff to getting better information about "what really works" and reducing practice variations might be extremely large. One study estimated the deadweight losses from practice variations to be about $8 billion annually.[25] A good case can be made for investing greater *public* resources in expanding knowledge about the effectiveness of medical procedures because the private rewards for developing such knowledge may be far less than its social value. Still, large managed-care organizations have the capacity to gather data that shed light on these issues, and the incentive to curtail ineffective or unnecessarily costly practices based on what research shows, so they offer some hope of reducing wasteful variation.

Another common indictment of American health care is the significant share of the population with neither private nor public health insurance coverage, 16.3 percent in 1998. In all 28 other OECD countries except Mexico and Turkey, at least 99 percent of the population had insurance in 1997. The high uninsured rate in the United States cannot reasonably be blamed on poor performance of the health care industry, nor can the industry be expected to rectify the situation on its own. If there is to be a solution, collective action through government policy changes will certainly be required.

Effects of Managed Care

Has managed care made a difference in health system performance, and, if so, in what ways? Despite the considerable attention focused on managed care by the media, policymakers, health care interest groups, researchers, and the general public, these questions are surprisingly difficult to answer with confidence. The recent slowdown of growth in real per capita health spending (Figure 10-2) closely followed the shift in health insurance to managed-care techniques (Figure 10-4). While it is tempting

---

[24]Study of variations in medical practice was pioneered by John Wennberg and his collaborators. See for example, John E. Wennberg and Megan McAndrew Cooper, eds., *The Dartmouth Atlas of Health Care in the United States* (Chicago: American Hospital Publishing, Inc., 1998).

[25]Charles E. Phelps and Stephen T. Parente, "Priority Setting in Medical Technology and Medical Practice Assessment," *Medical Care* 28 (August 1990): 703–723.

to infer that managed care has at least been effective in restraining spending growth, one would like to see stronger evidence than this simple correlation over time in the aggregate data. Researchers have approached the issue by looking for natural experiments, trying to exploit variation arising from the fact that managed care has been embraced at different times and to a different degree in different parts of the country. A few recent studies have shown that health care spending has grown less rapidly in places where managed-care market penetration is greater, but the evidence is not overwhelming.[26]

A great deal of research effort has also been devoted to whether and how managed-care organizations use resources differently than do traditional insurance providers. Such comparisons must be interpreted carefully for several reasons. Individuals still exercise some choice in the type of insurance plan they enter; differences observed across types of insurance might reflect differences among the kinds of people who enroll as much as differences in how the plans perform. Secondly, there is so much variation within managed-care plans that there may be little generalizability across studies. Variation extends to what is left of the traditional fee-for-service sector as well. As Figure 10-4 indicates, almost all fee-for-service insurance has adopted at least some utilization management techniques. The blurring of the lines between different forms of health insurance increases the difficulty of doing comparative studies of performance.

Despite these caveats, most of the evidence points in the direction of lower resource use for HMOs as compared to traditional fee-for-service medicine (there is much less evidence available as yet on the use of resources in the PPO form of managed care).[27] Studies show fairly consistently that HMOs reduce the use of inpatient hospital care. Evidence is more mixed for physician care outside the hospital, which is not surprising given the conflicting incentives at work. HMOs would be expected to scrutinize the use of all types of services more closely, but they might also provide more preventive care to deter future hospitalizations and substitute less expensive outpatient services for more expensive inpatient ones. Recent studies show more use of physician care in HMOs as compared to fee-for-service, but the difference is not large enough to offset the reduced use of hospital care. Studies that compare HMOs with fee-for-service in the use of particular expensive services where there is some discretion about use (such as cesarean section in childbirth) indicate that HMOs use such services less frequently.

---

[26]Evidence on this issue and other aspects of managed-care performance is summarized in Sherry Glied, "Managed Care," a chapter in A. J. Culyer and J. P. Newhouse, eds., *Handbook of Health Economics* (Amsterdam: North-Holland, forthcoming).

[27]Robert H. Miller and Harold S. Luft, "Managed Care Performance Since 1980," *JAMA* 271 (18 May 1994):1512–1519.

Effects on quality of care should be of at least as much interest as those that relate to cost. Here, the evidence is very mixed. In a recent review of the literature, Robert Miller and Harold Luft find equal numbers of statistically significant results showing higher or lower quality in HMOs.[28] The mixture of findings is not terribly surprising and does not imply that any of the studies were incorrect or poorly executed. A more plausible interpretation is that quality of care really is sometimes better, sometimes worse in HMOs, depending on the particular organization, type of disease, and other circumstances. One well-conducted study of chronically ill elderly people, for example, found that HMOs provided lower quality care for physical health but better quality for mental health.[29]

An optimistic view of the evidence is that the incentives faced by managed-care organizations, at least in the HMO forms, lead them to provide health care at lower cost than traditional fee-for-service arrangements, without systematically adverse effects on quality. Even such a guarded conclusion should be regarded tentatively, however, and we must be careful not to overgeneralize across the extremely diverse landscape of managed care.

Managed Care and Provider Compensation

Some observers believe that to the extent that managed care has reduced the cost of health insurance it has done so primarily at the expense of providers by exercising market power to bargain with them to accept lower payments. Although there are some indications that insurers have successfully used market power to put pressure on providers, there is little systematic data to show substantial adverse effects. In competition among managed-care plans, those that purchase services from independent hospitals and medical groups or IPAs appear to be winning out over more tightly vertically integrated organizations. This suggests that insurers can obtain hospital and physician services more cheaply by buying them in the marketplace rather than producing them "in-house." According to AMA survey data, median physician income grew about 1.4 percentage points per year more slowly than the CPI between 1993 and 1997. The extent to which this slow growth can be traced to the effects of managed care is not entirely clear. However, one study looking at data from the 1985–1993 period found that incomes of primary care doctors grew most rapidly and of hospital-based specialists most slowly in states where managed-care market share was growing fastest.[30] Because managed-care

---

[28]"Does Managed Care Lead to Better or Worse Quality of Care?" *Health Affairs,* 16 (September/October 1997): 7–25.

[29]John E. Ware, Jr., et al., "Differences in 4-Year Health Outcomes for Elderly and Poor, Chronically Ill Patients Treated in HMO and Fee-for-Service Systems," *JAMA* 276 (1996): 1039–1047.

[30]Carol J. Simon, David Dranove, and William D. White, "The Impact of Managed Care on the Physician Marketplace," *Public Health Reports,* 112 (May-June 1997), 222–230.

plans often emphasize primary care gatekeeping and appear to reduce inpatient hospital utilization, these findings provide evidence that demand from managed-care plans is influencing physician income in ways that health insurers traditionally did not.

A recent study in Massachusetts, although limited in scope, provides some fascinating information about the effect of managed care on provider payments. David Cutler and his colleagues looked at detailed information on treatment of heart attack patients who had insurance coverage through one large employer (which covered over 250,000 individuals), during the period between 1993 and 1995.[31] The employees could choose relatively unmanaged indemnity coverage or one of several HMOs. Heart attack care is an interesting case to study. While enrollees chose their insurance plans, they would have done so before the attack occurred, and there is little reason to think that the healthiness of heart attack patients would differ systematically across insurers. Heart attack survivors also receive different types of procedures of varying cost, and it is frequently claimed that the most expensive procedures, such as coronary bypass surgery, are overutilized in the United States. HMOs might be expected to be more selective in approving such expensive procedures than indemnity insurers.

Cutler and colleagues found that payments per heart attack treated were only about 61 percent as high in the HMOs ($23,600 as compared to $38,500). However, when they placed patients into categories by the type of treatment they received, the costs for HMO patients were lower by a similar ratio in each of the categories, suggesting that the overall difference in cost is not primarily a result of substituting to less expensive forms of treatment. At least in this case, it appeared that a large share of the reduction in cost must have come from lower payments to providers. Interestingly, they could also find no difference in quality between the HMOs and indemnity insurers as measured by deaths or rates of hospital readmissions due to complications.

Effects of Consolidation

In assessing the effects of recent developments in health care on the performance of the industry, another important issue is whether consolidation has been primarily efficiency-enhancing, with larger size making possible the exploitation of economies of scale and scope, or has been primarily in the service of greater market power for the organizations involved. Although interest in Integrated Delivery Systems is by no means dead, much of the recent consolidation activity has been horizontal,

[31] David M. Cutler et al., "Pricing Heart Attack Treatments," in D. Cutler and E. Berndt, eds., *Medical Care Pricing and Output,* (Chicago: University of Chicago Press, 2000).

across organizations engaged in similar activities, rather than vertical, across stages of production. We will consider the evidence about mergers among hospitals and among managed-care insurers.

Hospitals have increasingly chosen to affiliate in multihospital systems, frequently with other hospitals in the same local market, but also with hospitals in other geographic areas which had not been direct competitors. Some of these affiliations are rather weak, with the individual hospitals remaining largely autonomous, but joining forces to achieve some economies in activities such as the purchasing of supplies. Others are formal mergers or acquisitions. Over the last several years, between 100 and 200 hospital mergers have taken place per year. Public attention has focused heavily on acquisition of nonprofit hospitals by for-profit chains, especially by Columbia/HCA, the largest and most aggressive chain. Columbia acquired or negotiated joint venture agreements to manage 35 formerly nonprofit hospitals in 1995 alone. But for-profit chains have become less aggressive about expansion in the wake of a federal government investigation of Columbia, which began in March 1997. In any case, most hospital mergers occur within the nonprofit sector.

The managed care environment is more challenging to hospital managers than the relatively placid era that preceded it. One reason for affiliating with a larger hospital system that extends beyond one's market area is to get access to greater management expertise for coping with rapidly changing market conditions. Other reasons include better access to capital for modernization or expansion, or to gain some benefits (probably small) from shared activities such as joint purchasing. The direct effect on a hospital's local market power from this sort of consolidation is likely to be small.

Mergers with hospitals in the same market could be a different story. Research on economies of scale suggests that they are essentially exhausted at a moderate size of 200–300 beds. On that basis, we would not expect the merger of two hospitals—unless they were very small—to produce any significant economies through such avenues as the sharing of overhead functions. However, in a market with underutilized bed capacity or excessive duplication of services—a common state of affairs for U.S. hospitals today—a merger might facilitate reductions in capacity and more rational planning as new services are added, thereby reducing costs of care. On the other hand, mergers that increase market concentration always raise questions about effects on prices. It is not hard to believe that a primary aim of many hospital mergers is to gain bargaining power relative to managed care insurers, by reducing the insurer's ability to play off one hospital against the other.

As with many aspects of the changes wrought by managed care, a consensus view has not emerged about the effects of mergers on hospital prices. A reasonable inference to draw from recent research is that two opposing effects on prices are present in hospital mergers: an efficiency-enhancing or cost-reducing effect that tends to depress prices, and a market power effect that increases them. One study using a large national data set from 1986 to 1994 found that the price-reducing effect tends to be stronger.[32] However, the market power effect, which seems to exist for non-profit hospitals as well as for-profits, may be getting stronger over time.[33]

We know less about economies of scale in managed-care organizations, partly because there is so much diversity in how they behave. Existing research suggests an HMO may be able to exploit most economies of scale at a size as low as 50,000 enrollees.[34] In 1996, 73 percent of HMO enrollees were in plans with at least 100,000 enrollment, so 50,000 is a relatively small HMO. In theory, affiliation of HMOs operating in different markets, as has happened in many recent mergers, might offer some additional economies that have not shown up yet in research studies. A larger total enrollment base offers more data that can be used to analyze and improve the effectiveness of techniques for managing care. Although care must be delivered locally, for the most part, if an organization succeeds in developing a knowledge base and effective tools for managing care, there could be gains from exploiting this competitive edge in many markets simultaneously. Large multilocation employers might also find some advantages in dealing with managed-care organizations that are similarly far-flung.

Evidence suggests, not surprisingly, that HMO premiums are lower in markets with more HMOs.[35] Antitrust enforcement agencies should look closely at mergers that substantially increase local concentration. Mergers of managed-care organizations that formerly operated in different areas are not particularly troubling, as they do not increase market power in relevant market areas. Roger Feldman and colleagues found that between 1994 and 1997, concentration in the HMO industry increased at the national level, but fell in most local markets (note the steady increase in number of HMOs shown in Table 10-2).[36] They note that some of the larger recent mergers, such as Aetna with U.S. Healthcare, and FHP with Pacificare in 1996, and Aetna and Prudential in 1999, have, in many cases, merged plans that were already operating in the same markets. The concentration-increasing effect has nonetheless often been offset by entry of new HMOs at the same time.

---

[32]Robert A. Connor et al., "Which Types of Hospital Mergers Save Consumers Money?" *Health Affairs* 16 (November/December 1997): 62–74. "Prices" in this study and the next one referenced are measured by hospital revenue per admission.

[33]Keeler, et al., "The Changing Effects of Competition."

[34]Douglas Wholey et al., "Scale and Scope Economies Among Health Maintenance Organizations," *Journal of Health Economics* 15 (1996): 657–684.

[35]Douglas Wholey, Roger Feldman, and Jon B. Christianson, "The Effect of Market Structure on HMO Premiums," *Journal of Health Economics* 14 (1995): 81–105.

[36]"HMO Consolidations."

V. PUBLIC POLICY ISSUES

Can the Market Work in Health Care?

The most basic public policy question about the economics of health care concerns market versus nonmarket allocation. Is it best to harness the power of the market for allocating resources as effectively as possible, recognizing and adjusting for the peculiarities of the product and the industry, or is health care so special that it is better to rely on nonmarket mechanisms, as in the United Kingdom, Canada, or a number of other countries? Compared with other parts of the U.S. economy, the role of government as regulator and purchaser of health care is unusually extensive. Looking across countries, however, our health care system is easily the most market-oriented. Comparative data like that in Table 10-6 may lead one to wonder whether we have the right idea.

In a 1963 article generally considered the seminal paper in health care economics,[37] Nobel laureate Kenneth Arrow argued that uncertainty in the incidence of disease and the effectiveness of treatment, and the institutional adaptations to that uncertainty, largely account for the peculiarities of health care as an economic industry. Uncertainty about illness and the demand for care create a demand for insurance, which may be satisfied through private arrangements or through social insurance programs such as Medicare and Medicaid. Individuals do not want to have to worry about the cost of health care at a time of serious need, and they are willing to pay for insurance to protect them against that eventuality. As taxpayers, we also are willing to provide assistance for the poor to help them in meeting unpredictable medical needs. Arrow also emphasized the patient's uncertainty about the effectiveness of health care and the imbalance of information between doctor and patient. When a health problem presents itself, the doctor is expected to be much better informed than the patient about the consequences of alternative courses of action, and the patient will want to rely heavily on the doctor's advice.

In light of these features of health care, there seems ample reason for skepticism that unfettered market forces are the answer to resource allocation problems. The usual argument that markets will allocate resources efficiently relies on the discipline imposed by well-informed buyers spending their limited budgets shrewdly, assuring that only sellers who can deliver the best value for money will survive. Because of the imbalance of information, however, patients are poorly equipped for this role of responsibility. And while health insurance is surely, on balance, a good thing, it brings with it reduced price sensitivity at the time that care is re-

[37]Kenneth J. Arrow, "Uncertainty and the Welfare Economics of Medical Care," *American Economic Review* 53 (1963): 941–969.

ceived. We have long had social institutions, such as licensure and the code of ethics under which physicians practice, to help guard against under-provision of services or inferior quality. As insurance coverage grew and technological progress expanded the potential to spend money on health care, we got a system that promoted spending growth while creating few incentives to weigh cost against benefit at the margin.

But managed care may be changing that picture. Viewed in the best light, the success of managed care in the marketplace can be seen as a groping for a new way of dealing with the "moral hazard" problem in health insurance. Moral hazard, in this context, is the tendency of the insured to overuse services, which inevitably drives up premiums. Managed care might provide a countervailing force to other features of the system that push in the direction of insufficient attention to cost.

The best hope for the market is probably some version of "managed competition," a concept pioneered and tirelessly advocated by Alain Enthoven, among others.[38] The key idea is that consumers police the market by exercising informed choice and cost-conscious behavior primarily at the point of choosing a health insurance plan, not by shopping for individual services. Insurers compete for the consumer dollar, ideally by offering packages that are attractive in terms of both cost and quality of care. The insurers play the role of selecting providers and developing effective mechanisms for managing care. Differences in consumer preferences can be accommodated as long as individuals face the full difference in cost when they elect a more expensive plan. Some may be willing to pay for free choice of doctor and very comprehensive coverage, while others will accept greater restrictions on choice and benefits in exchange for lower premiums.

To make an analogy, most purchasers of personal computers do not pay great attention to the makers of the component parts, and most would find it difficult to assess the reliability of one hard drive or modem relative to another. They rely more on the incentives of the manufacturer assembling the package, be it a major corporation like Dell or Compaq or a local retailer, to make good judgments about quality and cost in selecting components. Performance in this market seems very satisfactory.

Choosing a health insurance plan is, of course, different from choosing a PC. To begin with, the adverse consequences of a bad choice are potentially much more severe. The proponents of managed competition have always recognized, as the name itself implies, that the environment in which insurance plans compete must be "managed" or regulated to achieve the best results. In the remainder of this section we will touch on

---

[38] An early version of the idea appears in his two-part article "Consumer Choice Health Plan," *New England Journal of Medicine* 298 (23 March 1978): 650–658, and 298 (30 March 1978): 709–720, and his book *Health Plan* (Reading, MA: Addison-Wesley, 1980).

some major public policy issues relating to how competition should be managed and what we can reasonably expect from this strategy.

Cost-Conscious Consumer Choice

Managed competition advocates envision a structure in which consumers select from a variety of health insurance plans. To the extent that insurance is provided as an employee benefit or subsidized through government programs, the individual should still face the incremental cost of a more expensive plan, and should reap the financial benefit of choosing a less expensive one. For most workers with job-related coverage, this is not the current reality, as most employers who provide coverage offer only a single plan. In 1997, according to a large national survey of employers, only 43 percent of enrollees in job-related insurance plans were offered a choice. Of those employers who did offer a choice of plans, only 28 percent made equal dollar contributions regardless of which plan was chosen as managed competition principles dictate.[39]

Greater consumer choice could be promoted through policies that encourage "purchasing cooperatives," insurance brokers that would pool workers from many firms and offer individuals a wider choice of plans. Federal tax policy might also be changed to encourage more cost-conscious choice. The open-ended nature of the current tax preference for employer-provided health benefits favors more expensive plans. Instead of excluding all employer payments for health insurance from taxable income, the size of the tax credit an employer or individual receives could be made dependent on the cost of the plan chosen.

Will Quality Suffer?

As employers and government programs have pushed insurers to compete more aggressively on price, there is already concern that competition will focus too heavily on price and cost, at the expense of quality and access to beneficial services. It is surely an exaggeration to claim, as some have, that "employers care only about cost"—firms have an interest in making the compensation package they offer as attractive as possible and will care about quality if workers do. A more serious issue is whether employers and consumers have or can get the information necessary to make reasonable judgments about the quality of health care plans. If those who choose among plans are unable to assess quality, the entire premise of the managed competition strategy is called into question.

Measuring health care plan—and health care provider—quality is a rapidly evolving field. Ratings of HMOs based on measures developed by

---

[39]M. Susan Marquis and Stephen E. Long, "Trends in Managed Care and Managed Competition, 1993–1997," *Health Affairs,* 18 (November-December 1999): 75–88.

the National Committee for Quality Assurance (see its Web site at *www.ncqa.org*) are now published in *U.S. News and World Report* and *Newsweek.* But measuring quality of such a complex product is difficult. Ideally, we would like to measure health plans' performance by their impact on the health of enrollees. However, it is difficult to separate the health plan's contribution from other factors that influence health. Hospitals that do poorly in mortality-based measures of quality, for example, consistently object that such measures do not adequately account for how severely ill their patients are. Current measures of health plan performance focus on "process" measures, such as the qualifications of network doctors, intermediate outcomes such as the percentage of pregnant enrollees who get prenatal care in the first trimester, and measures of patient satisfaction. Additional research to develop more reliable ways to measure health plan performance in the dimensions that most matter to consumers warrants public support.

Regulation is another way to influence quality. Congress and state legislatures have debated over the last several years the appropriate components of a "Patients' Bill of Rights" with respect to health plans.[40] A particularly contentious issue is the legal liability of health plans in disputes over coverage. Health insurance contracts cannot define precisely what services will be covered in every circumstance, and so generally contain language that services will be provided when "medically necessary," leading to disagreements over what this means. The Employment Retirement Income Security Act of 1974 (ERISA) has effectively limited a health plan's liability in such disputes to the cost of denied benefits; enrollees have not been able to sue plans for lost wages, pain and suffering, or punitive damages. Expanding liability would have a deterrent effect on improper denials and provide for more appropriate compensation of victims. On the other hand, health plans and employers contend that it could severely limit their ability to manage care in a cost-effective way, and, in light of the imperfections of the legal system, would add more to the cost of health coverage than would be gained from improved quality.

Is Competition Workable?

Aside from demand-side policies to give consumers the incentive to choose in a cost-conscious way among health plans and the information needed to do so wisely, managed competition relies on there being a sufficient supply of health plans to offer consumers a real choice. To consider the potential for competition on the supply side, we should examine the minimum efficient scale of a health care plan—the size that it needs to be

[40]Jill A. Marsteller and Randall R. Bovbjerg, *Federalism and Patient Protection: Changing Roles for State and Federal Government,* Urban Institute, August 1999 (available at *http://newfederalism.urban.org/html/occa28.html*).

to operate at minimum average cost per enrollee in relation to the size of relevant markets. One study did so by looking at the staffing patterns and use of hospital services in relation to enrollees in large staff model HMOs.[41] The authors found that a community of 360,000 could support three independent networks of physicians and three hospitals of about 240 beds each, but some types of acute services would not need to be available in all hospitals. A smaller community of 180,000 could still support three independent physician networks but would need to share all inpatient facilities to achieve productive efficiency. The authors noted that 37 percent of the American population lives in health care market areas smaller than 360,000 in population, and 29 percent in markets smaller than 180,000. At the other extreme, 42 percent are in markets with population greater than 1.2 million.

We might conclude that in major metropolitan areas market size is not a serious obstacle to competition among health care plans, but that a significant share of the population lives in areas where several fully independent delivery systems cannot compete and be productively efficient. As discussed earlier, however, independent delivery systems dedicated to a single HMO are the exception rather than the rule among managed-care plans. Several plans frequently contract with the same sets of doctors and hospitals. Other research that looks at costs per enrollee in relation to HMO size finds that costs may be minimized at a size as small as 50,000 enrollees. Gaining a better understanding of how managed-care plans compete in relatively small markets is an important objective for further research. Even in areas with a fairly large population base, market power exercised by health plans with substantial market share, combinations of providers, or providers of highly specialized services may still lead to less than optimal results. Vigilant antitrust enforcement will likely be a key component of a managed competition strategy, but we are still learning what appropriate antitrust policy entails.

High-Risk Populations and the Uninsured

In any year, the use of health care resources is highly concentrated among a small share of the population, with the highest percentile of users accounting for 30 percent of all expenditures, and the top 10 percent for 70 percent of spending. To the extent that high usage is predictable on the basis of such factors as age or preexisting conditions, a competitive market in insurance will tend to segregate, with higher risk groups paying higher premiums. If there are legal restrictions on premium differences or other reasons why they are not practical, health plans will have incentives

---

[41] Richard Kronick et al., "The Marketplace in Health Care Reform," *New England Journal of Medicine,* 328 (14 January 1993): 148–152.

to act strategically to attract healthy enrollees and avoid the sick. This has been a particularly significant issue for the Medicare program when it contracts with managed-care plans on a capitation basis. Until recently, it paid managed-care plans a capitation rate equal to 95 percent of what it would expect to pay for fee-for-service Medicare enrollees in the same geographic area. If those who join managed-care plans were typical Medicare beneficiaries, the program could expect to save 5 percent, on average, on each one. But it appears that managed-care plans generally attract relatively healthy Medicare enrollees, who would have spent less than 95 percent of the average had they stayed in the fee-for-service system—so the program actually spends more while paying at a "discounted" rate.

Any resources devoted to competition for a preferred set of enrollees are wasted from a social perspective—one group or plan's gain comes almost entirely from costs imposed on other groups, plans, or individuals. It also seems unfair that those unlucky enough to be struck with a serious and chronic illness should be burdened further with higher insurance premiums or difficulty in obtaining coverage. The conceptually appropriate solution is clear: Do not vary premiums by risk-status (at least for those elements of risk outside the individual's control), but adjust payments to insurers to reflect differences in expected cost. If risk-adjusted payments are made accurately, such a system would be fair to insurance plans and consumers, and would remove incentives for insurers to compete for preferred risks.

Two obstacles stand in the way of widespread adoption of risk-adjustment schemes. One is that despite considerable ongoing research, we are in the early stages of learning to do risk adjustment properly. The second is that to apply risk adjustment widely in the private sector, a mechanism would be needed for pooling premium payments very broadly across insured groups, and then redistributing them to insurance plans on a risk-adjusted basis. Such a pooling would be possible if most insurance were obtained through purchasing cooperatives (as it would have been, for example, under President Clinton's original reform proposal), but it is not in the current system.

A large uninsured population, as exists in the United States today, is also not compatible with effective managed competition. There are two related problems. First, the uninsured receive care in emergency situations that often costs more to provide than they themselves are able to pay. Providers must recover the unreimbursed costs of such care in some way, and, to the extent possible, will try to shift the costs forward into premiums paid by the insured. Because various providers and health plans will not bear the costs of uncompensated care equally, due to differences in location and other factors, these extra costs will distort competition among providers and among plans. Second, in order to survive in the competitive process, providers and plans have incentives to avoid bearing the costs of uncompensated care. The uninsured are likely to find it more difficult to get needed care in a market-driven system than in the earlier world of more passive insurers and employers. For these reasons, advocates of managed competition frequently argue that it will work best if accompanied by government action to assure universal health care coverage.

Technology and Spending Growth

A final question about market mechanisms in health care is whether they can provide the right incentives for new technology and spending growth over time. Managed care creates greater incentives than traditional insurance to adopt innovations that reduce cost and to eliminate those that add cost with no benefit. But what about innovations for which the expected benefits clearly exceed the risks, but at very high cost per unit of benefit? Most health economists believe that the long-term growth of health care spending has been most associated with the adoption of new technologies and treatment techniques offering at least some medical benefit, so this question has important implications for spending growth, and probably also for consumer welfare. Should an insurance plan pay for a cholesterol-lowering drug for a healthy 40-year-old with borderline high cholesterol, if the cost per expected life year gained is $200,000? What about a $20,000 surgery that would add half a year to a lung cancer sufferer's life with 10 percent probability—$400,000 per life year gained? How a managed-care plan responds in these situations may depend on its liability to a lawsuit, and on how the legal system defines "necessary care." What answer is right?

One can imagine a system in which, if legislation allows it, some insurance plans are liberal in their coverage of technologies, while others offer lower premiums but are much stricter, and consumers may choose among them. We may or may not be willing to live with the consequences of such a system, which, to some degree, already exists, but the issues are important for public policy to consider.

VI. CONCLUSION

In its account of recent developments in the health care industry, this chapter has emphasized managed care and the changes it has wrought, but there are those who expect, and certainly those who hope, that managed care will prove to be a passing fad. A former editor of the *New England Journal of Medicine* has written recently of "The Decline and Fall of Managed Care."[42] *USA Today* asks "Is the HMO Love Affair Over?" and

[42]Arnold Relman, *Hospitals and Health Networks* (5 July 1998): 70–71.

the same issue of *Newsweek* that rates the quality of 100 large managed-care plans features a cover story headlined "HMO Hell."[43] Is the "managed-care revolution" already history, or will it continue to reshape the American health care industry?

While managed care is evolving rapidly, in many cases loosening up on restrictions on choice and interference in medical decisions in response to consumer demands, reports of its demise are premature. Interest in controlling the growth of health care spending will not fade away, but neither will an interest in choice, quality, and access to beneficial services. Health insurers will need to respond to all of these concerns to be successful. If we continue to rely heavily on market forces to guide resource allocation, as seems likely for the foreseeable future, getting the incentives created by the legal and regulatory environment right, and supplementing private with public resources where appropriate, will remain significant challenges to policymakers and students of this industry.

Suggested Readings

Classic References

Arrow, Kenneth J. "Uncertainty and the Welfare Economics of Medical Care," *American Economic Review* 53 (1963): 941–969.

Enthoven, Alain C. *Health Plan* (Reading, MA: Addison-Wesley, 1980).

Fuchs, Victor R. *Who Shall Live?* (New York: Basic Books, 1974).

Joskow, Paul L. *Controlling Hospital Costs* (Cambridge: MIT Press, 1984).

Starr, Paul. *The Social Transformation of American Medicine* (New York: Basic Books, 1982).

Textbooks

Feldstein, Paul J. *Health Care Economics.* 5th ed. (Albany, NY: Delmar, 1999).

Folland, Sherman, Allen C. Goodman, and Miron Stano. *The Economics of Health and Health Care,* 3rd ed. (Upper Saddle River, NJ: Prentice-Hall, 2001).

Getzen, Thomas E. *Health Economics* (New York: John Wiley and Sons, 1997).

Phelps, Charles E. *Health Economics,* 2nd ed. (Reading, MA: Addison-Wesley, 1997).

A useful collection of somewhat more advanced papers is:

Culyer, A. J., and J. P. Newhouse, eds., *Handbook of Health Economics* (Amsterdam: North-Holland, forthcoming).

[43] *USA Today,* 20 October 1999; *Newsweek,* 8 November 1999.

CHAPTER 11

Telecommunications

—Manley R. Irwin and James McConnaughey*

As the United States begins the twenty-first century, telecommunications bandwidth assumes a role of critical importance. Bandwidth measures communications carrying capacity to deliver voice, data, video, and text to the end user. The United States is in the throes of a bandwidth crosscurrent. In one market, bandwidth is so plentiful that a capacity glut may well lead to a precipitous drop in transmission prices. In another market, a bandwidth shortage threatens to impose a limit on the quantity and diversity of information available to the public. The first market is the U.S. long distance market; the second, the U.S. local telephone market.

The characteristics of each market differ markedly. The long distance market is relatively open, invites market entry, and resides in an environment of de facto deregulation. Innovation in long distance facilities and bandwidth proceeds at a furious pace. The local telephone market, by contrast, is dominated by firms enjoying monopolist status. Rivalry in this market is at best stunted, entry remains episodic, and government regulation stands as an institutional reality. The local exchange market rests upon some 270 million lines of copper wire that connect telephone central office switches to a customer's home or office. The technology of twisted copper wire has changed little over the past 110 years.

It is the local telephone market—the copper wire pair—that emerges as a bandwidth bottleneck in today's economy; and it is local telecommunications that has invited the attention of Congress, regulatory agencies, and Internet users. That the local telephone monopoly is now a top policy priority is illustrated by the following questions: How can the United States promote competition in a market that is concentrated? How can public policy modernize telephone investment to accommodate an apparently insatiable demand for information bandwidth? Which industry should be allowed to compete in local telephony: Line resellers? Equipment suppliers? Long distance carriers? Cable television firms? Electric power companies? Wireless operators? Suppliers of aerospace hardware? Internet service providers?

---

*The views expressed in this chapter are those of the author and do not necessarily represent the views of the Commerce Department.

Is the current clamor for alternatives to the copper wire based on a technological imperative? Or does local telephony constitute the essence of a natural monopoly? If so, does local telephony call for more rather than less regulatory oversight? And if the former, which government agency should hold that power—a city, a county, the state, the U.S. government? How can the public resolve an inevitable jurisdictional clash between state and federal agencies?

In the final analysis, bandwidth capacity is not merely a question of more or less, but rather is an issue of economic incentives. What institutional setting best delivers future electronic goods and services to the firm and consumer—a competitive market, a regulated market, or admixtures of both? Whatever choice is taken, that policy option will surely configure a twenty-first century on-line economy. But first, what has the United States inherited from its telecommunications past?

I. HISTORY

Telecommunications, over the past 130 years, has traversed four somewhat loosely defined stages. These include the following: Monopoly (1876–1894); Competition/Regulation (1894–1920); Monopoly/Regulation/Antitrust (1920–1956); Antitrust/Divestiture (1956–present).

Monopoly

Consider the first stage: monopoly (1876–1894). The filing of two telephone patents on the same day of the same year presents an event unique in economic history. Suffice it to say that Alexander Graham Bell's patent prevailed over Elisha Gray's filing. The Boston Bell Patent Association, now in possession of a valuable property right, offered to sell the patent to the largest communication firm in the country—the Western Union Telegraph Company. Western Union management rejected the offer on grounds that the $100,000 asking price was exorbitant. Today's students of corporate history are virtually unanimously agreed that the Telegraph Company committed a commercial blunder of the first order.

To generate a return on its investment, the Bell Patent Association was forced to offer telephone service to the public. Service commenced in Boston, Massachusetts, and the Association assigned franchises in separate, exclusive geographic markets—especially populated cities. In 1878, the Patent Association hired a young manager from the U.S. postal service. Theodore Vail took a 50 percent cut in salary and accepted an assignment to convert a telephone patent into a viable commercial venture.

Recognizing its mistake, Western Union gave a research contract to the Thomas Edison laboratory to develop a rival telephone instrument. The Telegraph Company proceeded to establish a telephone subsidiary, the Home Telephone Company, but Vail was not intimidated by his $50 million rival. In fact, he took the offensive and charged Western Union with patent infringement. Vail not only threatened a patent suit, he pledged that Bell would enter the telegraph market.

The mouse roared; the lion blinked. Western Union agreed to withdraw from the voice market and to sell its operating subsidiary to Bell. Vail, in turn, renounced any intention of offering telegraph service. Historians mark the 1879 cartel agreement as the "Magna Carta" of the telephone industry.

Within the next 6 years, Vail put in place the foundations of what was to become known as the Bell System. He issued exclusive franchises to prospective telephone companies. Although Bell assumed an equity stake in each operating company, each company raised its own capital. In 1881, he acquired Western Electric Company, a manufacturer that had supplied telegraph equipment to Western Union, and assigned it a license to manufacture telephone apparatus under the Bell patent. Then in 1885, Vail established a company that connected long distance or toll lines to Bell's local telephone operations. The new American Bell Telephone Company provided both local and long distance service to customers or, in telephone parlance, its subscribers.

For reasons not entirely clear, Vail left the company in the late 1880s. By then, the American Bell Company had gone public, the stock was performing well, and Vail was now an individual of means. But he did not rest. He became a roving capitalist—starting traction and electric power companies in Europe and South America. And with his telephone holdings, Vail purchased a retirement farm in Vermont.

The basic Bell patent expired in 1893–1894. Though market entry became the order of the day, the company's structure was positioned to deal with competition. The company was horizontally integrated, vertically tied between long distance and local service, and vertically connected between telephone service and telephone manufacturing.

In place, too, were the company's policies and practices. For one thing, the company did not sell Bell's telephone instrument. Rather, the subscriber leased basic phone service. (At one time, Bell headquarters would not permit individual Bell affiliates to take ownership of the telephone handset.)

Bell refused to make its long distance lines available to competing telephone companies. The result of American Bell's policies was that a non-Bell customer required two phones, one for local calls, one for toll or long distance calls. To save money, a subscriber could lease a Bell instrument that permitted both local and toll calls. One by one, independent telephone companies found the logic of selling out to Bell compelling.

Competition/Regulation

Bell's patent expiration did foster the growth of independent or non-Bell phone companies—particularly in rural areas of the United States. The expiration also saw the rise of independent or non-Western Electric suppliers in the manufacturing market. Thus began an era of telephone competition. The results were predictable: telephone rates dropped, usage increased, and productivity surged. By the turn of the century, Bell—now known as the American Telephone and Telegraph Company, AT&T—saw its market share reduced to about half of the telephone service in the United States.

By the early 1900s, the J. P. Morgan Company, acquiring an equity stake in AT&T, prevailed upon Theodore Vail, now retired on his Vermont farm, to assume AT&T leadership. And once again, Vail's signature proved indelible. He instituted a personnel meritocracy, cut costs, improved service quality, pushed long distance facilities to the West Coast, and bought his old nemesis—the Western Union Telegraph Company. Indeed, Vail turned Western Union into a lean, vibrant, profitable operation.

Under Vail, AT&T continued to buy independent telephone companies, denied toll access to local rivals, leased—did not sell—telephone instruments to subscribers, and purchased equipment almost exclusively from Western Electric for Bell operating companies.

Vail also possessed the gift of foresight. He was cognizant that telephone handsets, central office exchanges, and transmission lines all had competitive substitutes. Marconi's vacuum tube-radio in particular posed a threat to AT&T's investment in wire and cable. By 1910, Vail had centralized AT&T's research activities, laying the groundwork for what was to become a world-renowned private laboratory, Bell Telephone Laboratory.[1]

Vail was aware of public sentiment, if not hostility, toward big business "trusts" as they were called at the turn of the century. The government-driven breakup of the American Tobacco Co., and the Standard Oil Companies loomed large on the corporate scene; and when AT&T's Western Union purchase was challenged by the U.S. government, Vail deferred to the government and divested the Telegraph Company from Bell ownership. Vail, nevertheless, remained convinced that competition in telephony was unworkable. The telephone industry, he maintained, constituted a "natural" monopoly.

The European response to natural monopoly—nationalization—appeared straightforward enough and Vail knew that the U.S. postal

---

[1]John Brooks, *Telephone: The First Hundred Years,* (NY: Harper and Row, 1975), 129.

service under the Woodrow Wilson administration coveted AT&T ownership. Vail responded by observing there was little difference between a private or a public monopoly. Both, in his opinion, remained unaccountable to the consumer. Vail's response to natural monopoly was regulation, government oversight, and a public watchdog—not unlike that of the Interstate Commerce Commission.

Exhorted by the Bell telephone companies, Congress in 1910 amended the Interstate Commerce Commission Act to extend the ICC's jurisdiction over interstate telephone service. The Bell System supported legislation to extend state commission oversight to telephone services and facilities. Populists and monopolists found common cause in a mandate for "universal telephone service" to the public at large.

To solicit, indeed, welcome government regulation was regarded as outright corporate heresy in the early years of the 1900s. Nevertheless, Vail insisted that a government board, not unlike a jury, would monitor AT&T's service, rates, investments, and earnings. Vail said that his company must tell the truth about itself or someone else would.[2] But regulatory due process carried a bonus; it immunized a telephone monopoly firm from antitrust assault. The result was that AT&T was to become the largest corporation in U.S. history.

Monopoly/Regulation/Antitrust

U.S. telephony was to grow and prosper over the next 40 years. In the 1920s, AT&T merged the R&D work of Western Electric and AT&T to form a single research entity, Bell Telephone Laboratories. AT&T also moved into broadcast radio, employing telephone lines to link the company's radio network as far west as Nebraska. Then the Bell System reversed itself and sold its broadcasting operations to RCA in the mid-1920s. Western Electric sold off its European operations to ITT in order to concentrate on supplying the domestic equipment needs of the Bell operating companies. AT&T not only survived the Great Depression, but continued its $9 dividend, a revenue flow so reliable that the company's stock was viewed as a bedrock investment for widows and orphans.

Franklin D. Roosevelt's New Deal inaugurated a serious of alphabet agencies, the FPC, SEC, CAB, FCC. The latter, the Federal Communications Commission, supplanted the ICC, and was assigned interstate telephone regulatory oversight. The Commission's first major investigation probed AT&T's control of both buyer and seller of telephone equipment. Were such internal transactions, asked the commission, in the interest of the telephone consumer? AT&T obviously said yes; but the Commission's staff wasn't sure. A task force recommended that the FCC seek

[2]Ibid., 143.

legislative authority over Western Electric's sales, prices, and earnings. Too radical even for the New Deal, the proposal was dropped in 1939. By then, foreign policy began to supersede U.S. domestic issues, as the clouds of another war descended over Europe.

Pearl Harbor brought World War II to the United States, and AT&T, the Bell Telephone Laboratories, and Western Electric made important contributions to the nation's defense effort. By 1946, the war over, the FCC wrestled with a post-war development to bring a new signal, television, to homes. Then, in 1949, another antitrust shoe dropped. The Justice Department charged that AT&T's ownership of an unregulated supply affiliate (Western Electric) violated section 2 of the Sherman Antitrust Law (monopolization). In 1956, the suit was settled by the Eisenhower administration, through a consent decree between plaintiff and defendant. AT&T agreed to open its patent portfolio to all users and to confine its activities to regulated telephone service. Under the agreement Western Electric was to remain part of the Bell System. The decree was not without controversy, however. The government claimed victory, and AT&T's response was somewhat muted. But from Bell's perspective, Vail's structure had been preserved; the institution of private monopoly and regulation was once again validated.

Antitrust/Divestiture

The next 28 years of the Bell System proved equally tumultuous. For one thing, regulation at the federal level began to question the underlying premise of AT&T's structure and policies. Worse, AT&T found itself caught in a crossfire between government antitrust and public utility regulation. Market entry into telephony clearly violated the premise of natural monopoly and it came from none other than the FCC. And this was but a first step. By the 1970s, the FCC had ruled that subscribers could attach their own telephone sets to the Bell System's lines; that new firms could enter private interstate long distance markets; that satellite companies could operate within the domestic United States; and that firms could lease and resell Bell's telephone circuits to end users.

Those decisions, a break from past practices, were opposed vigorously both by AT&T and state public utility commissions (PUCs). AT&T protested that entry would thwart economies of scale, raise telephone rates, degrade service quality and compromise the integrity of the best communications system in the world. AT&T took its case to Congress and sponsored the Consumer Communications Reform Act, legislation that sanctioned telephone mergers, banned market entry, blocked competitive substitutes, and reversed the wayward policies of the FCC. AT&T's legislative effort failed, however.

AT&T's response to market entry also had an unintended effect; it elicited private antitrust action. Soon some dozen firms filed complaints in the courts. In November 1974, the Justice Department filed an antitrust complaint alleging that AT&T had blocked the entry of suppliers of telephone service, foreclosed telephone equipment manufacturers from selling to the Bell operating companies, stalled competitors' private branch exchanges (PBXs) from plugging into Bell's networks, and orchestrated a Bell System response to deny local circuits to AT&T's long distance competitors.

Nor was the Department's proposed solution inconsequential. It sought both horizontal and vertical divestiture of AT&T, a dismemberment of the Bell System in the tradition of the Standard Oil breakup. Although the Bell System found an ally in the U.S. Department of Defense, President Reagan's Attorney General insisted that AT&T had manipulated the regulatory process to perpetuate its telephone monopoly. Perhaps more distressing, the suit challenged AT&T's conviction that public utility regulation superceded the nation's antitrust laws. AT&T, in fact, argued the company was subject to oversight by 50 state commissions, and its practices and tariffs sanctioned and approved by those regulatory bodies.

Assistant Attorney General Baxter served notice that he would litigate the case to "his eye balls." The government presented its brief before a District Court in Washington, D.C. After the plaintiff's case was concluded, AT&T asked that the suit be dropped. But Judge Harold Greene wrote that the Department's brief was not without merit—that AT&T indeed may have violated the nation's antitrust laws.

In January 1982, the parties reached an historic agreement. AT&T agreed to divest its 23 Bell operating companies and to reconstitute them as 7 independent regional Bell operating companies (RBOCs): NYNEX, Bell Atlantic, BellSouth, Ameritech, Pacific Telesis, Southwestern Bell, and US West. Restructured along geographical areas, the operating companies were to confine their activities to local, intrastate telephone services. AT&T retained Western Electric and Bell Laboratories and continued to provide interstate long distance service to the public. The agreement took effect in January 1984.

AT&T would reimburse local telephone companies—the RBOCs—for the use of local telephone facilities (the "loop" in telephone parlance). Known as an "access charge," the money payment would ensure that local telephone service would remain affordable to the public at large. Put differently, a universal service support system required that business users subsidize residential subscribers, and that urban subscribers contribute to the telephone bills of rural users. In essence, users in competitive toll markets subsidized consumers in noncompetitive local markets.

The fourth stage of telecommunications experienced the rise of the on-line computer. A legacy of the Second World War, the computer was devised to enable the Army's Corps of Engineers to calculate artillery tables. Unlike a voice or analog signal, the computer generated digital signals transmitted over telephone lines.

By the 1950s, computers began to move into commercial applications such as payrolls, accounts receivable, and sales data. Later, the intercontinental missile spurred the development of a U.S. early warning system across the North Pole. Radar dishes scanned the sky for intruders, fed information into computers, and relayed signals via telephone lines to the United States. The digital signal, modulated as an analog tone for line transmission, was then reconstituted at U.S. Air Force Headquarters. National defense needs sired the modem, the modulation–demodulation unit, as a device to accommodate a digital signal. AT&T's tariffs, known as the Sage network, were duly approved by the FCC.

Thermonuclear missiles raised the possibility of electromagnetic bursts capable of knocking out telephone circuits within the continental United States; the Department of Defense launched studies to address that potential threat. A Rand scientist, Dr. Paul Baran, proposed to assemble binary signals into packets routed through computers over many different telephone lines.[3] Reconstituted as a message at the receiver's terminal, packet switching was designed for digital transmission.

In the 1960s, computers permitted remote users to access the arithmetic and memory of a main frame computer. Sponsored by the Defense Department, computer terminal sharing suggested the possibility of distributed information processing not unlike that of an electricity utility—a computer utility.

In the mid-1960s, an FCC docket asked whether the U.S. analog telephone system could accommodate the impending needs of digital traffic. Did telephone rates and policies comport with growing on-line computers? Was telephone company investment responsive to the imperatives of a digital world?[4] The telephone industry's answer to the FCC's computer inquiry was reassuring: The computer required no fundamental change in the industry's regulation, investment, prices, or subscriber policies.[5] There was one exception: Subscribers could attach computers to phone lines via a modem provided by the telephone company.

The rapid pace of technology has kept public policymakers busy. Technological change successively made obsolete the FCC's rulings in the original (1970) "Computer I" inquiry and "Computer II" (early 1980s). "Computer III" (latter 1980s and the post-AT&T divestiture period generally) still stands but has been revised frequently to accommodate new technological, political, and legal realities. The attempts to draw a "bright

[3]Wilson Dizard, *MegaNet: How the Global Communications Network Will Connect Everyone on Earth* (Boulder, CO: Westview Press, 1997), 146.

[4]Before the Federal Communications Commission, Docket No. 16979, *In the Matter of Regulatory and Policy Problems Presented by the Interdependence of Computer and Communication Services and Facilities, Notice of Inquiry,* 10 November 1966.

[5]Stuart Matheson and Philip Walker, *Computers and Telecommunications: Issues in Public Policy* (Englewood Cliffs, NJ: Prentice Hall, 1970), 153; Appendix C, 242–243.

line" between unregulated computers and regulated telephone service proved frustrating as commissions continually searched for an optimum mix of regulation and market forces.

In the 1980s, the personal computer, born in a California garage, gained legitimacy when IBM and other suppliers entered the PC market. If the 1980s heralded the personal computer era, the 1990s were to become the era of the Internet. The Department of Defense's Advanced Research Products Agency network linked university computers over copper wire bandwidth. The introduction of a graphic user interface (icons and graphic signals) now required larger bandwidth—more than the 56 kilobits per capacity of local telephone loops.[6] Copper wire was beginning to impose a limit on computer access speed.

Today, the computer is the driving force behind long distance fiber networks. Internet speed, nevertheless, is constrained by copper wire loop capacity; and the local telephone line surfaced as an issue of public policy in the 1990s. Congress passed the Telecommunications Act of 1996 in an attempt to address local loop congestion.[7] The Act promised Regional Bell Operating Companies entry into the long distance market if competition were introduced into the local telephone market. The legislation represented a landmark endeavor to convert a monopoly market into a competitive market—to alter, in short, the structure of the telephone industry. It is to such structural matters we now turn.

II. MARKET STRUCTURE

Market structure includes elements of demand, supply, and entry barriers in both long distance and local exchange markets.

Demand

As a derived demand, U.S. buyers consume nearly $200 billion worth of telecommunication services annually. Of that total, local exchange revenues account for $100 billion; long distance, $90 billion.[8] The local exchange traffic growth approximates the growth of Gross Domestic Product (GDP); the toll market enjoys double-digit growth. The divide between voice and data traffic suggests a shift in buyers' tastes and preferences. Whereas voice traffic experiences single-digit growth, nonvoice or data

---

[6]Comments of Philip J. Sirlin, Schroder & Co., in "Cable Industry," *Wall Street Transcript,* 1 March 1999, 8.

[7]Dick W. Olufs, *The Making of Telecommunications Policy* (Boulder, CO: Lynne Rienner, 1999), 135.

[8]Seth Schiesel, "A Big Western Bell Rides East to Buy Connecticut Phone Company," *New York Times,* 6 January 1998, D1.

traffic demand increases at some 200 percent per year. Internet demand, a subset of data traffic, is estimated to increase by 500 percent annually.[9]

That the Internet ushers in a new era is seen by the following:

- Eighty percent of Internet traffic is driven by electronic commerce among business firms.
- The Intel Corporation states that its on-line microprocessor sales now total $1 billion per month.
- Cisco (Internet switches and routers) estimates that 80 percent of its sales are Internet driven.
- Dell computer (personal computers) observes that half its PC sales originate on the Internet.
- GE's Internet has cut procurement cycles in half and processing costs by a third.
- Amazon (books, music, etc.) sales on its Web site have increased 200 percent a year.
- The U.S. Department of Commerce projects that the current $100 billion e-commerce market will reach $1.3 trillion in 2002.

Electronic commerce (e-commerce) is beginning to assume a generic pattern. First, a firm adopts the Internet to multiply customer access and to achieve cost economies. To secure a first mover advantage, the firm reassesses its value chain and outsources high-cost activities. The firm's suppliers, no longer perceived as adversaries, tie their computers to its customers' database, quickening response time to consumer demand. Some e-commerce firms mandate that supplier operations be located within 15 minutes of final assembly lines. Lower transaction economies are passed forward to the customer as reduced prices.

The Internet, by direct access, permits a firm to circumvent traditional marketing or sales channels. Banks, for example, engage in on-line financial transactions and can bypass a rival's investment in "brick and mortar." On-line brokerage services today challenge conventional investment houses; an on-line MBA program can reach students beyond a traditional university classroom. Geography no longer protects or insulates.

Web sites enable a firm to compress response time to buyers' shifting tastes. Ford Motor Company, for example, links 120 design engines worldwide, permitting a 24-hour design cycle.[10] Toyota claims it can deliver a customized car to a customer in 5 days. And once a firm enjoys an Internet competitive advantage, rivals are sure to follow. Competitors have little choice. Failure to do so can prove traumatic. In an on-line

[9]Reinhardt Krause, "Web Weaving its Way Through Telecom Industry," *Investor's Business Daily,* 9 June 1999, A4.

[10]Ira Brudsky, "The Case Against Making Money the Old Fashioned Way," *Network World,* 3 May 1999, 47.

environment, nouns become adverbs—"Amazoned" or "Delled." (Ford Motor Company's Brazilian experiment to outsource its manufacturing activities has prompted the phrase "Ford Amazon.")[11]

That e-commerce occurs within an environment of accelerating change is seen in the observation of Mr. Jack Welch, CEO of General Electric. The Internet, he said, represents "the greatest change in business in (his) lifetime."[12] The president of Intel adds that "all companies will be Internet companies or they won't be companies at all."[13] Market pressure fuels the adoption of e-Commerce in the U.S. and throughout the world. By the year 2003, estimates have it that 90 percent of the global bandwidth will be carrying Internet traffic.[14] Bandwidth now constitutes the new paradigm. (Figure 11-1)

Supply

Long Distance Market Shares The $90 billion U.S. long distance, or toll, market is dominated by three firms, with hundreds of providers sharing the rest of the field. The approximate market shares (based on 1998 long distance carrier revenues) are depicted in Table 11-1.

MCI struggled for 6 years to enter the market, beginning in 1963. It prospered but was acquired by WorldCom Inc., in 1997 for $20 billion. Sprint, a midwestern company, has pushed fiber optics transmission, operates a long distance service, and has moved aggressively into wireless communications. And now, MCI WorldCom, outbidding Bell South, contemplates a $115 billion acquisition of Sprint.

Long Distance Market Entry Though classified as a loose oligopoly, the long distance market has experienced a rash of start-up firms, corporations investing in high-speed data routers, fast switches and optical fiber links. Six companies (Qwest, Global Crossing, Frontier, Williams, IXC and Level 3) have entered the "backbone" toll market. Other firms on the market's edge include the aerospace industry. Even electric power companies are exploring the potential of broadband telecommunications supply.

This entry pattern suggests that traditional market barriers may not be as formidable as they have been over the past 50 years. Certainly, one constraint that can give pause to any firm pondering market entry is the absolute size of the incumbent corporation. But in U.S. long distance, neither market share nor corporate assets appears to have arrested the entry process.

---

[11]"Internet Anxiety," *Business Week*, 28 June 1999, 86; also Tim Burt, "Ford to Farm Out Key Final Assembly Jobs to Contractor," *Financial Times*, 4 August 1999, 1.

[12]Matt Murray, "GE Now Views Internet as Crucial to New Growth," *Wall Street Journal*, 23 June 1999, 15.

[13]Matthew Benjamin, "Surf's Up: International Network Services Prepares to Ride Data Traffic Tidal Water," *Investor's Business Daily*, 29 June 1999, A9.

[14]Thomas Bonnett, *Telewars in the States: Telecommunications Issues in a New Era of Competition* (Washington, D.C.: Council of Governors Policies Advisors, 1996), 19.

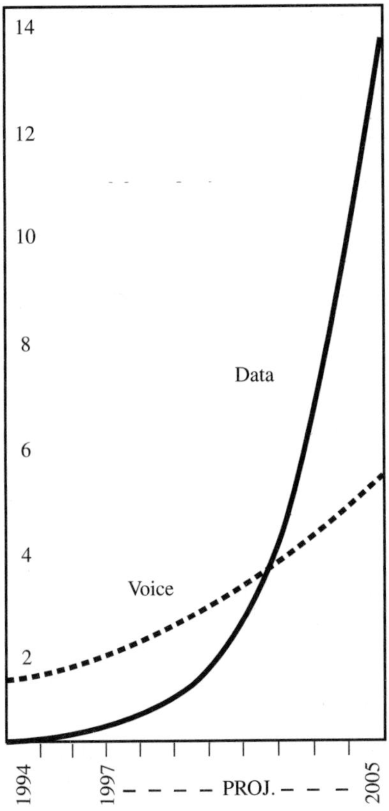

Source: Fortune, 13 October 1997, 112.
© 1997 Time Inc. Reprinted by permission.

FIGURE 11-1 U.S. Long Distance Traffic (in Billions of Gigabits per Year)

Government regulation, of course, constitutes a second barrier to market access. However, federal regulation of toll carriers is largely benign. A notable exception concerns the Regional Bell Operating Companies. Section 271 of the 1996 Telecommunications Act permits RBOCs to supply "in-region" long distance service providing that a number of

TABLE 11-1 Long Distance Market Shares

AT&T	43.1%
MCI WorldCom	25.6%
Sprint	10.5%
All other long distance carriers	20.8%
Total:	100.0%

Source: Federal Communications Commission, "Trends in Telephone Service," September 1999, Table 11.3.

obligations are met. These requirements include, among other things, the establishment of interconnection agreements that comply with a 14-point "competitive checklist" such as nondiscriminatory access to RBOC network elements and unbundling of certain functions for use by competitors. The Act authorizes the FCC to judge whether the applicants have met these standards. To date, the Commission has rejected five applications, although Bell Atlantic appears close to breaking the statutory ice in several states in which it provides local service.

Scale economies present still another hurdle to long distance entry. Apparently that constraint has diminished as entrants perceive incumbent carrier investment as a handicap rather than an asset to bandwidth efficiency. And although capital financing often poses as an impediment to market access, a vibrant U.S. equity market has allocated billions of dollars to long distance telecommunications and facilities.

Beyond labor, capital, and administrative expenses, long distance firms incur other expenses, namely, an access charge of $0.04 per minute for local loop facilities, and a contribution to a universal service fund including an education or "e-rate" assessment used to support telecom purchases by public schools and libraries. Such costs are borne by interstate carriers and their customers.

Competitive substitutes, such as IP (Internet Protocol) telephone services, pose a very real alternative to switched voice service. Tied to the Internet, a PC in one location can send a packetized voice message to another PC. Internet Service Providers (ISPs) deliver "voice" as data transmission. The 1996 Telecommunication Act exempted Internet traffic from local telephone access charges. Clearly, telephone users are attracted to IP cost savings: One company reports that its telephone bill between its New Jersey and Dallas offices dropped from $2,500/month to "pennies on the dollar."[15]

The RBOCs view IP telephony as a financial bypass around their loop plant investment. Two RBOCs, Bell South and U.S. West, have, in fact, imposed a local access charge on Internet service providers (ISPs) adopting IP telephone—a charge that implies that thousands of ISPs may fall under the category of long distance telephone companies.[16] In the meantime, ISPs now solicit customers by giving away personal computers or rescinding monthly lease charges.

Local Telecommunications Unlike toll telecommunications, barriers to market entry in local telephone service remain formidable. Local loop plant traditionally has embodied the essence of a natural monopoly and

[15] James DeTar, "Hearing a Pin Drop in Cyberspace, Phone Carriers Use Internet More," *Investor's Business Daily,* 6 June 1999, A6.

[16] "Telecommunications: Prognosis 1999," *Business Week,* 11 January 1999, 99.

few communities or towns would tolerate letting firms tear up streets in the name of consumer choice. State commissions, embracing the natural monopoly concept as equivalent to the public interest, have historically erected barriers to market entry. A firm contemplating offering local telephone service must obtain a license of public convenience and necessity, and must receive eligible telecommunications carrier designation before it can draw from the pool of universal service support monies. Entry in the local arena has not been for the faint of heart.

A second barrier to local competition turned on matters of plant depreciation schedules. Regulatory officials reasoned that stretching plant economic life (i.e., outside wire) to 25 years would result in low annual depreciation expenses.[17] Low expenses translated into reduced monthly telephone bills to the consumer but also distorted price and investment signals for potential entrants.

A third entry barrier derived from a policy brokered between state and federal regulatory agencies. Over time, long distance costs declined and local telephone costs increased. State commissions solicited a revenue contribution from long distance customers to subsidize local service. Prior to the breakup of the Bell System, this toll subsidy was subsumed within a complex cost-separations process. After the breakup, the toll subsidy was recycled as an access charge levied upon long distance subscribers using a local carrier's wire. The result found local costs higher than local rates—a shortfall made up by a long distance subsidy. Few firms would contemplate entering a local market where revenues did not cover costs. However well intentioned, that subsidy reinforced the notion of natural monopoly.

Today, the four Regional Bell Operating Companies, together with GTE, operate some 30,000 circuit switches, and 173 million local access lines.[18] With a plant investment of $320 billion, the RBOCs and GTE control about 90 percent of U.S. local lines. (See Figure 11-2.)

The Telecommunications Act of 1996 introduced the concept of the competitive local exchange carriers—CLECs—to compete with the RBOCs and independent local exchange carriers. But competition thus far remains less than robust. RBOCs' market share reductions are minimal. Southwestern Bell Corporation (SBC) has, for example, forfeited 2.2 percent of its lines to rivals since 1997; Bell Atlantic has lost 3.4 percent of its lines to new entrants.[19] The FCC found that, nationwide, local service competitors such as CLECs and resellers have managed to wrest

---

[17]Andrew Kupfer, "Transforming Telecom: The Big Switch," *Fortune,* 12 October 1997, 108.

[18]Stephanie Mehta, "Locked Out: Some Bells Less Friendly than Others Toward Newcomers," *Wall Street Journal,* 21 September 1998, C8.

[19]John J. Keller, "Phone Companies Scour the U.S. for Partner," *Wall Street Journal,* 13 May 1998, 4.

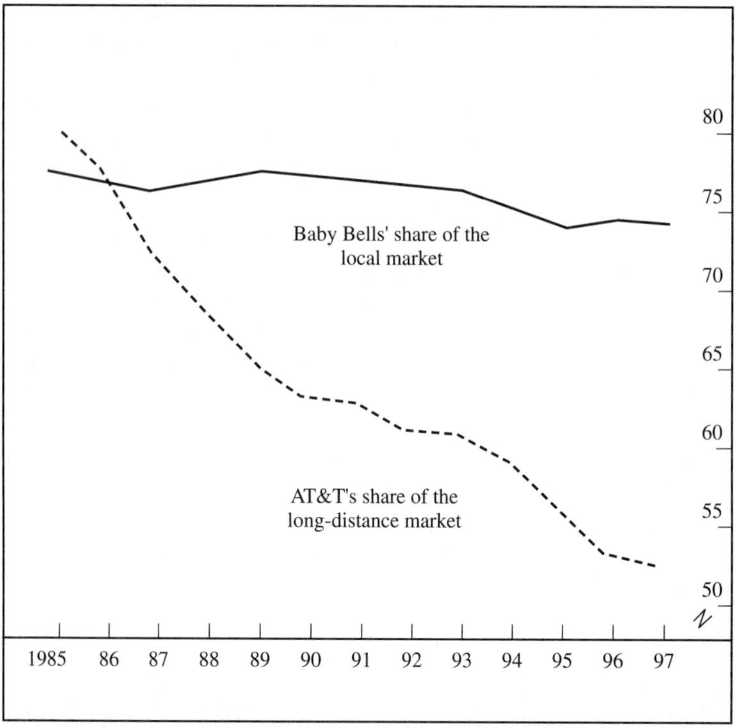

FIGURE 11-2 Share of U.S. Telephone Markets, % of Total

Source: The Economist, 27 June 1998, 62. © 1998 The Economist Newspaper Group, Inc. Reprinted with permission. Further reproduction prohibited.

only 3.5 percent of local service revenues from incumbent local exchange carriers.[20] The trend has been encouraging, though: In 1997, local competitors accounted for 2.3 percent of local service revenues, meaning the total for 1998 jumped 50%.[21] On the other hand, Dr. Robert Crandall, Brookings Institution, has concluded that local telephony remains concentrated because state regulators have succeeded in restricting entry into most intrastate markets.[22]

However uncertain the entry process, CLECs and Internet Service Providers have had some influence on the local bandwidth market.

---

[20]"Local Competition: August 1999," Federal Communications Commission, Table 2.1.
[21]Ibid.
[22]Robert W. Crandall, "Managed Competition in U.S. Telecommunications," Working paper 99-1, AE1 (Washington, D.C.: *Brookings Joint Center for Regulatory Studies*), March 1999, 15.

CLECs have introduced digital subscriber line equipment (DSL) that multiplies bandwidth capacity to 30 times that of a regular telephone dial-up modem; and cable TV modems offer bandwidth capacity that exceeds copper wire by as much as 50 times. Other loop alternatives include fixed wireless, satellite dishes, and third-generation wireless. Still, competitive substitutes fall short of converting local telephony into a contestable market.

Today, as the nation moves to e-commerce, the local telephone line persists as a bandwidth bottleneck. Rather than being competitive, the local market is becoming more concentrated. Horizontal merger is the culprit. Bell Atlantic, for example, has acquired NYNEX and now proposes to buy GTE. Southwestern Bell Communications (SBC) has purchased Pacific Telesis as well as Southern New England Telephone company, and the FCC has recently approved SBC's $120 billion acquisition of Ameritech. (See Table 11-2.) With the latter acquisition, SBC now controls 30 percent of all local access lines in the United States. As one SBC manager put it, "We love access lines."[23]

In sum, the market structure of U.S. telecommunications remains bifurcated. The long distance market experiences vibrant entry; the local market retains its monopoly structural trait.

TABLE 11-2 Top 10 Telecommunication Mergers

Announced	*Target (Country)*	*Acquiring company (Country)*	*Deal Value (in Billions)*
10/05/99	Sprint (U.S.)	MCI WorldCom (U.S.)	$127.27
05/11/98	Ameritech (U.S.)	SBC Comm. (U.S.)	72.36
07/28/98	GTE (U.S.)	Bell Atlantic (U.S.)	71.32
01/18/99	AirTouch Comm. (U.S.)	Vodafone Group (U.K.)	65.90
06/14/99	US West (U.S.)	Qwest Comm. (U.S.)	48.48
10/01/97	MCI Comm. (U.S.)	WorldCom (U.S.)	43.35
02/20/99	Telecom Italia (Italy)	Olivetti (Italy)	34.76
04/22/96	Nynex (U.S.)	Bell Atlantic (U.S.)	30.79
10/19/99*	Orange (U.K.)	Mannesmann (Germany)	30.00
04/01/96	Pacific Telesis (U.S.)	SBC Comm. (U.S.)	22.42

*Mannesmann confirms it is in talks to acquire Orange

Source: Wall Street Journal, 20 October 1999, A23.

[23]Gautam Naik, et.al., "Party Line: SBC and Ameritech Send Phone Industry Loud Wake-up Call," *Wall Street Journal,* 12 April 1998, 5.

III. MARKET CONDUCT

Long Distance

Price and nonprice competition manifest themselves in the long distance telecommunications market. To the extent that firms in the toll market are aware of rival pricing strategies, carrier prices tend to converge over time. A rate discount by one carrier is invariably countered by rivals. A firm, for example, may offer a discount on Sunday calls; but rivals trump the rate by extending discounts for calls to an entire weekend. Price competition is, in fact, so heated that carriers are not above employing "fighting brands" that require tapping digits to secure cheaper rates (i.e., "10-10-321"). Subscribers may be surprised to learn that some of those digit "brands" are affiliates of either AT&T or MCI WorldCom.[24] That price rivalry is standard operating procedure can be seen by rates offered by new long distance suppliers, especially firms relying on fiber optics transmission. Here, rates are not determined on the basis of time and distance but rather reflect bandwidth quantity used by the customer.

The toll market is characterized by nonprice competition as well. Long distance carriers encourage brand and customer loyalty, and "quiet as a pin drop" ads inform subscribers that circuit quality is unmatched by rivals. Toll carriers now package "bundled services" as a standard offering to their subscribers; some services may obscure once-clear demarcations between local and long distance traffic.

The enterprise or corporate market enables firms to generate Internet bandwidth for exclusive company use. Here, a firm leases bandwidth and purchases Internet routers or switches, to secure a state-of-the-art digital network. Such links, enabling the firm's Web site to link employees as well as customers and corporate suppliers, have emerged as a competitive strategy in markets where industry boundaries are now permeable.

Local Telecommunications

Local telephone companies control a critical piece of telecommunication real estate—the line between the end user and the company's central office switch. In the absence of competitive alternatives, local carriers enjoy pricing discretion at this last telecommunications mile—subject, of course, to regulatory approval. Every long distance call ends or begins on the subscriber's local premises; and each toll user is assessed a fee of several cents per minute. From the perspective of a long distance toll carrier, the access charge constitutes the carrier's largest expense. AT&T's access

[24]John J. Keller, "AT&T Prepares Campaign to Battle MCI's '10-321' Plan," *Wall Street Journal,* 8 April 1998, B7.

charge payments total $12 billion annually; since 1984, AT&T has paid the RBOCs about $200 billion.[25]

Whether the local access charge is reasonable or not is controversial. Long distance carriers argue that RBOC fees far exceed cost and are exorbitant. RBOCs, on the other hand, insist that the charges must remain high to ensure telephone availability to all. Be that as it may, long distance customers contribute $25 billion annually to local exchange users.

In addition to monthly service rates, local exchange carriers offer bandwidth options to corporate users. A local carrier, for example, will provide high-speed, broadband capacity T-1 leased lines that vary from $1,000 to $3,000 per month. The 1996 Telecommunications Act attempted to breathe competitive life into local telecommunications services. New entrants either resell RBOC circuits or place multiplex equipment in carrier central office locations. The former lease circuits wholesale at an 18 percent discount and attempt to compete with RBOC customers at the retail level. Lest one regard local competitors as fly-by-night operations, two major CLECs have attempted to lease local circuits and compete in basic telephone service—AT&T and MCI WorldCom.

AT&T invested $4 billion in an endeavor to enter the local lease service business, generating revenue of $86 million. But AT&T's new CEO halted this strategy of market entry and labelled the leased route option a "fool's errand."[26] MCI spent $2 billion as a CLEC and then backed off lease circuits as a vehicle to local entry. Many CLECs allege they are vulnerable to an RBOC wholesale/retail financial squeeze that, in effect, precludes them from effective customer access.

Another type of CLEC provides broadband access at the local level by employing DSL (digital subscriber line) equipment in the RBOC's central office and then leasing RBOC lines to the customer's premises. Although DSL CLECs have made some market penetration, they, too, are beholden to RBOCs positioned in the dual role as both supplier and rival. CLECs assert that RBOCs engage in dilatory tactics by claiming that the central office lacks DSL capacity, that CLEC equipment must be checked for safety, that CLEC filing papers are mislaid, and that CLECs' RBOC contract penalties lock in telecommunications customers.[27]

---

[25]Andrew Kupfer, "AT&T Gets Lucky," *Fortune* 9 November 1998, 114; also Leslie Cauley, "Ma Bell? AT&T Appears Close to a Deal to Acquire TCI for 30 Billion," *Wall Street Journal,* 24 September 1998, 1.

[26]"New Boss, New Plan," *Business Week,* 2 February 1998, 124.

[27]Henry Goldblatt, "The Real Target is your Dial Tone," *Fortune,* 24 November 1997, 116; also David Rohde, "RBOC Termination Penalties Challenger," *Network World,* 10 May 1999, 39; Ronald Rosenberg, "AT&T's Armstrong Hits Bell Atlantic," *Boston Globe,* 6 November 1998, C2; finally, Nick Wingfield, "No Mercy: Covad Communications Needs the Bell's Cooperation to Thrive. It Says It Isn't Getting Much," *Wall Street Journal,* 21 September 1998, R10.

AT&T, in particular, has alleged that 80 percent of RBOC lines have been tardy or late in availability. Moreover, potential entrants allege that RBOCs find central office capacity for their own DSL equipment often of the same make as their CLEC rivals. Some CLECs complain that when they approach RBOCs' customers, the RBOCs expedite DSL equipment as a device to foreclose competitive entry.

The venue for such market disputes more often than not rests with state regulators. And here, the playing field is not necessarily level. One CLEC hired three attorneys to make a case for market entry only to be confronted by 60 attorneys fielded by its RBOC rival. All of this suggests that market access at the local telephone market requires tenacity, deep pockets, and much patience.

IV. MARKET PERFORMANCE

Market performance parallels the dichotomy in long distance and local service.

Long Distance

Although the toll telephone market approximates an oligopoly, the softening of entry barriers has had a positive influence upon carrier price, productivity, cost, and innovation. Rivalry is, in fact, so keen that some experts claim that toll service is in danger of becoming a "commodity." In this market, price wars break out periodically. Recently, the average long distance call was posted at 10 cents per minute. One carrier announced 5-cents-per-minute rates on one or more weekend days. AT&T then countered with a 7-cents-anytime rate in response to a 5-cents off-peak plan by MCI WorldCom, and Sprint. In real terms, toll telephone rates in the United States have dropped 90 percent since 1984.[28]

Falling rates, of course, fuel and stimulate telecom usage. In 1984, U.S. consumers completed 1.2 billion toll calls. By 1995, toll call usage had exceeded 11.5 billion a year. Over that same period, AT&T saw its market share fall steadily. Long distance rivalry obviously places a premium on cost efficiency. AT&T allocates 22 percent of its revenue to overhead cost, but MCI WorldCom's smaller overhead is a benchmark for all carriers.[29] New toll optical fiber firms promise to make available further cost savings.

Competitive entry serves as a check on the modernity of capital spending in the toll market. In the 1980s, MCI and Sprint's adoption of fiber optics forced AT&T to write off $9 billion in investment and to in-

[28]Peter J. Howe, "Breakup, then Buildup," *Boston Globe,* 6 June 1999, F7.

[29]Seth Schiesel, "Long Distance Giants Report Solid Results for Quarter," *New York Times,* 30 July 1999, 14. (22 percent of revenue allocated to general, administrative expenses.)

augurate its own fiber investment program. Today, new fiber optic firms generate unrelenting pressure on toll costs and prices. Some industry analysts predict that fiber costs will soon approach a penny per minute.[30]

All of this suggests that the toll market is the beneficiary of transmission productivity. And that productivity has been breathtaking: In 1975, a single optical fiber delivered 8,000 circuits; by 1995, a single fiber could accommodate 1.5 million circuits.[31] More recently, new multiplexing techniques have lifted fiber capacity 16 times. According to the Council of Economic Advisers, the cost of transmitting one bit of data over a kilometer of fiber optic cable fell by three orders of magnitude between the mid-1970s and the early 1990s. Productivity gains convert into falling costs and dropping prices.[32]

Toll carriers are now providing Internet protocol equipment access in preference to conventional voice circuit switching technology. Here again, the telecommunications market reaps productivity gains from data routers and packet switching computers whose performance, in turn, follows Moore's Law. Moore's Law holds that microprocessor productivity doubles every 18 months. The result is that Internet protocol equipment prices are falling 20 to 30 percent annually.

All U.S. toll carriers have a presence in wireless technology and service, and wireless rates are declining about 20 percent a year. The cell phone industry now targets the Internet market, permitting subscribers to "surf the net" while on the move. If Finland serves as a U.S. prototype, wireless may overtake wireline facilities as the medium for voice communication.[33]

AT&T and CLECs employ broadband access in an attempt to bypass RBOCs' local loop wire. Some cable TV companies now offer long distance, local service, and Internet service packages, a prospect that raises the subversive notion that Internet telephony may very well become a "free" good.

Local Telecommunications

Local telephone service prices have increased moderately since 1984. Today, the average telephone bill is $45 per month in the United States. Local rates have not seen any dramatic price reductions, nor has the local telephone user enjoyed price wars associated with the long distance market.

---

[30]Quentin Hardy, "A Wireless World: For a Glimpse of U.S.'s Cordless World, Just Set Your Sights Overseas," *Wall Street Journal,* 21 September 1998, R16.

[31]Michael King, "Too Much Long Distance," *Fortune,* 15 March 1995, 107.

[32]*Progress Report; Growth and Competition in U.S. Telecommunications 1993–1998,* 8 February 1999, 35.

[33]Quentin Hardy, "A Wireless World," R16.

The $25 billion access subsidy paid by toll subscribers does stabilize local telephone rates. Still, the sunk investment of RBOCs conditions their performance. In contrast to the dynamics of the toll markets, capital expenditures and innovation proceeds at a more leisurely pace. Although CLEC resellers offer pricing and quantity options to local customers, it is the evolution of DSL CLECs that introduces new bandwidth hardware, and accords high-speed Internet access to users.

The RBOCs are obviously cognizant of CLEC digital line innovation, and some RBOCs have responded. US West, for example, offers a range of fast bandwidth packages accompanied by rates as low as $20 per month. Similarly, Bell Atlantic has upgraded its local network in New York City. However tentative, entry at the local level has had a therapeutic influence upon RBOC line performance.

Over the longer term, local carriers will encounter broadband cable modems as an alternative to copper wire. Time-Warner-AOL, a cable TV firm, offers toll, local, and Internet services as a frontal assault on RBOC services, pricing, and innovation. AT&T's $120 billion acquisition of cable giant TCI now looms in the RBOC future.

RBOCs offer wireless capability across the nation and compete with affiliates of long distance carriers. And although wireless rates have dropped in the United States, the 40-cents-per-minute cost stands in sharp contrast to an 8-cents-per-minute rate in Toronto, Canada.[34] Rate disparities once again suggest that an industry's economic performance is not unrelated to industry structure.

To sum up, it is difficult to ignore the performance disparity between the U.S. long distance market and the U.S. local market. One market embraces the productivity gains of computer and telecommunications; the other is apparently comfortable with its current technological lot while enjoying support monies from its long distance counterpart.

V. PUBLIC POLICY

Since 1996, U.S. public policy has focused on the local telecommunications market. How should the United States address such questions as RBOC collocation policy, universal service subsidies, local competitive substitutes, and corporate mergers?

Given these variables, the United States confronts three policy alternatives: maintain the status quo; enlarge regulatory oversight; or introduce competition in local telecommunications.

[34]Peter J. Howe, "U.S. Cell Phone Costs Fall But Stay Above Europe's," *International Herald Tribune*, 24 June 1999, 12.

Status Quo—Pro

Those who defend a status quo policy marshal several arguments. First, the Telecommunications Act of 1996 introduced competition—CLECs—into the local telephone market. CLECs offer new transmission bandwidth that competes with RBOCs in the retail market. Cable firms now offer a broadband alternative to the copper wire pair, and bundle Internet and local and long distance as a service offering. AT&T's cable acquisitions are an important new player in local service offerings. Proponents of the status quo insist that local access charges are declining and that the annual billion-dollar subsidy ensures the universality of telephone service—particularly to those economically disadvantaged.

Proponents of the status quo also assert that competitive substitutes do intrude into the local market, whether DSL, fixed wireless, cable modems, or satellite relay. Some RBOCs are employing satellite dishes as a device to confer fast Internet access to their customers.[35] The loop market, in short, does not constitute a technological backwater.

A status quo policy insists that RBOC horizontal mergers are monitored to comply with a public-interest standard. Adherents to the status quo challenge critics who contend government oversight—state PUCs, the Federal Communications Commission, and the Department of Justice—is incapable of divining the merits of corporate consolidation. These regulatory bodies can and will determine whether horizontal affiliation generates scale efficiencies that position RBOCs to participate in a world-wide information market. If regulatory opponents disagree, they can pursue their case in the forum of legal due process.

Regulatory institutions clearly possess the expertise and knowledge to monitor RBOC vertical diversification into the long distance market. The FCC is currently examining the merits of Bell Atlantic's acquisition of GTE and has approved the SBC-Ameritech merger. Congress, in fact, empowered the FCC to assess whether sufficient competition exists in local telecommunications as a condition for RBOC entry into long distance. The regulatory machinery, both state and federal, can and will strike a balance between competition and regulation.

Status Quo—Con

Critics of the status quo argue that the intent of the Telecommunications Act of 1996—to bring competition to local telecommunications—has failed. RBOCs and a number of state PUCs have opposed local competition at virtually every step, including filing briefs that the 1996 statute violates the U.S. Constitution. RBOCs, they say, will not tolerate competition in local facilities—irrespective of subscriber demand for high speed

[35]David Rohde, "Rivals Slams SBC/Ameritech Proposal," *Network World,* 19 July 1999, 29.

Internet access. And critics remind status quo defenders that the market share of DSL CLECs remains both fragile and insignificant as a market force.

Second, critics of the status quo submit that universal service and the local access charge are nothing but an incumbent's ploy to protect its local telephone monopoly. RBOCs that demand universal service be extended to the Internet are simply asking that their "natural" monopoly status be expanded in perpetuity, without reason or rationale.

Third, critics observe that local competitive substitutes subsist at the sufferance of RBOC economic power. For one thing, the RBOCs manifest a conflict of interest. They engage in both wholesale circuits and retail circuits. The result is that potential entrants are subject to a classic economic squeeze. Regulatory critics query, why did AT&T withdraw from leasing RBOC lines after spending $4 billion? The answer, they say, is that RBOCs effectively choked off market entry. Those critical of the status quo remind Congress that not one RBOC merger has ever been banned or enjoined by a state PUC, the FCC, the Department of Justice, or the Federal Trade Commission. The nation's antitrust watchdogs, say critics, are not unlike Rip Van Winkle. And the result is more than disquieting: RBOCs are gathering more and more copper wire into fewer and fewer hands. Certainly, RBOC horizontal acquisitions are not grounded on the premise of bringing high-speed bandwidth to the needs of electronic commerce. Rather, say critics, RBOC mergers are merely an accumulation of monopoly assets in an eternal search for guaranteed local subsidies.

Critics of a "steady as she goes" policy question the FCC's approval of SBC's $120 billion acquisition of Ameritech on the condition that SBC serve as a CLEC in 30 non-SBC markets. Presumably, FCC policy rests on the proposition that a marriage of two monopolies will somehow inspire "good" conduct—and that FCC oversight will inspire such conduct. Critics of regulation insist that nothing in the past prevented SBC from establishing competitive services in Ameritech's territory or vice versa. Thus, under the guise of pursuing the public interest, the FCC has eliminated two competitors from the market place, while simultaneously touting the virtues of an Internet economy. Regulatory critics insist that the Internet was sired, not by telephone monopoly, but by telephone competition.

Finally, critics of regulation submit that a status quo policy is a case of institutional amnesia. Telecommunications policy today has forgotten why AT&T was broken up in the first place. The courts approved the 1982 AT&T divestiture because of the manifest and obvious failure of government regulation. What, they say, has changed in the past 15 years to inspire the resurrection of the public utility principle?

Regulatory Option—Pro

Consider next the pros and cons of a second policy choice: regulation. Those supporting more rather than less public oversight insist that competition at the local facilities level constitutes an elusive dream. The reality, they say, is that the copper loop will long remain embedded in the telephone plant. The loop is, has, and will remain a local monopoly. No market force will dissolve or remove that stubborn fact. And incumbents can acquire or merge with LECs or CLECs, and markets thereby remain concentrated. Proponents of the regulatory option conclude that RBOC control of local facilities mandates more rather than less public oversight.

Regulatory advocates note that the CLEC phenomenon was created by the Telecommunications Act of 1996. CLECs are a creature of Congress; their life can be sustained by artificial means only. Stated differently, promoting both competition and regulation under our current policy is a prescription for telecommunications chaos. Proponents of public oversight insist that state regulatory commissions retain undiluted jurisdiction over local telephone plant. That policy has provided the United States with the best telecommunications system measured by any standard. Federal intrusion into local monopoly simply undermines the effectiveness of regulation at the state level.

Adherents to the regulatory option argue that not only has local telephone service been recognized as a universal subscriber right, but that universality can and must be extended to Internet users as well. The Internet market now reveals a "digital divide" that segregates those consumers financially endowed from those financially disadvantaged. Universal service has bridged a voice divide; universal service can also overcome an Internet divide. To ensure consumer equity, regulation must play an affirmative role. The FCC's e-rate makes available subsidies for K-12 schools and public libraries. Those constituencies must share the benefits of affirmative regulation.

Advocates for regulation insist that competitive substitutes are often misconstrued by free market advocates. New technology complements but does not replace existing telecommunications facilities and services. Regulation ensures a coordinated adaptation of assets by local telecommunications carriers. Moreover, few quarrel with the insistence that the Internet is endowed with elements of the public's convenience and necessity. If nothing else, widespread Internet access accords the United States a comparative advantage in a world of global competition and market rivalry.

According to some regulatory adherents, control over horizontal acquisitions by RBOCs must and should remain the province of state PUCs. They, not the federal government, are ultimately responsible for local telephone performance. Nor do state PUCs exercise that mandate alone. Some 30,000 U.S. local and county authorities are empowered to define and promulgate the interest of the consuming public. Certainly, no one can deny San Antonio or Detroit's right to judge whether cable modems are to be shared or will remain the exclusive property of cable TV firms.

Finally, regulatory advocates insist that RBOC vertical mergers do not occur in a vacuum. All acquisitions are studied and monitored for their public interest dimension. Only regulation can determine whether the public will benefit from local telephone competition.

Regulatory Option—Con

Critics of the regulatory option insist that the cause of local bandwidth gridlock is none other than regulation itself. Any shortfall in RBOC economic performance rests ultimately upon government disincentives. RBOCs are utilities. Not unexpectantly, they behave as utilities. And utilities institutionalize cost-plus. Critics suggest that regulation by state commissions masks and protects RBOC malperformance, and that the goal of "universal" access is simply a front for economic privilege.

Regulatory critics contend the local access charges reinforce market power under a "public interest" fig leaf. Both RBOCs and state commissions may proclaim local technical diversity but that is only because they have been unable to stifle new competitors. Regulatory critics contend that it is not the RBOC that is responsible for inadequate bandwidth or obsolete plant. Rather, responsibility rests with a public sector that aids and abets RBOC market power.

Local substitutes, say regulatory critics, have arisen in spite of, not because of enlightened government oversight. State utility commissions may proclaim local technical diversity but that is only because they have been unable to stop new entrants. After all, PUCs regard competitive substitutes as the antithesis of scale economies and a threat to the premise of public oversight. Potential rivals, in fact, clutter up otherwise clean regulatory dockets.

Finally, regulatory critics conclude that RBOC horizontal integration promotes market concentration. If nothing else, market concentration guarantees public sector job security. Professor James Buchanan's observations on public choice or Professor George Stigler's capture theory, suggest critics, merit reading.

Competition Option—Pro

The competitive option concurs with the observation that the source of local bandwidth gridlock is regulation. Free market advocates offer a simple policy remedy: Deregulate the local loop market. In fact, do more. RBOCs manifest a conflict of interest to the extent that they are both wholesalers and retailers of local circuits. Little wonder that CLECs subsist as bit players on the local telecom stage. RBOCs can throttle rivals through a time-honored vertical squeeze, accelerate new equipment, and then tie up rivals in regulatory due process where RBOCs hold a comparative advantage. That power was the thrust of the Justice Department's 1974 antitrust case against AT&T.

The remedy to the vertical squeeze, say procompetitive advocates, is restructuring, i.e., "divestiture II." The RBOCs must spin off their retail operations from their wholesale operations.[36] The RBOCs' conflict-of-interest boil must be lanced in the tradition of the AT&T divestiture I. Then and only then will the public have any real opportunity to enjoy the benefits of price, cost, productivity, and innovative performance—and, most importantly, adequate bandwidth capacity.

Free market proponents insist that universal service is an anachronism. Market forces now ensure customer price, choice, and quality. Internet Protocol telephony holds the promise of making toll calls a "free" service. Under a policy of open markets, bandwidth access will no longer be reduced to a zero-sum game.

Open market advocates demand that a thousand flowers can bloom in loop substitutes. Few in telecommunications, they argue, can predict which technology will prevail in the industry over the long term. Fewer still are regulatory bodies endowed with the gift of foresight. Rather, the give and take of market forces will reveal technical options appropriate to tomorrow's consumer requirements.

Finally, free market proponents question whether RBOCs should be permitted to engage in horizontal acquisitions. Whatever the answer, market advocates suggest that regulatory authorities are the least qualified to make that determination. Rather, RBOC mergers must meet the test of the nation's antitrust laws.

Competition Option—Con

Skeptics of the competitive/antitrust option reply that the odds favoring RBOC structural reform are virtually nonexistent. For one thing, the RBOCs surely possess sufficient political power to block any move toward their own restructuring or divestiture. State regulatory commissions, they argue, accept their mandate to protect local RBOCs, posing a united front against libertarians convinced that a new era of deregulation is upon us.

Skeptics of open competition insist that universal service evokes images of equity and fairness, and reflects regulation at its best. Any proposal to deregulate local telephone service is tantamount to abandoning the telephone subscriber to the illusion of free choice. In any case, RBOCs and state commissions stand opposed to any move toward open local markets.

Opponents of competition note that local loop subsidies represent the dilemma of the commons. Someone must rise above narrow self-interest and determine the public good. To assault the local access subsidy

[36]Peter Howe, "Breakup, Then Buildup," *Boston Globe,* 6 June 1999, F7.

is essentially to attack those citizens most vulnerable in our society. In exercising its mandate to impose an e-rate or Internet tax, the FCC is merely carrying out the wishes of Congress.

To ask the nation to desist from regulatory oversight is to contemplate a nonexistent world. Critics of competition insist that horizontal integration at the RBOC level is now U.S. telecommunications policy. The Bell Atlantic acquisition of GTE awaits final FCC approval; the FCC has now cleared the SBC/Ameritech merger. In a world of global competition there is now bipartisan agreement that the nation's antitrust laws are a legacy of a bygone era. Critics of competition insist that AT&T's entry into the RBOC market via cable TV constitutes a fact of telephone life. Local, state and federal regulators may debate whether AT&T's modem lines should be shared with the company's rivals. But if public policy rules that RBOCs must share telephone lines, cable firms will be under enormous pressure to do the same. Critics of local competition conclude that any policy must accept the fact that RBOCs exhibit market preeminence; that divestiture is not a serious proposal on any public agenda; that market entry in loop bandwidth will remain impervious to genuine competition; and that technical substitutes to copper wire remain speculative. Public utility regulation, in short, must not be consigned to the ashes of policy history.

VI. CONCLUSION

The drift of the U.S. economy toward electronic commerce is in its infancy. The long distance telecom market today experiences quantum jumps in bandwidth growth and productivity. Juxtaposed against that dynamism stands the quiescent local exchange market. Can these two markets—so distinct in tradition, technology, regulation, and access—be bridged? Thus far, no consensus has emerged as to the answer. Ultimately, the public must decide which policy options are appropriate. The process is likely to include an admixture of technology, economics, and political maneuvering. To that extent, the issues generated by an e-commerce economy will remain a front-burner controversy on the policy agenda for the foreseeable future.

Suggested Readings

Cairncross, Frances. *The Death of Distance: How the Communications Revolution will Change our Lives* (Cambridge: Harvard Business School Press, 1997).

Dizard, Wilson. *MegaNet: How the Global Communications Network Will Connect Everyone on Earth* (Boulder, CO: Westview Press, 1997).

McNamara, John R. *The Economics of Innovation in the Telecommunications Industry* (Westport, CT: Quorum Books, 1991).

Olufs, Dick W., III, *The Making of Telecommunications Policy* (Boulder, CO: Lynne Rienner, 1999).

CHAPTER 12

College Sports

—JOHN L. FIZEL AND RANDALL W. BENNETT

Sports is big business in the United States. Nike, Inc., the maker of athletic footwear, apparel, and equipment, had 1998 revenues of $9.5 billion. The Washington Redskins National Football League team was sold in 1999 for $800 million, a record price for a U.S. professional sports franchise. Kevin Brown signed for $105 million to pitch for the Los Angeles Dodgers.

Million- and billion-dollar sports transactions are not confined to athletic companies or professional sports. In 1997, the National Collegiate Athletic Association (NCAA) and its member schools generated over $3.5 billion in revenue. The big-time collegiate programs (Division I-A) alone produced $2 billion, almost doubling the $1.07 billion created in 1989. Major college football coaches, such as Steve Spurrier of the University of Florida and Phillip Fulmer of the University of Tennessee, make headlines when their compensation packages exceed a million dollars annually, ranking them the highest paid university and state employees. Coaches often earn additional income through sports camps, media shows, and endorsement contracts with athletic apparel companies. CBS paid $1.7 billion for television rights to the NCAA Division I basketball tournament for 1995–2002, and just negotiated an 11-year extension of the contract for a stunning $6 billion. Washington State University, one of the more modestly funded major college sports programs, reported intercollegiate athletic revenue of $15.4 million for 1997–1998.

College sports are a lucrative and growing business, but not without turmoil. Reports of athletes obtaining cash payments, cars, free tickets, and falsified academic credentials are widespread. Between 1977 and 1985, some football players at Texas Christian University were paid between $35,000 and $40,000 apiece to attend the school. In 1998, a former office manager at the University of Minnesota admitted to completing more than 400 pieces of course work for 20 basketball players over the 1993–1998 period. On March 8, 1999, NCAA Proposition 16 requiring freshman athletes to meet minimum SAT or ACT scores was ruled discriminatory. In 1995, a federal judge ruled that the NCAA could not limit the pay of assistant coaches as it had done since 1991; in a final settlement, the NCAA agreed to pay $54.5 million to approximately 2,000 assistant coaches affected by the rule.

Why the controversy in collegiate sports? The NCAA often depicts itself as a beleaguered, understaffed organization waging the good fight against dishonest coaches, lax administrators, and greedy athletes who violate the rules against under-the-table payments and other special favors. However, the situation is better analyzed by examining the economic incentives associated with a cartel: the universities operating college athletic programs are cartel members, and the NCAA is the cartel manager. A cartel is a group of rivals that suppresses economic competition by agreeing to coordinate individual behavior and to follow rules and practices that result in economic benefits for the cartel members. No less an insider than Walter Byers, the executive director of the NCAA from 1951 to 1987, describes the NCAA as a cartel that is "operated by not-for-profit institutions contracting together to achieve maximum financial returns."[1] Although cooperation among cartel members increases group profits, each member has an incentive to circumvent the group rules and increase its share of profits. For example, if one university would pay signing bonuses to the best high school athletes, it might be able to win more games, increase attendance at games, enhance private donations from excited fans, and reap the dollar rewards from being in a postseason tournament or bowl game. Yet, if many members cheat, the increased competition will cause an escalation in bonus payments and produce less certain and surely more limited benefits. Thus, if one or a few firms cheat, they can increase their individual profits; but if many cheat, all will receive reduced profits. The successful cartel must limit autonomous behavior by enforcing and monitoring its rules. However, the rules themselves are political, and no matter what policies the cartel promulgates, they will reflect a compromise among divergent views. As happens with any compromise, some cartel members will be more satisfied than others. Therefore, churning within the industry will occur as members constantly consider the benefits of joint versus individual action.

I. HISTORY

The original incentive for forming the NCAA, as well as the impetus for the early growth of the organization, was not based on financial goals related to cartel behavior. The catalyst for the development of the NCAA was the violence and lack of standard playing rules in college football. In the late 1880s, football was a cross between rugby and soccer, retaining some rules from each of its ancestors as well as developing additional rules of its own. College athletic teams constantly looked for new tactics

[1]Walter Byers, *Unsportsmanlike Conduct: Exploiting College Athletes* (Ann Arbor: University of Michigan Press, 1995), 374.

to win in this evolving sport. Many of the successful strategies involved increasingly violent player behavior: In 1905 alone, the college football season resulted in 18 player deaths and 159 serious injuries.

As the number of injuries and deaths grew, fan appeal fell. Some colleges attempted to limit violent tactics only to lose on the field to the colleges that continued to employ them. The industry was facing the classic "prisoner's dilemma": All colleges had much to gain from cooperatively banning violent play, but each college continued to have an individual incentive to use unilaterally successful tactics. Little could be done without some formal agreement or means to punish aberrant behavior.

President Theodore Roosevelt reacted to the carnage by calling on colleges to reform athletics. He organized a meeting with representatives of several schools hoping to create a cooperative plan to limit brutal and destructive play. No agreement could be reached. Shortly thereafter, a number of colleges dropped football as a sanctioned sport. A new sense of urgency developed, and a second meeting was called. Out of this latter meeting came the Intercollegiate Athletic Association of the United States, which changed its name to the NCAA in 1910.

Implementation of standardized rules and prohibition of violence in football quickly reduced the rate of injury. At the same time, the popularity of the game improved. NCAA membership grew rapidly as more schools sought the benefits of cooperation, while increasing acceptance of the NCAA allowed the organization to standardize rules for other sports.

The NCAA and its membership quickly realized that cooperation in the area of rules could be expanded to other areas of competition. The attention of the NCAA turned from standardizing rules to instituting the foundations for cartel control of college sports.

Input Controls

Cartel development began with an effort to limit competition for athletic talent. Contending that colleges should be limited to amateur athletics, the NCAA worked to remove professionals from collegiate sports. Many teams were packed with "hired guns," players who were not students, often had no link to the college, and participated for the paycheck. The NCAA declared that eligible athletes must be full-time students. In addition, eligibility was limited to 3 years (freshmen were ineligible). The NCAA also declared that "no student shall represent a college or university in any intercollegiate game or contest . . . who has at any time received, either directly or indirectly, money, or any other consideration."[2] To facilitate implementation of the rules, the NCAA recommended in 1919 that members should schedule games only with opponents who abided by NCAA rules.

---

[2]Ibid., 40.

Predictably, the result was widespread cheating because no enforcement mechanism was in place to police adherence to the amateurism and athletic compensation rules. Colleges that disregarded the rules and offered lucrative contracts to talented athletes reaped the financial benefits of having a winning program. With lax enforcement and incentives for noncooperative behavior, the labor restraint rules became nothing more than suggestions.

These shortcomings were addressed in the Sanity Code of 1948. It established standards for financial aid to student-athletes and set up an enforcement apparatus to deal with rules violations. In pursuit of amateurism, the NCAA enacted rules that athletes and nonathletes were to be treated identically: Aid could be based upon need or academic merit, but not on athletic ability; need grants were to make no distinction between athletes and other students. Student-athletes in the top 25 percent of their high school class, or who had a grade point average of B or better in college, were eligible to receive merit aid, even if there was no demonstrated need. The Sanity Code also established the NCAA Compliance Committee to handle allegations of rules violations. This first attempt to crack down on schools that violated the rules was hindered, however, because the only penalty available was to revoke membership. The rule breaker would be tossed out of the NCAA if two-thirds of NCAA members voted for expulsion. In 1950, the Compliance Committee voted to expel seven schools, the so called "Seven Sinners," for rules violations (Villanova, Boston College, Virginia, Maryland, Virginia Military Institute, The Citadel, and Virginia Polytechnic Institute). The two-thirds vote of NCAA members needed to confirm the expulsions was not obtained, indicating the reluctance of the NCAA membership to punish rule violators, at least when faced with imposing such a drastic penalty. This lack of will led to the abolition of the Sanity Code in 1951, and the Compliance Committee died in 1952. In 1953, the NCAA enacted a range of penalties less severe than termination of membership in an attempt to improve enforcement, and in 1954 established the Committee on Infractions to deal with rules violations. For the first time, the NCAA had the means and ability to successfully enforce athletic labor market restraints.

Output Controls

Having successfully limited competition for athletic talent, the NCAA began an effort to control industry output by asserting complete jurisdiction over all aspects of contract negotiations for college football telecasts. The NCAA Television Plan consisted of exclusive contracts with the television networks that limited the number of telecasts and the number of appearances by any one member over a specified period of time, and stipulated the times at which games could be televised. The financial gains from restricting output quickly became apparent: The initial television contract (1952) sold for $1.15 million; by 1962, the contract went for $5.1 million; $12 million in 1972; and $59 million in 1992.

This spectacular growth in broadcast revenues, combined with the NCAA's process for distributing these fees, created tensions within the organization. The few members that had football teams with sufficient fan interest to generate substantial broadcasting fees were sharing those fees equally with the large number of members whose teams enjoyed far more limited fan support. The revenue-generating members became disgruntled with the cartel's allocation mechanism. To save the cartel, the NCAA would have to address the diverse interests of its members.

In 1973, the NCAA responded by creating three homogeneous subgroups with the organization: Divisions I, II, and III. By having a common commitment to athletics and common revenue-generating capacity within divisions, more of the broadcasting fees earned within a given division could be distributed among the division membership. But several of the elite schools were still not placated. They threatened to leave the cartel unless they were provided even greater sovereignty within the organization. The response was more restructuring. Division I was further subdivided according to the size of football programs: I-A, I-AA, and I-AAA. Division I basketball remained unchanged. This divisional split brought stability to the cartel, at least temporarily.

The NCAA thus began as an organization dedicated to creating uniformity in playing rules and reining in brutal play. Once members began discussing these issues, however, there was little additional cost to determining how to control competition for inputs and outputs within the college sports industry. In short, the evolution of the NCAA provides a classic example of a cartel in action.

II. STRUCTURE

Successful cartels do not require that all firms in a market participate. Several firms that produce most of the output or purchase most of the input(s) can increase profits by colluding. However, power and influence are directly related to market share.

Colleges in the United States can belong to one of two organizations that oversee male and female intercollegiate athletics: the NCAA, and the National Association of Intercollegiate Athletics (NAIA). While all big-time college athletic programs belong to the NCAA, the size-diversity of NCAA membership is illustrated by the football attendance figures in Table 12-1. The major football programs of Division I-A schools play before tens of thousands of fans, led by the University of Michigan with a 1998 average home game attendance of 110,965. The next level, Division I-AA, has fewer athletic scholarships available and generally includes

TABLE 12-1 Attendance at NCAA Football Games

Division I-A			
Year	***No. Teams***	***Total Attendance***	***Per Game Attendance***
1978	139	25,017,915	32,407
1983	105	25,381,761	42,162
1988	104	25,079,490	41,454
1993	106	25,305,438	41,281
1998	112	27,674,217	42,510
Division I-AA			
Year	***No. Teams***	***Total Attendance***	***Per Game Attendance***
1978	38	2,032,766	10,113
1983	84	4,879,709	10,844
1988	88	4,801,637	10,326
1993	115	5,356,873	8,599
1998	119	5,555,862	8,805
Division II			
Year	***No. Teams***	***Total Attendance***	***Per Game Attendance***
1978	103	2,871,683	5,544
1983	122	2,705,892	4,429
1988	117	2,570,964	4,493
1993	142	2,572,053	3,582
1998	149	2,443,660	3,271
Division III			
Year	***No. Teams***	***Total Attendance***	***Per Game Attendance***
1978	204	2,447,366	2,629
1983	194	1,849,902	2,069
1988	215	1,871,751	1,883
1993	197	1,636,270	1,752
1998	215	1,817,339	1,790

Source: NCAA Football, National Collegiate Athletic Association, various issues, and *NCAA News,* National Collegiate Athletic Association, "Football Attendance Skyrockets to All-time Record of 37.5 Million," 21 December 1998, 3.

smaller schools. The average attendance is 10,000 or less, with the University of South Florida leading the way with a 1998 average of 27,143 per home game. NCAA Division II schools are allowed even fewer scholarships and average 5,000 or fewer in attendance per game, led by Tuskegee University with 13,269 fans per 1998 home game. NCAA Division III schools are not allowed to give athletic scholarships and average about 2,000 fans per game, with St. John's of Minnesota averaging a division-leading 6,562 spectators per game in 1998. The NAIA comprises a homogeneous group of smaller schools that do not place great emphasis on intercollegiate sports or have large fan bases, and so are similar to NCAA Division III schools. In sum, as noted by Fleisher et al., "(f)or all practical purposes, the NCAA today directs and controls all major revenue-producing collegiate athletic events."[3]

Entry and Entry Barriers

Unfortunately for the NCAA, its success at restricting competition and increasing profits results in a clamor for admittance to membership by outsiders eager to share in those profits. Rapid entry results in divergent interests and potential rule-breaking. The situation is exacerbated by heterogeneity in revenue generating capability. Also, monitoring and enforcing rules for member behavior becomes more difficult. In short, the stability of the cartel is at risk.

The NCAA currently has 973 college members. Multiply this by the number of coaches, players, potential recruits, alumni, and fans at each institution and it quickly becomes apparent that monitoring all potential rule-breaking activities would be prohibitively expensive, if not impossible. If monitoring is impossible, then cheating should be rampant. Although the NCAA cannot closely monitor each rule-related activity, it can use probabilistic evidence to infer when a member's behavior may deviate from the rules.[4] This process compares current performance with the historic performance of its members: If there is a significant improvement in current performance, then there is increased suspicion that the college has cheated. Resources can be allocated to launch a more intense investigation to determine whether cheating has actually occurred.

If cheating cannot be controlled, the cartel will disintegrate. The NCAA, however, can apply sanctions to punish cheaters who are caught, and these sanctions have become increasingly severe in recent years. For instance, the NCAA can reduce the number of athletic scholarships a college can grant. The NCAA can also limit television appearances and prohibit a college from appearing in lucrative postseason tournaments. An appearance in the Rose Bowl or in the Final Four of the NCAA basketball tournament can be worth over $6 million. The NCAA clearly has powers to enforce membership adherence to its rules, at least in most instances.

Although violations of NCAA rules are often cast in terms of legality or illegality, these rules are not law. The NCAA is a private organization governed by rules that have been adopted by representatives of its member institutions. It is not illegal for a college athlete to hold a job off

---

[3] A. Fleisher, B. Goff, and R. Tollison, *The National Collegiate Athletic Association: A Study in Cartel Behavior* (Chicago: University of Chicago Press, 1992), 55.

[4] For details, see ibid.

campus but such a job can be a violation of NCAA regulations. The perception that NCAA rules are law does, however, aid in enforcement. The "legal" ramifications of their actions may deter potential perpetrators of rule violations. Recently, though, NCAA rules have begun to seep into the legal system. In addition to the NCAA punishing an athlete and a college if an agent pays an athlete, many states now consider it a felony for an agent to offer anything of value to anyone as a means of inducing a student-athlete to sign with an agent. A federal bill proposes a nationwide ban on influence-peddling of sports agents. Although other students on campus and other workers in general are allowed to seek advice and representation as they see fit, athletes are not. The NCAA's influence seems to be steadily creeping beyond the narrow confines of college sports.

Entry considerations have traditionally focused on keeping peace within the college ranks. With so many member colleges in the NCAA, there has always been concern that a disgruntled group of members could form a league of its own if it desired. (Later we will discuss the rise and fall of the College Football Association (CFA) as an example of this course of action.) To be effective, the number of seceding teams must be sufficient to form an alternative league with a full slate of games and potential postseason play. The disparity among NCAA members has been reduced by the creation of divisions. As indicated earlier, the creation of subgroups within the organization increases the homogeneity of colleges within the division and reduces incentives for cheating. Division I-A football colleges can enact rules that apply only to them; they need not be impeded by the legislative dictates of the smaller, less sports-oriented colleges.

The entry barriers that do exist consist primarily of limiting admission to various NCAA divisions, especially Division I-A football. A Division I-A football entrant must offer a minimum number of male and female varsity sports, have a stadium with a minimum of 30,000 permanent seats, and average more than 17,000 in paid attendance per home game. A quick glance at Table 12-1 shows just how restrictive these rules are. If a college were to meet these minimum standards it would be accepted as a provisional member of Division I-A. Provisional status lasts for 3 years. During this time, the potential entrant must comply with Division rules without receiving Division benefits. Provisional entry can occur with movement between Divisions II and III. In 1994, when provisional status was first implemented, there were 41 provisional members. This number increased to 96 in 1995, 92 in 1996, 52 in 1997, and 67 as of 1998. The NCAA has clearly slowed migration between Divisions in an attempt to retain Divisional homogeneity.

A new and far more threatening type of entrant may soon confront the NCAA, however. The Collegiate Professional Basketball League is set to begin play in the fall of 2000. The league will offer salaries (starting at $17,000 per year) and scholarships to players to cover the full cost of attending college. The scholarships can be used during or after their playing careers. The likely size of the league is six to eight teams. The impact on the market for athletes should be significant, yet small, but the emergence of this college league outside the purview of the NCAA cartel raises the specter of other, competing leagues being initiated.

III. CONDUCT

Although the market share of the NCAA is near 100 percent, the threat of disharmony among the large number of members and the growing threat of new entrants put severe strains on the cartel. The stresses are so serious that much of the output control once held by the NCAA is being eroded. The NCAA today is better viewed as an input cartel, but even its labor controls are being tested.

Output Control

Control of broadcasting rights to college football telecasts is one key aspect of output control. As noted earlier, this control initially generated significant and rapidly rising broadcasting fees. Increased dissension about the distribution of the fees, however, fueled a restructuring of the NCAA. The resulting split into divisions in 1973 was only a temporary solution to the growing disparity in revenue generation across the membership, and dissatisfaction soon returned.

The College Football Association (CFA), founded in 1977, was an outgrowth of this dissension. The CFA included most of the Division I-A schools except those from the Big Ten and PAC Ten conferences. (Originally the CFA members threatened complete secession from the NCAA but stopped short when they did not have the support of the Big Ten and PAC Ten schools.) Instead, CFA focused solely on gaining control of football telecast revenues. The CFA also planned to garner more television appearances and generate more television revenue for its member schools. In 1981, the CFA signed an agreement with NBC that fulfilled these goals. The NCAA immediately threatened penalties that would apply to football and other sports. Later that year, the University of Oklahoma and University of Georgia filed suit against the NCAA, alleging that the NCAA Television Plan, by limiting television exposure by any one team, was an illegal restraint of trade.

The 1983 Television Plan allowed two networks, ABC and CBS, each to air 14 telecasts annually. These telecasts could be a mixture of national and regional games, but each network was required to telecast at least 82 different teams over a 2-year period. ABC and CBS together had to show at least 115 different teams over the 2 years of the Plan. The NCAA also mandated that teams be limited to four national appearances and six total appearances during this period. Finally, all teams involved in a telecast received equal remuneration, regardless of the attractiveness of the game to viewers and fans or the number of stations that broadcast the game. In some years, for example, Oklahoma, University of Southern California (USC), Appalachian State, and the Citadel each received the same compensation, even though the Oklahoma-USC game was broadcast over 200 stations while the Appalachian State-Citadel game was broadcast on only four.

The NCAA acknowledged that its Television Plan "restrained trade" but pointed out that professional sports had often been granted exemptions from prosecution when restrictive business practices were necessary to promote "competitive balance." The NCAA asserted that if colleges were given the right to negotiate their own contracts, a proliferation of telecasts would ensue with most appearances being awarded to traditional football powers. Because television appearances are a key aid in recruiting top athletes, a distribution of appearances skewed toward the traditional powers would accentuate the existing inequality among football programs; existing powers would prosper, while nonpowers would suffer.

Nevertheless, in 1984, the Supreme Court held that the NCAA Television Plan restricted output and fixed prices in violation of the Sherman Antitrust Act.[5] The ruling granted individual colleges the property right to their college football telecasts—a right the schools had an option to sell or assign at their discretion.

The demise of NCAA television control had three significant outcomes. Soon after the Court's ruling, colleges, conferences, and select organizations of colleges frenetically pursued local, regional, national, and cable outlets to televise their games. Network games alone doubled shortly after the ruling, while the price per network game dropped from \$2.3 million to \$0.6 million. As expected, the introduction of competition into a previously restrictive market resulted in a dramatic increase in the quantity of televised games and a decline in the price per game. Also, Bennett and Fizel, and Fort and Quirk, report that competitive balance on the field has been enhanced by the Court's decision.[6] Contrary to the NCAA's argument, NCAA control over television was not necessary to generate more equality of playing strength among Division I football teams. Finally, the case initially was a coup for the CFA and its partial secession from the NCAA. However, over time, the CFA began to face

[5]See *The National Collegiate Athletic Association* v. *Board of Regents of the University of Oklahoma and University of Georgia Athletic Association,* 468 U.S. 85 (1984).

[6]Randall W. Bennett and John L. Fizel, "Telecast Deregulation and Competitive Balance," *American Journal of Economics and Sociology,* 54 (1995): 183–200; R. Fort and J. Quirk, "Introducing A Competitive Economic Environment into Professional Sports," in *Advances in the Economics of Sports,* ed. W. Hendricks (Greenwich, CT: JAI Press, 1997), 11–26.

internal pressures similar to those experienced by the NCAA. Eventually, several prominent members left the CFA and, in 1997, the CFA ceased operations. The demise of the CFA underscores the difficulties facing the NCAA in maintaining its output cartel.

Another area that escapes NCAA control is postseason play in Division I-A football. Currently, 114 Division I-A football schools participate in the only sport for which the NCAA does not sponsor a national championship. Why would the NCAA ignore championship play in the sport that generates the largest revenue for the typical Division I-A school? The answer stems from the development of the postseason bowl system. Since the University of Michigan defeated Stanford University 49–0 in the 1902 Rose Bowl, a system of postseason bowls has developed as a reward for a successful football season: The Rose Bowl was first played in 1902, the Orange and Sugar Bowls in 1935, the Sun Bowl in 1936, the Cotton Bowl in 1937, the Gator Bowl in 1946, the Liberty Bowl in 1959, and the Fiesta Bowl in 1971. By 1998, the number of Division I-A postseason bowl games had grown to 22.

The mythical national champion of Division I-A football historically has been determined by polls of sportswriters or coaches, not by performance on the playing field as is done for Divisions I-AA, II, and III football. Dissatisfied with this arrangement, the major college football programs began tinkering with the bowl system in 1991 in an attempt to arrange for the Number 1 and Number 2 teams in the coaches' and press polls each year to play in a national championship game at an existing bowl. This initial bowl coalition became the bowl alliance for the 1995 season, in a system where the Orange Bowl, Sugar Bowl, and Fiesta Bowl would trade off as hosts for this national championship game. This game was not, however, a true national championship, because the finalists were determined through the polls and not by a playoff system, and two major conferences, the Big Ten and PAC Ten, were not initially involved. These conferences were not ready to sever the lucrative arrangement that tied their conference champions to the Rose Bowl—the bowl with the biggest payout—for the chance to play for the national championship. The Big Ten, PAC Ten, and the Rose Bowl did join the bowl alliance for the 1998 season, forming the Bowl Championship Series (BCS). The championship game will now rotate among the Orange, Sugar, Fiesta, and Rose Bowls. The compromise that brought the Big Ten and PAC Ten into the BCS allows their champions to still meet in the Rose Bowl when it is not hosting the championship game, and when they are not involved in the championship game in other years.

Bowl directors and major conference commissioners—not the NCAA—administer the BCS. The administrators have reduced the emphasis on polls to determine the championship game participants by relying on a combination of (1) team record, (2) Associated Press and

ESPN/USA Today poll rankings; (3) computer rankings, and (4) a measure of strength of schedule based on opponent performance. The 1999 Fiesta Bowl hosted the first BCS game, in which the University of Tennessee was crowned national champion after defeating Florida State University 23–16.

A true playoff system seems more likely as the potential payouts become more lucrative. The *Chronicle of Higher Education* reports that International Sports and Leisure, a sports marketing company, is proposing to pay $3 billion over 8 years to coordinate a 16-team, Division I-A football playoff tournament. The proposal is to pay the NCAA about $380 million per year for the 8 years—a huge increase over the approximately $140 million the bowls paid out following the 1998 season. DeLoss Dodds, the athletic director of the University of Texas, says that colleges are "leaving $2-million a year, per school, on the table" by not going to a playoff system.[7]

Although these parties argue that college revenues would be enhanced if the NCAA could gain control of postseason play in football, others offer counter arguments. One weakness of the argument for playoffs is that they would lengthen the college football season. The current proposal would play the championship game the week before the Super Bowl in mid-January. Graham B. Spanier, the chairman of the NCAA Division I Board of Directors and the President of Pennsylvania State University, says "There is a great concern about commercialization, professionalism, and extending the season, and I can tell you that most of the presidents I've spoken with are not persuaded by the money that's potentially on the table."[8] The existing bowls oppose a postseason tournament because they fear they would lose autonomy or even be eliminated entirely by a playoff system. Arguments that conference commissioners make against playoffs are that they would reduce the importance of the regular season for most teams, hurt or destroy existing bowls, and possibly eliminate the opportunity for postseason bowl play for many teams. Almost 40 percent of the 112 teams that played Division I-A football in 1998 participated in a bowl game. If a 16-team playoff destroys the minor bowl games, many fewer teams will earn postseason play. Walter Byers, former executive director of the NCAA, argues that major college football programs do not want a playoff system because they do not want the money generated from postseason play to be funneled through the NCAA, where it is likely that funds will flow to nonparticipating schools and to the NCAA itself.

Whether the postseason bowls can survive remains to be seen. Because the current cash cow of the NCAA is the postseason basketball

---

[7]Welch Suggs, "Can $3-billion Persuade Colleges to Create a Playoff for Football?" *Chronicle of Higher Education,* 6 August 1999, 2.

[8]Ibid., 3.

tournament it oversees (accounting indirectly or directly for 93 percent of NCAA revenues), there is no doubt that the NCAA will work diligently to develop a proposal for a postseason football tournament/playoff. But can the NCAA concoct a proposal that overcomes the academic concerns of college presidents, the distribution concerns of football power schools, and the lobbying that will inevitably come from bowl administrators?

Input Control

A cartel in the output market increases profits by enabling members to collectively limit output and increase prices. A cartel in the *input* market increases profits by enabling members to collectively reduce the price paid for the input. In effect, an input cartel attempts to exercise its collective monopsony power to the detriment of input suppliers.

The NCAA has created a voluminous system of rules aimed at controlling the cost of inputs in collegiate sports, with most of the regulations being directed at the recruitment and compensation of athletes.

The NCAA contends that the proliferation of its recruiting controls enhances competitive balance by standardizing rules within the organization. Yet a quick examination of some of the rules shows that they are effective monopsonistic ploys to reduce recruiting expenditures: Potential recruits are limited in the number of on-campus and off-campus contacts they may have with representatives of a college's athletic program. Direct contact is also limited to certain months of the year. Each of these stipulations directly lowers the per-recruit cost of recruiting. The total costs of recruiting are further diminished because colleges are limited in the number of athletic scholarships they can award. A college can grant in any year a maximum of 85 scholarships in football, and a total of 13 in basketball and 11.7 in baseball. Scholarship limits are applied to other sports as well. Freshman eligibility also reduces the total costs of recruiting by giving colleges 4 rather than 3 years of service by the athlete, and by reducing the number of costly ventures into the recruiting fray. Recruits sign a "National Letter of Intent" to indicate their chosen college. Once signed, the recruit cannot enroll in another institution without forfeiting 2 years of athletic eligibility. Once signed, the chosen college and all other colleges can immediately terminate expenditures for wooing this particular athlete.

Despite the importance of recruiting rules, the predominant feature of the NCAA cartel is the compensation package paid to athletes. Under the guise of "amateurism" the NCAA has severely limited athletes' compensation relative to their value to the institution, while coupling the ability to receive compensation with a variety of changing academic standards.

In 1956, the NCAA initiated athletic scholarships that were independent of need or academic merit. The scholarships were limited to tuition, room, board, and incidentals, "not to exceed the cost of attendance at the school." The compensation limits have changed little over the past 40 years. If anything, the development of NCAA Proposition 62 suggests that athletic compensation is declining: The NCAA now allows athletes to hold limited jobs to cover the *difference* between the full cost of attending college and the value of the athletic scholarship!

The NCAA strictly enforces the compensation limits. Departures from the rules, no matter how slight, can bring severe penalties. For example, UCLA's basketball team was prohibited from playing in the postseason tournament because recruits were given free UCLA shirts, and the team received a free Thanksgiving dinner from an athletic booster. These perks were violations because they were available to the basketball players but not to students on the campus at large.

The shrinking compensation paid to athletes occurs as the revenues of the NCAA are skyrocketing. College athletic programs are generating annual revenues greater than $1 billion in ticket sales and television. The 1998 bowl season alone paid out $140 million. Over 40 programs report annual revenues greater than $10 million. A winning basketball or football team can provide enough revenue to finance a college's entire athletic program. Clearly, monopsonistic exploitation is profitable.

A number of methods exist for assessing the extent to which athletes are underpaid relative to the revenue stream they generate. The Collegiate Professional Basketball League, a potential competitor, is proposing to pay each participant a minimum of $17,000 plus the cost of a 4-year degree. This compensation package can be construed as the "reservation wage"—i.e., the minimum monetary amount required to entice an athlete away from the NCAA. What if competition for athletic services were introduced across the entire NCAA? When this happened in Major League Baseball, player salaries increased to 50 to 60 percent of total team revenues. If 50 percent of the $840 million in Division I-A football revenue were allocated among the 11,000 players, each player would receive about $38,000 per year. Marginal revenue product analyses offer similar conclusions concerning the appropriate average compensation of athletes, and suggest that monopsonistic exploitation is even greater for star players: Brown concludes that the annual marginal revenue product of individual college football and basketball stars is about $600,000 and $1,000,000, respectively.[9]

The NCAA argues that amateurism is an essential part of the product it sells, and that these compensation rules are necessary to minimize commercialization of collegiate sports. Nevertheless, the NCAA does not prohibit other competitive and commercial activities: Athletes are

[9]R. Brown, "An Estimate of the Rent Generated by A Premium College Football Player," *Economic Inquiry,* 31 (1993): 671–684; and R. Brown, "Measuring Cartel Rents in the College Basketball Recruitment Market," *Applied Economics,* 26 (1994): 27–34.

courted with lavish stadiums, training facilities, locker rooms and specially outfitted athletic dormitories. Customers are wooed with college brand apparel, videos, logos, and advertisements. Business interests are captured with stadium billboards, electronic ads on scoreboards, sponsorship of bowl games, logos on team uniforms, and exclusive apparel/equipment contracts. Only the athletes seem to be barred from reaping the benefits of big-time college sports.

In 1965, the NCAA began developing academic-eligibility standards in response to the accusation that colleges were accepting ill-prepared student-athletes who had little chance of academic success. These standards also reinforced the NCAA claim that amateur sports required educational objectives to supercede profit-making objectives. The success of academic standards, however, has been limited both legally and practically.

The initial academic standard was the "1.6" rule, which restricted freshman athletic scholarships to those who could expect a freshman grade point average of 1.6, or above, based upon high school academic performance and standardized SAT or ACT scores. The 1.6 rule continued through the 1960s and early 1970s, when campus upheaval led many colleges to relax admission standards for all students. In 1973, the NCAA voted to rescind the 1.6 rule and to let colleges set their own admission standards for athletes. This led to a period of declining graduation rates, followed by college presidents leading a fight to reinstate academic requirements for incoming student athletes. The result was enactment of Proposition 48 in 1983. Freshman eligibility under Proposition 48 required that a student be a high school graduate, obtain at least a 700 on the SAT or a 15 on the ACT, and earn at least a 2.0 grade-point average in 11 core high school courses. Students who did not meet these standards were not eligible to practice or play during their freshman year of college and had only 3 years of eligibility left.

Proposition 16 was passed by the NCAA in 1996, replacing Proposition 48. It required college freshman to have a high school diploma, and a minimum grade-point average in 13 core high school courses, with this GPA linked to standardized test scores by a sliding scale: The higher the high school GPA, the lower the allowable standardized test score. For instance, a student with a 2.0 GPA in these core courses needed to score 1,010 or higher on the SAT in order to achieve freshman eligibility; an SAT score of less than 820 rendered the student ineligible for his or her freshman year regardless of high school GPA.

The reign of academic standards has been stormy. The effect on the allocation of athletic talent has been contentious, but the most contentious criticism has been that eligibility standards discriminate against African-Americans. For example, two African-American students who ranked 5th and 27th in their high school class of 305 could not attain the required minimum standardized test scores and were declared ineligible.

They filed suit and their case went to court. In March 1999, U.S. District Court Judge Ronald Burkhalter of Philadelphia ruled that the use of high school GPA and core classes in Proposition16 was acceptable, but that the Proposition relied too heavily on standardized test scores.[10] His ruling stated that reliance on standardized tests scores results in "an unjustified disparate impact against African-Americans." In fact, the NCAA's own research reveals that 1 in 5 potential African-American recruits did not meet the standards, as opposed to 1 in 25 white recruits.

A few weeks later the third U.S. Circuit Court of Appeals issued a stay of Judge Burkhalter's ruling until the NCAA's appeal was heard. The stay reinstated Proposition 16 until and if the full appeals court ruled against the NCAA. During the stay, the NCAA began examining alternative initial-eligibility rules having less racial disparity, including absolute ineligibility of freshman, use of minimum core class GPA only, and a revised sliding scale of test scores and GPA.

On December 22, 1999, however, the Third Circuit Court of Appeals overturned Judge Burkhalter's decision in a 2-1 opinion, and ruled that the NCAA may continue to employ minimum standardized test scores in determining freshman eligibility. The court held that because the NCAA did not directly receive federal funding, it was not subject to Title IX.

These decisions assuredly will not end the battle over test scores: Counsel for the African-American students involved has already begun preparing its appeal, while the NCAA continues to assess alternative initial-eligibility rules. Meanwhile, the executive committee of the Faculty Athletics Representatives Association has issued a statement strongly supporting the use of standardized test scores for initial eligibility, declaring that "in light of the fact that a combination of grade-point average and standardized test score is the best available pre-college predictor of collegiate academic success, we believe that both grade-point average and standardized test score should be an integral part of any initial-eligibility standard."[11] An alternative view is expressed by Bob Goin, the athletic director at the University of Cincinnati, who argues that "we're going to have to take a hard, hard look at the merits of basing eligibility on the basis of test scores. Some people feel very strongly that they are a valid measuring stick. My gut feeling is that good old hard work is the best evidence of academic success."[12] (It should be noted that the University of Cincinnati failed to graduate a single basketball player from its 1985–1991 freshman classes.)

Despite the SAT and high school course requirements of Propositions 48 and 16, athletes continue to have average SAT scores below those

---

[10]See *USA Today,* 17 March 1999, 1A.
[11]*NCAA News,* 26 April 1999.
[12]*USA Today,* 10 March 1999, 7C.

of other students.[13] While the initiation of these propositions may have reduced differences between the academic backgrounds of athletes and nonathletes, measurable differences continue to exist. These data are consistent with admission policies that pave the way to recruit excellent athletes who are marginal students, but also create a situation where the student-athlete will continually be at a disadvantage in competing with peers in the classroom. Athletes also appear to opt for less rigorous curricula, and are significantly slower in advancing to an academic degree. Football players, who often represent the largest number of college athletes and the largest sports revenue source for the college, have average grade point averages comparable to the 39th percentile of the student body. The exploitation of the big money collegiate athlete, it seems, has been extended to the classroom.

The market for coaches provides a stark contrast to the market for athletes. Head coaches operate in a market close to the competitive ideal. They are free to accept whatever salary and fringe benefits they are offered in the freely competitive bidding among colleges. The existence of potential National Football League or National Basketball Association assistant and head coaching positions intensifies the college-level competition over coaches.

In 1991, however, the NCAA instituted a restricted-earnings rule that limited the income of assistant coaches: Restricted-earning coaches could be paid a maximum of $16,000 per year and faced other limitations. For example, the third assistant coach for a Division I men's basketball could receive only $12,000 in salary with up to $4,000 additional summer earnings, but was prohibited from off-campus recruiting, and could hold this job for a maximum of 5 years. The NCAA's stated intentions were to provide low cost, entry-level positions for young and inexperienced coaches, and to prevent a bidding war for assistant coaches that would result in competitive imbalance as the sports powerhouses outbid others for the best assistants. A group of restricted-earnings coaches disagreed, however, and sued the NCAA alleging that the rule limiting their pay was an illegal restraint of trade in violation of antitrust law. The NCAA argued that the restricted-earnings rule was a reasonable restraint of trade, similar to other restraints the courts have allowed. For instance, the NCAA is allowed to limit the size of coaching staffs, the number of games played per season, and financial aid to athletes in order to foster competitive balance. The NCAA also argued that the rule was enacted as an alternative to completely eliminating these coaching positions to cut costs.

---

[13] J. Fizel and T. Smaby, "Participation in Collegiate Athletics and Student Grade Point Averages," in *Sports Economics: Current Research,* eds. J. Fizel, E. Gustafson, and L. Hadley, (Westport, CT: Praeger, 1999), 161–171.

In 1995, a U.S. District Court found that the restricted-earnings rule did indeed violate antitrust law, and it ordered the NCAA to cease and desist from setting assistant coaches' pay. After the appellate court upheld the verdict in 1998, a jury awarded damages of $11.2 million for restricted-earnings basketball coaches and $11.1 million for coaches in other sports affected by the restricted-earnings rule. These damages of $22.3 million were then tripled under antitrust law to nearly $67 million. After an appeal that ended in March 1999, the NCAA settled the case for $54 million.

This decision prompts once again the nagging question: Why are restricted earnings illegal when applied to coaches, but not when applied to the players themselves?

IV. PERFORMANCE

"Most college sports lose money." This is an assertion commonly made by representatives of collegiate athletic departments, and increasingly believed by the media.[14] For example, school officials at Michigan and UCLA regularly claim financial shortfalls in their athletic budgets, yet these schools play football in stadiums seating more than 100,000, traditionally have strong basketball teams that play to sell-out crowds, compete regularly in the NCAA postseason tournament, and are located in heavily populated metropolitan areas. Their revenues typically exceed $20 million. These schools are also supported by the NCAA's power to control pricing of output and payments to inputs. How is it that these schools operate in the red?

The answer lies in accounting practices that cause reported profits to dramatically understate true economic profits. The two most important of these practices are overestimating the cost of athletes, and omitting the positive promotional effects sports teams have on admissions and financial contributions to colleges.

Consider first the data reported by the NCAA for the major revenue sports—Division I-A football and Division I basketball (see Table 12-2). These profit statistics differ dramatically from media reports implying athletic department losses. The revenue growth from 1989 to 1997 was approximately 76 percent for football and 74 percent for basketball.[15] During the same period, expenses for football and basketball grew by only 42 percent and 37 percent, respectively. The result of this disparity in growth rates is a doubling of profits per team and profits per player. In other

[14]See *USA Today,* 14 October 1991, 1C; *USA Today* 15 July 1999, 16C; and Murray Sperber, *College Sports, Inc.* (New York: Henry Holt, 1990).

[15]The revenue data do not include $3 million in "Unrelated Revenue" which may, at least partially, be attributable to one of these two sports, and include only a portion of the billion-dollar contract the NCAA signed with CBS for the postseason basketball tournament.

TABLE 12-2 Revenue and Expenses

Division I-A Football

Year	*Total Revenue*	*Revenue per Team*	*Revenue per Player*	*Total Expenses*	*Expenses per Team*	*Expenses per Player*
1989	$447,400,000	$4,340,000	$31,120	$342,320,000	$3,112,000	$31,120
1993	$693,000,000	$6,300,000	$63,000	$443,410,000	$4,031,000	$40,310
1995	$708,290,000	$6,439,000	$64,390	$450,780,000	$4,098,000	$40,980
1997	$839,190,000	$7,629,000	$76,290	$486,750,000	$4,425,000	$44,250

Division I Basketball

Year	*Total Revenue*	*Revenue per Team*	*Revenue per Player*	*Total Expenses*	*Expenses per Team*	*Expenses per Player*
1989	$498,560,000	$1,640,000	$136,667	$288,192,000	$948,000	$79,000
1993	$643,568,000	$2,117,000	$176,417	$331,664,000	$1,091,000	$90,917
1995	$760,912,000	$2,503,000	$208,583	$370,576,000	$1,219,000	$101,583
1997	$865,488,000	$2,847,000	$237,250	$394,592,000	$1,298,000	$108,167

Note: In 1997, Division I-A football consists of 110 teams with approximately 100 players each and Division I basketball includes 304 schools with about 12 players each.

Source: Daniel L. Fulks, *Revenues and Expenses of Divisions I and II Intercollegiate Athletics Programs*, 1997. NCAA Publications.

words, accounting profits are escalating and they understate the true economic profits.

Also, the reported expenses overstate the true economic expenses of each athlete. This report indicates costs of approximately $44,000 per football player and $108,000 per basketball player. However, the NCAA sets the maximum allowable payment to athletes including all in-kind and direct payments for the "cost of attending school." Brown claims that the ceiling for such payments is $20,000.[16] If correct, the total expenses for football players are about half, and the total expenses for basketball players about one-fifth of what the NCAA claims.[17]

The story concerning the expenses allocated per athlete is still incomplete. Thus far we have considered only the "potential" average cost of the athletes rather than the marginal cost to the college of enrolling these students. Given that few colleges operate at full capacity, the marginal cost of admitting an additional student is near zero. The colleges will not hire new faculty or build new classrooms to educate the athlete. The college may have no dormitory costs and little food and utilities expenses in housing the athlete. Booster contributions, rather than college resources, finance many of the scholarships. When scholarship payments are based on marginal costs, athletic department profits increase substantially.

Athletic department accounting practices also underestimate revenue attributable to the signing of athletes. In addition to providing games for consumption, athletic departments can also be construed as a public relations branch of the college. Athletic events provide a large amount of advertising for the colleges. Such promotions can increase student applications as well as enhance endowments and gifts from boosters. Each can be a significant source of income for the institution.

Collegiate sports are profitable. Appropriate cost and revenue adjustments turn apparent deficits into million-dollar profits. Borland, Goff, and Pulsinelli show that the alleged loss of $1.5 million in the athletic department at Western Kentucky is actually a net gain to the college.[18] Noll provides evidence that a $3 million deficit at the University of Michigan should more accurately be interpreted as a $5 million profit.[19] Obviously, institutions may wish to mask these surpluses as they pump boosters for money, but the fact is that sizable cartel profits continue to flow.

---

[16]Brown, "Measuring Cartel Rents."

[17]The source of the expenses can vary from one university to another. For details on expense allocation, see M. Borland, B. Goff, and R. Pulsinelli, "College Athletics: Financial Burden or Boom?" in *Advances in the Economics of Sports,* ed. G. Sally, vol. 1 (Greenwich, CT: JAI Press, 1992), 215–235; and Roger Noll, "The Economics of Intercollegiate Sports," in *Rethinking College Athletics,* eds. J. Andre and D. James (Philadelphia: Temple University Press, 1991), 197–209.

[18]Ibid.

[19]Ibid.

V. PUBLIC POLICY

College athletics has clashed with a number of public policies legislated by Congress, and courts have become increasingly embroiled in determining the extent of violations of law and appropriate remedies. Recent cases have held that NCAA rules have violated antitrust laws enacted to promote economic competition and prevent anticompetitive practices. Recent judicial decisions have also held that NCAA rules have violated anti-racial discrimination laws. Battles concerning gender equity and athlete compensation are apt to be the next major legal challenge faced by collegiate athletics. How these challenges are resolved will have a significant impact on the structure and functioning of the college sports cartel.

Title IX

Perhaps no issue has caused more controversy for athletics departments and the NCAA than gender equity or Title IX compliance. As Cedric Dempsey, the president of the NCAA, says, "I do not know of any topic in college athletics that brings emotions to the surface more quickly than Title IX. People from all perspectives on this issue have assailed me. It is absolutely impossible to engage this topic without frustrating or even angering somebody."[20]

Title IX of the Education Amendments of 1972 states that "no person in the United States shall, on the basis of sex, be excluded from participation in, be denied the benefits of, or be subjected to discrimination under any education program or activity receiving federal funds."[21] Uncertainty about what Title IX meant was clarified by the U.S. Supreme Court in 1984, when it ruled that violations of Title IX only affected federal money going to areas directly involved in the violation.[22] Since college athletics receive very few federal funds, movement toward Title IX compliance was slowed due to the lack of effective penalties. This dramatically changed, however, with the 1988 enactment of the Civil Rights Restoration Act, which barred institutions that violate civil rights laws from receiving any federal money *in any area of their entire operations.* The particular activity need not receive federal funds; it is enough that the institution receives federal funds for any of its activities to be covered under Title IX.

The impact of Title IX on women's athletics has been immense: The number of women's sports offered and the number of female athletes participating in them has skyrocketed. At the high school level, female

---

[20]"NCAA's Commitment to Title IX Still Strong," *NCAA News,* 15 March 1999, 2 (Internet).
[21]20 U.S.C. section 1681(a).
[22]See *Grove City College* v. *Bell,* 465 U.S. 555, 573–74 (1984).

participation in athletics has risen from 1 in 27 in 1972 to 1 in 3 in 1998.[23] The NCAA had no interest in women's athletics prior to Title IX. The Association of Intercollegiate Athletics for Women (AIAW) was the primary organization for women's athletics at the time. Title IX forced the NCAA to take more interest in women's sports. The AIAW was in trouble once the NCAA started sponsoring intercollegiate championships for women's sports in the early 1980s, since the NCAA funds most of the expenses associated with participating in its championships. This was something the poorer AIAW could not afford, and the organization folded in 1983.

The conflicts arising from Title IX are mainly due to disputes about how compliance with the law should be determined. The Civil Rights Office of the Department of Education, which enforces Title IX, has promulgated three criteria for determining compliance with the law. If at least one of these three criteria is fulfilled, compliance is met.

The first is the "proportionality" test. This test requires that the participation of women and men in intercollegiate sports should reflect the gender proportions of the full-time undergraduate student body at the institution. A school with 60 percent women and 40 percent men should have women comprise approximately 60 percent of the intercollegiate athletes at the school. Athletic scholarships and other forms of support should also reflect the gender proportion of students. The second compliance test is to show a continuing expansion of programs for the under-represented sex that is "responsive to developing interests and abilities of that sex."[24] If programs for the under-represented sex are expanding fast enough to satisfy the student body, then the school is complying with Title IX. The third test for compliance is to show that existing programs have satisfied the under-represented group's "interests and abilities" in intercollegiate sports.

A recent court case illustrates the primacy of proportionality in determining compliance with Title IX. In 1991, Brown University sponsored 16 men's sports and 16 women's sports. Brown decided to cut university funding for four sports—men's golf and men's water polo, and women's gymnastics and women's volleyball. Members of the women's teams sued the university for violating Title IX. The 1990–1991 school year's athletic participation was 63 percent men and 37 percent women while the student body was 51 percent women. Brown argued that the disparity was due to a lower level of interest by women in athletics, and that the school was complying with Title IX by matching offerings with interests. A survey of potential students found that 50 percent of the men and 30 percent

---

[23]Ruth Conniff, "The Joy of Women's Sports," *The Nation,* 10/17 August 1998, 26.

[24]"Comment: Use of Proportionality Test is Out of Control," *NCAA News,* 12 April 1999, 4 (Internet).

of the women had an interest in playing intercollegiate sports. It was also noted that 8 times as many men as women participated in intramural sports at Brown.[25]

The District Court, however, issued a preliminary injunction to reinstate the women's teams in 1992, and, in 1995, the Court ruled that Brown had violated Title IX. The court said that Brown did not meet any of the three criteria set by the Office for Civil Rights: The participation relative to enrollment numbers violated the proportionality standard; the demotion of two women's programs did not correspond to expanding opportunities; and the two demoted programs had the necessary interest of women students since Brown was able to field teams in them.

Brown appealed this decision to the U.S. Court of Appeals for the First Circuit in Boston, which upheld the lower court's finding. The court said that "to assert that Title IX permits institutions to provide fewer athletics participation opportunities for women than for men, based upon the premise that women are less interested in sports than are men, is (among other things) to ignore the fact that Title IX was enacted in order to remedy discrimination that results from stereotyped notions of women's interests and abilities. . . . Interest and ability rarely develop in a vacuum; they evolve as a function of opportunity and experience. . . . [W]omen's lower rate of participation in athletics reflects women's historical lack of opportunities to participate in sports."[26] This ruling makes it extremely difficult to demonstrate Title IX compliance on any basis other than proportionality.

The U.S. Supreme Court declined to review this decision in 1997, and Brown settled the case the following year. It agreed to maintain women's sports participation within 3 percentage points of the women's undergraduate student body percentage. The focus on proportionality is typical. For instance, the California State University System is under court order to have gender participation in sports within 5 percentage points of gender enrollment.[27] Michigan State University announced that it would comply with Title IX by increasing women's participation from 40 percent to 49.3 percent, in part by adding women's crew as a varsity sport, and by dropping men's lacrosse and men's fencing as varsity sports.[28]

Adding women's sports and cutting men's sports has been common in the era of Title IX. This, in turn, has provoked heated protest by those involved with men's nonrevenue sports: They charge that athletics

---

[25]Walter Olson, "Title IX from Outer Space," *Reason,* February 1998, 50–51.

[26]"Brown Title IX Decision Upheld on Appeal," *NCAA News,* 2 December 1996, 2 (Internet).

[27]"California State's Division I Colleges Struggle to Meet Gender-Equity Goals," *Chronicle of Higher Education,* 4 June 1999.

[28]"Title IX Ticker—Michigan State Presents Plan for Title IX Compliance," *NCAA News,* 27 January 1997.

departments facing limited budgets and the Title IX proportionality standard expand women's programs by eliminating nonrevenue men's sports. Statistics offer some support: The number of men's gymnastics teams has fallen from 133 in 1975 to 26 in 1999.[29] More than 250 men's wrestling programs were eliminated between 1972 and 1997. The 1997 NCAA Gender-Equity Study points out that in the previous 5 years, 20,800 male opportunities were eliminated, or more than 10 percent of the positions, while women gained 5,800 opportunities over the same time period.[30]

A study done for the *Chronicle of Higher Education* indicates that attainment of proportionality is far from complete. In the 1997–1998 season, 40 percent of the athletes at NCAA Division I schools were women, while females made up 53 percent of the undergraduate population.[31] Women also received only 40 percent of the athletic scholarship budget and 32 percent of the recruiting budgets.

If the demands of Title IX to increase the athletic participation of women and the athletic funds devoted to women represent increases on top of existing male teams and budgets, then the NCAA and its members will face significant cost increases. With the exception of some women's basketball programs, women's sports are not net revenue producers. The escalation of expenses can be reduced if colleges continue to substitute nonrevenue women's teams for nonrevenue men's teams. In either case, the composition of college sports programs will forever be changed. More important, the current profit levels of the NCAA will be threatened by an acceleration toward Title IX compliance.

Finally, all these costs and concerns are compounded by the fact that male athletes in sports dropped to conform with Title IX have begun filing "reverse" gender discrimination lawsuits against universities—these in addition to the gender discrimination lawsuits filed by female athletes!

Historically, when profits are imperiled, the NCAA attempts to extend its cartel reach. What rules will it create to meet these mounting challenges and dilemmas?

Eliminate the Monopsony

Current NCAA policies governing athletic compensation violate the spirit of antitrust laws, but the NCAA claims that these policies are needed to protect the competitive balance and amateur status of collegiate sports. These defenses may no longer be valid, if they ever were.

---

[29]"Mercantile Decisions Cost Non-revenue Sports," *NCAA News,* 26 April 1999; Olson, "Title IX From Outer Space," 50; and "Men Treated Unfairly by Title IX," *NCAA News,* 20 January 1997.

[30]"Quest for Equity has Been Misguided," *NCAA News,* 4 August 1997.

[31]Welch Suggs, "More Women Participate in Intercollegiate Athletics," *Chronicle of Higher Education,* 21 May 1999.

The NCAA has used the competitive balance argument in previous cases involving restrictive practices. This argument failed in the NCAA's attempt to maintain control over college football telecasts. Without control of telecasts, the NCAA claimed that broadcasts would be skewed to the traditional football powers, allowing them to recruit more successfully and thereby increasing the on-field disparity between the traditional powers and their lesser rivals. The Supreme Court rejected this claim and assigned control of telecasts to the individual schools. Empirical evidence suggests that competitive balance has increased since the telecast restrictions have been lifted. The "competitive balance" argument also failed when the NCAA imposed a salary cap on assistant coaches. Without the salary cap, the NCAA claimed that the best coaches would all go to a few schools and destroy competitive balance. But the fact is that with or without a salary cap, the coaches already had an incentive to go to the best sports schools because these programs provide better training and exposure. A change in the compensation structure does not affect competitive balance, but it does change the allocation of resources: A salary cap transfers monies from coaches to the colleges. The same is true for college athletes—compensation restrictions transfer monies from the players to the colleges without affecting competitive balance.

The NCAA's second line of defense is that it provides amateur sports contests. If athletes were paid and collegiate sports commercialized, demand for the NCAA product would decline. This argument is commonly and uncritically accepted, but for most colleges that engage in big-time sports, the game is not now broadly viewed as amateur. Audiences do not view the players as student-athletes; they accept the commercialization of college sports. Billions of dollars in NCAA revenues indicates that acceptance, too. We agree with Noll who states that "[c]ollege sports are already professionalized at universities that house their athletes separately, that advertise themselves as preparatory schools for a career in professional sports, and that fail to graduate nearly all of their players. America wants big-time sports, professional and collegiate, and as long as they do, colleges will supply it. [T]he damage of professionalism has been done, and is probably irreversible even if one wanted to undertake the task of changing the system."[32]

It is also doubtful that colleges would lose a significant portion of their audience and revenue if the athletes were paid. Fan support has been steadily growing even as the sport has become commercialized. Boosters—the biggest supporters of college sports—are typically the ones attempting to pay athletes to recruit them to play on their teams. Perhaps popularity and demand would even accelerate if the hypocrisy tainting the

[32]Noll, "The Economics of Intercollegiate Sports," 208.

amateur status of collegiate sports were removed. Certainly, the Olympics has lost none of its appeal and has generated increased revenues since it abandoned the requirement that its participants be amateurs.

Occasionally, supporters of the NCAA monopsony will argue that underpayment is a temporary phenomenon, with athletes soon to make millions as professionals. The soon-to-be-rich athletes are subsidizing the less fortunate. This claim is invalid on two counts. First, fewer than 1 percent of all collegiate athletes actually make it to the professional ranks. Second, collegiate athletes typically come from poorer households than the average college student; often they come from quite disadvantaged backgrounds. Thus, the NCAA not only blocks the functioning of this labor market, it does so in a regressive way that hurts the poorer students the most. The question remains, how should athletes be paid? Several alternatives have been suggested.

The players could unionize. A fundamental factor in the NCAA's current power is that colleges do not recognize athletes as employees. If athletes were viewed as employees, then they would be eligible to unionize and bargain for pay. They would also be eligible for workers' compensation for injuries sustained in practice and play. This arrangement would be similar to that used in the four major professional sports, where an alliance of teams bargains with a union of players to establish rules and compensation packages. Teaching assistants at many colleges are currently fighting for employment status and, if they are successful, athletes might soon follow.

A compensation fund could be set up for each college, with limits determined by an estimation of monopsony rents. Colleges could then distribute the funds among the players as they saw fit: Colleges could pay athletes a signing bonus to enroll, pay them rewards for competitive performance, or establish trust funds.[33] To emphasize the concept of student-athlete, athlete compensation could be linked to graduation: If athletes do not graduate, they would forego a portion of their agreed-upon remuneration.

Player compensation does have its side effects. If a college currently uses profits from its basketball and football programs to subsidize nonrevenue sports, the nonrevenue programs may suffer unless they can obtain financial support from the college or other sources. Many colleges might drop some sports due to the diminished profits. These financial difficulties are exacerbated by Title IX requirements for women's collegiate athletic programs. The basic issue is whether athletes in profitable sports should bear the cost of supporting less profitable programs. An increase in the cost of athletic talent might also precipitate a significant decline

[33] Ibid., 209.

in the salaries of coaches. However, fans might get to view higher quality collegiate sporting contests as the top athletes continue to play college sports rather than jumping early to professional leagues. Most important, collegiate athletes would earn a competitive salary in exchange for their services.

VI. CONCLUSION

The NCAA and its member schools have created a college sports cartel that pays its most important resources, the athletes, far below what they would earn in a competitive market. The NCAA operates behind a veil of amateurism as its members generate revenues comparable to professional sports, practice and play in facilities that rival those found in professional sports, and pay their top coaches salaries comparable to those paid to coaches of professional teams. Only the student-athletes are bound to amateur status and restricted in their ability to share in the bounty generated by their play.

However, as the wealth of the cartel increases, its strength may be eroding. A recent string of losing court battles is pulling down the veil of amateurism. Gender equity requirements are causing serious profit allocation difficulties. The specter of competing leagues portends the possible necessity of bidding competitively for human resources. Employee rights may soon be granted to athletes. Meanwhile, points of conflict multiply with the ever-increasing size and diversity of NCAA membership. The cartel has responded to threats in the past by expanding its reach—in membership as well as in its private rules and regulations—but now it is beginning to crack. How will it respond to the new challenges it confronts?

Suggested Readings

Bennett, R., and J. Fizel. "Telecast Deregulation and Competitive Balance: Regarding NCAA Division I Football." *American Journal of Economics and Sociology* 54, no. 2 (1995): 183–200.

Borland, M.; B. Goff; and R. Pulsinelli. "College Athletics: Financial Burden or Boom?" In *Advances in the Economics of Sport,* edited by G. Scully, vol. 1, 215–235 (Greenwich, CT: JAI Press, Inc., 1992).

Brown, R. "Measuring Cartel Rents in the College Basketball Recruitment Market." *Applied Economics* 26 (1994): 27–34.

——. "An Estimate of the Rent Generated by a Premium College Football Player." *Economic Inquiry* 31 (1993): 671–684.

Byers, W. *Unsportsmanlike Conduct: Exploiting College Athletes* (Ann Arbor: University of Michigan Press, 1985).

Fizel, J. "Free Agency and Competitive Balance." In *Stee-rike Four! What's Wrong with the Business of Baseball?,* edited by D.R. Marburger, 61–72 (Westport, CT: Praeger Publishers, 1997).

Fizel, J., and R. Bennett. "Telecasts and Recruiting in NCAA Division I Football: The Impact of Altered Property

Rights." *Journal of Sport Management* 10, no. 4 (1996): 359–372.

Fizel, J., and T. Smaby. "Participation in Collegiate Athletics and Student Grade Point Averages." In *Sports Economics: Current Research,* edited by J. Fizel, E. Gustafson, and L. Hadley, 161–171 (Westport, CT: Praeger Publishers, 1999).

Fleisher, A., B. Goff, and R. Tollison. *The National Collegiate Athletic Association: A Study in Cartel Behavior* (Chicago: University of Chicago Press, 1992).

Fort, R., and J. Quirk. "The College Football Industry." In *Sports Economics: Current Research,* edited by J. Fizel, E. Gustafson, and L. Hadley, 11–26 (Westport, CT: Praeger Publishers, 1999).

———. "Introducing a Competitive Economic Environment into Professional Sports." In *Advances in the Economics of Sports,* edited by W. Hendricks, vol. 2, 3–26 (Greenwich, CT: JAI Press, Inc., 1997).

Koch, J. "The Intercollegiate Athletics Industry." In *The Structure of American Industry,* edited by Walter Adams, 325–346 (New York: Macmillan Publishing Co., 1982).

Noll, R. "The Economics of Intercollegiate Sports." In *Rethinking College Athletics,* edited by J. Andre and D. James,197–209 (Philadelphia: Temple University Press, 1991).

Sperber, M. *College Sports, Inc.* (New York: Henry Holt, 1990).

CHAPTER 13

Public Policy in a Free-Enterprise Economy

—JAMES W. BROCK

Controlling power in a free society and guarding against its abuse are at the core of the American political-economic experience. Indeed, the American nation was forged from the colonists' protest against the arbitrary power of the British Crown.

Once liberated, the nation's founders understood that in creating a governance structure for a free society, they must provide for a government strong enough to prevent individuals from infringing on the liberties of one another. At the same time, they understood that additional safeguards were required in order to prevent government itself from being transformed into an instrument for oppressing the citizenry. Throughout their deliberations, the founders displayed a deeply rooted, dyspeptic view of human nature. They recognized (as Thomas Burke put it in 1777) that "power of all kinds has an irresistible propensity to increase a desire for itself"; that "power will sometime or other be abused unless men are well watched, and checked by something they cannot remove when they please"; and that the "root of the evil is deep in human nature."

Their solution for resolving this dilemma was incorporated in the Constitution and predicated on two transcending principles: First, that it is the *structure* of government, not the personal preferences and predilections of those who govern, that is of utmost importance; and, second, in Jefferson's words, that "it is not by the consolidation or concentration of powers, but by their distribution, that good government is effected." The master plan was to construct a system of checks and balances—a Newtonian mechanism of countervailing powers—operating harmoniously in mutual frustration. The goal was to prevent what the founders considered the ultimate evil: the concentration of power and the abuses that flow from it. "It may be a reflection on human nature that such devices should be necessary to control the abuses of government," James Madison reflected in *Federalist Paper 51,* "But what is government itself, but the greatest of all reflections on human nature? If men were angels, no government would be necessary. If angels were to govern men, neither external nor internal controls on government would be necessary. In framing a government which is to be administered by men over men, the great difficulty lies in this: you must first enable the government to control the governed; and in the next place oblige it to control itself. A dependence on the people is, no doubt, the primary control on the government; but experience has taught mankind the necessity of auxiliary precautions."

I. THE AMERICAN ANTITRUST TRADITION

Subsequent events, however, demonstrated that in a free society the power problem is not confined to the political realm alone. A century after the Constitution was ratified, during the post-Civil War era, an explosion of pools, trusts, cartels and monopolies revealed the need to control economic as well as political power. In order to guard against excessive private, as well as governmental, concentrations of power, Americans perceived the necessity of preventing "autocrats of trade" from ensnaring the people in a new kind of feudalism. "If we will not endure a king as a political power," Ohio's Republican Senator John Sherman warned, "we should not endure a king over the production, transportation, and sale of any of the necessaries of life." Unless Congress addressed the private economic power problem, he urged, there would "be a trust for every production and a master to fix the price for every necessity of life."[1]

In theory, Adam Smith had shown how the competitive marketplace would regulate and neutralize economic power—how it would disperse economic decision-making power in the hands of a multitude of rivals, how it would compel each to perform well in the public interest, and how it thus would transform the private vice of self-interest into the public virtue of good economic performance. In theory, Adam Smith had demonstrated how the competitive market system would channel private economic decision making into socially beneficial outlets—how it would compel innovation, technological advance, productivity, and efficiency in allocating resources in accordance with society's preferences. In theory, he showed how the competitive market system would maintain economic freedom and opportunity for all, while rendering private economic decision making accountable to the public.

In reality, however, the corporate combination and trust movement of late nineteenth-century America demonstrated that as a system of governance, the competitive market is neither self-perpetuating nor an immutable artifact of nature. It showed that without strictly enforced rules of the game, the competitive market can be eroded and subverted, through agreements not to compete as well as through mergers, combinations, and monopolization by dominant firms.

---

[1]Quoted in Hans B. Thorelli, *The Federal Antitrust Policy: Origination of an American Tradition* (Baltimore: Johns Hopkins University Press, 1955), 180.

Maintaining competition as the prime regulator of America's economic affairs is the central objective of the antitrust laws. Like the Constitution, the American antitrust laws provide for a structure of governance—a social blueprint for organizing economic decision making and for guarding against its abuse. Like the Constitution, the antitrust laws aim to disperse power into many hands rather than tolerating its concentration in the hands of a few. Just as the purpose of the Constitution is to prevent any political "faction" from monopolizing the coercive power of the state, so the basic objective of the antitrust laws is to prevent private organizations from monopolizing economic decision making in a free society.

The Sherman Antitrust Act, the nation's first antitrust law, enacted in 1890, outlaws two major types of interference with competitive free enterprise: cartels and monopolization. Section 1 of the Sherman Act, dealing with cartels, states: "Every contract, combination . . . or conspiracy, in restraint of trade or commerce among the several States, or with foreign nations, is hereby declared illegal." As interpreted by the courts, this renders it unlawful for businesses to engage in such collusive action as agreeing to fix prices, agreeing to restrict output or productive capacity, agreeing to divide markets or allocate customers, or agreeing to exclude competitors by systematic resort to oppressive tactics and discriminatory practices—in short, it enjoins all collective actions by competitors aimed at controlling the market and short-circuiting its regulatory discipline.

Section 2 of the Sherman Act, which addresses structural concentrations of power, provides that "every person who shall monopolize or attempt to monopolize, or combine or conspire to monopolize any part of the trade or commerce among the several States, or with foreign nations, shall be deemed guilty . . . and . . . punished." Section 2 makes it unlawful for firms to obtain a stranglehold on the market, either by forcing rivals out of business or by absorbing them. It prohibits a single firm (or group of firms acting jointly) from dominating an industry or market. Positively stated, Section 2 encourages a decentralized economic structure in which there is a sufficient number of independent rivals to ensure effective market competition.

The Sherman Act's provisions are general, perhaps even vague, and essentially negative. Directed primarily against *existing* dominant firms and *existing* trade restraints, the Sherman Act proved incapable of addressing specific practices that could be employed to realize the proscribed results. Armed with the power to dissolve existing monopolies, the enforcement authorities could not, under the Sherman Act, attack the growth of monopoly in advance and prior to its realization. For this reason, Congress passed supplementary legislation in 1914 in order "to arrest the creation of trusts, conspiracies and monopolies in their incipiency and before consummation." In the Federal Trade Commission Act of

FIGURE 13-1 The Antitrust Challenge

Source: Thurman W. Arnold, *Cartels or Free Enterprise?* Public Affairs Pamphlet 103, 1945. Reproduced by courtesy of Public Affairs Commission, Inc.

1914, Congress established an independent regulatory commission to police the economic field against "all unfair methods of competition," as well as to undertake expert studies of conditions of competition and monopoly in the American economy. In the Clayton Act of the same year, Congress targeted four specific practices which experience had shown to be favorite means for creating monopoly positions: (1) price discrimination (that is, cutthroat competition and predatory price cutting); (2) tying contracts and exclusive dealership agreements; (3) mergers and acquisitions; and (4) interlocking boards of directors among rival firms. These practices were declared unlawful, not in and of themselves, but where their effect might be to substantially lessen competition or tend to create a monopoly. Price discrimination, for example, would be illegal only if used as a systematic device for destroying competition, as it was in the hands of the Standard Oil and American Tobacco trusts. Similarly, the Clayton Act's merger provisions (as amended in 1950 by the Celler-Kefauver Act) prohibit any corporate merger and acquisition whose effect may be to substantially lessen competition or tend to create a monopoly. The emphasis in the Clayton Act is on preventing anticompetitive problems from occurring in the first place, rather than struggling to remedy them after they already are entrenched.

The essence of American antitrust policy was perhaps most cogently articulated by Judge Charles Wyzanski:

> Concentrations of power, no matter how beneficently they appear to have acted, nor what advantages they seem to possess, are inherently dangerous. Their good behavior in the past may not be continued; and if their strength were hereafter grasped by presumptuous hands, there would be no automatic check and balance from equal forces in the industrial market. And in the absence of this protective mechanism, the demand for public regulation, public ownership, or other drastic measures would become irresistible in time of crisis. Dispersal of private economic power is thus one of the ways to preserve the system of private enterprise. . . . [Moreover,] well as a monopoly may have behaved in the moral sense, its economic performance is inevitably suspect. The very absence of strong competitors implies that there cannot be an objective measuring rod of the monopolist's excellence. . . . What appears to the outsider to be a sensible, prudent, nay even a progressive policy of the monopolist, may in fact reflect a lower scale of adventurousness and less intelligent risk-taking than would be the case if the enterprise were forced to respond to a stronger industrial challenge. . . .

Progress, he concluded, "may indeed be in inverse proportion to economic power; for creativity in business as in other areas, is best nourished by multiple centers of activity, each following its unique pattern and developing its own esprit de corps to respond to the challenge of competition."[2]

II. ANTITRUST POLICY UNDER FIRE

Over the years, these precepts periodically have been attacked from both ends of the political-economic spectrum.

---

[2]*United States* v. *United Shoe Machinery Corp.*, 110 F. Supp 295 (1953), affirmed per curiam, 347 U.S. 521 (1954).

The Challenge from the Left

On the left, an antitrust regime of competition enforced by law has long been dismissed as a counterproductive anachronism; instead, concentration and market dominance are considered the inevitable products of industrial advance, and more direct social control, typically involving some form of bargaining among labor, industry, and government, is advocated as the preferred policy.

This was true of the trust and consolidation wave at the turn of the century. Pioneer labor leader Samuel Gompers, for example, dismissed antitrust policy (the early enforcement of which had been directed against a number of labor unions for restraining trade in labor markets): "We have seen those who know little of statecraft and less of economics urge the adoption of laws to 'regulate' interstate commerce, 'prevent' combinations and trusts," he charged, but the state "is not capable of preventing the legitimate development or natural concentration of industry."[3] Strong unions, he believed, would neutralize the power of the trusts, while enabling labor to bargain for a fairer share of the economic gains generated by industrial combines. Herbert Croly, a leading progressive spokesman of the day, was certain that monopolistic trusts marked "an important step in the direction of the better organization of industry and commerce," and he advocated scrapping the Sherman Antitrust Act in favor of a new national policy aimed at nurturing "a more positive mode of action and more edifying habit of thought" among corporation and labor leaders.[4] Socialists, meanwhile, declared with Biblical certitude that we "have left the Egypt of competition . . . and are now wandering in the desert of monopoly, which we must pass through to reach the promised land of universal co-operation."[5]

Criticism of antitrust policy from the left re-emerged during the 1930s, and became the touchstone for the National Industrial Recovery Act of 1933. The NRA was enacted in order to implement a new economic regime of "constructive cooperation" which, it was believed, would lift the country from the depths of the Great Depression: Business would get self-government, relief from "destructive" competition, and immunity from the antitrust laws. Labor leaders saw the NRA as ushering in the kind of planning and industrial self-government they had long advocated, including the right to organize and collectively bargain. For progressive government officials such as Rexford Tugwell, the NRA demonstrated

---

[3]Quoted in Joseph Dorfman, *The Economic Mind in American Civilization,* vol. 3 (New York: Viking Press, 1949), 217.

[4]Herbert Croly, *The Promise of American Life,* Harvard Library ed.(Cambridge: Harvard University Press, 1965), 358–59, 397.

[5]Quoted in Jack Blicksilver, *Defenders and Defense of Big Business in the United States,* 1880–1900 (New York: Garland, 1985), p. 68.

that "cooperation and not conflict" was a superior principle for restoring confidence and getting the economy moving again.[6] These objectives, many New Dealers believed, could be achieved only by scrapping competition and replacing it with a system of planning along individual industry lines—sectoral planning jointly undertaken by business and labor, and overseen by government in the public interest.

In the 1980s, the anemic performance of the U.S. economy, coupled with the specter of a world-triumphant "Japan, Inc.," triggered yet another resurgence of cooperation and coalitionism on the left—under the rubric of "industrial policy"—as an alternative to America's antitrust tradition. Pointing to the flood of foreign imports into American markets, slumping U.S. productivity and savings, high inflation, mass layoffs and stagnating living standards, industrial policy advocates charged "What used to work won't work. For the world has changed."[7] The only viable course, they contended, lay in a consciously constructed, national "industrial policy" comprising tripartite planning, negotiation, and compromise among management, labor, and government. They pointed to postwar economic "miracles" in Japan and other East Asian nations as proof of what such cooperation could achieve. And they dismissed traditional antitrust concerns about disproportionate economic size and power as outmoded and destructive in a new global age. They "don't care whether General Motors is the only car manufacturing company. It's still in a competitive fight for its life with the Japanese and Germans. And it doesn't make sense to hamstring General Motors or anybody else with antitrust laws since they must operate in an international competitive environment. . . ."[8]

As a guide for national economic policy, however, the left's infatuation with "cooperationism" and organizational giantism suffers from a number of congenital defects.

The first drawback is the inevitable tendency toward the coalescence of power among organized groups, which are predisposed to protect their parochial private interests rather than promote the well-being of society. Advocates of "coalition capitalism" presume that powerful private groups will act in ways, and toward ends, that will promote good economic performance. But such power blocs may instead recognize their mutual interest in preserving the status quo, opting to aggrandize their own power and influence at the public's expense.

---

[6]See Ellis W. Hawley, *The New Deal and the Problem of Monopoly* (Princeton, NJ: Princeton University Press, 1966), 19–33.

[7]House Subcommittee on Economic Stabilization, *Hearings: Industrial Policy, Part 1,* 98th Cong., 1st sess., 1983, 173.

[8]Lester C. Thurow, "Abolish the Antitrust Laws," *Dun's Review,* February 1981, 72. See also Thurow, *The Zero-Sum Solution* (New York: Simon & Schuster, 1985).

This concern is not idle conjecture. The consequences of the National Recovery Administration (NRA), for example, were scarcely what its proponents promised: The NRA enabled business groups to cartelize industries and labor groups to raise wages, while government rubber-stamped their self-serving activities. In 1934, at the conclusion of congressional hearings on the NRA, Senator Gerald P. Nye (Republican, North Dakota) was "forced to the conclusion that the power of monopoly has been greatly increased during the stay of the NRA; that invitation to monopoly in the United States is greater than ever before. In view of what amounts to suspension of the antitrust laws, the small independent producers, the small business man generally, whether buyer from, competitor of, or seller to large monopolized industries, and the great mass of ultimate consumers, are seemingly without protection other than that given by the NRA. And the NRA is not giving this protection. On the contrary, it has strengthened, not weakened, the power of monopoly."[9]

The nuclear electric power debacle provides a more modern example of the problem.[10] Here is a field where government and industry cooperated for decades to promote what both considered to be a "sunrise" technology. Tens of billions of dollars were expended in government subsidies for research and production of nuclear power plants, equipment, and fuels which, the industry's advocates believed, would produce electricity "too cheap to meter." Nuclear power provided cost-plus revenues for the monopoly utility firms which commissioned the plants. It was a gravy train for the labor unions and construction trades that built the plants, dismantled them when they required redesigning, and then rebuilt them, drawing their pay all the while. But the consequences for the country have been less than inspiring: Billions of dollars of abandoned nuclear power plants; a steadily mounting bounty of highly radioactive wastes for which no acceptable method of disposal has been devised; and an uneconomical source of electricity whose "stranded" costs pose a daunting obstacle to current efforts to interject competition into this traditionally monopolized field.[11]

Defense weapons procurement provides another example of coalescing power in action:[12] Here, too, has been an intimate degree of cooperation among government, industry and labor—so close, in fact, that company executives and Pentagon officials regularly exchange jobs through a well-lubricated "revolving door." But with what consequences

---

[9]Quoted in Leverett S. Lyon et al., *The National Recovery Administration: An Analysis and Appraisal* (Washington: Brookings Institution, 1935), 709; for an equally critical appraisal, see Clair Wilcox, *Public Policies Toward Business* (Homewood, IL: Irwin, 1971), 680.

[10]For details and sources, see Walter Adams and James W. Brock, *The Bigness Complex* (New York: Pantheon, 1987), chapter 21.

[11]See Barnaby J. Feder, "The Nuclear Power Puzzle," *New York Times,* 3 January 1997, C1.

[12]For a general background, see Adams and Brock, *The Bigness Complex,* chapter 24.

for the public that pays the bills? Mind-boggling cost overruns; weapons that fail to deliver contracted-for performance levels; and a bonanza of pork-barrel projects for constituents back home.[13]

In professional sports, mutually agreeable accomodation between owners and players has hardly protected the public or fans from the brazen kind of blackmail which the "sports-industrial" complex routinely inflicts on communities in extracting astronomical subsidies, stadiums, and salaries.[14]

Antitrust critics on the left also harbor a misplaced faith in the virtues of corporate giantism and megamergers.

General Motors has long ranked as the world's largest automobile producer and, indeed, as the world's very largest industrial concern: Its annual sales revenues exceed the gross national product of all but a handful of nations. Yet, GM suffers from a seemingly intractable case of bureaucratic sclerosis. Its unit costs are the highest in the industry, while its productivity and efficiency are the lowest: "Size and complexity have a price," *Fortune* observes, "and GM pays double or triple the going rate"[15]—hardly a stirring testimonial to the economic virtues of corporate bigness.

In steel, a century of merger-induced bigness did not produce paragons of efficiency or technological innovativeness. Instead, America's steel giants—and the steelworkers' union—became backward, hide-bound bureaucracies that lost sales, market shares, and hundreds of thousands of jobs when confronted, first by competition from abroad, and later, by small U.S. "mini-mills"—state-of-the-art operators who have revolutionized steel production, and have captured one product market after another from such allegedly "invincible" foreign producers as "Japan, Inc.," and South Korea. Meanwhile, Big Steel cooperates with Big Labor to lobby government for trade restraints that inflate American steel prices, handicap America's steel-using firms and industries, and impose a net *loss* of jobs in the U.S. economy generally.

In transportation, the megamerger of the Union Pacific and Southern Pacific railroads in 1996 produced a continental-sized fiasco for the nation's shippers. "For nearly a year, freight train service west of the Mississippi River has been all but derailed by the merger of the Union Pacific and Southern Pacific railroads," *Fortune* reports. "Billions of dollars worth of freight shipments, supposed to arrive in 3 or 4 days, have been taking 30 days, 45 days."[16] Little wonder that industrial shippers are

---

[13]See, for example, Kevin Sack, "Taking turns, G.O.P. Takes Care of South," *New York Times,* 18 November 1997, 1.

[14]Generally, see James Quirk and Rodney Fort, *Hard Ball: The Abuse of Power in Pro Team Sports* (Princeton, NJ: Princeton University Press, 1999).

[15]Alex Taylor, "GM's $11,000,000,000 Turnaround," *Fortune,* 17 October 1994, 66.

[16]Brian O'Reilly, "The Wreck of the Union Pacific," *Fortune,* 30 March 1998, 94, 96.

outraged by the prospect of the continuing consolidation among the continent's rail giants.[17]

Similar consequences are evident abroad, where merger-induced gigantism failed to provide salvation for West European nations (especially Britain and France), which became enthralled in the late 1950s with the bigness mystique. The putative "national champions" that were merged together to dominate their national industries (including British Leyland in automobiles, British Steel, and Bull in French computers) became lame ducks in the 1970s and 1980s. After suffering billions of dollars in losses, they became dependent on financial life support from their home governments in order to forestall their collapse. According to analysts Paul Geroski and Alexis Jacquemin, the "new super firms did not give rise to a new competitive efficiency in Europe. Indeed, by creating a group of firms with sufficient market power to be considerably sheltered from the forces of market selection, the policy may have left Europe with a population of sleepy industrial giants who were ill-equipped to meet the challenge of the 1970s and 1980s."[18]

Advocates of coalitionism may also have neglected an important strength of Japan's postwar economic "miracle," while celebrating what the recent East Asian meltdown reveals to be a key weakness of "crony capitalism" founded on incestuous industry-banking-government relationships.

The strength of Japan's postwar performance may be due in important part to a competitive domestic market structure put into place by American occupational authorities during the years immediately following World War II. Under the leadership of General Douglas McArthur, a massive deconcentration program was implemented: Sixteen of Japan's largest holding companies were dissolved outright; twenty-six were dissolved and reorganized; eleven were reorganized with dissolution; and another nineteen firms with "excessive concentration" were dismembered. The two largest Japanese holding companies, Mitsui and Mitsubishi, were divided into hundreds of successor firms, while an accompanying divestiture program forced the sale of possibly half the 1945 paid-in value of all Japanese corporate securities.[19]

Later, during the 1950s and 1960s, concentration trends in Japan and the United States diverged, with average market concentration drifting downward in Japan but rising in the United States. At the same time,

---

[17]Daniel Machalaba and Steven Lipin, "Burlington Northern Agrees to Merger," *Wall Street Journal,* 20 December 1999, A3.

[18]Paul A. Geroski and Alexis Jacquemin, "Industrial Change, Barriers to Mobility, and European Industrial Policy," *Economic Policy,* November 1985, 175; also see Walter Adams and James W. Brock, "The Bigness Mystique and the Merger Policy Debate: An International Perspective," *Northwestern Journal of International Law & Business,* Spring 1988, 1.

[19]Adams and Brock, "The Bigness Mystique," 36–43.

Japanese industrialists strenuously resisted government efforts to promote oligopoly giantism by limiting major industries to a few favored "national champions." In automobiles, for example, Honda and other new entrants overcame government efforts to limit the field to the two existing producers, while in electronics, Sony overcame Ministry of International Trade and Industry (MITI) efforts to stifle it by denying the then-unknown company's request to purchase transistor production rights from Western Electric.[20] More generally, George Gilder points out that "in every one of the industries in which the Japanese did prevail, they generated *more* companies and *more* intense domestic competition than the United States." He observes that it was entrenched American oligopolies in consumer electronics, such as RCA, Zenith, and General Electric, that gave up the color-television industry to the more entrepreneurial Japanese, while the highly concentrated, vastly integrated U.S. auto firms succumbed to the more fragmented, more specialized, more entrepreneurial Japanese auto makers.[21]

Meanwhile, systems of cross-corporate and bank stockholdings ("keiretsu")—bolstered by government support—in the 1990s have been revealed as a trap: In Japan, groups of interconnected companies grew dependent on each other for subsidies and financial bailouts, while their reliance on assured sales to corporate family members may have rendered them complacent and vulnerable to competition from abroad.[22] Likewise, in South Korea, huge conglomerates of firms ("chaebol") were supported by the government as engines of economic growth. "But in the process the cosy links between the chaebol's bosses and the country's politicians and bureaucrats fostered corruption that still needs to be cleaned up. As they grew, the conglomerates became ever harder to challenge. . . . Banks fear that if they do not keep handing out cash to their biggest creditors, they themselves may be dragged down too."[23]

At bottom, the Achilles heel of coalitionism, "industrial policy," and other variants of economic syndicalist schemes is the problem of power and interest-group politics. As Henry C. Simons pointed out long ago, "Bargaining organizations will contest over the division of the swag, but we commonly overlook the fact that they have large common interests as against the community and that every increase of monopoly power on one side serves to strengthen and implement it on the other." To encourage such coalescing power, Simons warned, would be to "drift rapidly into political organization along functional, occupational lines—into a

[20]Christopher Wood, *The End of Japan Inc.* (New York: Simon & Schuster, 1994), 77.

[21]George Gilder, *Microcosm* (New York: Simon & Schuster, 1989), 341 (emphasis in original).

[22]"Fall of a Keiretsu: How Giant Mitsubishi Group Lost Its Way," *Business Week,* 15 March 1999, 90.

[23]Cutting Down the Chaebol," *Economist,* 14 November 1998, 18.

miscellany of specialized collectivisms, organized to take income away from one another and incapable of acting in their own common interest or in a manner compatible with general prosperity."[24]

The Challenge from the Right

On the right of the political spectrum, economic Darwinists recurrently have deprecated America's traditional antitrust philosophy, and urged that it be scrapped and replaced by a policy of untrammeled laissez-faire. This, they contend, would enhance the nation's economic performance by unleashing the benefits of natural selection of the most economically fit.

Concentration of economic control in the trusts, William Graham Sumner declared at the turn of the century, "is indispensible to the successful execution of the tasks which devolve upon society in our time. . . . The concentration of power (wealth), more dominant control, intenser discipline, and stricter methods are but modes of securing more perfect integration. When we perceive this we see that the concentration of wealth is but one feature of a grand step in societal evolution." Monopolists, he believed, are "the naturally selected agents of society for certain work. They get high wages and live in luxury, but the bargain is a good one for society."[25] John D. Rockefeller, the father of the Standard Oil trust, put it in horticultural terms: "The growth of a large business is merely a survival of the fittest. The American Beauty rose can be produced in the splendor and fragrance which bring cheer to its beholder only by sacrificing the early buds which grow up around it. This is not an evil tendency in business. It is merely the working-out of a law of nature and a law of God."[26]

The leading modern-day exponent of this view, Robert Bork, sees a striking analogy between a free-market system and Darwinian evolution: "The familiarity of that parallel, and the overbroad inferences sometimes drawn from it, should not blind us to its important truths. The environment to which the business firm must adapt is defined, ultimately, by social wants and the social costs of meeting them. The firm that adapts to the environment better than its rivals tends to expand. The less successful firm tends to contract—perhaps, eventually, to become extinct." There is little justification, Bork argues, to interfere with the "natural" operation of a free-market system. Laissez-faire, he believes, can be trusted to produce optimal results. Private monopoly and market power should be of no social concern because neither has any significant durability: "A mar-

---

[24]Henry C. Simons, *Economic Policy for a Free Society* (Chicago: University of Chicago Press, 1948), 119, 219.

[25]William Graham Sumner, "The Concentration of Wealth: Its Economic Justification," in *On Liberty, Society, and Politics: The Essential Essays of William Graham Sumner* ed. Robert C. Bannister (Indianapolis: Liberty Fund, 1992), 149–150, 155.

[26]Quoted in Richard Hofstadter, *Social Darwinism in American Thought,* rev. ed. (Boston: Beacon Press, 1955), 45.

ket position that creates output restriction and higher prices will always be eroded if it is not based upon superior efficiency."[27] Of course, if it is based on superior efficiency, Bork would say, it serves the best interest of society and should therefore be immune from antitrust attack.

In this view, a firm achieves market power or giant size because of superior economic performance, and it would be foolish for public policy to punish the superior firm for its success. The winner of the race deserves the prize. Prosecuting industrial size, the economic Darwinists contend, only diminishes consumer welfare and destroys incentives to excel.

Alas, this doctrine, too, suffers from a number of fatal defects.

It is based on a *post hoc ergo propter hoc* fallacy: The mere existence of a monopolist, oligopolist, or giant firm proves that it must have achieved its position solely because of superior performance. This is no more than an assertion—devoid, more often than not, of any empirical substantiation.

Although economic Darwinism makes superior economic performance the centerpiece of its policy position, its advocates concede that such economic performance is difficult, if not impossible, to measure scientifically. Judge Bork, for example, admits that "the real objection to performance tests and efficiency defenses in antitrust law is that they are spurious. They cannot measure the factors relevant to consumer welfare, so that after the economic extravaganza was completed we should know no more than before it began."[28] Bork seems to despair about the possibility of measuring performance, even though he posits superior performance as the ultimate goal of economic policy.

Economic Darwinism is concerned primarily with static, managerial efficiency rather than with dynamic social efficiency. It thus falls victim to the sin of suboptimization: Perhaps the relevant policy question is not whether Ford Motor Company produces three-and-a-half ton, gas-guzzling sport utility behemoths at the least average cost, but whether it should be producing such vehicles at all. The relevant policy question is not whether Microsoft writes its Windows operating software efficiently, but whether other, fundamentally different operating systems would be the preferred choice of computer users if software rivals were free from Microsoft's monopoly control to innovate and compete.

Economic Darwinism assumes that any firm which no longer delivers superior performance will automatically be displaced by newcomers. This neglects the ability of powerful established firms to build private storm shelters—or to lobby government to build public storm shelters for them—in order to shield themselves from the Schumpeterian gales of creative destruction. It ignores the difference between the legal freedom

[27] Robert H. Bork, *The Antitrust Paradox* (New York: Basic Books, 1978), 118, 133.
[28] Ibid., 124.

of entry and the economic realities deterring the entry of potential newcomers into concentrated fields. The American airline industry provides a case in point: Having deregulated the field in order to enable competition to function, an extremist laissez-faire policy permitted merger-mania and "alliances" to transform the industry into a tight-knit oligopoly of giants that dominates hubs across the country, and whose abuses have precipitated cries for passenger "bills of rights" in Congress.

Proponents of laissez-faire overestimate the disciplining effect of international competition in the "new" global market. They underestimate the capacity of powerful domestic firms, once dominant, to join with their international rivals to subvert foreign competition at home and abroad.

Since 1992, for example, the Justice Department has uncovered and prosecuted a plethora of global cartels, collecting more in fines than the combined amount collected throughout the Antitrust Division's century-old history. These include Swiss giant Roche ($500 million fine), Germany's BASF ($225 million fine), SGL Carbon ($135 million fine), American agri-giant Archer Daniels Midland ($100 million fine), and Japan's Takeda Chemical Ltd. ($72 million fine). Recent Justice Department prosecutions of the world's dominant producers of food additives, food preservatives, and vitamins vividly reveal the capacity of international rivals to fix world prices, allocate global market shares, and eliminate international competition. In the case of the $5 billion global vitamin business, for example, top executives from around the world gathered regularly at clandestine meetings to rig prices and allocate market shares for ingredients contained in products in every refrigerator and kitchen cabinet, from milk and orange juice to breakfast cereals, bread, butter, and meats. In the case of the global citric-acid cartel, the president of the Archer Daniels Midland Company was recorded on videotape assuring his foreign conspirators that "[o]ur competitors are our friends and our customers are our enemies."[29]

Sir Alfred Mond, organizer of the British chemical combine Imperial Chemical Industries, long ago elucidated the global nature of the monopoly problem: "The old idea of the heads of great businesses meeting each other with scowls and shaking each other's fists in each other's faces and . . . trying to destroy each other's business may be very good on the films, but it does not accord with any given facts."[30]

Economic Darwinists decry counterproductive government policies which, they say, are the prime evil to be avoided. But this ignores the fact that in a democracy, government does not operate in a vacuum, and that

---

[29]Quoted in Kurt Eichenwald, "U.S. Wins Another Round in Fight Against Additive Cartel," *New York Times,* 30 January 1997, C1.

[30]Quoted in George Stocking and Myron Watkins, *Cartels in Action* (New York: Twentieth Century Fund, 1946), 429.

the anticompetitive government policies they condemn are typically the product of lobbying by powerful economic groups bent on manipulating the state. It ignores the fact that in a representative democracy, disproportionate economic size entails disproportionate influence in the political arena, as corporate giants mobilize the vast political resources at their command—executives and labor unions, suppliers and subcontractors, governors and mayors, senators and representatives, Republicans and Democrats—in their efforts to pervert public policy for their private antisocial ends.[31] It fails to recognize that when an American baron of bananas contributes millions of dollars to political campaigns, it might be for something other than good government, and that bananas might, in response, be annointed by the President's Special Trade Representative as constituting a "vital national interest"!

Thus, corporate bigness complexes can lobby government for import restraints to immunize them from foreign competition at exorbitant expense to the economy. They can obtain billions of dollars in tax favors, tax loopholes, and subsidized government loans by whipsawing states and communities against one another in bidding wars for plants and facilities. They are accorded special treatment because, as Federal Reserve Bank Chairman Alan Greenspan observes of merger-induced megabanks, they are "entities that create the potential for unusually large system risks in the national and international economy should they fail."[32] If they are big enough and incompetent enough, corporate giants can achieve the ultimate perversion of private enterprise—government bailouts—because they are considered to be too big to be allowed to fail. As Lockheed, Chrysler, and Long Term Capital Management Company show, large firms can survive, not because they are better, but because they are bigger—not because they are fitter, but because they are fatter.

Because they tolerate private economic size and power while ignoring its political ramifications, the economic Darwinists are like Henry David Thoreau's neighbors who, he observed, "invite the devil in at every angle and then prate about the garden of Eden and the fall of man."

Economic Darwinism fails to make the critical distinction between individual freedom and a free economic *system.* As Jeremy Bentham recognized long ago, it is not enough to shout "Laissez-faire!" and oppose all government intervention: "To say that a law is contrary to natural liberty is simply to say that it is a law: for every law is established at the expense of liberty—the liberty of Peter at the expense of the liberty of Paul."[33] If

---

[31]For a debate on this important point, see Walter Adams and James W. Brock, *Antitrust Economics on Trial: A Dialogue on the New Laissez-Faire* (Princeton, NJ: Princeton University Press, 1991), 117–127.

[32]*The Evolution of Bank Supervision,* Remarks by Alan Greenspan, American Bankers Association, Phoenix, AZ, 11 October 1999.

[33]J. Bowring, ed., *The Works of Jeremy Bentham* vol. 3 (Edinburgh: W. Tait, 1843), 185.

individual rights were absolute and unlimited, they would, as Thomas Hobbes recognized 4 centuries ago, mean license to commit the grossest abuses against society, including destroying the freedoms of others. As Lord Robbins emphasized, public policy must "distinguish between [government] interventions that destroy the need for intervention and interventions that tend to perpetuate it." Viewed in this light, the Darwinist admonition not to penalize the winner of the race is irrelevant to public policy purposes. Rather, the relevant problem is how to reward the winner without including in its trophy the right to impose disabling handicaps on putative competitors, or the power to determine the rules by which future races shall be run, or the discretion to eliminate the institution of racing altogether.

Finally, economic Darwinism fails to appreciate the link between industrial structure and market behavior and the ultimate consequences for economic performance. As John Bates Clark warned 80 years ago,

> In our worship of the survival of the fit under free natural selection we are sometimes in danger of forgetting that the conditions of the struggle fix the kind of fitness that shall come out of it; that survival in the prize ring means fitness for pugilism, not for bricklaying nor philanthropy; that survival in predatory competition is likely to mean something else than fitness for good and efficient production; and that only from strife with the right kind of rules can the right kind of fitness emerge. Competition is a game played under rules fixed by the state to the end that, so far as possible, the prize of victory shall be earned, not by trickery or mere self-seeking adroitness, but by value rendered. It is not the mere play of unrestrained self-interest; it is a method of harnessing the wild beast of self-interest to serve a common good—a thing of ideals and not of sordidness. It is not a natural state, but like any other form of liberty, it is a social achievement, and eternal vigilance is the price of it.[34]

The "gangster capitalism" flourishing in postcommunist Russia—what House Majority Leader Richard Armey has called "a looted and bankrupt zone of nuclearized anarchy"—underscores the continuing relevance of this point.

III. CONCLUSION

The overarching purpose of American antitrust policy is to sustain the structural preconditions for the maintenance of effective competition. The purpose is to substitute the decentralized decision-making system of the competitive market for central planning, whether by the state or, alternatively, by private monopolists, oligopolists, or cartels. The purpose is

[34]John B. Clark, *The Control of Trusts* (New York: Macmillan, 1912), 200–201.

FIGURE 13-2 The Public Policy Choice

Source: Thurman W. Arnold, *Cartels or Free Enterprise?* Public Affairs Pamphlet 103, 1945. Reproduced by courtesy of Public Affairs Commission, Inc.

to substitute regulatory control by the invisible hand of the competitive marketplace for the visible fist of corporate power blocs operating as despotic private governments—free from competitive checks and balances, free from accountability, and with no compulsion or assurance that their decisions will promote the public good.

But as a new millennium dawns, amidst the clamor about "cyberspace," and "new economic paradigm," are these traditional antitrust goals still relevant? Are these traditional antitrust concerns still valid? Or have events and developments rendered them obsolete?

In contemplating this question, it is helpful to consider the observations of Professor Horace Gray.[35] Throughout human existence, he once

---

[35]Senate Subcommittee on Antitrust and Monopoly, *Hearings: Economic Concentration, Part 3, Concentration, Invention, and Innovation,* 89th Cong., 1st sess., 1965, 1155–66.

pointed out, "determinism, in one form or another, has served as the ultimate rationalization by which men have sought to justify their acts or to explain their condition." Whether labelled "cause," "principle," "fate," "necessity," "nature," or "deity," the allure of deterministic rationalization exerts a powerful hold on mankind. This is especially the case, Gray noted, of those who wield market economic power: "They can avoid responsibility and escape jeopardy only by appeal to some deterministic force that appears to require monopoly and monopolistic behavior. In short, they must invent some superficially plausible rationalization to 'prove' that monopoly has been thrust upon them by necessity; that fate, not art, has decreed monopoly; that they are helpless victims of some blind process which predetermines both organization and behavior." During the twentieth century, these rationalizations variously included Darwinian adaptation; the inexorable concentration of capital; "natural" monopoly; risk minimization; technology; planning; "synergy;" and a host of socio-cultural forces.

In recent years, "global competition" has become the talisman du jour for rationalizing economic power. It is incessantly invoked (but seldom objectively scrutinized) to justify virtually anything that is proposed or undertaken, no matter how anticompetitive or threatening to economic performance.

Trillions of dollars of corporate mergers and acquisitions are attributed to the dictates of "global competition"—even though a century of evidence overwhelmingly demonstrates that "the real disappointment about mergers is that, on average, they do not result in higher profits or greater efficiency; indeed, they often damage these things."[36]

In airlines, joint ventures involving the nation's largest carriers are rationalized in the name of "global competition"—even though the American airline oligopoly is allying itself with its largest potential foreign rivals!

In oil, megamergers are undertaken among the world's biggest producers (British Petroleum/Amoco/ARCO, Exxon/Mobil) because, according to Exxon's chairman, "[i]t's a lot cheaper to go buy the stuff you already know than to take a chance on exploration"[37]—even though doing so obviously fails to expand the nation's crude reserves, fails to reduce America's dependence on geopolitically volatile foreign supplies, and thus fails to enhance America's economic security.[38]

---

[36]"The Trouble With Mergers," *Economist,* 10 September 1994, 13; see also Leslie P. Norton, "Merger Mayhem," *Barron's,* 20 April 1998, 33–37; and "After the Deal," *Economist,* 9 January 1999, 21–23.

[37]Robert Lenzer and Toni Mack, "The John D. Way," *Forbes,* 28 December 1998, 51.

[38]Bhushan Bahree, "Oil Mergers Often Don't Live Up to the Hype," *Wall Street Journal,* 23 July 1999, A10.

In banking, megacombinations among the nation's largest financial concerns (Citicorp and Travelers, BankAmerica and Nationsbank) are rationalized by appealing to the dictates of the "global marketplace"—despite the absence of any compelling evidence that giantism enhances efficiency in banking;[39] despite considerable evidence to the contrary indicating that disproportionate size breeds *dis*economies of scale;[40] despite the fact that the home of the world's biggest banks (Japan) has suffered the world's biggest banking bailout crisis; and despite the fact, noted by *Wall Street Journal* columnist Holman W. Jenkins, that the "advocates of bigness say big banks can diversify their risks and afford the best in technology. But neither stopped them from pouring money into Indonesia and South Korea. . . ."[41]

In commercial jet aircraft production, the merger between America's only two manufacturers—Boeing and McDonnell Douglas—is celebrated in the name of bolstering America's ability to compete with the European Airbus consortium—even though, according to *Business Week,* "[a]lmost from the time Boeing completed its merger with McDonnell Douglas Corp . . . the company has been racking up writedowns caused by production problems and product cancellations"; even though following the merger Boeing suffered its first loss in a half century; and even though the firm's chief executive admits that acquisitions have distracted attention from Boeing's core operations.[42]

And in pharmaceutical drugs, the nation's and the world's biggest firms have been merging with each other at a furious pace—despite the fact, according to the *Economist,* that "Few drug mergers in the 1990s produced the promised flood of novel drugs from 'research synergies' used to justify the deals; nor did they add to shareholder value."[43]

In the final analysis, Professor Gray concluded, such recourse to determinism is a ruse and a delusion. Neither "fate" nor "technology"—nor

---

[39]Fred Furlong, "New View of Bank Consolidation," Federal Reserve Bank of San Francisco, *Economic Letter,* 24 July 1998; John H. Boyd and Stanley L. Graham, "Investigating the Banking Consolidation Trend," Federal Reserve Bank of Minneapolis, *Quarterly Review,* Spring 1991, 3.

[40]See, for example, Timothy L. O'Brien, "Analysts Ponder Banks' Woes," *New York Times,* 18 August 1998, C1; "Merger Mania, Sobering Statistics," *Economist,* 20 June 1998, 89; Matt Murray, "KeyCorp Fails to Prove It Can Unlock Promise of a Merger of Equals," *Wall Street Journal,* 25 August 1998, 1; Bernard Wysocki, "After Big Bank Merger, CoreStates Customers Prove Ripe for Taking," *Wall Street Journal,* 2 July 1998, 1; Stephen E. Frank, "Consumers Wonder If Deals Will Deliver Better Service," *Wall Street Journal,* 14 April 1998, A3; Jim Carlton, "Wells Fargo Discovers Getting Together Is Hard to Do," *Wall Street Journal,* 21 July 1997, B4.

[41]Jenkins, "Let's Not Shoot All the Bankers," *Wall Street Journal,* 1 July 1998, A19.

[42]Aaron Bernstein, "Lost in Space at Boeing," *Business Week,* 27 April 1998, 42; Howard Banks, "Slow Learner," *Forbes,* 4 May 1998, 54; Laurence Zuckerman, "$1.4 Billion Boeing Charge to Force First Yearly Loss Since '47," *New York Times,* 22 January 1998, C5.

[43]"Drug-Induced Seizures," *Economist,* 13 November 1999, 20.

the "global market"—predestines an economy's organization and structure. Instead, individual free will and social choice prevail. And because they do, the antitrust challenge of controlling economic power in a free society remains a vital concern. As Alan Murray points out, the economy may be new, but human nature isn't.[44]

Suggested Readings

Adams, Walter, and James W. Brock. *The Bigness Complex.* (New York: Pantheon, 1987).

———. *Antitrust Economics on Trial: A Dialogue on the New Laissez-Faire* (Princeton, NJ: Princeton University Press, 1991).

Adams, Walter, and Horace M. Gray. *Monopoly in America: The Government as Promoter,* (New York: Macmillan, 1955).

Bork, Robert H., *The Antitrust Paradox,* (New York: Basic Books, 1978).

Brandeis, Louis D. *The Curse of Bigness,* (New York: Viking, 1934).

Breit, William, and Kenneth G. Elzinga. *The Antitrust Casebook.* 3rd ed. (New York: Dryden Press, 1996).

Brock, James W., and Kenneth G. Elzinga. *Antitrust, the Market and the State: The Contributions of Walter Adams,* (Armonk, NY: M.E. Sharpe, 1991).

De Jong, H.W., ed. *The Structure of European Industry.* 3rd ed. (Boston: Kluwer Academic Publishers, 1993).

Dewey, Donald. *The Antitrust Experiment in America,* (New York: Columbia University Press, 1990).

Edwards, Corwin D. *Maintaining Competition,* (New York: McGraw Hill, 1949).

Friedman, David. *The Misunderstood Miracle: Industrial Development and Political Change in Japan,* (Ithaca, NY: Cornell University Press, 1988).

Galbraith, John Kenneth. *The New Industrial State.* 3rd ed. (Boston: Houghton Mifflin, 1978).

Graham, Otis L. *Losing Time: The Industrial Policy Debate,* (Cambridge: Harvard University Press, 1992).

Hadley, Eleanor M. *Antitrust in Japan,* (Princeton, NJ: Princeton University Press, 1970).

Harrison, Bennett. *Lean and Mean: The Changing Landscape of Corporate Power in the Age of Flexibility,* (New York: Basic Books, 1994).

Hawley, Ellis. *The New Deal and the Problem of Monopoly,* (Princeton, NJ: Princeton University Press, 1966).

Hofstadter, Richard. *Social Darwinism in American Thought,* (Boston: Beacon Press, 1944).

Kuttner, Robert. *Everything For Sale,* (New York: Alfred A. Knopf, 1997).

Kwoka, John E., and Lawrence J. White, eds. *The Antitrust Revolution,* 3rd ed., (New York: Oxford University Press, 1999).

Lippman, Walter. *The Good Society,* (Boston: Little, Brown, 1937).

Lowi, Theodore. *The End of Liberalism.* 2nd ed., (New York: Norton & Norton, 1979).

Machlup, Fritz. *The Political Economy of Monopoly,* (Baltimore: Johns Hopkins University Press, 1952).

[44]*Wall Street Journal,* 24 May 1999, 1.

Martin, Stephen. *Industrial Economics: Economic Analysis and Public Policy,* (New York: Macmillan, 1994).

May, James. "Antitrust in the Formative Era: Political and Economic Theory in Constitutional and Antitrust Analysis, 1880–1918." *Ohio State Law Journal,* vol. 50 (1989), 257–395.

Nader, Ralph, and William Taylor. *The Big Boys,* (New York: Pantheon, 1986).

Olson, Mancur. *The Rise and Decline of Nations,* (New Haven, CT: Yale University Press, 1982).

Peterson, Wallace C., ed. *Market Power and the Economy,* (Boston: Kluwer Academic Publishers, 1988).

Peritz, Rudolph J.R. *Competition Policy in America, 1888–1992,* (New York: Oxford University Press, 1996).

Porter, Michael E. *The Competitive Advantage of Nations,* (New York: Free Press, 1990).

Reich, Robert B. *The Work of Nations,* (New York: Alfred A. Knopf, 1991).

Rosenbaum, David I. *Market Dominance,* (Westport, CT: Praeger, 1998).

Shepherd, William G. *The Economics of Industrial Organization,* 4th ed., (Upper Saddle River, NJ: Prentice-Hall, 1997).

Simons, Henry C. *Economic Policy for a Free Society,* (Chicago: University of Chicago Press, 1948).

Spencer, Herbert. *The Man Versus the State,* (Indianapolis: Liberty Fund, 1982).

Stocking, George W., and Myron W. Watkins. *Cartels in Action,* (New York: Twentieth Century Fund, 1946).

———. *Cartels or Competition?,* (New York: Twentieth Century Fund, 1948).

———. *Monopoly and Free Enterprise,* (New York: Twentieth Century Fund, 1951).

Sumner, William Graham. *On Liberty, Society, and Politics.* Robert C. Bannister ed., (Indianapolis: Liberty Fund, 1992).

Thorelli, Hans B. *The Federal Antitrust Policy: Origination of an American Tradition,* (Baltimore: Johns Hopkins University Press, 1955).

Thurow, Lester C. *The Zero-Sum Solution,* (New York: Simon & Schuster, 1985).

Waldman, Don E., and Elizabeth J. Jensen. *Industrial Organization,* (New York: Addison-Wesley, 1998).

Weaver, Paul H. *The Suicidal Corporation,* (New York: Simon & Schuster, 1988).

Wills, Garry. *A Necessary Evil: A History of American Distrust of Government,* (New York: Simon & Schuster, 1999).

Name Index

C

D

E

F

G

H

I

J

K

L

M

N

O

P

Q

R

Y

Z

Subject Index

A

B

C

D

V

W